BENNY HILL
Merry Master of Mirth

THE COMPLETE COMPANION

Robert Ross

B. T. Batsford

DEDICATION

To that great character actor, Norman Mitchell, a vital part of the indispensable band of players who made post-war British film and television such a rich treasure trove of delights. A wonderful friend, encouraging voice and cheerful spirit, you won't find your name anywhere beyond this page, but this book is for you, Norman.

First published 1999

Printed by Polestar Wheatons Ltd, Exeter

Published by B. T. Batsford,
9 Blenheim Court,
Brewery Road, N7 9NT
A member of the Chrysalis Group plc

ISBN 0 7134 8422 5

FOREWORD

'He touched the funny bone of the whole world!'
Henry McGee

'One thing that should be mentioned about his career is its sheer longevity – it was quite amazing. He was an extremely generous, kind man. Anything he set his mind to, he could do. His work had to be just right but he was always modest. He was a kind, lovely man whom I miss greatly – a great liver who lived his own way.'
Peter Charlesworth

'That small group of people who worked with him, we would have done anything for him, because we really did love him. He was totally unpretentious, kind and all the things that weren't like the man the press made him out to be. A great man, a wonderful man, and an enormous talent. I know I'll go to my grave knowing my shows will be screened all over again – when they're all watching it on kid's television in 2090.'
Dennis Kirkland

'Benny was great fun to work with.'
June Whitfield

'I think he had this deep concern that some people hated his comedy because it was branded sexist. Benny continually said, 'My comedy is not like that – I never chase the girls, the girls chase me!' He was marvellous.'
Phil Collins

'Benny was imbued with the knowledge and understanding of comedy tradition. He knew instinctively as a professional, and learning from others, what was right for his work. People to this day, say, "Oh, Benny Hill was so politically incorrect." Well, maybe some of it isn't acceptable by today's standards, but if you say, "Was Benny Hill a funny man?", the answer is "Yes, he was." That's all you need to know. He was of the music hall and the saucy postcard. He wasn't consciously trying to offend, he was simply of his time, and that humour doesn't date, however much our moral consciousness may change. He made millions laugh – end of story.'
Nicholas Parsons

ACKNOWLEDGEMENTS

I owe tremendous thanks to Benny's major BBC collaborator, Dave Freeman, and major Thames Television collaborator, Dennis Kirkland, for giving so much of their time and support to this project, also to Ian Carmichael, Peter Charlesworth, Phil Collins, Pamela Cundell, Nicholas Parsons, Graham Stark, Frank Thornton, Stanley Unwin, June Whitfield, Alec Brgonzi and Norman Rossington for their incisive, affectionate memories. Thanks also to Henry McGee, Gary Morecombe for his enthused encouragement, Barry Took for being such a legend and still having time for a newcomer like me...

Thanks again to Mr Richard Reynolds, my main man at B.T. Batsford, for continuing to pay me for something I would probably (I said probably) do for nothing, his assistant Andrie Morris, Max Tyler of the British Music Hall Society for pointing me in the right direction, those gloriously helpful folk at the British Film Institute Library, and latterly those other helpful folk at the Newspaper Library in Colindale, Alan Coles for a wonderfully dodgy copy of a wonderfully dodgy movie, that cool dude Rick Blackman for a cool dude-like programme for Fine Fettle, the late George W. Brown and my selfless friend Maxine Ventham of The Goon Show Preservation Society for invaluable information regarding Third Division – Some Vulgar Fractions, David Graham of Comic Heritage for valued support, me darlin' Annalie Howlett for those glorious university days (remember when a session in The Vulture's Perch seemed much more attractive than an evening of Benny Hill at the National Film Theatre?), Mum, Dad and Fiona for everything, and a fond farewell salute to Mr Cool himself, Frank Sinatra, who, apart from touching the human soul with everything from 'One For My Baby' to 'That's Life', was a dedicated Benny Hill fan. Sock it to 'em ....

Stills are copyright to the production comapanies as credited in the accompanying text. The author would like to thank the British Film Institute, The BBC, Pearson and Canal+ for their help with illustrations.

INTRODUCTION

'In relations between the sexes, the male is always disappointed.' **Benny Hill**

As Jimi Hendrix some time before 1970, a bigwig at RCA in 1977 and some bloke at Parlophone in 1980 all reputedly said: to die young is the best career move you can make. Benny Hill, for many years British television's most successful comedian, died in 1992 at the age of 68. His youth and golden years gone, Hill was trapped in a twilight zone, rejected by the new blood of programme planning, held up as the epitome in tired, old-fashioned and offensive comedy by the new breed of comedian, and fast disappearing from the collective consciousness of the new generation of home viewers. While Tony Hancock, Eric Morecambe and Peter Sellers saw their legends soar and Frankie Howerd was riding the crest of a wave with renewed student stardom, Benny Hill had become the forgotten giant of British comedy.

In over a hundred countries across the world, the story could not have been more different. From Angola to Belgium, his shows were screened constantly. In France, his genius for mime was considered to be on a par with Chaplin and Keaton, in Russia his television shows were one of the few Western images to break through the Iron Curtain, and most importantly of all, in America he was by far the most popular comic import with his classic ITV Thames Television shows re-edited for repeated prime-time screenings. However, despite a strong, loyal following in Britain, the work of Benny Hill is still in limbo, stereotyped and castigated as embodying all that's bad about British comedy.

But there was far more to his work than a neverending line of suspender-clad dolly birds. This book will attempt to redress the balance by simply detailing the varied and endearing work of one of Britain's best-loved clowns. Unlike biographies written by those family and friends close to Hill, this book is not a life story, nor is it a hagiography of the man – indeed, it's impossible to deny that in later years, with his freedom restricted by the moral minority, Hill's comedy became jaded and uninspiring. But writing all his own material, performing it with pride and embracing a trusted, tested troupe of colleagues, Hill was the all-conquering Citizen Kane of his own Xanadu before Thames Television finally pulled the plug.

His much-celebrated work for Thames between 1969 and 1989 typifies his enormous contribution to popular culture, and programmes from his 1970s golden age capture him at his assured peak. However, it must not be forgotten that Hill was the first comedian to attain stardom through the medium of television with his hugely popular BBC series from 1955 – programmes that, due to both the BBC's distaste for all-out smut and the more restrained social climate of the time, allowed Hill to cleverly inject innuendo into his comedy. His radio assignments of the 1950s reveal a fine patter comedian in the mould of Max Miller, excellent character work opposite Archie Andrews, and latterly, the starring vehicle *Benny Hill Time*, which, heard today, reinforces the brilliance of his 1960s writing. Hill attempted cinema stardom with one of the last Ealing comedies, played Shakespeare, sparred with Michael Caine in an archetypal swinging sixties heist comedy and soared to number one in the British pop charts with his comic lament, *Ernie (The Fastest Milkman in the West)*.

Unlike the ensemble dexterity I have previously tackled in *The Carry On Companion* and *Monty Python Encyclopedia*, this is a study of one man's career. Regardless of the familiarity of his regular team, Benny Hill single-handedly summed up a tradition of saucy seaside-postcard comedy, delivered at breakneck speed, peppered with knowing grins, rustic comments and innuendo-drenched songs. While the aim of this book is to present in full detail all the television, stage, radio, recording and cinematic ventures which made up Hill's career, personal autobiographical information will be scattered between the dates and cast lists, sometimes to back up a point, or merely to highlight for the reader what Benny Hill the man was up to, as opposed to Benny Hill the comedian.

Totally aware of his own limitations (although his acting in the film *Light Up the Sky!* is a revelation that was sadly never repeated), Hill's ambition was simple. From watching touring revue shows docked at Southampton, Hill remembered: 'I used to watch comedians in shows like *Oo La La* always surrounded by pretty girls. That's going to be the life for me one day!' 'The girls' – like Bob Todd, custard pies or clown shoes – were just part of the act, but in the end they would prove to be his downfall. Despite the fact that Hill correctly argued that 'My would-be lovers never succeed. A man who succeeds is not funny. A man who fails is funny ... if my sketches teach anything it is that, for the male, sex is a snare and a delusion. What's so corrupting about that?', his shows were axed in 1989, to the anguish of his fans and the delight of those who thought him politically incorrect. This book will look at the evidence and opinions from both sides of the argument, as well as Hill's continued popularity with 100 million viewers in over eighty countries and his place in the annals of British comedy heritage alongside other beloved losers, such as Basil Fawlty, Harold Steptoe, Derek Trotter, Victor Meldrew and Anthony Aloysius St John Hancock.

When Sue Upton called Benny 'the hapless clown', she was dead right. Here was a comic talent without malice, bumbling through his own tightly controlled comic universe with the sole aim of making us laugh. He succeeded beyond his wildest dreams. This is the story of one towering comic figure who dominated British television entertainment for over forty years. His name may still be held in unjustified contempt by some, but his legacy, unfolded here, tells a tale of struggle, hard work and sheer talent.

BLUE BENNY HILL:
The early days of a comic legend

'I'm the saucy comic!'   **Benny Hill**

Benny Hill was destined to became the most universally successful comedian of the modern era. Marching the well-worn path of the European clowning tradition of the seventeenth and eighteenth centuries, he reshaped visual antics from his childhood cinematic heroes like Buster Keaton, Harry Langdon and, most importantly, Charlie Chaplin. The mixture included BBC radio snatches of music hall comedian Max Miller-like innuendo, thrilling early visits to local stage revues and the healthy tide of Donald McGill's saucy seaside postcards coming in from Brighton. A transatlantic edge was grafted onto the sub-consciousness with influences from New York arriving at his hometown port of Southampton. The end result: the only British comedian of the post-war era to fully crack the international market, arguably one of the most instantly recognizable British icons, and the one clown who can rightfully challenge Chaplin for his crown.

Born Alfred Hawthorne Hill in a flat above a lamp shop in Bernard Street, Southampton, on 21 January 1924 (not 1925, as several reference books and Hill himself would have had us believe), he was the youngest son of Alfred and Helen. Performance was clearly in the blood of Hill's family. Helen's sister, Louise Cave, had been a semi-professional singer, his father's father, Henry, had been a street clown, his father's brother, Leonard, had been killed in a circus high-wire accident, and father Alfred Snr himself, born in Leytonstone, London, in 1894, had run away from home at the age of 16 to join in the excitement of Fossett's Circus. Not surprisingly, throughout his life Benny Hill loved the small-town country circuses of France and Spain. His earliest memories were of his mother making him a clown suit out of an old pair of pyjamas and of his father donning the old make-up and walking on his hands up the stairs. This clownish sense of the absurd contrasted with the military strictness which earned Alfred Snr the title of 'The Captain' from his children.

Hill's father's life was marred by hardships, near misses and abandoned opportunities. His career in entertainment was prematurely curtailed by First World War

service, and having fought on the Western Front, been gased in France at the age of 19 and survived a period as a prisoner of war in Belgium, he nursed an understandable hatred for authority shared by many of his shattered generation, promised homes fit for heroes, but returning as heroes fit for homes. Alfred had met and married Helen Cave in 1920, when he was a clerk at Toogoods Rolling Mills. In the same year as his marriage, a further failed business prospect had really turned Alfred sour – for he was now the sole employee in a company which would make a certain Jack Stanley a millionaire. Alfred had been offered a partnership in the firm, but couldn't borrow the necessary money from his father. The business, a backstreet affair selling surgical appliances, abdominal supports, vigour-inducing medicines and contraceptives, dealt with many customers by post. With a new wife and just about to start a family, regular pay was far more important than risky business ventures.

Leonard Hill was born in 1921, followed by young Alfie Hill three years later, and sister Diana in 1933. They spent their childhood in a small terraced house, 164

The Future Looks Bright!

Wilton Road, Southampton, enchanted by their mother's readings from *Bubbles* annuals and other Christmas books – throughout his life, Hill maintained that the Giant in *Pompety Finds a Needle* was the most terrifying creation in literature.

As a small boy, Benny faced taunts from schoolyard baiters along the lines of 'Hillie's dad sells French letters.' Latching onto these cheeky jibes, piecing together limited sexual knowledge, and in the clichéd tradition of all great comedians, playing the classroom fool to win appreciation, Hill developed a knowing way with smutty comedy to entertain his contemporaries – he used this technique for the rest of his career. In his 1992 book, *Star Turns*, Barry Took points out the embarrassment with sexual matters and his father's position as appliance fitter as the root of the deep-rooted, insecure fear of copulation that prevented Benny's humour from escaping a nudging, giggling world of childish smut. In my opinion, Hill knew exactly what the score was, playing to his youthful audience, getting the required reaction, and sticking with it.

While his father may have been the dictatorial master of the household, Hill's mother was open and affectionate, happy to protect her 5-year-old son's female flirtations at Shirley Infant School, Wilton Road, and eager to discuss at length bodily functions of all kinds. It was hardly a sheltered upbringing, and before long Benny was cracking the first of many risqué treasures:

Teacher: '*Where have you been?*'
Late Boy: '*Up Shirley Hill.*'
Teacher: '*Who are you?*'
Late Girl: '*I'm Shirley Hill.*'

Just the kind of thing to get the other boys to stop hitting you in the dinner break, this little story was given added credibility as Shirley Hill was a local beauty spot.

Painful experiences that shaped Hill's comedy include tales of a brief clash with a child molester, dreadful parental rows at home, bereavement (his mother's parents, Gran and Granpa Sims, died in 1929 and 1930 respectively) and deeply hurtful female rejections, but the star himself would often relate happier times with his father, skipping along to his shop in Market Street with his lunch and playing the Jewish card game Kiobbiyos – which his father would as often as not let him win. However, this myth of an idyllic childhood served the public persona of a star remembering his dead father, as in a 1983 *TV Times* interview by Jennifer Farley, headed 'The Clown who Made his Old Dad Very Happy' (12–18 March), whereas privately, he often confided to his equal-

ly embittered brother that he could have cheerfully killed his father!

The power of his father was vitally important to Benny Hill – reflected comically in his stupid, aged, misunderstanding comic sketch parents, and in his fearful respect of police, doctors, lawyers and every other authority figure – but the spectre of female rejection remained the overwhelming aspect of his comic expression, although he had no fear of women, simply respect, and there was no shortage of female playmates and hand-holding in the early years. Aged 5, he would playfully frolic with little Peggy Bell, but later the usual teenage angst led to depressions, nail-biting and long walks.

At the age of 12, Hill discovered his ideal woman. In September 1936, he was staying with his cousin in nearby Eastleigh for Carnival Week when a vision of dark-haired loveliness with a green coat caught his imagination. The crush was, he explained in later years, 'the biggest I've ever had', and on his return home he would walk six miles just to get a glimpse of her. Four years later, 16, streetwise and much more confident, Hill saw her again, asked her to the pictures, but felt 'no sparks' on their date, and called it a day. Now, whether this mysterious young lady is Citizen Hill's Rosebud is debatable, but the repeated impetuous proposals that marked his life have their roots here. Gallant, caring and kind to women throughout his life, the victim of his humour was always the man – and more importantly, *himself*, his younger, love-struck 12-year-old self from Southampton adolescence. Therapy, inspiration or self-mockery, Hill the comedian continually used this inner catalogue of emotions to fashion a universal language of classic television comedy.

Coming from a family of frustrated performers and acting the schoolroom clown through necessity and enjoyment, his early years were spent transfixed by cinema. Allegedly, by the age of 3 he had already perfected the staggering walk of Charlie Chaplin! And it wasn't just the magical movies inside – Hill was fascinated by the cinema building itself, spending many happy childhood days riding his bicycle to new picture palaces just to check out the elaborate decor. But those glorious stories from his mother gave him a love for language, even though his party piece, a ballad concerning Mustapha and Hussan, was hardly his best use of it. Word games with brother Leonard and a shared delight in the world of Damon Runyon pointed him in the right direction.

Hill delighted in entertaining his friends and family, discovering a gift for impersonating everyone from Louis Armstrong to Jack Buchanan, which became his main obsession at the time. BBC radio voices of Max

Miller and Robb Wilton delighted him, he perfected the unique vocal delivery of George Bernard Shaw and H.G. Wells, while cinema provided the source for his first female impersonation, Mae West, and his first real character technique as Claude Rains, using a kitchen knife to create a set of false teeth from orange peel and painting on a moustache with his mother's eyebrow pencil. Performances as sexy Maurice Chevalier, grouchy Edward G. Robinson and buoyant James Cagney, or comic monologues wearing his George Robey hat were all part of his childhood love of becoming somebody else to entertain people. Naturally, this talent would become an important part of his classic television shows, although, on reflection, his inspired performances as W.C. Fields, Peter Lorre and Max Miller himself are unfairly forgotten in light of the clichéd 'dirty old man' misunderstanding.

Another important but often underrated string to his performing bow was music, a skill also embraced while Hill was still at school. At an early age, he sang to the accompaniment of his father's one-string violin, and later, he loved to play music himself, realizing its impor-

tant place in the overall structure of a show. In later years, Hill would become proficient on guitar and cornet (once playing at a big concert with Ted Heath and His Orchestra), but during these formative days he supported himself by playing drums in a local band – a talent which united him with contemporary struggling comic genius Peter Sellers in nearby Portsmouth.

The young Hill delighted in sound, and one of his earliest party pieces was a sound-only 'walk through the countryside', complete with golf balls hitting animals and other surreal audio pictures. His position of family clown at the age of 9 or 10 even impressed his father, although he would usually walk out of the room to laugh rather than let his son see his appreciation of the performance. Father's weekly trips to his Freemasons' lodge would inspire Benny with a flurry of comic observation – sending up his father's well kitted out attire with mini gangster kaleidoscopes, elongated James Cagney death scenes and George Raft coin-tossing or flamboyant orchestra situations with exaggerated conducting movements and mimed violin solos.

Around this time, Hill was briefly part of the choir of St Marks Church, but – typically – solely for the 6d a week fee and a trip to the Isle of Wight. By 1935, he had won a scholarship to the Richard Taunton School, but life there was just boring enough to allow him plenty of daydreaming moments. Disinterest was reflected in his poor academic achievements at school, although art was a favourite subject, and the boy was good – his old teacher kept a statue from among Benny's work and bequeathed it back to the star in his will, while actress Connie George bought a carving of an Aztec head by the talented 11-year-old. This artistic bent was pinpointed by a *TV Times* piece ('A Dream in the Life of Benny Hill', 25–31 May 1985) for which Hill posed for a Lord Patrick Lichfield photograph, typically depicting him with a glamorous model reflected in his abstract portrait, and equally typically, balanced by fond memories of his own saucy mind: he had peppered a school project entitled 'The City of Dreadful Night' with a montage of prostitutes and sailors looking for action.

School also gave him the chance to play goalkeeper for the football team – which allowed him to fill quiet spells with impromptu gorilla impressions from the crossbar – and to develop a profitable cottage industry removing 14 carot gold nibs from discarded pens and swapping them for gold coins, jewellery, and eventually, semi-precious gemstones. Hill enthralled his small audience with a

Always happy to reclaim milk round memories.

The serious face of war - stunning publicity pose for the 1959 film *Light Up The Sky!*

three-dimensional boot-box peep-show depicting scenes from *Treasure Island*. He was also a dab hand at flicking his well-worn cigarette cards. Most importantly, school days presented him with his first real taste of theatrics. Apart from art, Hill loved his French lessons, but even more influential than these was English, with his guiding teacher Dr Horace King. Later to enjoy a hugely success-ful political career, become Speaker of the House of Commons and enjoy the title Lord Maybray-King, King spotted acting potential in his young pupil, encouraged his flamboyant comic expression, and vitally, cast him in his first scripted stage performance. Yes, Hill's earliest offi-cial work was as a rabbit in a school production of *Alice In Wonderland*. Hardly the most taxing of beginnings, he had to wear a sign round his neck reading 'Rabbit', and found his dialogue consisted almost entirely of emitting the occasional squeak, although the role did showcase Hill's first painful pun – crying out ''Ear! 'Ear!' during the courtroom scene.

From the age of 13, Hill tried his hand as an amateur entertainer in and around Southampton, tuning his natur-al talent for impression, but overloading his act with the familiar sounds of Harry Roy, Horace Kenny, Claude Dampier and Stainless Steven, giving nothing more than a reheated, albeit impressive, presentation of each artists' act.

In these days before the Second World War, BBC radio comedy was tightly guarded against smut and innu-endo. Before armed conflict allowed Tommy Handley's *It's That Man Again* and Max Miller to become vital home front comforts, BBC Director General Lord John Reith deplored any hint of suggestive material, and Miller was banned from the BBC for allegedly cracking the joke about an optician whose client complained: 'Every time I see F you see K' (think about it). Miller found refuge on the less morally censored Radio Luxemburg, and of course, the variety theatres, which were packed for his every performance.

One of those faithful millions who warmed to the cheeky chappie's irresistible charm was a certain Benny Hill, and without a doubt, no single comic was more influential on him. While eulogizing fans later placed Hill firmly in the tradition of Chaplin and Keaton, it is essen-tial to highlight the influence of Max Miller, Donald

McGill's saucy seaside postcards and Brighton end-of-pier variety shows throughout his work. A fresh, streetwise, confident figure – in contrast to the hugely successful comic characterizations of, say, George Formby or Frank Randle – Miller embraced an air of American-styled fast banter while embodying the British spirit. It's true that American comedians fascinated the young Hill during trips to the cinema, and as with Liverpool's 1950s influx of pure rock 'n' roll, Southampton was full of sailors arriv-ing with the latest recordings from New York. As a result, Hill was brought up on a staple diet of Louis Armstrong, Fanny Brice, The Two Black Crows and Whispering Jack Smith, savoured on the family wind-up gramophone. However, it was Miller, 'The King of the South of England', who captivated the young Hill. Miller's brightly coloured suit, blue and white books and jauntily angled trilby embodied the essence of fish 'n' chips, kiss-me-quick

Love is in the air...
Benny turns on the romantics
with *Who Done It?* co-star
Belinda Lee.

The young hopeful...

and thrilling trips to see American speedway ace Sprouts Elder as diverting distractions – with varying degrees of success – but the excitement of performance was all-consuming. Even Benny's refereeing of his brother's scrappy boxing bouts would resolve into a perfect 'cocky cockney' routine. Finally, several visits to the music hall culminated in a guided tour of the Southampton Hippodrome. The object of the exercise was to dampen the young man's ambitions rather than fire his imagination, but predictably, he became even more stagestruck, so his father finally relented and bought him his first professional make-up box. Some sources claim that Hill made his official stage debut as early as the age of 9, with an appearance at Southampton's Palace Theatre in 1933. Whatever the truth in that, Hill's performing career really began to take off during the days immediately before the Second World War. His father was secretly impressed by Benny's talent, and encouraged him with back-handed comments and half-hearted actions, but continually damped the boy's aspirations with knowing asides that showbusiness was nothing like a Betty Grable picture. His son wasn't really bothered. In the summer of 1938, he had seen Albert Hunter and the Jitterbugging Maniacs in *The Cotton Club Revue* at the London Palladium. As J. Worthington Foulfellow was about to sing, 'It's an actor's life for me', and the young Alfie was hooked.

hats and naughty weekends by the sea.

When at the start of the Second World War he began to experiment with his own material, Hill embraced the cheeky innuendo of his idol. He couldn't have hoped for a better role model. Hill's father was less than impressed, introducing bike riding, swimming, boxing

THE STAGE

Despite the best intentions and best efforts of his father to dissuade him from a career on the stage, the natural clown was in Hill's genes, he revelled in the buzz an appreciative audience's laughter gave him, and the glamorous prospects were more than enough to attract a wide-eyed teenager. Along with his older brother, Leonard, Hill had run through his collection of vocal tricks – playing Crosby, Wilton, Durante, Buchanan and the Ritz Brothers in their double act depicting three different radio broadcasts: BBC programming, Radio Luxemburg and American commercial radio. The climax had Benny being bashed over the head with a gong – it was that sort of show. These performances were for charitable events for the Fellowships Supporters Council, but for Leonard, the future lay in teaching, eventually becoming a headmaster.

In 1938, at the age of 14, Hill landed his first semi-professional position with Bobbie's Concert Party. His two spots were very short, and the deal was only struck because six performances were imminent and nobody else was available, but he relished the chance. Firstly, he would come on in woolly hat and heavy coat, toss a handful of shredded paper in the air to serve as a cheap snow effect, and chatter about the bad weather. A better characterization had him playing a vicar, wearing one of his dad's collars back to front and made up with lipstick and rouge borrowed from his mother. Hill performed as 'second comic', and all the gags were stolen from various source material he had filed away. One-liners such as 'The Young Mother's Club seems to have a shortage of young mothers – in spite of all the efforts of myself and the Bishop' were probably beyond the young comedian's powers of delivery, but it was invaluable early experience – albeit short-lived, since after the six shows, his contribution was curtailed. However, he was learning the business. Offered the fee of 2s 6d or a bottle of pop and a taxi home, the young Benny took the money and walked!

Hill dabbled with a guitar group, The Hill Brothers, supporting leader Eric Vincent, fooled around with his guitar-plucking pal Tex Southgate, and hastily resurrected his Bobbie's Concert Party turns for a talent show held at the Plaza Cinema, Northampton, in which he came second to a glass-eating act! He tirelessly refined his slapdash patter act with countless Sunday lunchtime shows at working men's clubs. With an audience in the mood for bluer, rougher material than that approved of by the BBC, Hill found an eager reception for his Max Miller-style performances. Lacking the nerves that curtailed stage work when he became a star, and eager to learn about the business, he frequently visited the theatre, whether to see Charlie Poland's band on Southampton's Royal Pier or the grand revue at the Palace Theatre.

Despite his father's lack of interest, Hill's paternal grandfather was much more supportive. Although he was a stolid pillar of the local community, he was part-time critic for *The World's Fair* journal, so he could secure free tickets to most productions, get the best seats in the house, create fever pitch in the expectant cast and excite a polite welcoming nod from the orchestra leader – young Benny loved all this. The Hippodrome Theatre was his ultimate treat – studying the various comedians on the bill, being enchanted by the illusionist Horace Goldin, and most importantly, delighting in presentations of popular travelling revue shows such as *Naughty Girls of 1900*, *Scandals of Broadway* and *Ooh La La!* The shows boasted a straightman who doubled as a baritone, a saucy soubrette, an older comedienne and loads of girls, but it was the star comedian that most impressed young Hill, and his lifestyle seemed like paradise: 'I used to watch all these great fat women in the audience laughing at the comic and I would think how wonderful it would be to be that man. He was surrounded by pretty girls, he obviously got more money than anyone else and everyone loved him. They laughed and clapped when he came on stage – you could feel the warmth going out to him.'

Evacuated briefly to Bournemouth, Hill's family moved from Westrow Gardens to temporary accommodation in Hounsdown, near the New Forest, although it wasn't long before everything was back to normal at home in Southampton. Bournemouth had introduced him to the delights of a pierrot show, falling in love with the pierrette and instantly in awe of the star comedian's physical comedy routines. The comic was Willie Cave, and he remains one of the unsung influences of Hill's life. The acting bug was still gnawing at its latest victim, and he would often take the train down to Basingstoke to meet the star comedians headlining the Grand Theatre – now the glorious Haymarket Theatre. One such act was the Smeddle Brothers, who auditioned him, liked what they saw, and promised him a chance if anything presented itself.

He left school at the age of 15 without taking the scholarship certificate for which he was studying, and found employment as a weighbridge operator with the Phoenix Coal Company. He lasted in the job for just three weeks, and after the outbreak of the Second World War in September 1939, he supplemented his full-time job as stockroom clerk cum trainee manager for his local Woolworth's store by entertaining in pubs, halls and air raid shelters. The shelter at Catchcold Tower rang to reheated music hall routines, and young Benny enthralled the easily delighted audience. During his six months at Woolworth's, he was surrounded by a workforce totally made up of charming young ladies, lovingly calling him 'Sonny Boy' and smothering him with their California Poppy scent. Hill fell for the toiletries counter assistant, although most of his time was spent clearing up dog mess in the store, and he came to dread Mr Dean the manager's yell of 'Hill!'

To escape this and to allow him more time to rehearse his act, he took a job as a milkman with Harry Hann & Son's Dairy for 28s a week – complete with Daisy the horse and a cart, an experience later immortalized in 'Ernie (The Fastest Milkman in the West)'. Lodging with a Mr and Mrs Brown in Eastleigh, he began as an assistant milkman, and only secured that post because of war shortages. This was a step down from the promotional hierarchy of Woolworth's, but that didn't matter: his biggest thrill came from entertaining.

By 1940, one of his Woolworth's girlfriends had suggested he join a local dance band, Ivy Lillywhite and Her Friends. Soon he was strumming a guitar, pounding drums, telling jokes and singing popular hits like 'Who's Taking You Home Tonight?' and 'Careless Love', once receiving the hefty fee of 5s, and finally playing at the Spitfire Concert, Eastleigh. Hill introduced the technique of joking between numbers, and his comedy spots soon became hugely popular with the crowds, appearing at the local Conservative and Liberal Clubs. Basing his entire persona on his worshipped Max Miller, his stage attire consisted of a white felt hat with a sewn-up brim, loud blue-check jacket (which he had bought from the Eastleigh Co-op for 10s) and a garish red tie (which he cheekily brought into the act – 'That's all right dear, it's just me tongue hanging out!'). This Miller-like rapport with his audience made up for his catalogue of stolen jokes, hastily written down during theatre trips, and his ad-libs marked him out as a promising fledgling comedian – allegedly, one night a lady was breast-feeding in the audience and Hill shouted out: 'After you with that!' He completely embraced Miller's irresistible technique addressing the audience with friendly conspiracy, and Hill's throwaway interjections of 'Mrs Woman' hinted at this attempt to emulate the affection of his hero.

BENNY GOES TO LONDON

At the age of 17, Hill took a life-changing decision, sold his beloved drum kit for £6, supplemented his savings with a few extra pounds from his father, and left home to try to become a full-time performer. His parents were totally against his gamble, but Hill was determined, and in September 1940, with the blue serge suit on his back and a few possessions packed in a cardboard suitcase, he made the journey to London. However, rather than streets paved with gold, the young hopeful found streets paved with used bus tickets.

Arriving at Waterloo, he made his way to Leicester Square, bought a copy of *The Stage*, and asked a policeman if there was anywhere outside the West End which had a few theatres in close proximity. Having the common sense not to go straight for the top, Hill was told that the Empress, Brixton, and the Streatham Hill Theatre were near each other, and he took the bus to Brixton. Sid Seymour and the Mad Hatters were in residence at the Empress, and Hill asked for Seymour at the stage door. He told Hill that there was nothing for him, but struck by the boy's keenness, he pointed him in the direction of his brother, Phil Seymour, who was an agent currently presenting a show called *Follow the Fun* at the Chelsea Palace. The star comedian was Hal Bryan, and on a Thursday, the manager, a kindly man by the name of Harry Frockton Foster, listened to young Benny's dream of turning professional, and told him to come back the following Monday, when there might be a position for him. Although he had enough money for digs, since he had no guarantee of work, Hill decided to conserve his money, spending the first four nights sleeping rough on Streatham Common, initially on the grass, eventually finding a slightly more comfortable place to rest his head in an unfinished concrete air raid shelter. He washed and shaved at the toilet in Lyon's Corner House cafe.

On the Monday, he turned up at the office of

producer Harry Benet at 11 Beak Street, Soho, and landed himself a £3 10s a week job with *Follow the Fun*, which was due to open that night at the East Ham Palace. Despite his ill-advised cocky attitude and Jimmy Cagney swagger, Hill clearly had something, but the offered position really was the lowest of the low. Informed that Benet's star comic, George Lacey, had started at the bottom, he was offered the post of Assistant Stage Manager, with the promise of small parts in the show (later, he would typically joke: 'I'm not an ASM anymore but I've still got the small parts!'). He was aware that this apprenticeship was going to be difficult. The stage parts would be very small, if any, and the job mainly involved humping props, baskets and scenery around, as well as looking after the ponies, monkeys and dogs involved in the 'Pino's Circus' section. However, now in secure employment, he rented a room in an East End lodging house and revelled in the theatrical experience.

On his first night, he was shown how to use Leichner grease sticks and appeared as a policeman in a court sketch. In the finale, a patriotic tableau, Hill strolled on as John Bull (complete with a cushion stuffed up his waistcoat to fill out his physique) to shake hands with another player as Uncle Sam, culminating in a glorious flag-waving singalong of 'Land of Hope and Glory'. The whole thing was a cheerful knees-up, from the cheerful arrival by stage prop boat to the important three-handed sketch concerning gaining a girl's favours by offering her drink. Hill cropped up in this as well, naturally.

On the Wednesday night, he was setting up props for the next scene when he heard a pause on stage. Instead of the usual cross-talking double act based round the military call-up poster promotion 'Go To It', the star comic, Hal Bryan, had launched into a desperate-sounding barrage of one-liners. Instantly realizing that the straightman, who liked the occasional drink, hadn't turned up, Benny, already made up and quickly donning a boiler suit over his policeman costume, took a deep breath, thought for an instant and went on. Although he had only heard the routine during the previous two nights, he managed to feed the opening remark, 'Hello, Hal. Going to it?' Bryan was off, answering 'No, coming from it!', and they completed the sketch without a hitch. One of Hill's favourite memories was Bryan whispering 'Thank God you've shown up' on stage, and the young man came off with a huge grin of pleasure. Congratulated by all the crew and cast, as Bryan was leaving the theatre he walked over to Hill, put a 10s note in his hand and muttered: 'You're going to be a trouper, son.'

When *Follow the Fun* folded, Hill was retained by

Harry Benet as baggage master for the pantomime *Robinson Crusoe* at the Bournemouth Pavilion. Principal comic was Walter Niblo, and the show-stopping speciality act was Gary Hickson tap-dancing on his xylophone – perhaps mercifully overshadowing Hill's blacked-up, bone-through-the-nose antics with four chorus boys in 'The Cannibal Dance'.

Hill enjoyed further less high-profile employment as firewatchman at Benet's scenery workshop in Walworth Road, South London – an old haunt of young Charlie Chaplin. Some of his handiwork found its way onto the stages of the London Palladium and the Prince of Wales Theatre – where, less than a decade later, Hill would be headlining. However, in 1947 his fledgling stage career was going very nicely thank you – he was back on the road in a touring revue, *Send Him Victorious*. Starting with a successful run at the Hackney Empire, Hill found himself travelling round the country for several months, a different venue each week. Initially, snooker star Joe Davis was enlisted as an added attraction, but even without him, London dates in Camden Town and at the Brixton Empire went well. Further afield in the North of England, the company played the Victoria, Burnley, followed by the Salford Hippodrome.

THE ARMY YEARS

Due to his wandering lifestyle, Hill's call-up papers were repeatedly redirected but never caught up with him, until the military police finally tracked him down in November 1947 on the fourth night of *Send Him Victorious* at Cardiff's New Theatre and dragged him away. One can imagine the farcical scene as Hill was arrested in the theatre, confused and complaining at the treatment, and carted off, under guard, to Catterick induction camp in Yorkshire.

During his war service, he became Craftsman A.H. Hill, No. 14332308 in the Royal Electrical and Mechanical Engineers (REME). In later, more affluent, years, he was typically dismissive of his military career, explaining that his mechanical knowledge wasn't sufficent to put a lavatory chain together, but all that enforced saluting certainly came in handy for his later character, Fred Scuttle. He underwent an intensive driving course (which he hated, and although fully licensed, he never drove in civilian life) and a six-week fitter's course in Brighton before being posted to Dunkirk, just after D-Day. Although he never faced action during his time in France and Germany, he was continually in the combat zone. He became fluent in French and German, and the countries made an impression on him which remained throughout his life.

After serving with the Third Light Anti-Aircraft Searchlight Battery workshop at Arnold, near Nottingham, he was accepted into the Central Pool of Artists. He was pronounced A1, and during leave time in London visited the Mayfair headquarters of Stars in Battledress. Initially dismissed by Sergeant Charlie Chester with the regret that the organization had no need of scriptwriters, in spring 1946 Hill found himself stationed near the Grosvenor Square HQ, and three weeks later opened in the frightfully dated 1930s musical comedy revue *Happy Weekend*. Hill was the bespectacled juvenile lead, Riki, made famous in the West End by Steve Geray, but this was hardly the stuff servicemen wanted. The aspiring comic spiced up the dialogue with contemporary references and knowing mockery, building up the minor part of the barman with a self-penned song, 'They Call Me the Yodelling Bar Man', and stumbling through the delicate number 'We Go Together Like Sausage and Mash, Bacon and Egg' in heavy Army boots. It was perfect fare for the cramped Nissen huts that served as makeshift venues, but was somewhat lost on the vast stage of the Opera House, Calais, where they finally arrived.

He toured British military bases with the piece, and was finally sent through the Combined Service Entertainment (CSE) HQ in Hamburg and AEM in Lüneburg to start rehearsing a variety band show which he was to host. The list of stars who were discovered by services entertainment units during the war is lengthy and impressive, with Peter Sellers, Tony Hancock, Spike Milligan, Kenneth Williams, Harry Secombe, Jon Pertwee, Kenneth Connor and countless others taking the post-war years by storm following their experience of entertaining the troops.

Hill was confident from the outset that he was destined to be a star, while the stammering Private Frankie Howard, who was serving in the same unit, was full of the nervous doubts that were the trademark of his unique and timeless act. Both admired each other's work, and they remained close friends, dying within hours of each other over the Easter weekend of 1992. Never fully coming to terms with Howerd's depressive attitude, Hill's total conviction that he would become a major star within months of leaving REME made for a fascinating contrast in the barrack room, but his self-assurance was dented when his clever, breathtakingly intricate linking banter between the acts was lost on a certain Major McGregor, who dismissed the effort as simply 'not funny' – hardly the most confidence-building review for a comedian.

Hill's solo piece was hastily cut from the show, and his compering links were delivered by McGregor himself.

Thankfully for Hill's bruised ego, a young man by the name of Harry Segal was also watching, and was far more impressed. Segal, an old pro on the halls since childhood, spotted a raw energy in Hill's comic performance that immediately struck him. Whisking the private off to the NAAFI for a cup of tea, Segal gushed with admiration, quickly explaining that he was running a touring military revue called *It's All In Fun*. Segal took Hill on as stage manager, with assurances that the work would also include on-stage performance once the troupe moved away from the headquarters and the critical eye of Major McGregor. Hill slowly regained confidence, although he was never quite so ebullient as a stage personality again – indeed, it was a very hard struggle to finally coax him back on stage at all, with Segal leading him into the cockney knees-up finale, then a brief part in a comedy sketch, and finally, the five-minute spot he had performed previously. Segal literally ordered him onto the stage, but with justification – his sophisticated comic monologue, delivered clad in a silk dressing gown, received huge applause.

At the time, Hill and Howerd were still basing their delivery style on Max Miller's, and naturally, with an audience of servicemen in the middle of world conflict, the material was expected to be as fruity, raucous and unsubtle as possible. Hill's variety style of Miller-like bonding with his audience against the strict moral code of the authority figure was perfect for the situation, and is a technique still employed by comedians such as Ben Elton in his live performances.

Encouraged by warm reactions from his comrades in arms, Hill's stage persona became stronger, and finally, during one of the last German shows, he finished to a standing ovation. Luckily, the audience included Colonel Richard Stone, in charge of Combined Service Entertainment throughout the whole of Europe, who became Hill's life-long agent after the war. Stone also signed up former Captain Ian Carmichael from Hill's unit, and the two performers were reunited in the 1959 war film *Light Up the Sky!* Hill's Army days later came back to haunt him when a certain ex-Major McGregor approached agent Richard Stone to book Benny for a cabaret evening at his New Forest pub. Initially the star refused, finally accepting a massive £30 fee for a brief fifteen-minute turn. In the end, due to bad advertising of the event, no audience turned up, the show was cancelled and Hill was paid off with his fee in full. Almost immediately, he bumped into his old champion, Segal, in the Charing Cross Road. Segal was back in the business, but lacked the necessary cash to secure costumes for a prospective pantomime offer, so Hill gave him the required funds – exactly £30.

Perhaps the most formative moment of Hill's military days came with a fumbled date with an attractive NAAFI girl by the name of Maria. Hill invited her out to the cinema, scraped together some money for a meal afterwards, and donned his finest clothes for the occasion. When he picked her up, she explained that another soldier had also asked her out, he was there as well, and the young lady suggested all three go to see the film. Understandably upset at this, the razor-sharp comic mind of Hill was working overtime. Turning to the other soldier, who was equally put out, he invited him to the cinema and left the girl standing, foreshadowing Hill's reversed-sexual-situation comedy which would reach genius with his 'The Collector' parody, Mervyn Cruddy's ageing chorus boy and the powerful female figures which would become so misunderstood. Whether it be Patricia Hayes during the BBC days or Stella Moray in the early Thames Television escapades, Hill delighted in defending himself against the predatory, man-eating vamp with sexual designs uncomprehensible to him. Right until the late 1980s, Hill planned to film the original, inspirational wartime encounter as it happened, but never got round to it – perhaps the memory was better reflected in other comic situations rather than starkly recreated.

BACK TO CIVVY STREET

When he was demobbed in autumn 1947, Hill gratefully received his £50 Army gratuity money, made a fleeting trip back to Southampton, and resumed his hunt for theatrical employment, journeying to the haven of returning military personnel entertainers, the Windmill Theatre in Windmill Street, Soho, with its famous nude revue. His first audition on returning home was for the Windmill's Vivian Van Damm. Continually on the lookout for fresh, willing and, above all, cheap comedians to keep the theatre's pledge to never close, Van Damm was happy to give newcomers a chance.

Military service and countless service shows had changed audience expectations of comic delivery, a skin as thick as a rhino's was needed to withstand the reaction of the audience, who were much more interested in staring than laughing, and the comic became nothing more than a hasty distraction as the nude girls changed scenes. Many tried, but few succeeded, and for every career that Van

Damm helped (Peter Sellers, Tony Hancock, Jimmy Edwards), there was disappointment for future comic stars (Spike Milligan, Bob Monkhouse, Norman Wisdom). Hill was one of the unlucky ones. Having written a new skit around famous Jewish/Irish tenors of the time, he failed his audition – indeed, he didn't deliver one gag before being shown the door. The turnover of talent was very quick, and Van Damm had no time to waste.

In the autumn of 1947, Hill was down to his last 14s when he accepted badly paid and sporadic variety theatre spots. Living in a flat at 62 Ambler Road in Queensway, just fifty yards off Bayswater Road, London, sharing with two young ladies called Dorothy and Hazel, Hill performed at venues like the Tottenham Liberal and Radical Club or the Edmonton Working Men's Club, earning £1 per turn or £1 10s for two performances. Terry-Thomas was the big star from the military training ground, and held court at a celebratory party for CSE folk, but nobody could touch the spiralling genius of Michael Bentine in Hill's eyes – even years later, a gem from Benny's own show would be subjected to the question, 'How does it compare with "The Chair Back"?', one of Bentine's early routines.

Hill was still concentrating on lacklustre Max Miller-like material, teasing the audience with Southampton-based tales of his family's bull-shipping, then expressing amazement that some thought it all bullocks. He was going nowhere fast, and with his Army payoff dwindling, no quality work and the depressing task of keeping cheerful, he decided to return home. Trying to convince himself this would just be a trip to see his parents, he secretly harboured the fear that his future lay as a bank clerk in Southampton. Having bought himself a ticket for the coach, he was advised there would be a two-hour delay, so, strolling to fill the spare time, he stumbled across the Biograph Cinema, Victoria, screening Danny Kaye's classic comedy *The Kid From Brooklyn*. He watched the film, was captivated by Virginia Mayo (who isn't?) and struck by the fact that Kaye was playing character comedy Hill himself could perform. With renewed faith, he tore up the coach ticket, returned to his flat, cooked his last two eggs, washed his last two shirts and was back in showbusiness with a vengeance.

At this stage of his struggle, Hill was still performing under his own name – billed as Alf Hill. His brother, Leonard, advised him that the name didn't look very impressive on a theatre bill, and besides, it made him sound too cockney – like a third-rate Max Miller. The fact that at the time Hill *was* a third-rate Max Miller notwithstanding, the seed of radical change had been sown. He had already began peppering his innuendoes with impersonations and character comedy, delighting in rustic bumblers and Germanic fools, and delivering the beloved, corny one-liners through his own created characters rather than his breathless 'self' persona. Like Peter Sellers, Hill found it easier and more successful to encase himself in myriad hilarious characters and let them tell the jokes. He toyed with the stage name Leslie Hill, but felt it sounded like a tea dance pianist. With a life-long respect for the American comedian Jack Benny, he first adopted the stage name Ben K. Benny, but this quickly became Benny Hill.

By now living in very cheap digs in Cricklewood and earning £1 per performance in working men's clubs and pubs, the comedian travelled the entire London Underground system for his performances, and began to effortlessly fall back on cutting responses to rowdy hecklers ('There's a bus leaving in two minutes!' – 'Be on it!') and skilfully embarrassing punters who had to visit the toilet during the performance by asking them, 'Could you hear us in there?', gratefully receiving the stunned response 'No!', and finishing them off with: 'Well we could hear you in here!' It was a gag that Hill used shamelessly and frequently, even resurrecting it for a lacklustre *Streetcar Named Desire* sketch in his very last show from 1992.

With his pianist, Bill Randall, in tow, Hill travelled round London by tube and bus to each gig. It was hardly the glamorous showbusiness life he had expected during his days with REME. However, things were on the up and up. A few months after his demob he appeared in a *Spotlight* revue at the Twentieth Century Theatre in Notting Hill Gate in November 1947. Hill's material was now more refined than the working men's club stand-up fare he had peddled previously – he played character parts like the Dreadful Dancing Sisters, an alcoholic baritone, a Peter Lorre/Sydney Greenstreet two-hander, and most telling of all, an overtly cockney send-up of his own front-cloth routine. By parodying the form, his audience laughed at the old jokes in a knowing, deconstructed way. The bill also included Bob Monkhouse, and Hill's performance remains typical of his late-1940s variety turn. *Spotlight* was used as a showcase for producers looking for new talent, so Hill received no payment, although he was quickly picked up for a BBC radio slot. Boosted by positive reactions, Hill once again tried his hand at a Windmill Theatre audition, only to receive a second rejection, before gratefully polishing his act round the working men's clubs of Dagenham, Harlesden,

Lambeth and Stoke Newington. Once in these early days he was incorrectly billed as 'Bennie Hill', but he didn't really care as long as he earned enough money to pay for his next tube journey. Other performers like Max Bygraves and Bob Monkhouse would help out their friends, recommending Benny Hill if they themselves couldn't make a date. He worked at the Metropole, Edgware Road, and enjoyed a week at Collin's Music Hall, Islington, but this invaluable experience was as nothing compared to the hefty £5 a week he could earn.

By early 1948, Hill had graduated to more sophisticated, respectable ventures like entertaining after Masonic dinners, when he could pocket anything up to 3 guineas a performance. A week at the Kilburn Empire was a high point, while a five-times-a-night engagement in a Cine-variety Christmas show on Bognor Pier was less impressive. The show combined film and live entertainment, and Hill struggled valiantly to fill in between movie treats, but the bookings were pitiful and the run folded prematurely. To supplement these irregular earnings, Hill moonlighted the old working men's club circuit as comic impersonator Bob Job – he gave his disgruntled audience everybody from Gordon Harker to Ned Sparks to Janet Gaynor, and the few pounds boosted his pocket without denting his reputation.

It was around this time that ex-Captain Richard Stone signed Benny Hill up as his client and eagerly presented him to the hugely influential impresario Hedley Caxton. Always on the lookout for interesting, funny and keen comedians with an appeal for the family working-class audience, Caxton's forte was seaside variety show bills for the summer season market. His star name comedian was Reg Varney. Richard Stone did a convincing enough job promoting Hill to secure him an audition for a part in the up-coming revue. Primarily, the position was for supporting player and comic stooge for Varney, and Hill landed the job, notably beating a certain Peter Sellers, who left Caxton rather unimpressed by giving a straight rendition of a George Formby number on his ukelele. Hill, accompanied by his own guitar-playing, sang a self-penned calypso satire on the Atlee/Bevin government. It clearly blew the competition out of the water – sweetest of all, the rehearsal room was Mac's, just opposite the Windmill Theatre, which had twice turned him down. As previously agreed, the winner bought coffee and cakes for Sellers at Velotti's Cafe, nipped over to see Edith Piaf in Paris to celebrate, and returned home for his £14 a week summer season. Hill was headed for the bright lights of Margate.

Gaytime

This comic revue for 1948 enjoyed a hugely successful trial run at Cliftonville Lido, Kent, before a pre-season tour and the great opening at the Lido, Margate. Bursting forth with the jolly invitation, 'Gaytime,/Let's have a gaytime,/Gaytime,/Let's have some fun!', this was a real feelgood holiday experience.

Like a low-grade Sid Field and Jerry Desmonde, Varney turned on the campness with skill, brilliantly playing a terribly shy tennis player (based on the French champion Suzanne Lenglen), while Hill's petulant instructor fed the laugh-lines with aplomb. Entitled 'What the Deuce!', Hill had crafted a wonderfully flamboyant part for his partner, allowing himself time to develop his own comedy through long pauses, disconcerted looks and innocent, innuendo-drenched comments like 'Balls to you!' Varney thought the teaming was inspired and many people considered Hill's perfectly timed amazed facial reactions the making of the act. However, whether because this hired hand was outshining his star name or not, Caxton was left totally unimpressed by Benny Hill. Indeed, his solo spot, hated by Hill himself, was so badly received that the management's unpromising reaction was that the man had no potential for comic stardom.

It was hardly the ground-breaking venture that Hill had hoped for, although he tirelessly worked alongside Varney for three seasons of *Gaytime* before they were given an impressive escape route. At the Royal Theatre, Bournemouth, cockney Reg was treated like a king by the holidaymakers, the performance played like repertory theatre, with five sketches for five different versions of the piece, and even the top-lining guest performers for this one stint, The Radio Revellers, couldn't outshine the comedy team. There was a return performance for summer 1949 at the Cosy Nook Theatre, Newquay, although this time Hill was teamed with comic Ron Clark, while Varney was retained at Cliftonville. Back at the Lido, Margate, in 1950 with Reg, Benny continued writing gems for the team – notably an audience-threatening boxing skit which saw Varney flamboyantly swing his punch and send his glove shooting off into the audience – who said William Castle was first?

Did You Know?

It was during the 1950 run of *Gaytime* that Hill made his first marriage proposal to a showgirl in another production in Margate. Hill was so embarrassed at the possibility of being overheard that he popped the question from a phone box, and the subsequent rejection was the first of several heart-breaking engagement flops. Years later, when Hill was the most famous comic on television, the lady in question invited him to reunite for a meeting with her dentist husband and family. Hill declined.

Hill was now based with friends Bill and June in Cricklewood, but it was a time of much moving, decamping to another couple's tension-filled home, a lodging house in Finsbury Park, and finally, the packed Kilburn Victorian abode of Mrs Birkitt. However, towards the end of the decade his star was on the ascendant, and he was on the move to a better place to rest his head.

In 1949, he appeared in revue at Bolton's Theatre, South Kensington, Chelsea. The payment was £7 a week, but the high prestige of these shows was worth far more. One performance was even attended by Queen Mary. Ferrier's *Searchlight* cartoon caricatured all the performers involved – speciality act The Burt Twins, Latin-styled dancer Lucille Gaye, satirist Marcella Salzer, drag act Stanley Beard, forever limber Larry Drew, musical director Ann De Nys and her keyboard player Judith Dolman, glamorous singer Patricia Morne, and crooners Michael Harding and Eugenie Sivyer – highlighting the venue's reputation for harbouring future stars and wondering who would be the West End hit of tomorrow.

For this hugely important run, Hill introduced a perennial favourite. Billed as 'A gem of purest razz serene – Benny Hill as a "deutsche komiker"', he took on the character of misunderstanding Toto the German. He would ram a hat down over his head to make his ears stick out comically, and ramble on about life, girls and London in the unique 'Deutschspeak' he had perfected during the war. Comically saucy with his talk of 'Marble Arse' and 'Golders Groin', Hill, never one to let ideas slip into obscurity, happily resurrected the turn for a 1980 edition of *The Benny Hill Show* on television. Accepting any offer that would allow his face to be seen around London, Hill even undertook cycling antics as compere for a bicycle exhibition at Olympia, and of course, he was always willing to judge a beauty contest such as for *Blighty Magazine* at the Albert Hall.

More structured, progressive work was offered with John Alexander's touring production of the West End smash *Montmarte*, which had starred Alfred Marks and Paddie O'Neil. Once more teamed with headlining Reg Varney, Hill enjoyed a notable hit with the show during its November run at the East Ham Palace – their comic bumbling alongside Bill Gordon, Donan O'Dea, Audrey Cranston and Johnnie Downs in a super Continental show was far too good to miss.

Aladdin

In another rare appearance in pantoland, Hill appeared opposite Sydney Arnold, Rowena Gregory and Russell Thorndike at the Richmond Theatre for the December 1949/January 1950 season, while Varney was headlining at the Dudley Hippodrome.

Sky High

Impressed by Hill and Varney's work in *Gaytime*, George and Alfred Black hired the team for the autumn 1950 touring version of a successful Palladium revue, *Sky High*, which had starred Windmill graduate Jimmy Edwards. From the Chelsea Palace to Northampton, Varney and Hill worked the audience relentlessly. Again Hill was the stooge to Varney's comedian, but he had another solo spot which Hill, once more, loathed with a passion. Later holiday audiences were rather more tolerant of the material, but certain crowds weren't impressed, and this was the end of a beautiful friendship.

The problem, contrary to newspaper reports at the time of Hill's death, did not lie between the two performers – indeed, Hill helped Varney struggle through a performance at the Royal Theatre, Chatham, just after he had heard of his father's death. The two were bonding like never before, but the magical bubble was about to burst. Following a particularly disastrous performance of Hill's solo spot in Sunderland, the crowd began to slow handclap and let the comedian walk off stage to the sound of his own footsteps. The manager, Mr Challen, was outraged, stormed off to the Black brothers, and the result was that Hill was told his solo spot was cut from now on. Hill was hardly besotted with the monologue and decided to leave the show. Varney fought to keep him but Hill was adamant – he was nobody's stooge. Varney, who within a few short years would be shocked to see his old stooge become the first mega-star of this powerful new medium called television, struggled on through life in variety before, over a decade later, he hit the small screen big time with the comedy series *The Rag Trade* and, most notably, *On the Buses* for Frank Muir's 'beans on toast'-audience-geared London Weekend Television.

IF AT FIRST YOU DON'T SUCCEED ...

After this brief but eye-opening excursion into stage nightmare, Hill almost turned his back on a struggling performing career. However, he heavy-heartedly returned to what he had peddled before, developing his variety turn with impish, hand-rubbing delivery, impersonations and songs. Even an ill-fated attempt to interest George and Alfred Black backfired. Richard Stone presented an ambitious five-handed boxing sketch starring Hill, Ian Carmichael, Ian Wallace, Philip Dale and Reg Varney at Poplar Town Hall, London, which came to naught, although the performers all received £50. At least Hill was happy with the self-penned material he was performing, and the variety bill proclaimed him 'Britain's Brightest Boy'.

Writing reams of routines at the time, he continued in variety until the early 1950s, meeting Peter Charlesworth in his dressing room at the Alma Theatre, Luton, who was struggling to progress from often-unemployed musician to manager. Hill, displaying the kindness that often marked his private life, took Charlesworth on as his driver for six months, continually paying him well over the odds, and eventually he stood in as Benny's straightman at Sunday concerts. However, the Sunderland debacle had seriously damaged Hill's confidence and reputation, and his stage career never recovered. He made another attempt at pantomime with *Dick Whittington* at the Devonshire Park Theatre, Eastbourne, for the 1950 season, and enjoyed the summer of 1951 at Ramsgate, where bandleader Billy Merrin topped the bill, with singer Penny Nichols and comic duo Low and Webster in support. As well as his own spots, he would occasionally fill in for an ailing member of the double act. Hill was also writing a regular column for the journal *Show World*, a cheaper weekly alternative to *The Stage* or *The Performer*. Although he was never paid for these, his brilliantly topical gags kept his name in the limelight. Indeed, one comedian would collect all the columns and use them as material during his American assignments, where nobody could match their cleverness.

Although his stage career was faltering, by the start of the 1950s Hill had made a substantial impact on radio and was becoming a television celebrity. His fame didn't deter stage performance completely, and his continued variety spots reached their zenith with a prestigious summer season on Wellington Pier, Great Yarmouth, for Billy Marsh in 1953. His variety masterpiece was an intricate performance of the *Romeo and Juliet* balcony scene – but on his own. Perfectly timed, it was a stunning and, above all, hilarious performance. Hill played the

Finsbury Park Empire with singers Pearl Carr and Teddy Johnson, and his booking at the Chelsea Palace, immediately following the record-breaking stint of singer Dickie Valentine, broke the box office record. Hill even doubled for bandleader Joe Loss when illness forced him to pull out of concerts at the Metropolitan, Edgware Road. For a few weeks' engagements around London, Hill flamboyantly waved his arms and let the band get on with it, playing halls, Sunday concerts, the Gaumont, Lewisham, the Elephant and Castle, the Brixton Empress, finally filling in for flu-ridden Larry Gretton with an Al Jolson medley.

Another important booking for 1953 came from entertainment officer Dave Freeman, ex-policeman, newspaper employee, failed electrician (taking the job to remain in the London area, and quickly dropping out after almost blowing up Ben Lyon) and a regular in the Navy, who signed Hill for a Saturday dance cabaret spot at Winfield House, the US Air Force officers' club in Regent's Park. Chatting after the performance, Hill and Freeman found they shared the same sense of humour, and once he became successful on television, Freeman became Hill's writing partner.

At the time, Hill was part of Bernard Delfont's touring *Showtime* variety bill, with the new added attraction of television stardom thanks to *The Centre Show*, and receiving very positive responses from the audiences. One venue was the notorious Sunderland Empire, where Hill had been slow-handclapped off stage during the Reg Varney days. The all-conquering television star couldn't resist peppering his routine with exactly the same jokes that had bombed just two years earlier. This time they received tremendous applause.

The Benny Hill Show

Although 1953 was a highly successful year on stage for Benny Hill, with television taking up more of his time, the lure of the boards was becoming less and less potent. Hill's last major stage tour was to promote the first batch of television Benny Hill shows in early 1955. Television was completely reshaping his career – the beloved 'Romeo and Juliet' stage performance was replaced by a more risqué version of his Lady Isabel Barnett impression from *The Centre Show* (her 'dress' would slip on occasion). During the second half of 1954, he toured the provinces with a stage version of *The Benny Hill Show*, tuning his stock collection of comic characters, inventing new ones and, importantly, revelling in the renewed celebration of his work in light of small-screen success. In November 1954,

he scored a major hit at the Hippodrome, Manchester. This was planned to be the culmination of his stage work before he fully concentrated on television. However, in 1955, Hill received a rare stage offer that even he couldn't turn down. The West End came a-calling.

Paris by Night

In 1955, the same year that saw the BBC launch the very first edition of *The Benny Hill Show*, Hill headlined in this spectacular West End Folies Bergère revue which ran for eighteen months at the Prince of Wales Theatre, but only after Richard Stone barraged his client with the prospect of working in the West End for the monumentally important impresario Bernard Delfont.

Never one to avoid obvious clever career moves, Hill scored a hit with Delfont (he was often photographed together with Delfont and his wife at Variety Artists' dinners), and became a revue sensation. It was the biggest advance booking for any Bernie Delfont production, and the man himself brought Maurice Chevalier for the opening night. Also on the bill was fellow ex-star in battledress Tommy Cooper. For Hill, this was major work overload – *Paris by Night*, Ealing studios by day, and Shepherd's Bush during any spare time! However, he was keen to take on this challenge, not least because he was using the old dressing room of one of his idols, Sid Field. Besides, Hill's dream of being the beloved comedian surrounded by a seemingly never-ending line of glamorous girls had come true.

The sketches included the Michael Bentine-inspired 'Male Fashion Parade', with Hill as the embarrassed Digby and, in a nightmarish flashback to those dreaded times playing *Sky High* in Sunderland, a seven-minute solo spot. But now, he was at the top of his profession, a situation that wouldn't change much for the next thirty years. However, even at this stage in his career, Hill was keen to drop out of stage work completely.

Hill cannily realized that many of his audience were coachloads of foreign tourists simply there to see some sort of show rather than Benny Hill's performance. Indeed, the comedian noticed that most of these international eyes were focused on the scantily clad girls – a realization that, although it made him furious at the time, remained with him throughout his work and dictated the appearance of Hill's Angels and visual material for the world comedy market.

Paris by Night: Val Parnell and Bernard Delfont. Prince of Wales Theatre, Piccadilly Circus, 1955, 6.15/8.50

Already stealing all his own material. A touch of the Noel Cowards before a performance of *Paris By Night*.

embrace Frankie Howerd's style of feigning nerves, delivering his gags and masking the silence or muted laughter with asides to himself:

She was a really robust girl. All ro and no ... wonder [to himself], otherwise she was quite nice really. This girl was so thin she could stand in a shower without getting wet. [to himself] Which is quite extraordinary, I can't believe it myself even though I said it.'

p.m. twice nightly. Starring BENNY HILL with TOMMY COOPER and 30 girls (count 'em!). Orchestra conducted by Harold Collins.

The Royal Command Performance, 1955

As a natural extension of his West End run, Hill was invited to perform before royalty in this, the most prestigious show of the year, in November 1955. Still packing them in for *Paris by Night*, Hill appeared early, to allow him to play both houses at the Prince of Wales and, in between, gallop across to the Victoria Palace for the royal appointment. In attendance were the Queen, the Duke of Edinburgh, Princess Margaret, the Queen Mother and Princess Alexandra. Fellow performers that night included Lena Horne, George Jessell and Johnnie Ray.

With West End success under his belt and his own BBC television series soaring, Hill still continued to tread the boards, nurturing his comic characters and allowing them to mask his nervousness on stage. Bob Monkhouse recalled an occasion in the number one dressing room of the Prince of Wales Theatre with Benny discussing his comic impression of Frankie Laine, a stunningly accurate resurrection of the current hit 'The Cry of the Wild Goose', complete with flamboyant, outstretched-arms stage delivery. The real Hill couldn't have been so free on stage, but Hill as Laine found it easy. This move away from the cocky, confident stand-up comedy delivery of Max Miller (which Hill struggled with) allowed him to develop as a performer. When talking as himself, he would

With wringing hands and tremendous self-doubt, this is how Hill survived the variety circuit. Richard Stone gingerly persuaded him to take the Black brothers' offer of three weeks filling in for an ailing Dave King at the London Hippodrome in November 1955, but Hill, cannily, only accepted when he secured a percentage of the takings. He performed in a summer season for Delfont at the Wellington Theatre, Great Yarmouth, in 1957 with Frederick Ferrari, The Konyots and Roger Carne. He turned out, with the glamorous Sabrina on his arm, for the final burst of fun – Terry Scott and Hugh Lloyd – at the doomed Chelsea Palace, his box office record intact, for a special farewell gig organized by Richard Stone, and in 1958 he starred at the Floral Theatre, Scarborough, with Renee Strange, Jack Beckitt and Peter Vernon. He later appeared at the Brighton Hippodrome, by now adopting Arthur Askey's ploy of mocking his own jokes before the audience could – thus defusing groan reactions and endearing himself to the crowds.

Television exposure helped enormously. He performed at charity benefit concerts under the direction of BBC director Ernest Maxim, helping raise funds for children with cerebral palsy at a London Palladium midnight matinee, and for poor children from the East End in need of money for synagogue reconstruction at the Coliseum. Hill happily did several charity performances at the Prince of Wales, usually giving his 'This Is Your Life' spot as a load of different guests battling the Eamonn Andrews host figure played by either

Inspired madness for the beatnik generation - *Fine Fettle*.

PALACE THEATRE
SHAFTESBURY AVENUE - W.1   GERRARD 6834
Proprietors : London Palace Limited   Chairman and Managing Director : Emile Littler
Licensed by the Lord Chamberlain to Emile Littler

FINE FETTLE

A REVUE
IN
CLOTH-CAP AND TAILS

PROGRAMME : ONE SHILLING

Peter Vernon or Nicholas Parsons. He compered Marlene Dietrich's sell-out run at London's Café Anglais, and compered again for a special show in honour of his old English master, Horace King. There were hugely successful Sunday night concerts at Felixstowe and sell-out appearances at the Finsbury Park Empire, but treading the boards night after night was never his style, and he liked it less and less each time he did it. However, once again he put aside a huge amount of time to tackle a further West End appearance in the revue *Fine Fettle* – the promise of major theatrical stardom and the chance to reinvent a key influence was too good to miss.

Fine Fettle

Hill returned to the West End stage in 1959 with *Fine Fettle*, 'a mid-summer frolic in cloth-cap and tails', exploiting his position as one of the country's top television comedians and simply bringing his collection of comic characters to a live audience. Based on Robert Dhery's *La Plume de ma Tante*, the script was written by Benny Hill and Dave Freeman. Emile Littler suggested the title should be *Boo to a Goose*, much to the star's indignance. Disarmingly he told Freeman, 'I don't fancy a title with the word "Boo" in it, it might give the audience ideas,' muttering as a follow-up, 'I don't much care for the word "goose" either!' Freeman's original suggestion, *Layabout Laughing*, was far superior, but *Fine Fettle* it became. In an astounding piece of work, Hill played some twenty characters through the performance, and secured a popular seven-month run at the Palace Theatre.

Hill mugged with glorious abandon, playing a centaur, giggling through a 'This Is Your Life' skit with Bunny Hare, turning on the wide-eyed amazement as the eager stable-boy to Lady Godiva, delivering bumpkin mannerisms on his way to a country market, and presenting the full stage version of 'Milk Marketing Board', adopting cropped hair to enable quicker wig changes. Much of this material would be revamped for years to come as part of *The Benny Hill Show*.

The *Daily Mirror* theatrical reporter was less than impressed, pinpointing – albeit unknowingly – exactly why the audience loved it so much when he snootily commented: 'It's very much a seaside show masquerading

as a West End one.' The *News Chronicle* described the show as 'fresh and zealous', while the *News of the World* thought it included 'choice, catchy tunes and laughs aplenty'. Hill's final bow to the peer pressure of Stone and Delfont, this was his second and last big, starring stage production. Television was the future.

Fine Fettle. Bernard Delfont and Emile Littler. Palace Theatre, London W1 from 6 August 1959, 8 p.m. Friday/Saturday 6.15/8.45 p.m twice nightly. Closed February 1960. Prices: Stalls, 25s, 20s, 15s. Dress circle, 25s, 17s 6d, 12s 6d. Upper circle: 10s 6d, 8s 6d. Balcony 6s. Starring BENNY HILL, SHANI WALLACE, ROBERTSON HARE with IRVING DAVIES, PETER VERNON, MILDRED MAYNE, MARIO FABRIZZI, CLEMENCE BETTANY, VIVIENNE MARTIN, ROSE HILL. First half – 'Something Out of ...': Shani Wallis, Irving Davies, Mildred Mayne, Clemence Bettany and the dancers. 'Trunk Call': Benny Hill. 'Work Song' (music and lyrics by Robert Gould): Shani Wallis, Irving Davies, Rose Hill, Vivienne Martin, Malcolm Macdonald & David Spurling. 'The Open Book': Benny Hill, Robertson Hare and Peter Vernon. 'Boy in a Hurry': Shani Wallis. 'Sea View': Robertson Hare and Rose Hill, with Vivienne Martin, Peter Vernon, Mildred Mayne and Clemence Bettany. 'Re Percussion' (by John Law and Lance Mulcany): Irving Davies and the dancers. 'The Pride of Lower Tidmarsh': Benny Hill, Vivienne Martin, Peter Vernon, Kenneth Toye, Peter Thornton,

Brett Stevens, Bruce Gordon and Frank Davies. 'Early Worm': Robertson Hare, Rose Hill, Peter Vernon, Mildred Mayne, James Dark and Bruce Gordon. 'Rickshaw Boy' (by Robert Gould and Delores Clayman): Shani Wallis, Irving Davies, Vivienne Martin, Mildred Mayne, Frank Davies, Brett Stevens, Peter Thornton, Kenneth Toye and Malcolm Macdonald. 'Turkish Bath': Robertson Hare, Kenneth Toye, Tommy Shaw and James Dark. 'Preamble': Benny Hill. 'Carry On Zeus' (by Leslie Bricusse): Pan – Irving Davies, Zeus – Robertson Hare, Venus – Rose Hill, King Priam – Peter Vernon, Helen – Vivienne Martin, Hope – Shani Wallis, Hercules – Bruce Gordon, Hector – Kenneth Toye, Paris – Peter Thornton, and full company. Second half – 'In Formation, Please': Benny Hill, Shani Wallis, Irving Davies, Rose Hill, Mildred Mayne, Clemence Bettany, Terry Day and the dancers. 'Midnight' (Music and lyrics by Robert Gould): Robertson Hare, Shani Wallis & Irving Davies. 'To See a Fine Lady': Benny Hill, Peter Vernon, Rose Hill, Bruce Gordon, Mildred Mayne and Oliver. 'Falling': Shani Wallis and the male dancers. 'Boy at the Fair': Benny Hill. 'Spice of Life': Irving Davies, Tommy Shaw and David Spurling. 'The Observer': Robertson Hare. 'Scarecrow' (by Ron Moody): Vivienne Martin. 'Moment Musicale': introduced by Peter Vernon. 'Small Town Episode' (by Tony Tanner and Neville McGrah): Shani Wallis and the dancers. 'The Traitor': introduced by Vivienne Martin, Benny Hill and Robertson Hare. 'Finale': The full company. Revue directed by Kenneth Carter. The dancers: Janet Hall, Nita Howard, Heather Lynn, Maureen Sims, James Dark, Malcolm Macdonald, Tommy Shaw and David Spurling. Choreography: Irving Davies. Scenery and costumes: Louden Sainthill. Lighting: Michael Northern. The Palace Orchestra under the direction of Bert Rhodes. Music: Ronnie Hazlehurst and Ron Grainer.

Did You Know?

With bookings declining, Delfont replaced the usual television extravaganza *Sunday Night at the London Palladium* with edited highlights of *Fine Fettle*. Attendances soared.

The Palace Theatre, bearing the legend 'Benny Hill in *Fine Fettle*', also crops up in the French documentary film *The World By Night*, representing London entertainment.

Juggling television, radio, film and stage commitments in 1955 had physically exhausted Hill, but once he was released from his contract with Bernard Delfont, he could finally concentrate on his first love, television. However, he still had a summer season agreement to fulfil for agent Richard Stone

Lets Make a Night of It

Headlining the new Pavilion Theatre, Weymouth, in 1960, Hill fulfilled his promise to Richard Stone to star in this, his agent's first stage presentation. A typical summer season revue, it naturally capitilized greatly on Hill's television stardom.

Let's Make a Night of It: Starring BENNY HILL, CYRIL STAPLETON AND HIS BAND. Featuring RAY MERRILL, JANET RICHMOND, THE FREDIANIS, PETER VERNON, CHRIS CARLSEN, JUNE POWELL, JEAN AND PETER BARBOUR, HELEN GRAY, THE TWELVE KING DANCERS. Choreography: Rita King. Producer: Bill Roberton.

Immediately afterwards, Hill departed for a long-standing engagement of variety appearances and television specials in Australia. His last stage appearance at this time was in 1960, at Sydney Town Hall – the Lord Mayor's Command Performance, with local talent June Bronhill and John Larson. After that, Hill turned his back on live theatre for many, many years.

At the height of his international fame in the early 1980s, with American television screening his Thames Television material on a daily basis, he turned down huge amounts of money to appear in cabaret in Las Vegas and Atlantic City. He simply wasn't interested in performing live, and certainly wasn't prepared to go through 'fingernails and asprins' for an entirely new audience. No, the one show that would see his belated return to theatrical performance was a very special salute to a fellow comic genius, Eric Morecambe.

Bring Me Sunshine

A Tribute to Eric Morecambe, OBE

Although Hill performed to a studio audience within the comfortable confines of the television studios and would even perform at the drop of a hat for overseas promotional purposes, the only event which coaxed him back to performing in a theatre was the death of his friend and contemporary, Eric Morecambe.

The major tribute show, *Bring Me Sunshine*, performed at the London Palladium, was Hill's first stage appearance in twenty-five years. During their parallel time at Thames Television during the 1970s, Eric and Benny would chat in the corridors and canteen of Thames's Teddington Lock studio, each respecting the other's totally different gifts for laughter-making. Indeed, Eric would cheekily rib his friend over the enormous international success of *The Benny Hill Show* – a level of world-wide fame unequalled by any comedian at the time or since. Hill's determination to be in the Morecambe tribute show despite his terror at performing in front of a theatre audience speaks volumes. His eight-minute solo spot as a word-muddling, befuddled schoolmaster stopped the show. Helped by the fact that he could hold a huge book, both as prompt and prop to stop his hands shaking, it was a triumph and a moving return to live theatre.

The glorious tradition of Jimmy James variety was recreated by Jimmy Casey (aided and abetted by Roy Castle and Eli Woods), Kenny Ball blew up a storm, familiar Morecambe and Wise co-stars Hannah Gordon and Angela Rippon provided glamour, while that master pro, Dickie Henderson (himself, sadly, soon to be honoured with a tribute show), turned on the style. Other performers on the bill that night included Jim Davidson, Des O'Connor, Bruce Forsyth, Jimmy Tarbuck, Cannon and Ball (whom Eric had, incorrectly, predicted would take over the Morecambe and Wise crown as Britain's best-loved double act) and impressionist Mike Yarwood – who set the pace for the evening by cheerfully answering Benny's comment that this was his first stage work since 1960 with the throwaway, 'You should get a better agent!' Ernie Wise bravely hosted the evening in front of the guests of honour for the night, Eric's widow, Joan Morecambe, and Prince Philip. Hill stood next to Tommy Cannon and Bobby Ball in the royal line-up, and sent a huge wreath to the funeral. Eric's son, Gary Morecambe, later wrote *The Illustrated Benny Hill*, published in 1989. Thames filmed the show for later television transmission on Christmas Day 1984.

Bring Me Sunshine – A Tribute to Eric Morecambe, OBE: London Palladium. Starring MICHAEL ASPEL, KENNY BALL, ALISON BELL, LIONEL BLAIR, MAX BYGRAVES, TOMMY CANNON AND BOBBY BALL, JAMES CASEY, ROY CASTLE, PETULA CLARK, LESLIE CROWTHER, BARRY CRYER, SUZANNE DANIELLE, JIM DAVIDSON, DICKIE DAVIES, FRANK FINLAY, BRUCE FORSYTH, JILL GASCOINE, CHERRY GILLESPIE, HANNAH GORDON, THE HALF WITS, SUSAN HAMPSHIRE, DICKIE HENDERSON, BENNY HILL, DIANE KEEN, BONNIE LANGFORD, LULU, FRANCIS MATTHEWS, FULTON MACKAY, NANETTE NEWMAN, DES O'CONNOR, MICK OLIVER, ELAINE PAGE, MICHAEL PARKINSON, BERTICE REDDING, ANGELA RIPPON, WAYNE SLEEP, JIMMY TARBUCK, JOHN THAW, THE TILLER GIRLS (Choreographed by Fred Peters), ARTHUR TOLCHER, BRYN WILLIAMS, ELI WOODS, MIKE YARWOOD, THE IRVING DAVIES DANCERS, THE STEPHEN HILL SINGERS. Orchestra: Harry Rabinowitz. Choreography: Irving Davies. Script: Barry Cryer and Sid Colin. Staged and directed by Mark Stuart and Robin Nesbitt.

Salute to Thames

To mark the presentation of a National Academy of Television Art and Sciences award for American television work to Thames Television, Philip Jones was invited to celebrate with a live stage show at the Lincoln Center in New York in March 1987. Naturally, Benny Hill – both as the company's biggest star and the key figure in America's understanding of the Thames catalogue – was the first to be considered. Jones was less convinced. On many occasions he had approached Hill for special appearances on Thames Christmas television galas and the like, only to be greeted with the oft-repeated comment that he was only concerned with his own hour-long specials and nothing else. However, encouraged by the emotive Eric Morecambe tribute, Hill gingerly agreed to take part. After all, Thames had been good to him.

The planeful of Thames artistes flew into New York's Kennedy Airport on 24 March 1987, and Benny Hill was aboard. A major Broadway exercise, the venture set Thames back about £1 million, and all the stars gathered for an after-show soiree in the luxury Plaza Hotel on 5th Avenue.

Performed in front of 2,000 people at the Lincoln Center, Broadway, *Salute to Thames* was a real gala affair. Mike Yarwood and Suzanne Danielle did their celebrated 'Charles and Diana' act, Janet Brown impersonated Margaret Thatcher, actor Edward Woodward interjected with running commentary, Richard Stilgoe tickled the ivories and the funnybone, while archetypal cockney musical turn Chas 'n' Dave let rip with a knees-up celebration. The performance also featured Hill's back-up buddies, Henry McGee and Hill's Angels. In front of an audience of pros, Hill performed his usual stand-up routine of reading from a mock diary – again both prompt and prop – while the audience went wild on his first appearance, adopting the beloved Fred Scuttle salute and stumbling through his stagehand duties sporting an 'I Love New York' T-shirt. By the time he reappeared as himself, in dinner jacket, he was totally relaxed.

RADIO

Fresh-faced and rearing to go.

While it is fair to accept the oft-quoted description of Benny Hill as the first British comedian made by television, his rise to fame was little different to some of his contemporaries'. For instance, there are many parallels with the career of Tony Hancock, beginning with military service shows, Windmill Theatre experiences (Hancock was accepted, Hill was not), variety performances, fledgling radio spots, sparring with Archie Andrews, and eventually achieving television stardom. Benny Hill hit the BBC big time in 1955, Hancock saw his radio classic, *Hancock's Half Hour*, transfer successfully to television in 1956. The only real difference was that Benny Hill never really became a star of radio, whereas Hancock most certainly did. However, radio was vitally important in the development of Hill's comic personality, and it gave him many opportunities to impress would-be producers, build up a substantial country-wide following and skilfully develop his vocal mannerisms without the visual comedy which would became such a cornerstone in his work.

Ironically, the closest Hill came to becoming a major radio attraction was on the printed page, as the star of his own hugely popular comic strip in *Radio Fun* from 1956, billed as 'Britain's Brightest Boy!' With no defined radio persona to mould the comic strips around, the story writers cast Hill in a series of misadventures involving a bumbling detective agency resembling the one in the film *Who Done It?* The Benny Hill strip lasted until the demise of the comic in 1961, by which time the comedian's caricatured likeness had graced the coveted *Radio Fun* annual cover in 1958. Indeed, his likeness was endorsing products in that other respected journal, *Radio Times*, in 1955 and 1956, featuring several appearances of his advert for Mars bars. A tasty steal at just 6d each, 'It's that Magic Melting Moment that Makes Mars,' said Benny Hill. Jon Pertwee was saying the same thing during a lengthy campaign, but Benny's choc-stuffed beaming features could have sold anything. He also cropped up endorsing Rufflette, a line of curtain tape, hooks, rings and curtain tracks from M. Thomas French & Sons Ltd: 'Benny Hill pops the question – What's behind your curtain?' with poses from him as his clean-cut young self and his own aged, kindly old dear of a mother.

By 1956, Hill was far more famous for his own television hours than any radio interludes. Despite notching up an estimated two hundred broadcasts, ranging from *Variety Roundabout* to *Starlight Hour*, during the immediate post-war era, it would never be a medium he wanted to conquer. Once his fight for television stardom had been won, he would flirt with the airwaves on his own terms when he wanted to, but the long radio journey was an interesting and important one.

Beginners Please!

Hill's very first radio appearance was on 30 August 1947, on this long-forgotten variety show. Designed to showcase new talents fresh to radio, billed as 'A variety programme featuring new radio personalities', *Beginners Please!* was hardly the most inspiring start, broadcast for 30 minutes from 11.45 on a Saturday morning. Brian Reece was the compere, with musical assistance from Eric Robinson and His Players. It was hard-working producer Roy Speer who struggled to secure a more convenient slot, and from 6 September, just after Hill's appearance, the show went out

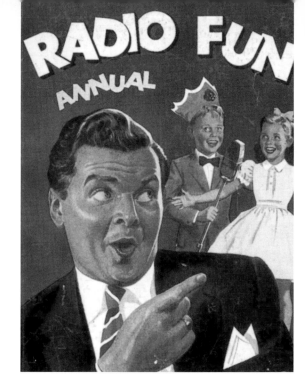

at 5.40 p.m. with new compere Nigel Neilson.

The struggling comedian made his mark with a sparkling four-minute routine, culminating in his dead-pan delivery of Lincoln's Gettysburg Address – '345a Main Street, Gettysburg'. Broadcast on the BBC Light Service from Camberwell Palace, Hill had enjoyed encouraging words from Phil Brown and Joe Collins before the main star-maker himself, Carroll Levis, recommended him for radio work. His spot was a hit, and Hill was recommended to Joy Russell-Smith, the producer of *Variety Band-Box*.

Variety Band-Box

What the Windmill Theatre was to the stage, *Variety Band-Box* was to radio. Indeed, the legendary Soho establishment proved the perfect showcase for *Band-Box* producers, and every returning military-experienced comedian worth their salt (and a few who weren't) struggled into the limelight of BBC radio. Originally conceived as *Band-Box Variety* but rearranged by a typing error and never corrected, this cheap and cheerful training ground for post-war comedy giants was billed as 'the people of variety to a variety of people' – the sights were, wisely, never aimed any higher than that.

An intrinsic part of post-war Britain – like lingering rationing and the rise of Denis Compton – the series had started as far back as 27 December 1942 on the BBC Overseas Programme. The brainchild of producers Cecil Maddern and Stephen Williams, the first *Variety Band-Box* came from the Queensbury All Services Club, London Casino, and featured the talents of Issy Bonn, Anona Winn, Edmundo Ros and others. It proved so popular with home audiences that it was given a regular slot on 27 February 1944. The initial, uninterrupted run lasted an amazing seven years, during which time Benny Hill made several appearances.

As did all his contemporaries, Hill simply stuck to his regular variety theatre routines, and his very first performance was on the same bill as ventriloquist Peter Brough and his dummy Archie Andrews in the show broadcast on 5 October 1947. Hill was greeted with muted reaction from the BBC hierarchy. In a report dated 10 October 1947, Ronald Waldman, who was taking into account both Hill's contribution to *Band-Box* and *Beginners Please!*, unpromisingly commented: 'He didn't-

make me laugh at all – and for a comedian that's not very good.' Ironically, the major *Variety Band-Box* hit was Hill's old REME pal, Frankie Howerd, who muttered, jittered and oohed his way into the nation's subconscious.

Howerd had struck gold with this laid-back, working-class variety collection of songs, jokes and star guests. The major talking point was inspired, tongue-in-cheek interviews with major film stars. Dirk Bogarde, fresh from huge success and killing Dixon of Dock Green in the film *The Blue Lamp*, was probed about his continued impulse to rob people. Other guests Howerd interrogated included former regular *Band-Box* comedian Tony Hancock, Robert Newton, Margaret Lockwood, Richard Burton, Richard Attenborough, Gilbert Harding and Cary Grant, who was totally bemused by Howerd's seemingly unrehearsed delivery.

In an attempt to emulate the popular radio rivalry of Jack Benny and Fred Evans in America, Howerd was pitted against Derek Roy for an ever-heightening battle of wits. Indeed, Benny Hill and Bob Monkhouse established a similar on-stage 'feud', with Monkhouse describing his companion as 'Fanny Hill's son', and Hill retaliating by dubbing him 'Blob Monkhouse'. Hill abandoned this short-lived and uneasy sparring relationship almost immediately.

Although Frankie Howerd would crop up as a guest in the *Variety Band-Box* broadcasts of the early 1950s, his departure as full-time link on 2 April 1950 saw the development of the comic soap opera 'Blessem Hall', with Peter Sellers and a procession of resident comics like

Arthur English, Al Read and Harry Secombe. What had started as a morale-boosting wartime programme hosted by a mistress of ceremonies (usually stars like Googie Withers and Margaret Lockwood – later editions were hosted by Philip Slessor), with the band playing a burst of 'I Love to Sing', Billy Ternent's 'She's My Lovely' and closing with rousing audience participation on 'Let's Have Another One', ended its life in 1952 as arguably the most influential of BBC radio comedy platforms, inspiring *Hancock's Half Hour*, *The Goon Show* and many others.

Producer Bryan Sears fashioned *Variety Band-Box* as a talent contest for comedians, trying out young hopefuls in front of the studio audience as warm-up acts before the actual recording. Some of these comedians would graduate to an appearance on air, and although Benny Hill was hardly the most prominent of these, *Variety Band-Box* offered invaluable experience in working an audience, firing his imagination with more and more fresh material. The very last broadcast, on 28 September 1952, fittingly ended with a turn from Frankie Howerd, the show's brightest discovery.

Variety Band-Box: Series 1 (373 editions: 27 February 1944–29 April 1951) broadcast on the BBC General Overseas Programme and later the BBC General Forces Programme. Series 2 (44 editions: 8 October 1951–28 September 1952), broadcast Mondays 9–10 p.m. for the first eight shows, then Sundays 9–10 p.m. on the Light Programme. Locations: Queensbury All-Services Club, Camberwell Palace, People's Palace at Mile End, Hippodrome at Golders Green, Cambridge Theatre, Kilburn Empire. Regular features: 'Composer Cavalcade', 'Continental Corner', 'Songs of Yesterday', 'The Middle Eight', 'Ring in the New' and 'Blessem Hall' with Peter Sellers and Miriam Karlin. Starring REG DIXON, ARTHUR ENGLISH, TONY HANCOCK, JIMMY HANLEY, FRANKIE HOWERD, BILL KERR, HARRY LOCKE, BERNARD MILES, ALBERT MODLEY, HAL MONTY, ROBERT MORETON, BERYL REID, DEREK ROY, GEORGE WILLIAMS, VIC WISE. Featuring JOHN BLORE AND HIS ORCHESTRA, THE BBC REVUE ORCHESTRA conducted by FRANK CANTELL, WOOLF PHILLIPS AND THE SKYROCKETS, CHARLES SHADWELL AND THE BBC VARIETY ORCHESTRA, CYRIL STAPLETON AND HIS ORCHESTRA, THE BILLY TERNENT ORCHESTRA. Regular guests included: Avril Angers, Dick Bentley, Harold Berens, Janet Brown, Max Bygraves, Violet Carson, Charlie Chester, Clapham and Dwyer,

Petula Clark, Betty Driver, Percy Edwards, Dick Emery, Cyril Fletcher, Ronald Frankau, Stephane Grappelli, Benny Hill, Claude Hulbert, Jimmy Jewel and Ben Warris, Pat Kirkland, Alfred Marks, Nat Mills and Bobbie, Bob Monkhouse, Richard Murdoch, Tessie O'Shea, Vic Oliver, Ted Ray, Cardew Robinson, Harry Secombe, Terry Scott, Mrs Shufflewick, Terry-Thomas, Max Wall, Jack Warner, the Western Brothers and Jimmy Wheeler. Producers included: Philip Brown, John Foreman, Cecil Maddern, Tom Ronald, Joy Russell-Smith, Bryan Sears and Stephen Williams.

Listen My Children

From its first broadcast on 1 June 1948, this entertainment slot for children invited its audience to 'Listen my children and you shall hear the strangest thing.' The strange things were often written by the fledgling team of Frank Muir and Denis Norden. With no studio audience and no recurring characters, *Listen My Children* was Pat Dixon's experimental attempt at presenting 'comedy with a gently satirical note'. Musical accompaniment came from Vic Lewis and his Orchestra, with an injection of avant-garde jazz from the Swinging Strings. The starry cast included Robert Beatty, Carol Carr, Patricia Hayes, Benny Lee, Jon Pertwee, Harry Secombe and Peter Watson.

Following his moderate success on *Variety Band-Box*, Benny Hill was contracted for this show, recording his single contribution on 29 May 1948 to be broadcast on 29 June 1948. His *Listen My Children* appearance was repeated on 1 July 1948, and from then on in Hill would be a popular, albeit fairly infrequent, radio guest.

Third Division – Some Vulgar Fractions

A sort of semi-sequel to *Listen My Children*, with some original cast members, the same writers and the same producer, Pat Dixon. Indeed, Dixon set out the mission for the series *Third Division – Some Vulgar Fractions*: 'We shall try above all to avoid the whimsy-whamsy, and the whole thing will be made as radiogenic as possible.' Hill appeared in all six programmes, alongside Robert Beatty, Patricia Hayes and, in a historic first teaming, Michael Bentine, Harry Secombe and Peter Sellers, three-quarters of the original Goons.

The most famous legacy of the show is the classic 'Balham – Gateway to the South'. Later immortalized by Peter Sellers' tour de force 1958 recording, performing the entire piece single-handed (other than record producer George Martin's brief undertaker interjection), the piece was divided between all the cast members of *Third Division*. Hill intoned the unforgettable, toothbrush holesmanship piece ('He stopped by for a couple of words – I didn't understand either of them!'). Sadly, no recordings of this show exist in the archives.

Third Division – Some Vulgar Fractions: Broadcast on the BBC Third Service, Wednesday – show 1, 26 January 1949, 8–8.35 p.m. (recorded at 200 Oxford Street, 6 December 1948), show 2, 2 February 1949, 8.20–8.50 p.m. (recorded at Broadcasting House, 8 December 1948), show 3, 9 February 1949, 8–8.30 p.m. (recorded at Broadcasting House, 11 December 1948), show 4, 16 February 1949, 8–8.30 p.m. (recorded at Broadcasting House, 16 December 1948), show 5, 23 February 1949, 8.55–9.25 p.m. (recorded at Aldenham House, 18 December 1948), show 6, 2 March 1949, 8–8.35 p.m. (recorded at Broadcasting House, 29 December 1948). Starring ROBERT BEATTY, BRUCE BELFRAGE, MICHAEL BENTINE, CAROLE CARR, BENNY HILL, MARGARET LINDSAY, ROBERT MORETON, HARRY SECOMBE, PETER SELLERS (except show 4) with THE GEORGE MITCHELL CHOIR, VIC LEWIS AND HIS ORCHESTRA (strings under Reginald Leopold). Script: Frank Muir and Denis Norden. Additional material: Paul Dehn and Benny Hill. Producer: Pat Dixon.

Starlight

This hour-long musical comedy spectacular for the Light Programme teamed wide boy Alfred Marks with the ever so humble Benny Hill as 'Scrubber' in autumn 1948.

Petticoat Lane – You Want It, We've Got It

A popular and unfairly forgotten comedy journey through London's famous market, this was a starring vehicle for Elsie and Doris Waters as the nationally beloved Gert and Daisy. The catchy theme song captured the spirit of the thing with:

'*Petticoat Lane,*
There's not another street like
Petticoat Lane,
Petticoat Lane,
It may be poor and tumble down,
It's the Sunday morning rendezvous of London Town.'

A cockney romp in which the duo 'meet unexpected peo-

ple in the most unexpected places', the show was a sequel to the ten-episode run of *Our Shed* (July–September 1946), a vehicle for legendary comedian Max Wall (who starred and wrote the scripts) which hastily filled the gap between two seasons of *It's That Man Again*, and was a resurrection of Wall's manic contributions to a show called *Hoop-La*. *Petticoat Lane* also featured Wall in a supporting role, included other familiar characters from *Our Shed* (the snobbish Auntie and Humphrey – originally played by Harold Berens, but replaced here by Benny Lee), and saw an important role going to Benny Hill, in charge of the books and sheet music stall.

Importantly, this was Hill's first comedy character acting assignment on radio, but unfortunately, the show didn't run to the hoped-for second series, and besides, Hill had already been replaced by Peter Sellers for the last seven episodes. Interestingly, two of the three producers (Pat Dixon and Tom Ronald) subsequently had important parts to play in the development of *The Goon Show*.

Petticoat Lane – You Want It, We've Got It: Recorded at the People's Palace, Mile End Road, East End, London. Broadcast on the BBC Home Service. 23 editions (29 July–28 December 1949), broadcast Friday, 9.30–10.15 p.m. (programmes 1–8), Wednesday, 7–7.45 p.m. (programmes 9–21), Wednesday, 6.30–7.15 p.m. (programme 22) and Wednesday, 7.15–8 p.m. (programme 23). Starring ELSIE AND DORIS WATERS, MAX WALL, BENNY HILL (programmes 1–16), MICHAEL HOWERD, MAURICE KEARY, JOAN YOUNG, DORIS NICHOLS, IAN SADLER, KENNETH BLAIN, ALBERT AND LES WARD, BENNY LEE, PETER SELLERS (replacing Benny Hill in programmes 17–23). Music: BBC Variety Orchestra directed by Rae Jenkins. Producers: Pat Dixon (programmes 1, 8-16), Charles Chilton (programmes 2–7) and Tom Ronald (programmes 17–23).

Did You Know?

Although *Petticoat Lane* was Hill's big radio break, he was still very much seen as a team with stage cohort Reg Varney. Inspired by the surreal banter of Gert and Daisy, Hill wrote reams of similar cross-talk ramblings for himself and Varney. Dubbed 'Bill and 'Arry', the duo enjoyed several notable radio assignments, including a high-profile appearance on *Henry Hall's Guest Night*. However, as was the norm for Hall, guests were not billed in *Radio Times* or advertised, so if you caught Hill's contributions, you did so without warning.

Happy-Go-Lucky

A widely remembered if fairly uninspiring 'light-hearted blend of comedy and music'. Hosted by Derek Roy, *Happy-Go-Lucky* featured items including 'Wedding Anniversary', when a celebrating couple were treated to a rendition of their favourite song, and 'Rhapsody at Random', another request segment (this time open to anybody) presented by Peggy Cochrane ('You call the tunes and composer's styles, and Peggy gives you her impromptu interpretation.'). Benny Hill was signed up for a guest comedian spot on the very first programme (recorded on 28 July 1951 at BBC Broadcasting House, serial number SLO 92598, broadcast Thursday 2 August 1951, 9–10 p.m. on the Light Programme. Producer: Roy Speer). Very much along the lines of his old *Variety Band-Box* contributions, with the laughs punctuated by a 'Naughty Nineties' song from Doreen Harris and the Bar-Room Ballard Four or a duo from Jack and Daphne Barker, Hill's fellow guests were Suzette Tarri and John Hanson.

Not surprisingly, the programme was in trouble from the start. Tradition had it that any show with the word 'Happy' in its title failed immediately. However, help was at hand when the original squadron of writers were replaced by up-and-coming talents Ray Galton and Alan Simpson. Historically important, *Happy-Go-Lucky* was the first collaboration between the writers and Tony Hancock, who was starring as Scout Master Mr Ponsonby in the only memorable section, 'The Eager Beavers'. Hardly world-shattering, these low-brow romps were enough to raise the required smile, and featured a dream team of scouts in Graham Stark as Creep, Bill Kerr as Dilberry and Peter Butterworth as Botterill.

The 'Beavers' sketch seemed the most problematic. Hancock hated the scripts (originally written by Australians Ralph Peterson and E.K. Smith), and Bill Kerr had walked out after show 5. Galton and Simpson were drafted in for show 10's 'Beavers' antics, Hancock missed show 11, and show 12 saw Peter Butterworth replaced by Benny Hill. He played the role of 'Botterill' for one broadcast only on 12 November 1951. Although he rehearsed, Hancock missed show 13 (later subtly mocked by Galton and Simpson in *Hancock's Half Hour*) and for show 14, Butterworth's original character was played by Dick Emery. In the face of such turmoil, the BBC held their hands up and pulled the series from the air.

Happy-Go-Lucky. 14 editions (2 August–10 December 1951), broadcast Thursdays 9–10 p.m., fortnightly from show 8, and moving to Monday from show 9 (9.05–10 p.m.), alternating weekly with *Variety Band-Box* on the Light Programme. Starring DEREK ROY, PEGGY COCHRANE, TONY HANCOCK, BILL KERR (shows 1–4), PETER BUTTERWORTH (shows 1–11), GRAHAM STARK, JACK AND DAPHNE BARKER (shows 1, 3–5,7–8 only), DOREEN HARRIS AND THE BAR-ROOM BALLAD FOUR. Guests: Avril Angers, Janet Brown, Charlie Chester, Leon Cortez, Dick Emery, Benny Hill, Miriam Karlin, Ken Platt, Beryl Reid, Suzette Tarri, Terry-Thomas. Script: Ralph Peterson, John Law, Bill Craig, Laurie Wyman and John Vyvyan, Rona Ricardo, E.K. Smith, Ray Galton and Alan Simpson. Script editor: Gale Pedrick. Music: Stanley Black and the Augmented Dance Orchestra, with Harry Noble and Francis King and the Sam Browne Singers. Producers: Roy Speer (shows 1–12) and Dennis Main Wilson (shows 13 and 14).

Anything Goes

This short-lived half-hour comedy variety series originally broadcast on BBC West Region was soon transferred to the Light Programme. Co-written by Benny Hill, who starred and compered, support came from Cherry Lind, Johnny Morris, Jack Watson and the Ivor Raymonde Seven. A variation on the *Worker's Playtime* format, the group travelled round service camps in the West of England and put on a show.

Starting with a performance in Bristol, one less than impressed reviewer described it as something which had just 'crawled out from under a stone'. Broadcast from 21 February 1952, it was produced by Duncan Wood. (It should not be confused with the 1954 BBC radio show *Anything Goes* that starred singing duo Pearl Carr and Teddy Johnson.)

The Forces Show

Following four classic seasons of the comedy show *Much-Binding-in-the-Marsh*, an ill-fated Radio Luxemburg relaunch, a handful of editions simply called *Much Binding* and another name change to *Over to You*, the winning team of Kenneth Horne, Richard Murdoch and Sam Costa were rounded up for this reunion, christened *The Forces Show*.

An hour-long variety presentation, the first show welcomed comedian Cardew Robinson, while Jack Hawkins and Phyllis Calvert enacted a scene from their film *Mandy*. Reflecting the heavy reliance on services comedians as guest artistes, Benny Hill was once again called on to enliven the proceedings. Indeed, the supporting cast reads like an edited season of *Variety Band-Box*.

The Forces Show: Series 1 (30 September 1952–24 March 1953) – broadcast on the Light Programme every Tuesday (fortnightly from show 23), 8–9 p.m. Hosted by KENNETH HORNE, RICHARD MURDOCH, SAM COSTA with THE PETER KNIGHT SINGERS, LESLIE WELCH (the Memory Man), THE AUGMENTED DANCE ORCHESTRA (conducted by Stanley Black) and, from show 19, LANA MORRIS. Special sections: 'The Singers', 'Show Time' (which lasted just one week and featured a clip from the film *The Sound Barrier*), 'Novelty Corner' (kicking off with Sirdani 'the Gully-Gully Man' performing conjuring tricks on the radio!) and 'Solo Pianist'. Script: Bob Monkhouse and Denis Goodwin. Producers: Leslie Bridgmont and Frank Hopper. Series 2 (from 7 April 1953) – hosted by JIMMY JEWEL, BEN WARRIS with BETTY DRIVER, WINIFRED ATTWELL, WOOLF PHILLIPS AND THE SKY-ROCKETS. Special sections: 'Can You Beat Pharos and Marina?' (mindreading act), 'Forces Quiz' (hosted by Michael Miles). Script: Ronnie Hanbury and George Wadmore. Producers: Bill Worsley and Trafford Whitelock. Series 3 (from 15 September 1953) – hosted by JACK BUCHANAN, with GERALDO AND HIS ORCHESTRA, THE HEDLEY WARD TRIO, MAX JAFFA, LYSBETH WEBB, DIANA DORS. Special section: 'Forces Jazz Session' (with Humphrey Lyttelton). Series 4 (from 9 May 1954) – hosted by ALFRED MARKS with SALLY ROGERS, FRED YULE, EVE BOSWELL, DICKIE VALENTINE, THE PETER KNIGHT SINGERS, PETER YORKE AND HIS ORCHESTRA. Special sections: 'The Ultimate in Magic' (with David Berglas), 'Sport Corner' (with Raymond Glenndenning), 'Forces Instrumentalist' (with Julian Bream). Script: Gene Crowley, Alan Blair, Maurice Rogers and Jimmy Grafton. Series 5 (from 3 November 1954) – hosted by JOY NICHOLS, KENNETH HORNE, DEREK ROY (starring in 'The Dean of Detectives – Kenneth Horne finds himself Without A Clue: Fantastic Adventures To Be Continued In Our Next!') with LESLIE WELCH, RAYMOND GLENDENNING, ALBERT AND LES WARD ('The Harmonious Discords'), DAVID HUGHES (with 'Forces Request'), THE CORONETS, MALCOLM LOCKYER AND THE CONCERT ORCHESTRA. Guest comedians included: Arthur Askey, Max Bygraves, Peter Cavanagh, Dick Emery, Cyril Fletcher, Denis Goodwin, Benny Hill, Bill Kerr, Bob Monkhouse, Jon Pertwee, Ted Ray, Stan Stennet, Terry-Thomas, Jack Train, Max Wall, Jimmy Wheeler. Producer: Trafford Whitelock.

Showband Show

The stage antics which had seen Bob Monkhouse and Benny Hill create a cross-talking battle of wits were transferred to radio for this musical comedy show. Hill was dubbed 'Belly Hill' or 'Benny Hell', and 'B.H.' was explained as standing for 'Broadcasting House', 'Benny Hill' and 'Big Head'. Monkhouse's brilliant patter contrasted with Hill's bizarre character performances perfectly. One such figure, a German psychologist, even decided to spice up their orchestra conductor, Cyril Stapleton, by bashing him over the head.

Mid-Day Music Hall

This 30-minute slice of old-fashioned entertainment, presented by Michael Miles and dished up by the finest talents to emerge during the immediate post-war era, began on 2 January 1953. Benny Hill was a regular top-of-the-bill guest artiste, alongside legends like Peter Sellers, Jon Pertwee, Michael Bentine, Peter Butterworth and Terry Scott. Trafford Whitelock produced the popular programmes, and Malcolm Lockyer's Revue Orchestra kept the listeners' feet tapping. By 6 May 1953 the show went twice-weekly, with a Wednesday edition hosted by Bill Gates, while on 10 April 1961 the programme was elongated to an hour slot, marking the occasion with the presence of super-guest Max Miller.

The show's tenth anniversary was marked with a title change from 7 January 1963, when the programme became simply *Music Hall*, although by then the original stars were too busy with movies and television to make an appearance.

Variety Cavalcade

Benny Hill hosted this marginally popular regional revue show. One edition featured guest comedian Tony Hancock, and Hill kept the fun ticking over with consummate ease, but this was hardly going to set the world alight. It should not be confused with the seven-hour history of wartime radio comedy broadcast from 11 February 1946.

Variety Cavalcade: Produced by Duncan Wood for the BBC West of England Service only. Recorded 19 May 1953 at the BBC Bristol studio, broadcast 30 May 1953, 8–9 p.m.

Archie's the Boy

When I was at school, one class wag told a gag about a hopeless performer who became a hit on radio as a ventriloquist. Oh, how we laughed – and oh, how little we knew that, over thirty years earlier, the very talented ventriloquist Peter Brough had fashioned one of the most popular and important comedy radio shows with his irascible dummy, Archie Andrews. Brough's father, Arthur Brough, had marked his swansong with chilling work in the classic Michael Redgrave closing segment of Ealing's chiller compendium *Dead of Night,* while Peter and Archie had charmed post-war radio audiences with guest appearances on *Music Hall, Navy Mixture, Variety Band-Box, Workers' Playtime* and *Henry Hall's Guest Night.*

After several false starts (including a 1947 pilot, *The Archie Andrews Radio Programme,* with Jon Pertwee and Bonar Colleano), Brough secured a series, *Educating Archie,* which started on 6 June 1950. Within weeks, the original line-up (Max Bygraves, Hattie Jacques and Robert Moreton) was attracting a regular audience of 12 million, and the show won the Top Variety Award in 1950's *Daily Mail* National Radio and Television Awards. Alongside stage productions, a surreal venture into Goonland, a wealth of merchandising and the honour of being the first dummy to be immortalized in wax at Madame Tussaud's, Archie's hit show, *Educating Archie,* proved an invaluable training ground for comic talents like Bernard Bresslaw, Dick Emery, Bruce Forsyth, Tony Hancock, Sid James and Alfred Marks. Benny Hill was not one of them! However, he did get to battle the wooden-headed wonder with the short-lived and unsuccessful spin-off series *Archie's the Boy.*

The show was an experiment to move Archie out of the classroom and into early teenage antics, although his chief cohort was Beryl Reid's snooty schoolgirl, Monica ('She's my best friend and I hate her!'), who also added to the fun as Birmingham youth Marlene ('Good evening, each!'). Indeed, the show's chief saviour, Eric Sykes, left his post as writer after a mounting argument about Reid proffering one-liners for the script while he struggled to develop *Educating Archie* as a character-driven piece.

By the time of *Archie's the Boy,* Sykes (whom Brough considered the cornerstone of the show's success)

was gone, and Beryl Reid was still very much at the helm. Despite comic support from Graham Stark as the bombastic Nigel Bowser-Smythe and the seductive tones of Shirley Eaton adding to the mix, the great British public missed the original format of naughty boy versus bemused schoolteacher. Benny Hill's place in all this madness was really an extended combination of the master authority/comic relief role of old, sparring with the wooden star and feeding him laugh lines/catchphrase links for all his worth. The level of humour was hardly staggering, but Hill kept his delightfully feminine convention ribbing style intact with best man gags, such as that marriage equals a three-ring circus – 'engagement ring, wedding ring and suffer-ring'.

The BBC quickly returned to the old format, resurrecting *Educating Archie* for its sixth season from 26 September 1955. Retaining Graham Stark and Beryl Reid from the run of *Archie's the Boy,* they abandoned Hill in favour of turning the clowning/authority duties over to Ken Platt and James Robertson Justice. *Educating Archie,* which featured performing and scripting duties by Warren Mitchell and Marty Feldman, eventually came to an end after its tenth season on 17 February 1960. In its 219th edition, Sid James provided most of the laughs.

Archie's the Boy: 20 editions, 11 November 1954–24 March 1955, broadcast Thursday 7.30–8 p.m. on the Light Programme. repeated on each following Sunday, 14 November 1954–27 March 1955, 1.45–2.15 p.m. Starring BERYL REID, BENNY HILL, GRAHAM STARK, SHIRLEY EATON, PETER MADDEN, THE CORONETS, THE AUGMENTED REVUE ORCHESTRA conducted by Harry Rabinowitz. Script: Eddie Maguire, Ronald Wolfe and Rex Dawe. Producer: Roy Speer.

Desert Island Discs

From its very first broadcast on 29 January 1942, when Vic Oliver selected the eight favourite records that would be stranded with him in palm-tree solitude, Roy Plumley's long-running programme *Desert Island Discs* was hugely popular. Benny Hill was never fully comfortable with appearing as himself in the public arena, so interviews were rare, but he made a single appearance as castaway number 465, patiently going through his life and work, digging out his favourite sounds and seeming very relaxed. The show also proved a useful platform to plug his new stage show, *Fine Fettle.*

In 1992, Hill agreed to make a second appearance

on *Desert Island Discs* during Sue Lawley's tenure in the chair – typically claiming he only accepted because he liked her legs! Hill asked Louise English if she had a recording of her singing Ivor Novello's *Glamorous Nights* – to remind him of a joyous theatre trip to see her at the Mill Theatre, Sonning.

Desert Island Discs: BBC, the Home Service, Monday 16 November 1959, 1.10–1.40 p.m. Producer: Monica Chapman.

Holiday Music Hall

A popular, hour-long variety spectacular hosted by that glorious master of the 'odd ode', Cyril Fletcher, Hill topped the bill on one edition in June 1961.

Holiday Music Hall: Saturday 10 June 1961, 7.30–8.30 p.m. Host CYRIL FLETCHER invites the family to listen to CON TRAVERS, ANDY COLE, MICHAEL HOWARD, JAMES B. CHRISTIE, JULIE DAWN, BENNY HILL. Featuring PERCY EDWARDS

('Country Calendar'), CY GRANT ('Calypso Time'), RAWICZ AND LAUDAUER ('Memories in Music'). BBC Variety Orchestra led by John Jezard. Conductor: Paul Fenoulhet. The Adams Singers directed by Cliff Adams. Producer: Bill Worsley.

Variety Playhouse

Yet another class showcase for Britain's top light entertainment personalities, this hour-long jamboree was hosted by Vic Oliver. Allowing new talents to stand alongside respected performers, each month featured a guest comedian, and for November 1961 it was Benny Hill. Comic support came from his familiar stooge, Peter Vernon, while fledglings Leslie Crowther and Ronnie Barker successfully picked up the pieces.

Variety Playhouse: BBC, the Home Service. Introduced by VIC OLIVER .Comedy: LESLIE CROWTHER, RONNIE BARKER. Comedy guests: BENNY HILL, PETER VERNON. Storyteller: FLORA ROBSON. Variety Playhouse Orchestra leader: John Jezard. Conductor: Vic Oliver. Saturday 4 November 1961, 7.30–8.30 p.m. (recorded Sunday, 28 October 1961) –

Benny Hill, the dummy and Peter Brough - *Archie's The Boy.*

Singers: Monica Sinclair, Leon Greene, John Heddle Nash and The George Mitchell Choir. Violin: Anthony Gilbert. New talent: Margot Barry. Saturday 11 November 1961, 7.30–8.30 p.m. (recorded Sunday 5 November 1961) – Singers: Victoria Elliott, Catherine Wilson and Edward Byles. Piano: Clive Lythgoe. New talent: Bernard Turgeon. Saturday 18 November 1961, 7.30–8.30 p.m. (recorded Sunday 12 November 1961) – Singers: Glenice Halliday, Niven Miller and The George Mitchell Choir. Flute: Wilfred Shaw. New talent: Angela Jenkins. Saturday 25 November 1961, 7.30–8.30 p.m. (recorded Sunday 19 November 1961) – Singers: Elizabeth Vaughan, Raimund Herinex and Alberto Remedios. New talent: Bruno Schrecker.

Star Parade

Variety on television may have been less popular than it had been, but variety on radio continued to enjoy large audiences, so it still attracted the cream of the crop for guest-geared, sketch-heavy entertainment. *Star Parade* headlined such stars as Edmund Hockridge, Bernard Cribbins and Harry Secombe, while the show was topped and tailed with Ronnie Hazlehurst's theme tune, 'Seconds Out'. Billed as 'the world's greatest layabout', Hill claimed top billing twice.

His first appearance, in February 1963, reflected the star's longing to return to variety, dragging orchestra leader Malcolm Lockyer into the comedy antics, hamming things up as a German tourist babbling on about the intricacies of British telephone boxes, teaming up with Peter Vernon as a couple of unsuccessful dance hall Don Juans, condemning the gutter press as a relentless exposé journalist, and celebrating the great British holiday as the entertainments manager for the lacklustre summer resort, Dimpton-on-Sea.

So popular was Hill's first guest appearance that he returned in August, when Fred Scuttle stumbled about as an amateur space captain, Arnold Cruddy rambled on about his less than respectful scribblings, Amos Thripp proudly discussed the fascinating facts behind his huge vegetable marrows, and a disgruntled baboon bemoaned his zoo-bound fate of turning somersaults for nothing more than a wet biscuit. All of them were brought to life by Benny Hill – and all without the need for make-up.

Star Parade – The Benny Hill Show. BBC, the Light Programme, Sunday 31 March 1963, 2–2.30 p.m. Repeated Sunday 31 March 1963, 2–2.30 p.m. Starring BENNY HILL. Featuring PETER VERNON, LYN-NETTE RAE, THE HIGHLIGHTS. Script: Benny Hill. BBC Revue Orchestra conducted by Malcolm Lockyer. Producer: Eric Miller.

Star Parade – The Benny Hill Show. BBC, the Light Programme. Sunday 25 August 1963, 2.30–3 p.m Repeated Thursday 29 August 1963, 8–8.30p.m. Starring BENNY HILL. Featuring PETER VERNON, JAN WATERS, THE MICHAEL SAMMES SINGERS, THE JOHNNIE SPENCE ORCHESTRA. Script: Benny Hill. Producer: John Browell

Benny Hill Time

Benny Hill's one and only headlining radio series came at the peak of his BBC television success, and displayed the effortless brilliance of his comedy writing at the time. If he could spare material of this quality for his radio shows, then imagine the standard of writing for his more beloved television specials. These radio escapades were a thankful return to the sketch format he always preferred. In between the experimental sitcom *Benny Hill* and his triumphant return to television's *The Benny Hill Show*, the star threw himself into the first season of this classic radio venture.

Although television had taken pole position in public popularity, radio was still an important medium, but few radio shows generated such publicity as *Benny Hill Time*. Heralded with a *Radio Times* front cover flash alongside William Hartnell's first *Dr Who* cover appearance (22–28 February 1964) and a lengthy introductory Hill interview, the show extended his television sketch personae. Producer John Browell commented, 'I haven't laughed so much since I produced *The Goons*', to which Hill disarmingly replied: 'Who are they?'

Just as polished and finely tuned as his television classics, Hill returned to full-time writing duties as well as gathering round him a competent team of supporting players and guest stars. Pitching the shows away from the free and easy style of other radio revues, Hill proudly described these perfectly timed productions as 'full-grown', giving them the same loving attention he had devoted to his more high-profile television assignments. The half-hour would be centred round one excellent, fairly lengthy sketch, a few shorter, less polished ones would be thrown in, and – typical of his BBC era – the gaps were filled by variety turns. A typical example from 1965's second season was resurrected for BBC Radio 2's 1994 nostalgia season, *The Golden Age of Radio*, with Raymond Baxter rather snootily introducing a prime piece of Benny Hill class.

This particular show kicked off with the universally feted Fred Scuttle, surprisingly revelling in new-found wealth, in conversation with interviewer Peter Vernon. Living the life of a rich business tycoon, Scuttle, complete with flamboyant title Fred Scuttle 'the Third', ran on auto-pilot, with Hill just winding the character up and letting him go. There were laughs aplenty to glean from his self-aware excesses (embracing Mae Westisms with peeled grapes, a huge cigar in each hand, and abandoning his car because it was facing in the wrong direction), counterbalanced with more bitter-sweet comic observations (having his television stolen while watching his prized jewellery) and tongue-in-cheek twisted economics while discussing his sausage-less sausage rolls – 'the roll with the hole'. Endearingly peppered with 'Sir!' this and 'Sir!' that, Hill shamelessly mocked his latest film appearance with talk of his position as the housewives' friend since *Those Magnificent Men in Their Washing Machines*, and exploited his ability to drag gags out of the most obvious of wordplays. The exchange 'Inveterate smoker?' – 'No, cigarette smoker!' was a model of comic timing. The pay-off concerning his inheritance of a million pounds leads to a rather lame ending, but it's still hilarious, and Peter Butterworth used a similar narrative ploy a decade later in *Carry On Behind* – written by Hill's old partner, Dave Freeman.

A brief musical interlude saw Hill presenting Jan Waters singing 'The Other Side of the Track' from *Little Me!* before the show's masterpiece, welcoming Waters back as the glam girl. Far too often cast as the emasculated male, Hill made a hilariously confident charmer, and this classic boating pond sketch is a perfect example. This was one of the regular spots for cheerful teddy boys Harry and Lofty (played by Hill and Peter Vernon), brilliantly escalating sketches which made up the backbone of all the best series entries. Here Hill could cascade through the obvious (his cohort reading the boat number upside down), crack into gear with suggestive comments about stroking an all-girl rowing team, and convince his pal that some kinky girls go for ugly fellows like him. The comedy was milked with mounting concern about one girl with two handbags, ranging from a thought that she had a lot of money to her having a boyfriend on the scene (as Hill exclaimed – 'What sort of people!').

The female figures were also the comic butt, particularly Patricia Hayes as the regular character Edie Grimthorpe ('not pretty – not horrible ... pretty horrible!'), who was likened to a dog, and only gained Hill's interest with talk of her father's new yacht. But again, as with all of Hill's comedy, it was the man who lost in the end, finding

out that she was really working-class, finally being coaxed into asking her out despite everything, and after a long pause, receiving the humiliating 'No!' from Hayes. Hill was allowed a bellowed 'Women!', but his cool dude was left with egg on his face, the fall from comedy confidence making the situation all the funnier. In those censorious days at the BBC, his jokes were all the more funny and inventive because he had to work within an accepted definition of what constituted dubious material.

Pearl Carr and Teddy Johnson broke into song for 'The Girls That Boys Dream About' from *Robert & Elizabeth* before it was back to Benny for a fairly average if enthused cinematic parody. Part of the regular 'Benny Go Round' slot, it was a look at the latest country yokel western being shot at Pinetree Studios, with plenty of bungled bank robbery discussions, innuendo-packed comments, some fine Max Miller-like throwaways (making the female carry the case to make them look more like a married couple) and the final lavatorial error which signalled the gang's quick exit. Probably a piece not considered strong enough for television, it was enlivened by Hill's obvious enjoyment, cracking up with laughter as he struggled to deliver the corny gags with a straight face.

Compulsory listening for anybody who thinks Hill was simply a fine visual clown, *Benny Hill Time* allowed him to develop new characters (Peter Vague and Mervyn Twit the awful actor), prolong the life of old favourites (notably the eternal Fred Scuttle), and most importantly, begin to sharpen his teeth on more satirical ideas, notably Peter Nobble, his merciless parody of respected film critic Peter Noble, and Hans and Lotte Hill, a couple of underwater explorers not a million miles from Hans and Lotte Haas, searching for the forward-walking crab. A regular spot featured 'The Sunday Ben', with songs performed by The Raindrops, while frequent vocal drag madness would be included with Hill's plummy-voiced Duchess figures. Harry Hypocrite would eagerly visit a strip joint six times in succession in order to fully comprehend how disgusting he thought it was, and the delightfully suave Anthony Sharp would often keep things in order as the refined man from the BBC.

So successful was the series that it ran for three seasons before Hill became preoccupied with regular television specials. The BBC released a compilation record in 1966, and a cassette of four complete episodes in 1995.

Benny Hill Time: Series 1 – 13 editions broadcast on the Light Programme, Sundays, 2–2.30 p.m. Starring BENNY HILL. Featuring PETER VERNON, JAN WATERS, THE MICHAEL SAMMES SINGERS.

Clowning with The Dagenham Girl Pipers at the Earls Court Radio Show - 1955.

Show 1: 23 February 1964, guest artists – Patricia Hayes and Frank Thornton. Show 2: 1 March 1964, guest artist – Patricia Hayes. Show 3: 8 March 1964. Show 4: 15 March 1964. Show 5: 22 March 1964, guest artist – Anthony Sharp. Show 6: Easter Day, 27 March 1964, guest artist – Anthony Sharp. Show 7: 5 April 1964. Show 8: 12 April 1964, guest artists – Patricia Hayes and Anthony Sharp. Show 9: 19 April 1964, guest artist – Patricia Hayes. Show 10: 26 April 1964. Show 11: 3 May 1964, guest artist – Patricia Hayes. Show 12: 10 May 1964, guest artist – Patricia Hayes. Show 13: 17 May 1964, guest artists – Patricia Hayes and Anthony Sharp. Series repeated on each following Wednesday, 26 February–20 May 1964, 7.31–8 p.m. BBC Revue Orchestra conducted by Malcolm Lockyer (shows 1, 2, 4, 7, 9, 11 and 12). BBC Variety Orchestra conducted by Paul Fenhoulet (shows 3, 5, 6, 8, 10 and 13). Script: Benny Hill. Producer: John Browell. Series 2 – 6 editions broadcast on the BBC Light Programme, Sundays 1.30–2 p.m. Starring BENNY HILL. Featuring JAN WATERS, PATRICIA HAYES, PETER VERNON, PEARL CARR AND TEDDY JOHNSON. Show 1: 21 February 1965. Show 2: 28 February 1965. Show 3: 7 March 1965. Show 4: 14 March 1965. Show 5: 21 March 1965. Show 6: 28 March 1965. Series repeated on each following Wednesday, 24 February–31 March 1965, 7.31–8 p.m. Script: Benny Hill. The Hill Time Band conducted by Malcolm Lockyer. Producer: John Browell. Series 3 – 7 editions broadcast on the Light Programme, Sundays, 2.30–3 p.m. Starring BENNY HILL. Featuring PETER VERNON, PATRICIA HAYES, ELAINE TAYLOR (except show 4), THE RAINDROPS. Show 1: 27 February 1966. Show 2: 6 March 1966. Show 3: 13 March 1966. Show 4: 20 March 1966. Show 5: 27 March 1966. Show 6: 3 April 1966. Show 7: Easter Sunday 10 April 1966. Series repeated on each following Monday, 28 February–11 April 1966, 7.31–8 p.m. Script: Benny Hill. The Hill Time Band conducted by Malcolm Lockyer. Producer: John Browell.

Woman's Hour

Making a very rare radio interview appearance, Hill was guest of the week for *Woman's Hour* between the second and third series of *Benny Hill Time*. Hosted by Marjorie Anderson, the other items that week were 'Back to Burnley', following Joan Cannon's diary of life as a Northern housewife after her move to the South-East, 'Young Widow', featuring memories of Anne Batt, whose husband had died when she was aged just 22, 'Reading Your Letters', 'Live and Learn', with Sally Holloway presenting views, facts and developments in the field of education, and Shakespearian actress Patience Collier reading the sixth of seventh instalments of *All Passion Spent* by Vita Sackville-West. How Benny coped in this company heaven only knows, but he seems to have come through the interview with flying colours, dignity intact, enjoying loyal fan

appreciation from the women around him, and plenty of plugs for his upcoming screen and radio ventures.

Woman's Hour: Broadcast on the Light Programme, Wednesday 16 February 1966, 2–3 p.m. Introduced by MARJORIE ANDERSON. Guest of the week: BENNY HILL.

The final series of *Benny Hill Time* came quickly on the heels of this *Woman's Hour* interview, and that collection of seven half-hour comic cascades pretty much wrapped up Hill's radio career. However, he would occasionally agree to headline in other variety spectacular shows under the direction of *Benny Hill Time*'s producer,

John Browell. Often, these would be last-minute, unheralded favours that allowed Hill the chance to fall back on vintage material he hadn't used since the days of *Variety Band-Box*. Working frequently with the BBC Light Orchestra, Hill would effortlessly spread his unique comic magic on the airwaves, although by 1969 he was rarely heard on the old network. He finally came back to the BBC for a selective interview contribution to Barry Took's celebration of the history of British comedy, *The Best of British Laughs*, broadcast in 1976

SOUND RECORDINGS

'Who Done It' / 'Memories are Made of This"

Hill's first and rarest single, released in 1956, was a natural tie-in with his classic Ealing comedy film, *Who Done It?* With gorgeous 1950s flourishes and flamboyant strings, this is a straight ballad of besotted love coupled with detective work to organize his confused romance. His voice is pleasant enough, but without any hint of parody of British pop conventions, this sounds like your average sentimental warble. A delight, nevertheless, and well worth searching out – pay any amount of money for it.

The B-side is of equal interest, another straight, sentimental treatment of Dean Martin's hit, 'Memories are Made of This'. There's a hint of drunken, laid-back ease about the performance, but again, although a charming, tongue-in-cheek edge is apparent, he sings it straight. Deliciously performed, rousingly orchestrated and a classic piece of rare Hill, the single failed to chart.

'Who Done It?' (written by Green/Newell/Stellman)/'Memories are Made of This' (written by Gilkyson/Dehr/Miller). Columbia DB 3731 (= SCM 5238).

'Teach Me Tonight'/'I Can't Tell a Waltz from a Tango'

Benny Hill tried unsuccessfully to break into the charts again in the 1950s with this ultra-rare 78 r.p.m. release, a Peter Sellers-like pastiche on a couple of popular tunes of the day. Both numbers feature Hill in fine comic form, accompanied by Woolf Phillips and His Orchestra.

'Teach Me Tonight' is a brilliant two-handed conversation with a sexy-voiced French Hill begging a coy female Hill for a few lessons. It's wonderful stuff, with the stuttering, nervous counter-comments building up to a hilarious twist on the old Tommy Handley *It's That Man Again* routine of finishing other people's sentences with a myriad of comic alternatives.

The B-side is another Hill conversation with himself, taking place on the dance floor, firstly with an American waltz partner and then a Noel Coward-styled Englishman.

One can only assume that this disc's failure put paid to Hill's recording attempts for a time, but this little gem is well worth searching out.

'Teach Me Tonight' (written by Hoffman and Manning)/'I Can't Tell a Waltz from a Tango' (written by Cahn and de Paul). Decca F.10442.

'Gather in the Mushrooms'/'Pepys' Diary'

This single was released on 16 February 1961, reaching its highest chart position at number 12 in March, and staying in the charts for eight weeks. The added hip appeal of songwriter and producer Tony Hatch was enlisted to bring a sense of modern musical production to this classic Hill song from his early BBC shows. Almost banned by the BBC, owing to its dubious sexual content, sales were unsurprisingly healthy after that back-handed endorsement.

Musical numbers had always been important to Hill's comedy, and this third, more high-profile attempt to enter the pop charts is an excellent piece of work. Learning a lot from Peter Sellers and his use of recording techniques, it begins by calling for a 'worthy and respected' introduction for choirmaster Ted Grumble, mispronouncing and misunderstanding the music jargon of the day before bursting straight into an upbeat, guitar-heavy rant about mushroom-gathering and other country quirks. A full decade before 'Ernie', Hill embraces the corny 'pasteurized' milk gag, innuendo-dripping delivery and joyful, rousing energy – there's even the expected reference to 'dumplings boiling over'. There's a great altered-harmony climax as well. Pure class.

'Pepys' Diary' is a classic Hill number which, despite its feeble single joke of reading Pepys as 'Peeps', bristles with comic style. One of the best-remembered pieces from the 1950s *Benny Hill Shows*, it reappeared several times, finally appearing in the very last Thames Television special in May 1989. Hill hams with delight as Mr Grimley, supported by his madrigal group, who continually chorus 'it's all written down in his diary'. Typically well-worn gags (leaving the eyes in a sheep's head 'to see us through the week') jostle alongside neat observations (a plaque marking the birth of a duke halfway up a wall). All blend perfectly in a jaunty, energetic performance. It's also the first time Hill recorded the gag about 'a house to be let, and the landlady to be let alone'.

'Gather in the Mushrooms'/'Pepys' Diary' (written by Benny Hill). Pye 7N 15327. Re-released on the EP *Benny Hill Parade No. 1*, Pye nep 24144.

'Transistor Radio'/'Gypsy Rock'

Released on 1 June 1961, this single's highest position was number 24 during its six weeks in the charts. 'Transistor Radio' is arguably Hill's finest 1960s chart entry, completely avoiding joyful, if sometimes rather tired, innuendo in favour of addressing the conventions of the record industry he was working in. The basic hook to hang the number on involves Hill's radio-obsessed girlfriend – from courtship to marriage – but the real meat comes with tasty, perfectly judged chunks of pop parody: squeaky choruses inspired by the high-pitched monster fad started by 'The Purple People Eater' and 'Witch Doctor', a stunning burst of Elvis in the 'Are You Lonesome Tonight?' monologue and 'Wooden Heart' tuba oomphing, international radio dedications, and finally, the wailing tones of 'Big Fat Mama'. An absolute classic from start to finish, the continual sexual undertones of Hill's comedy are firmly in place (the closing passionate advance is blocked by Hill's enquiry about the radio, and the female's amazed 'Music he wants ...'), but the real heart comes from Hill's incisive understanding of the industry he is affectionately sending up.

'Gypsy Rock' begins with a flamboyant violin intro and Hill's murmured warbling, before this embrace of Gypsy harmony quickly bursts into a high-speed rant. A completely incongruous jaunty style and the joyfully obvious jokery ('Hair long and black with fingernails to match/Hide 'n' seek and if you can't find me I'll be right behind this tree') were later successfully calmed down for the more sedate 1971 effort, 'Anna Marie'. Of course, the whole thing is a tongue-in-cheek piece of nonsense, with the climactic resurrection of Gypsy murmuring greeted by an outraged 'Now what good's that done yer ...?', but this is clearly a desperate B-side all the way.

'Transistor Radio' (written by B. Hill and M. Anthony)/'Gypsy Rock' (written by Benny Hill). Pye 7N 15359. Re-released on the EP *Benny Hill Parade No. 1*, Pye nep 24144.

'Lonely Boy'/'The Piccolo Song'

This stolid pop number from 1961 could quite easily have come from the Adam Faith stable, but gets the full smitten, rejected, regretful comic treatment that typified Hill's comedy. Hill allows a cascade of unsubtle love-obsession references to bounce the disc along, but his performance lacks the enthusiastic power of 'The Piccolo Song' – still, the cheeky gag concerning Pat, her name-emblazoned top, and Benny's court case which comes up next year redeems it.

The B-side, the heartwarming story of young Lucy and her piccolo ('Life is full of heartache – life is full of woe'), is brilliantly fashioned in rousing, cheerful Music Man style. Whether it be the sharp disinterest in her father's gift ('I don't know!'), Hill's passionately energetic delivery or all-conquering flamboyance, 'The Piccolo Song' remains one of his best musical performances. Smothered in the usual dubious references (the virgin/virtuoso playfulness), patriotic pride (a piccolo burst of 'Rule Britannia') and cartoon violence (the young lady ends her days as a musical fairground attraction thanks to the instrument being forced down her throat), this is sublime stuff – heaven alone knows why it didn't chart.

'Lonely Boy' (written by Benny Hill)/'The Piccolo Song' (written by Benny Hill and C. Ornadel). Pye 7N 15405. Re-released on the EP *Harvest of Love*, Pye nep 24174.

Kent Walton Presents ... Honey Hit Parade

This priceless slice of pre-Beatles 1960s pop selected from favourite tracks featured on the hit Radio Luxemburg show, *Honey Hit Parade*, sponsored by *Honey* magazine was released in 1962. Beginning with DJ Walton's usual introduction, Benny Hill's only appearance is with his classic 1961 single, 'Transistor Radio'. The record is nevertheless worth finding for Lonnie Donegan's brilliant juxtaposition of traditional/contemporary refrain, The Marcels reaching the zenith of doo-wop, The Viscounts hamming it up with introspective harmonies and every other class track on the album. This is a unique opportunity for the uninitiated to savour Hill's gloriously tongue-in-cheek knob-twiddling parody set among an outstanding collection of songs which formed the backbone of his inspiration. The cover notes were penned by the show's producers, Roy Tuvey and Morris Sellar.

Kent Walton Presents ... Honey Hit Parade: Side 1 – 'Ain't Gonna Wash for a Week': The Brook Brothers, 'Midnight in Moscow': Kenny Ball, 'Romeo': Petula Clark, 'Goodbye Cruel World': James Darren, 'Blue Moon': The Marcels, 'A Little Bitty Tear': Miki and Griff Side 2 – 'Who Put the Bomp (In The Bomp, Bomp,

Bomp)': The Viscounts, 'Come Along Please': Bob Wallis, 'But I Do': Clarence 'Frogman' Henry, 'Have a Drink on Me': Lonnie Donegan, 'Transistor Radio': Benny Hill, 'There Goes That Song Again': Gary Miller, 'Because They're Young': James Darren. Pye Golden Guinea GGL 0129.

'Harvest of Love'/'BAM-ba 3688'

Released on 16 May 1963, this single climbed to number 20 and lingered in the charts for eight weeks. Not only was it one of the earliest recordings accompanied by syncopated farmyard noises, it was the most successful marriage of country bumpkinisms and pop music hipness. One of the very best examples of Hill's songwriting, there's a real sense of musical style and comedy fever-pitch at work here. Basically, this is Hill's usual charming yokel, making sexual references in terms of nature, comparisons between his beloved and a horse's face and other farm-related tit-bits – 'happy as a pig in ... spite of the way you look at me'. However, the real class comes with the spring-is busting-out-all-over chorus, as Hill rips into 'Sow the seed of deep devotion/Fertilize it with emotion/Water it with sweet desire/And then I'll reap the harvest of love'. Class stuff, it builds to a Roy Orbison-like crescendo as the rustic element breaks in with a perfectly timed pig snort.

The B-side is a well-crafted one-way telephone conversation with Hill's beloved Ethel, kicking in with the overtly friendly introduction and an apology to the girl's father. A samba rant-a-thon, with homage elements from 1950s stars Ritchie Valens and The Big Bopper, it's all about Hill's female flirting, date lateness, financial trickery and all-out caddishness. Brilliantly conceived, recorded with great style and showcasing a thoughtful, rounded Hill performance, it's a real humdinger of a flip side.
'Harvest of Love' (written by B. Hill and M. Anthony)/'BAM-ba 3688' (written by Benny Hill). Pye 7N 15520. Re-released on the EP *Harvest of Love*, Pye nep 24174.

Benny Hill Sings?

Tony Hatch's first major assignment was to spice up Hill's classic collection of songs featured on *The Benny Hill Show* for a 1965 album release. The singles had clearly done very well in the marketplace, and with a cool, happening cover design – Beatles turtle-necked sweater, wailing to his own guitar accompaniment – Pye launched this bumper crop of hits and newly recorded tracks. Hill was happy to put the album's direction completely in

Hatch's hands, although, like John Lennon, he wanted to record fast. As a result, it was an exhausting schedule of four songs per day over a three-day period for the entire album.

'Moving on Again' is 'Freight Train' skiffle meets Johnny Cash's 'Ghost Riders in the Sky'. This may repeat familiar Hill lyrics ('let with the house ... let alone.' Again! Claire the fat tattooed lady from the fair, previously heard in 'Lonely Boy'), sound uneasy in performance and feature the most contrived situations (a chocolate cake being fed to a Scotsman's sporran, no less), but it still remains a total delight.

'The Andalucian Gypsies' is another variation on 'Gypsy Rock', a standard Hill track, lightly sprinkled with corny, groanworthy gags, basking in a wall of sound thanks to the use of four guitars. Performed with real gusto and delighting in one inspired reference to a chicken cooking on a spit being mistaken for an organ grinder's monkey on fire, it also features a well-crafted, atmospheric chorus.

'In the Papers' sees Hill employing a Bob Dylanesque delivery, tackling political satire, commenting on tabloid journalism, and more typically, deploying barrel-loads of sweet innuendo. The first appearance of Dr Jollygood the medical expert (whose 'Suffering from acne? Move to Walthamstow!' diatribe would resurface for *Benny Hill Time*'s 'The Sunday Ben'), this track enjoys a hip, mid-sixties Britpop beat with George Harrison-styled guitar riffs, a compelling performance and a hint of snook-cocking at the establishment. Hill's gruff, rocking, raucous fade into the 'Read all about it ...' close is a masterstroke.

'Golden Days' isn't much more than a bland piece of wistful whimsy, sounding like subdued West Coast of America pop meets rambling bumpkin Hill. The sweet harmony conjures up tongue-in-cheek childhood nightmares of repression, sentimental days of yore countered by typical abuse ('Big, fat, ugly crow you turned out to be') and shared sexual desire (a young boy and old man share miserable failure).

'Flying South' features a neat guitar intro, and Hill's wondrous, Chevalier-like burst of French passion kickstarts this dry run for 1971's 'Beaches of San Tropez'. Wallowing in unflattering humour (the female topless bather whom everyone calls 'Sir') and soon-to-be-repeated gems (the boating crew 'stroke' joke cropped up in *Benny Hill Time* the following year), this is a rampant performance from Hill which effortlessly reflects his Continental affiliations while still tapping into Max Miller territory with the mention of Annie from Brighton.

'My Garden of Love' was later totally restructured for the superior 'Broken-hearted Lover's Stew', complete with groanworthy references to turnip ('turn up late') and beetroot ('be true to me'). This heartwrenching ditty of self-regret moves along brilliantly, stumbling over dubious comic moments ('ash tree – I ashed you to be true'/'friends Ferdie and Liza' – oh work it out for yourself!), lent undeserved dignity by Hill's romantic, laid-back delivery. Crooned with affectionate style, this is a classic Hill cut. It was originally relased as a single, with 'The Andalucian Gypsies as the B-side (Pye 7N 17026).

'I'll Never Know' comes straight from the heart, in which Hill complains about all the silly things in life that don't make sense – from the schoolboy howlers ('Why is a horse so hard when it's always full of hay?') to clever social observation ('Why do nurses knock when they can see exactly what you've got?'). Packed with deliciously obvious jokes, a fine touch of wedded misery ('Why ruin a perfectly good mouth by putting a tongue in it?') and enjoyable, energetic style, it features set harmonies styled after The Platters – a real cracker!

With 'Wild Women', Hill's back in country bumpkin territory, accompanied by a cooking country guitar and rambling through his experiences with females – be it the strange one who sleeps under her bed and is called Potty, the all-image-and-no-money movie star, or the Chelsea jet-setter whose sexual identity is never crystal clear. However, the song's hook, the rousing chorus of 'Beware wild women', is not only corrupted from Red Ingle but doesn't even feature Hill's lead vocal.

'Jose's Cantina' is a manic tale of an overindulgent drinker, sung to the relaxed lilt of a Spanish guitar while avoiding any really hard-hitting Hill punchlines. Going nowhere from the start, there's one bonus in the couplet 'Young hot head/Get knotted', but a lack of musical cohesion, and the sudden, more than abrupt ending makes this an unsatisfactory offering.

'Rose' is a real piece of pop power. One of Hill's 1960s classics, this perfectly adapts the raw rock 'n' roll power of The Rolling Stones for family comedy. The gags don't really matter here (although the best one concerning the 18 candles on one slice of birthday cake would reappear in 'Anna Marie'), it's the relentless tambourine lead beat and Hill's convincingly raucous vocals (particularly on the 'summer time' chorus) that make this a timeless, head-banging, groovy sixties anthem. There's even a cultural icon namecheck for *The Avengers*-inspired 'kinky boots'.

'The Egg Marketing Board Tango' is a true classic of comedy recording, presenting the dance of love in terms of the push for British eggs, injecting telling comment on the modern dance trends of twisting miles away from your partner, and reaching the heights with a throwaway comment about hitting his beloved with a soft-boiled egg – surrealism or stupidity: you decide.

'Those Days', like 'Rose', latches onto current pop trends and reconstructs the Sonny and Cher hit 'I Got You Babe' (the intro is nearly identical) with a hint of Nina and Frederick harmonies as a farmyard-based duet of love with Maggie Stredder. As usual, Hill is the sex-starved predator (offering to switch off the lights when his unkeen beloved doesn't want to see him), bemoaning his lady's infidelities merely from financial concerns ('kissing the butcher when we owe the milkman so much'). But it's Stredder's grating, whining performance that makes this such a classic. Blending with Hill's understated singing, this is a British farming community reaction to pre-Summer of Love hipness.

'The Old Fiddler' is not so much a song, more an accompanied, rustic, Billy Bennett-styled monologue with a touch of the Stanley Hollways thrown in for good measure. Hill tells the poignant tale of a poverty-stricken old man who entertains the assembled masses with a wailing, cat-like violin rendition. He promptly dies upon completion, and fades out with frantic playing from the grave, and that's about it – fairly nondescript save for Hill's breathless gallop through the classical delights the old fiddler rattles through.

'What a World' works like pure folk social comment. Bob Dylan was always a rich and fruitful source of Benny Hill parody, but nowhere is this better illustrated than in this hilarious, perfectly performed and, yes indeed, thought-provoking piece of singer-songwriting genius. Don't be fooled by the throwaway opening verse concerning the penal system denying prisoners their treacle-covered puddings (later reworked in definitive terms for the 1971 track 'Interview'), for Hill merely uses it as an example of the folk singer's right-on attitude, only to be counterbalanced with the truth behind the American folk singer – shouting about equal rights for the starving millions at an Albert Hall concert, only to get into his Rolls-Royce and travel back to his exclusive penthouse. It veers between Home County-aimed topical satire (the BBC typist who speaks openly about her imprisoned family, but never about her dad's private radio station) and unsubtle sexual reference (the three old maids who dote on a cat, before one one gets married and makes the others let the poor creature enjoy life), but there's no denying that Hill scores a personal triumph with the final verse. Strip away the Dylan parody and the constant smile of Hill familiarity to wallow in the apocalypse of nuclear destruction. A sole survivor, unable to face the future alone, launches himself off the seventh floor of the Empire State Building, only to hear the telephone ring as he falls to his death – deep, powerful stuff, closing with an equally powerful guitar fade-out. This unfairly neglected gem was originally released as a single, with 'I'll Never Know' as the B-side (Pye 7N 15974).

Benny Hill Sings?: Side 1 – 'Moving on Again', 'The Andalucian Gypsies', 'In the Papers', 'Golden Days', 'Flying South', 'My Garden of Love', 'I'll Never Know'. Side 2 – 'Wild Women', 'Jose's Cantina', 'Rose', 'The Egg Marketing Board Tango', 'Those Days', 'The Old Fiddler', 'What a World'. Accompaniment directed by Tony Hatch. All songs written by Benny Hill, except 'The Old Fiddler', written by Benny Hill and Tony Hatch. Pye Castle PACD 008. Re-released as *Benny Hill Sings?*, The World Record Club Ltd/Pye T825: W8920.

Golden Hour of Benny Hill

A showcase for Benny Hill's three chart-busting hit singles from the 1960s, 'The Harvest of Love', 'Transistor Radio' and 'Gather in the Mushrooms', this 1965 release also included all the A- and B-sides from his other singles of that swinging decade. The cover, a garish cartoon comic postcard with a bizarre black and white, floppy-haired, vacant groover pose from Benny himself, gives the release a sense of psychedelic with-itness. The ultimate collection of Hill's recorded work from the period, this compilation is a must.

Golden Hour of Benny Hill: Side 1 – 'The Harvest of Love', 'Gypsy Rock', 'Piccolo Song', 'Pepys' Diary', 'Transistor Radio', 'Lonely Boy', 'BAM-ba 3688', 'Gather in the Mushrooms', 'Moving on Again', 'The Andalucian Gypsies', 'The Egg Marketing Board Tango'. Track 1 ATV-Kirshner Music, Tracks 2, 4, 5 and 8 Essex Music, Tracks 3 and 6 Chappell, Track 7 Ivy Music, Tracks 9–11 Copyright Control. Side 2 – 'In the Papers', 'Golden Days', 'Flying South', 'My Garden of Love', 'I'll Never Know', 'Wild Women', 'Jose's Cantina', 'Rose', 'Those Days', 'The Old Fiddler', 'What a World'. Tracks 1–4 and 6–9 Copyright Control, Tracks 5, 10 and 11 ATV-Kirshner Music. Pye GH 524, electronically rechannelled for stereo.

Benny Hill Sings Old Favourites

This less conclusive collection of prime 1960s Benny Hill tracks released in 1966 is charmingly packaged with a montage of sepia images of Hill in musical mode.

Benny Hill Sings Old Favourites: Side 1 – 'The Harvest of Love', 'I'll Never Know', 'Gypsy Rock', 'The Piccolo Song', 'Jose's Cantina', 'Pepys' Diary'. Track 1 Welbeck, Tracks 2 and 5 Copyright Control, Tracks 3 and 6 Essex, Track 4 Chappell. Side 2 – 'Transistor Radio', 'Lonely Boy', 'BAM-ba 3688', 'What a World', 'Those Days', 'Gather in the Mushrooms'. Tracks 1 and 6 Essex, Track 2 Chappell, Track 3 Ivy, Track 4 Welbeck, Track 5 Copyright Control. Arranged and produced by Tony Hatch. Pye Golden Guinea Popular Series GGL 0363.

Benny Hill Time: Benny at the BBC

A classic 1966 compilation from series two of the popular Light Programme radio series, *Benny Hill Time* is a refreshing, well-paced 40-minute slice of fine Hill comedy. Without the variety turns and half-hearted show songs, this is a priceless record of Hill's only major radio series, opening with a welcome to the show and a brief, Dick Emery-like interview section.

As with his more familiar television work, Hill embraces the medium he is working in and discusses the popularity of radio (Peter Vernon's opening gambit, 'I work for the BBC!', is hilariously greeted by Hill's female concern, 'I *am* sorry!'). The Swedish misunderstandings sag a bit (despite the truly wonderful wordplay: 'Officiate!' – 'It was a herring he ate!'), but Hill's whining old-timer is an early prize. It's all aimed at resurrecting Hill's old stage rivalry with Bob Monkhouse, but the muttered listening schedule ('... all the plays ...') cracks me up every time, and I'm still not quite sure why. The lengthy picnic sketch, with Hill's passenger, ton-up boy Harry, and the fate-worse-than-death encounter with Patricia Hayes's Edie Greenthrop, falls in with the running innuendo-encrusted brilliance of the familiar radio characters. Typically, Hill's sex-mad ambitions are scuppered, only to be put aside in favour of an individual fruit pie obsession. The nasal, moronic complaints of Lofty work superbly opposite Hill's overly confident man-about-the-countryside, but it's Hayes, the butt of a cascade of abusive comments, who allows Hill to shine – even the oft-repeated three-tier 'Oh look ...' – 'Why did you tread in it ...?' gag sparkles afresh.

Scuttle's cinematic pretensions are brilliantly coaxed and mocked, his latest film venture is analysed with amazed seriousness, and old jokes are revisited in preparation for the sneak preview of a clip from his new 'James Bond – 0017' movie, *From Moscow With Love*. Mervyn Cruddy, later immortalized in the Thames Television masterpiece 'The Grass is Greener', goes through the frightfully British agent motions and runs through the complete gamut of espionage jokes (yes, even the 'shepherd spy' gag gets in). Reflecting the polished Bond parody of *Carry On Spying*, with over-obvious British conventions in food and 'Fat Man' as codename, this painfully mugged piece of comedy works with gusto, thanks to the classic Hill playing of Cruddy, injecting mispronunciations ('Long live the Gremlin!') and flamboyant nationalistic outbursts ('The swine!') – no wonder he's my favourite Hill creation.

'The Sunday Ben', a newspaper in sound, runs like the sex-crazed moral outburst of Peter Sellers on *A Round World*, with Hill's Councillor Bilgewater disgruntledly muttering an indignant 'Hello' before complaining that the country is going to the dogs. Like Sellers, his crusader for an end to 'temptation and wickedness' isn't averse to sampling the sins on offer, resurrecting the sexy-corset-adverts-on-escalators diatribe from Hill's contribution to 1964's *Christmas Night With the Stars*, running into the violence of children's television, and naively relating his Soho experiences (setting out his store of party shocks later used in 'The Grass is Greener' – sideboards full of drink/Gomorrah).

Dr Jollygood's cockney problem slot (a reprise of 'Suffering from acne? Move to Walthamstow!') and a half-baked piece on the funny things kids say complete this Hill gem before it's radio convention-twisting again with the 'Down Your Way' slot. This is prime rustic mumbling coupled with pre-'Birds and Bees' japery (very small village), pre-feminist jibes (photo of wife feeding the pigs – 'the one with the hat on!') and experimental farming techniques for a happier farmer ('plant gin cress instead of water cress').

The epic historical film, 'Warlords of East Grinstead', is an enjoyable if lightweight tale of jostling, frantic wedding nights and rusty armour. Its star, Mervyn Twit, a Cruddy by any other name, adds much to the fun, Patricia Hayes as the mother is her peerless self, and there's a charming gag (no medieval magarine – 'too young to have middle-age spread!') to keep you awake.

Benny Hill, in straight persona, introduces Peter Vernon's interview with 'Holiday King' Fred Scuttle. A typical bit of Scuttle nonsense, a Clacton holiday is cited at 96 guineas ('Popular price!' – 'I like it, Thir!'), grass-skirted beauties attract punters by 'rotating their crops', and the sheer awfulness of the national dish/paws gag will get to you every time – guaranteed.

The Pinetree Studios country bumpkins bank robbery extract is enjoyably played, with Jan Waters particularly effective as the endearingly innocent 'gangster's mole'. Hill cracks up at another priceless Pat Hayes characterization (this time a chatting Welsh landlady), there's some nice drunken banter, and a Max

Miller sensibility eagerly breaks into Hill's laid-back criminal mastermind with the suggestion that a married woman would carry the cases. An invaluable chunk of radio Benny Hill.

Benny Hill Time: Benny at the BBC: The following actors, actresses and announcers also assisted BENNY HILL in the above abstracts: PETER VERNON, JAN WATERS, PATRICIA HAYES, ANTHONY SHARP, TEDDY JOHNSON, JOHN HOBDAY, JIMMY KINGSBURY. Side 1 – 'Interviews', 'Layabouts' Picnic', 'Film director-producer: J. Arthur Scuttle ... "From Moscow With Love"' Side 2: 'The Sunday Ben', '"Down Your Way" Visits Dalton Abbott', 'Warlords of East Grinstead', 'The Holiday King – Mr Fred Scuttle', 'The Jolly Robbers'. Producer: John Browell. Album compilation by John Browell and Michael Vernon. Released by arrangement with BBC Radio Enterprises. Decca LA 4723.

The World of British Comedy

This classic comedy compilation from 1969 boasts refreshingly bizarre cartoon cover pictures for most of the twelve tracks and is a much prized salute to the British sense of humour. A wonderful overload of Spike Milligan (with five classic cuts), a brief snippet of Tony Hancock and a priceless piece of rural gibberish from Marty Feldman rest alongside Benny Hill's sole contribution – 'The Sunday Ben' from the 1965 radio series *Benny Hill Time*. Previously available on the BBC/Decca record release of material from the shows, it is rather uninspiringly represented on the cover as a newspaper with the headline 'Going to the Dogs!'

The World of British Comedy: Side 1 – 'The Great Bell': Marty Feldman, 'Ten Guinea Cruise': Frankie Howerd, 'Cold Porridge': Spike Milligan, 'Eeh! Ah! Oh! Ooh!': The Goons, 'The Sunday Ben': Benny Hill, 'Pontius Kak – Story': Spike Milligan. Side 2 – 'Hand Up Your Sticks': Kenneth Williams with Lance Percival, 'Holy Smoke': Spike Milligan, 'The Ballad of Bethnal Green': Paddy Roberts, 'The Missing Page': Tony Hancock, 'The Great Man – Story': Spike Milligan, 'Father and Son': Peter Cook and Dudley Moore. Decca MONO PA39. The Decca record company limited, London.

'Ernie (The Fastest Milkman in the West)'/' Ting-a-Ling-a-Loo'

The 'Strawberry Fields Forever'/'Penny Lane' of Benny

Hill's recording career, from the first flurry of strings, this is a masterpiece, perfectly combining wonderfully dubious lyrics with an impossibly catchy tune. With references to his Thames Television stardom (Ernie's rival is a certain Two Ton Ted from Teddington) and basking in the widespread knowledge that he was a milkman made good (Hill continued to describe his extensive travelling as a 'European milk round'), this disc really grabbed the fun-hungry, Christmas-geared British audience of winter 1971.

In an awe-inspiring mixture of down and dirty innuendo (getting his cocoa twice a week) and the pseudo-innocence brought by the angelic backing refrains of The Ladybirds, this plays like a cheeky, winking variation on Spike Milligan's semi-surreal 'Postman's Knock'. Whether it be the gloriously groanworthy gags ('happy if it comes up to me chest'), the dodgy bit of scansion ('a rock cake caught him underneath his heart'), the comically touching, slowed, lower-key haunting verse ('Ernie was only 52, he didn't want to die') or the spirited, uproarious climax ('they won't forget H'ernie!'), this is priceless stuff. The totally knowing, confiding tones Hill employs for 'but a woman's needs are manifold' alone make it worth buying, and besides, while there's Bing Crosby, John and Yoko and Slade, no Christmas could be complete without a return visit to the milk-strewn streets of Southampton in the company of Benny Hill.

The single was released on 13 November 1971, and its highest chart position was the coveted number 1 slot for the festive season. It stayed in the charts for an amazing 17 weeks, holding onto the top spot for four weeks over Christmas/New Year with over 700,000 copies sold. The record knocked Slade's 'Coz I Luv You' from the top on 11 December 1971, and poor old 'Ernie' himself was booted from pole position by 'I'd Like to Teach the World to Sing' from the New Seekers on 8 January 1972.

Hill eventually achieved a total of 39 weeks in the charts (rising to 43 weeks with the 1992 re-release of 'Ernie'), and secures him a place between The Highwaymen and Chris Hill in *The Guinness Book of British Hit Singles*. At the end of the 1970s, Hill's finest made it onto the list of the decade's 100 best selling singles, coming in at number 59 – outstripping hits by Abba, Blondie and Chuck Berry's equally risqué 'My Ding-a-Ling'.

Inspired by his days as a milkman in Southampton (the marketplace reference was part of his round –

through Station Hill, into Leigh Road and onto Market Street), when Hill spent his time daydreaming about cowboys and indians, he enjoyed recreating his humble past, notably for a 1959 publicity pose on a B. & H. Davies dairy cart, Southsea, for the *Evening Echo*, and a decade later, several milkman-based publicity shots with Michael Caine for *The Italian Job*. A fellow dairy employee, Ernie Carrington, maintained the song was a tribute to him, having served the dairy for 42 years. Whatever the truth in that, this joyous classic Christmas novelty recording remains easily the most popular and successful comedy record of them all.

Without doubt Benny Hill's most lasting contribution to British pop, 'Ernie' was originally written in 1955 as the introduction to an unfilmed screenplay about Hill's milkman experiences. The song finally surfaced as part of *The Benny Hill Show*, and formed part of Hill's EMI album of 1971. With its rip-roaring, affectionate send-up of Frankie Laine, it had number 1 potential written all over it, but Hill was less than keen to make public appearances to promote the song. Although The Beatles had invented the pop video back in 1966, it wasn't until Queen's 'Bohemian Rhapsody' in 1975 that it became widely used, but Hill did make a special promotional film for 'Ernie' in 1971. Riding through the streets, battling Henry McGee's evil Two Ton Ted and featuring studio recording footage of Hill with The Ladybirds chorus singers, this proved perfect for television promotion on *Top of the Pops*.

After his death, the song hit the charts again,

Drinka pinta milka day -
The milkman back in harness for a number one hit record.

prompting one self-important BBC Radio 1 disc jockey to walk out of the studio in disgust. Given the new release number EMI ERN 1, the song hit the charts on 30 May 1992, reached a peak position of 29, and hung around for four weeks.

It remained one of Hill's proudest achievements, mainly because it so reflected his formative years as a struggling performer. Indeed, when picking up Dennis Kirkland in a chauffeur-driven car before departing for the airport, Hill would always pick up his milk, hand the bottles to him and perform an impromptu duet of 'Ernie'.

The recording earned Benny Hill his only gold disc, and remains arguably the best-loved comedy record of all time. Indeed, the influence of 'Ernie' staggers down the history of pop, not only in the continued market for novelty nonsense from Mr Blobby to the Teletubbies, but even in serious pop classics – just check out that stirring flourish at the start of The Lighthouse Family's December 1997 hit 'High'! Promoting the February 1972 edition of *The Benny Hill Show*, the star dismissed any ideas of performing his Christmas hit again – 'As far as I'm concerned Ernie's been and gone.' How wrong could he be?

In the face of such classic comic musical nonsense, any track chosen to back 'Ernie' was destined for obscurity. The needle rarely ventured off side A over the festive season for 1971, but 'Ting-a-Ling-a-Loo' ranks among Hill's finest and funniest tracks, certainly in the same league, if not the same ballpark, as 'Ernie'. Performed with a delightfully winning lisp, Hill's aged old codger cheerfully promotes the all-conquering technique to fight the blues, illness or political conflict – 'Just stick your finger in your ear and go ting-a-ling-a-loo'. This man's been round the block a few times, suffered both world wars, had a bomb dropped on his shed, happily gone under the surgeon's knife, and uncomplicatedly getting through life without a care in the world. According to Leonard Hill's book *Saucy Boy*, the suggestion for this song came from Ben's big brother Leonard himself, although the two were in the middle of a non-talking feud.

'Ting-a-Ling-a-Loo' does work as a comic antidote to all those relentlessly happy and upbeat late sixties tunes which gleefully employed nonsense lyrics and feelgood tunes to put the world to rights with a smile. Hill takes the standard form, puts a brilliant comic twist on the cliché, and even employs some rare but expertly moulded political satire with his condemnation of Prince Philip's infamous 'Get your fingers out' command to those in government – 'Be like Jenkins, Heath and Wilson and stick 'em back again!' Years later, Benny phoned his brother Leonard and told him to listen to the current

Spitting Images hit record, 'Stick a Chicken up Your Nose'. Sounds familiar? Hill's 'Ting-a-Ling-a-Loo' was ripe for plagiarism, since nobody remembered the original. 'Ernie (The Fastest Milkman in the West)'/'Ting-A-Ling-A-Loo'. Columbia DB 8833.

This is Benny Hill

A 1971 showcase for the classic 'Ernie', this album features both sides of the number 1 single as well as copious amounts of prime Benny Hill. All taken from his Thames Television series *The Benny Hill Show*, these songs and sketches were newly recorded at EMI's Abbey Road Studios. Indeed, split into two halves, concentrating on songs on side A and sketches on side B, this works like a comic variation of The Beatles' *Abbey Road*. Highlighting Hill's obsession with songs based around pretty girls, the tunes do tend to blend into one after a while, but Hill is clearly enjoying himself throughout, and there are enough classic jokes, thickly spread, to make this an essential purchase.

'Anna Marie' is an exotic samba dedicated to a tantalizing female, laden with passion from Hill's lovesick fool. Her feminine charms undermined by suggestions of ageing glamour (the cake has '28 candles on the slice that she had') and inability to cook a decent meal (her pastry tastes 'like a wet book'), this is typical Benny Hill, wallowing in wonderfully contrived lyrics, and as usual, finishing up as the embarrassed victim caught waiting for a sexual encounter at a packed party.

'Broken-hearted Lover's Stew' is one of his finest songwriting ventures, and a deserved single release if ever there was one. Again, the recipe of relevant food jokes is bent, rearranged and forced to fit the tune, but it's all so endearingly done that no one seems to care. Indeed, some of the gags ('You've got truffles of your own!') are beyond corn and touch some sort of mad genius. The repeated 'That's all he ever did' categorizing of the religious cousin (loaves and fishes) and little boy (wine and water) is a masterstroke of developing comic lyric.

'Colleen' is less impressive, a standard lament to a gorgeous young lady. Hill brings a much-needed touch of charm to the piece with his sweeping Irishness, brilliantly employed on the lyric 'Lovely figure she's got!'

The saga of Gypsy 'Rachel' is much more boisterous and energetic, although the gag level is equally low. Still, Hill's Elvis Presley-like restyling of 'Suspicion' is a treat, throwing himself with hammed delight into the hook line 'Why do they call you evil?' with unrestrained passion. Despite undermining his powerful performance with the camp 'I think I've done myself a mischief!' and labouring the climax with an elaborate musical burst for a finale, this is an interesting, undervalued example of Hill's artistry.

'The Beach at San Tropez' makes up for lack of comic brilliance with Hill's stunning Frenchman performance – a glorious cross between Charles Boyer and Maurice Chevalier. Blessed with a stirring organ accompaniment, the best joke (vocal impediment fun with an 'All white?' – 'Absolutely wavishing!' exchange) creates enough laughter to breeze through a frenzied close.

'Suzy' plays like a musical morality play, telling the stark story of Hill's fate as a country boy corrupted by drink and ladies of the night. The gags are so old and painful that the humour is stretched to breaking point, but naturally, the frantic Hill delivery gives all the old chestnuts a bright sheen, and there's real outraged passion in his 'I wish I'd heeded the warning!' lament. Besides, the truly brilliant glasses/contact lenses joke is worth a dumper truck of corn, and even redeems the maddening, relentless, rhyming nightmare of the song's close. It drags you into insanity, but it's worth it.

Side 2 begins with applause, laughter and Hill getting stuck into the Stanley Holloway-styled monologue 'Ted'. Hill's rustic chap is in envy of the smooth, cool dude title character of the piece, finding solace in sexual near misses, farmyard antics and playful cows. Contrasted with Ted's West End pleasures, Hill's uncertain, put-upon butt of the joke wins at the end of the day and finds happiness in financial gain.

The throwaway 'Tour Guide' is an excuse to showcase Hill's skilful command of several foreign languages. There's glorious smut to be dug out of his multi-linguistic gags, an unforgettable John Major-like German tourist and a brilliantly effete Englishman. Certainly, the punchline, Hill's smart Alec guide being foxed by an oriental enquiry, pales in comparison with the spirited build-up.

Much, much better is to follow, with 'Interview', conducted by Lesley Goldie. Hill, working like Peter Sellers *circa* 1959, grabs the character of cocky, cockney, working-class and proud of it poet John Barson, and creates a mini-masterpiece. An ultra-hip, with-it guy, Hill's East End artiste wallows in the mystic praise of his work 'Life is Like a Double Bed', but is, hilariously, less than precious about it all – he doesn't want to 'bleeding argue about it'. Steeped in the by 1971 rather old-fashioned style of bohemian London as represented in Tony Hancock's 'The Poetry Society', this is a brilliantly constructed flight of comic deconstruction, coaxed along superbly by Goldie. Hill is at his comic peak, detailing his whole family's aim not to conform, going against conventions, dismayed that everybody thinks he's a

smoked haddock – sorry, smoke addict – and celebrating the natural poetic abilities of the average occupant of a public convenience. Akin to Sellers and the 'So Little Time' popster Twit Conway, Hill gallantly struggles past misconceptions and malapropisms ('How can you define the intangerine?') to plug his latest work, 'Now is the Winter of My Discotheque'. Relating the sad tale of a soldier and his forbidden pudding, Hill breaks under the comic pressure, just managing to get his dialogue out in between laughter – this is pure comedy.

'Making a Commercial' begins with a rare chance to enjoy Benny Hill as himself, introducing the concept of this frontcloth monologue and endorsing his sexually charged persona with his personal memory of making an advert and strolling over to a scantily clad soap girl at '65 miles an hour'. Hill's director characterization employs the usual sketch voice/John Major tones to denote someone sad, pathetic and hopeless. Drooling over the stunning Miss Hargreaves, the soap/soup misunderstanding may not be the greatest punchline in the world, but the earthy atmosphere of tensely charged television is a Hill speciality. Employing comedy of mistaken identity, embarrassment and lusty male yearning, this is a great piece.

Finally, 'The Birds and the Bees' presents Hill's knowing, rustic bumbler in definitive terms. Familiar from all sorts of documentaries and compilations, including the invaluable feature film *The Best of Benny Hill*, this sketch is rightly regarded as a masterpiece. Perfectly illustrating Hill's wonderful ability with character comedy and gentle innuendo, it includes everything from an affectionate homage to Max Miller (there's a mention for 'Mary from the Dairy') to a touching, pathos-ridden, multi-layered love story between man and pigeon. The final, stark reality pay-off ('I thought, "That's bloody rude!"'), notions of eating the injured bird and cheeky, grin-inducing delight in his bird's bird-pulling power, this is classic Benny Hill from start to finish.

This is Benny Hill: Side 1 – 'Ernie', 'Anna Marie', 'Broken-hearted Lover's Stew', 'Colleen', 'Rachel', 'The Beach at San Tropez', 'Suzy', 'Ting-a-Ling-a-Loo'. Side 2 –'Ted', 'Tour Guide', 'Interview' (featuring Lesley Goldie), 'Making a Commercial', 'The Birds and the Bees' (piano accompaniment Sid Lucas). Words and music: Benny Hill. Arranged and conducted by Harry Robinson. Vocal backing: The Ladybirds. Producer: Walter J. Ridley. EMI THIS 27.

Did You Know?

Hill picked out a couple of lines from *This is Benny Hill* to use in everyday life – when a fellow performer or crew member was low on the set, he would relate the 'so unfair' days of the month piece from 'Interview', while interviewers, usually male, who enquired about why he had never married would be met with the observation 'Why buy a book when there's a thriving lending library?' from 'The Birds and the Bees'. It was his standard comic, macho answer, alongside the complex, self-deprecating/boastful retort, 'Why make one woman miserable when I can make so many happy?'

Benny Hill Sings Ernie The Fastest Milkman in the West

This hasty re-release of Hill's 1971 classic *This is Benny Hill* album on the budget label Music For Pleasure made no bones about its major selling point – that Christmas single. The colour cover depicts Benny Hill in typical milkman guise. The photograph is entitled 'Ernie – The Farmer's Wife Milkman' by courtesy of Unigate Ltd, and tied in with Hill's contemporary advertising campaign for Farmer's Wife Bread. (For Hill completists, the registration number for the dairy float is 983 CMX.)

Benny Hill Sings Ernie The Fastest Milkman in the West: Music For Pleasure 50040, YAX 4278 – Stereo.

Words and Music

This is yet another repackage of *This is Benny Hill*, with 'The Birds and the Bees' portrait adorning the front cover and a trio of black and white sketches (military Scuttle, aged bumpkin, camp Cruddy) on the back. Some editions, capitalizing on the eternal appeal of Hill's number 1 hit, included an official sticker as a speech bubble coming from Benny's lips, explaining – ''Ere, ERNIE's on this!'

Words and Music: EMI Records/Columbia SCX 6479 – 1E 062 04918: YAK 4278 – Stereo.

The World of Benny Hill

This is a reissue of the 1966 BBC recording of *Benny Hill Time*, featuring classic excerpts from the second series of hit radio shows.

The World of Benny Hill: Starring BENNY HILL, PETER VERNON, JAN WATERS, PATRICIA HAYES, ANTHONY SHARP, TEDDY JOHNSON, JOHN HOBDAY, JIMMY KINGSBURY. Side 1 – 'Interviews', 'Layabouts' Picnic', 'Film director-producer: J. Arthur Scuttle ... "From Moscow With Love"'. Side 2 – 'The Sunday Ben', '"Down Your Way" Visits Dalton Abbott', 'Warlords of East Grinstead', 'The Holiday King – Mr Fred Scuttle', 'The Jolly Robbers'. Producer: John Browell. Album compilation by John Browell and Michael Vernon. Released by arrangement with BBC Radio Enterprises. Decca MONO PA 116.

'The Dustbins of YourMind'/'Fad-Eyed Fal'

The 1972 follow-up single to the almighty 'Ernie' failed to chart, despite being a classic example of Hill singer-songwriting. It was his last attempt at chart success. 'The Dustbins of Your Mind' is a surprisingly emotive number, packed with sentimental, wistfulness. Auntie Lil's fading, serious words of wisdom, handed down and ignored, surround the expected innuendo-drenched scenarios. There's a good musical feel to the piece as well, although hardly as potent as Noel Harrison's 'Windmills of your

Who is this Bob Dylan bloke anyway? - The serious musician at work.

Next stop Shea Stadium! - the recording star in the studio.

Mind', whose title it comically corrupts.

'Fad-Eyed Fal' is better, funnier and brilliantly performed by Hill's lisping fountain of all knowledge. This is wonderful stuff, threading deliciously dreadful mispronunciations (F for S – the title's really 'Sad-Eyed Sal'), and reaching a peak with 'Let me feel it, let me feel it with a kiss!' But the whispered, downbeat climax is stunning stuff, with Hill's intense delivery bringing real dramatic tension to the poignant fate of the song's heroine.

'The Dustbins of Your Mind'/'Fad-Eyed Fal': Columbia DO 10048.

All Aboard

This comedy compilation headlining Benny Hill's masterpiece, 'Ernie (The Fastest Milkman in the West)' also included 'Right Said Fred' from Bernard Cribbins, Charlie Drake's frantically funny 'My Boomerang Won't Come Back' and the vintage gem 'The Laughing Policeman' by Charles Penrose. This collection charted in the top 20 albums on its first release for Christmas 1979.

All Aboard: EMI EMTX 101.

Smile!

A rare and fascinating compilation album for a special 1979 promotion for 'Mellow Bird's – The kinder cup of coffee', its cover, a blue background with yellow title design and the familiar smiling face from the coffee commercials, boasts a roll-call of class British comedy talent. Heroes like Bernard Cribbins, Peter Sellers, Charlie Drake, Kenneth Williams, Bernard Bresslaw and Michael Bentine are joined by Benny Hill for his contribution, 'Fad-Eyed Fal', and if you're not laughing by the close of 'Narcissus', check for a pulse. Mostly culled from the early 1960s, Hill's piece is the most contemporary, and happily rounds off the first side with pathos-ridden lisping and innuendo-fuelled laments.

Smile!: Side 1 – 'Goodness Gracious Me': Sophia Loren and Peter Sellers, 'Right Said Fred': Bernard Cribbins, 'My Boomerang Won't Come Back': Charlie Drake, 'You're a Pink Toothbrush': Max Bygraves, 'Football Results': Michael Bentine, 'Mad, Passionate Love':

Bernard Bresslaw, 'The Gnu Song': Flanders and Swann, 'Fad-Eyed Fal': Benny Hill. Side 2 – 'Boom-Oo-Yatta-Ta-Ta': Morecambe and Wise, 'Any Old Iron': Peter Sellers, 'Narcissus (The Laughing Record)': Joyce Grenfell and Norman Wisdom, 'The Hole in the Ground': Bernard Cribbins, 'Tip-toe Through the Tulips': Mike and Bernie Winters, 'Shame and Scandal in the Family: Lance Percival, 'Song of the Australian Outlaw': Kenneth Williams, 'The Chandler's Wife': Adge Cutler and The Wurzels. EMI BIRDS1.

20 Golden Giggles

More of the same, with Hill's milkman adventure introducing a bizarre, mixed bag of classic British comedy cuts. Pure genius from Spike Milligan, Peter Sellers and Lance Percival rests alongside a forgotten gem from Shag Connor and The Carrot Crunchers, but it's a neat cross-section of what tickled the British funnybone. The cover features 'The Laughing Cavalier' sporting a red nose.

20 Golden Giggles: Side 1 – 'Ernie (The Fastest Milkman in the West)': Benny Hill, 'If': Yin and Yan, 'Ode to Barry Island': Max Boyce, 'Don't Tell I, Tell Ee': Adge Cutler and The Wurzels, 'And the Same to You (Colonel Bogey)': Dudley Moore, 'Worms': Instant Sunshine, 'Kippers for Tea (Save Your Kisses for Me)': Bob Williamson, 'Nagasaki': Windsor Davies and Don Estelle, 'Metamorphosis': Mari Griffith, 'A Little of What You Fancy (Does You Good)': Shag Connor and The Carrot Crunchers. Side 2 – 'The Combine Harvester (Brand New Key)': The Wurzels, 'Singing the Blues': Morecambe and Wise, 'The Highway Code': The Master Singers, 'Keep Yer 'and on Yer 'Alfpenny': Fivepenny Piece, 'Pheasant Plucker's

The lighter side of Britpop -
Benny Hill and Tony Hatch down for the cameras during the making of *Benny Hill Sings*?

Son': Bill Maynard, 'Madeira, M'Dear?': Michael Flanders and Donald Swann, 'Shame and Scandal in the Family': Lance Percival, 'The Hole in the Ground': Bernard Cribbins, 'Wormwood Scrubs Tango': Spike Milligan, 'A Drop of the Hard Stuff': Peter Sellers. Compiled from EMI Archives by Chris Ellis. EMI Note NTS125.

Hit Kaleidoscope

Yet another EMI compilation featured 'Ernie', this time joining other comic chart toppers from the *It Ain't Half Hot, Mum* duo, Windsor Davies and Don Estelle, and an even more aged variation on *Dad's Army*'s Corporal Jones from Clive Dunn.

Hit Kaleidoscope. Side 1 – 'The Combine Harvester (Brand New Key)': The Wurzels, 'Whispering Grass': Windsor Davies and Don Estelle, 'I Don't Believe in If Any More': Roger Whittaker, 'Tears': Ken Dodd, 'Morningtown Ride': The Seekers, 'Rodrigo's Guitar Concerto De Aranjuez (Theme from 2nd Movement)': Manuel and the Music of the Mountains, 'Look Around (and You'll See Me There)': Vince Hill, 'Watercolour Morning': Fivepenny Piece, 'Grandad': Clive Dunn, 'El Bimbo': Bimbo Jet. Side 2 – 'The Last Farewell': Roger Whittaker, 'Think of Me (Wherever You Are)': Ken Dodd, 'I (Who Have Nothing)': Shirley Bassey, 'Ernie (The Fastest Milkman in the West)': Benny Hill, 'My Kind of Girl': Matt Monro, 'Eye Level (Theme from *Van der Valk*)': Simon Park Orchestra, 'If':

Yin and Yan, 'Paper Doll': Windsor Davies and Don Estelle, 'One Two Three O'Leary': Des O'Connor, 'May I Have the Next Dream with You?': Malcolm Roberts. EMI NTS 101 stereo (OC 054 06210).

'We are Most Amused' – The Very Best of British Comedy

Prince Charles's well-known passion for British humour led to this successful charitable comedy compilation in aid of The Prince's Trust in 1981. The gatefold cover features all the artists on the balcony of Buckingham Palace, with Hill's rather effete worker pictured as a red-nosed clown. A glorious collection, reflecting the multi-faceted history of post-war British comedy, Mike Yarwood gives the proceedings that regal touch with Charles-like interventions, and Hill, staggering into view with his 1963 classic, 'Harvest of Love', may have found his audience rather laughed out by the penultimate track, but still delivered. The promised volume two compilation, alas, never appeared.

'We are Most Amused' – The Very Best of British Comedy. Side 1 – 'Points of View': *Not the Nine O'Clock News*, 'Ying Tong Song': The Goons, 'Excerpt from 'The Blood Donor': Tony Hancock, 'Massage from the Swedish Prime Minister': Monty Python, 'Welly Boot Song': Billy Connolly, 'The Drivers' Meeting': Peter Ustinov. Side 2 – 'Ingle, Jingle, Jangle, Jong': Spike Milligan, 'Society Wedding Stakes': Roy Hudd, 'Take a Pew': Alan Bennett, 'Best Man's Speech': Rowan Atkinson, 'Return to Sorrento': Spike Milligan, 'The News In Welsh': *I'm Sorry I'll Read That Again*, 'The Day that Gareth was Dropped': Max Boyce, 'Sir Marcus Browning MP': Rowan Atkinson. Side 3 – 'Les Patterson, Australian Cultural Attache': Barry Humphries, 'Niceness': Dame Edna Everage, 'Excerpt from 'The Health Inspector': *Fawlty Towers*, 'Excerpt From *The Comedians*: Frank Carson, 'Balham': Peter Sellers, 'The Jeweller's Song': Morecambe and Wise, 'The Party': Griff Rhys-Jones, Rory McGrath and Company, 'The Protest Song': Neil Innes. Side 4 – 'Yangtse Kiang': Monty Python, 'The Nutter on the Bus': Jasper Carrott, 'The Restaurant': The Two Ronnies, 'Manuel': Mike Harding, 'The Women's Institute': Joyce Grenfell, 'Harvest of Love': Benny Hill, 'Excerpt from *The Comedians*': Frank Carson. Ronco/Charisma, album RTD2067, cassette 4C RTD2067.

Benny Hill ... The Best of

The idea of a specially commissioned American release of

Hill's songs was grabbed by producer Nick Cowan, and resulted in some of Hill's last and finest work. Instead of the usual reissue, this album was a unique re-recording of all his old studio hits, including the most poignant, heart-breaking rendition of 'Please Let Me Go Round Again' he ever gave.

A fraught time was spent with Hill miming to some numbers under the direction of Dennis Kirkland for an American promotional video, but the venture kept him busy during those final television-free days. Some material was filmed at Universal Studios, Orlando, and the place was packed with tourists – all of whom seemed to be Benny Hill nuts. Frustrated, nervous and irritated, Hill still had time to save face and oblige with countless autographs and photo opportunities. Other filming venues included Greece, with Hill dressed as an ancient Greek soldier.

Benny Hill: The Best of: 'Yakety Sax', 'Ernie (The Fastest Milkman in the West)', 'Bianca', 'Gypsy Dance', 'New York Rap', 'Star Names', 'Just Wanna Be in Your Band', 'Down on the Farm', 'Unlucky Luke', 'Pepys' Diary', 'Older Woman', 'Cafe Ole', 'Graffiti', 'Lifeguards', 'Please Let Me Go Round Again', 'Yakety Sax'. Festival D 197, 1991. Continuum Records, USA, 1993. D19792 (19206-2).

Ernie

Whether you see this as an affectionate tribute to a lost comic talent or a hasty repackaged cash-in, this first release on CD of the classic 1971 *Ernie* album in 1992 was a welcome addition to the shops immediately after Benny Hill's death. Backing up the reissue of 'Ernie' as a single, the CD version rearranges the old track listing for the musical numbers as well as adding the bonus tracks from Hill's 1972 single, 'The Dustbins of Your Mind' and 'Fad-Eyed Fal'. The colour cover shot is of a grinning Hill with peaked cap in Scuttle persona, with the image on the reverse that of rustic Ben in 'Birds and Bees' mode. Despite the incorrect and hastily penned programme notes from Replay's Chris White (claiming that Hill was born in Bournemouth, indeed!), this is a priceless, albeit cynical, celebration of a great laughter-maker.

Ernie: 'Ernie (The Fastest Milkman in the West)', 'Ting-a-Ling-a-Loo', 'Anna Marie', 'Colleen', 'The Dustbins of Your Mind', 'Rachel', 'Suzy', 'Fad-Eyed Fal', 'Broken-hearted Lover's Stew', 'The Beach at San Tropez', 'Ted', 'Tour Guide', 'Interview' (featuring Lesley Goldie), 'Making a Commercial', 'The Birds and the Bees' (piano accompaniment Sid Lucas). Arranged and conducted by Harry Robinson. Vocal backing: The Ladybirds.

Producer: Walter J. Ridley. Compiled by Vic Lanza. Digitally remastered by Chris Blair, Ron Hill and Vic Lanza. Programme notes by Chris White. Replay Tracks taken from the Thames TV series *The Benny Hill Show*, 1971, except 'The Dustbins of Your Mind' and 'Fad-Eyed Fal', 1972. EMI 0 7777 99733 2 3, CD GO 2040. Stero/Mono tracks 11-15.

A Golden Hour of Comedy

This splendid 1992 compilation of British comedy hits features a colourful collection of Spike Milligan, Tommy Cooper and Morecambe and Wise alongside Hill, typically being kissed by two glamorous blondes. Despite the rather incongruous inclusion of Lenny Henry's bizarre 'Boiled Beef and Carrots' and Bernard Cribbins wandering through 'Paddington Bear', highlights like Dick Emery's cocky rhumba and Tommy Cooper's bumbling imbue both sides with total class. There's a huge chunk of classic Max Miller, and Benny Hill's only selection resurrects his Elvis parody for 'Transistor Radio'. A great gift for anybody who questions the quality of British comedy.

A Golden Hour of Comedy. Side 1 – 'The Sheik of Araby': Tommy Cooper, 'Olympic Team': Spike Milligan, 'Save Your Kisses for Me': Hylda Baker and Arthur Mullard, 'Airport Routine': Bobby Knutt, 'Just Another Pretty Face': Larry Grayson, 'When Father Papered the Parlour': Roy Hudd, 'The Reddest Sports Car': Dick Emery, 'Pidey Pipeload of Hamblin': Stanley Unwin, 'Transistor Radio': Benny Hill, 'Boiled Beef and Carrots': Lenny Henry. Side 2 – 'You are Awful but I Like You': Dick Emery, 'Twelve Days Of Christmas': Morecambe and Wise, 'Banjo Boy': George Formby, 'Paddington Bear': Bernard Cribbins, 'Max at the Met': Max Miller. Castle Communications, cassette KGHMC 171, CD KGHCD 171.

The Laughing Box

A lot more of the same from 1993, and in many cases, exactly the same as the previous Castle Communications release, but worth buying for Hancock's hour of genius and the second tape presenting a feast of musical comedy numbers. There's some classic Frankie Howerd, Tommy Cooper brilliantly hamming 'We'll Meet Again', more Spike Milligan, and more importantly, more Benny Hill. Two self-penned songs, 'The Andalucian Gypsies' and 'The Egg Marketing Board Tango' bring some added fizz to the final selection. Hill again joins the cover stars, Hancock,

Milligan, Emery and Howerd, with the same Fred Scuttle pose used on the *Ernie* CD release.

The Laughing Box. Tape 1, side 1 – 'The Blood Donor': Tony Hancock. Tape 1, side 2 – 'The Radio Ham': Tony Hancock. Tape 2, side 1 – 'The Reddest Sports Car': Dick Emery, 'Up Je T'aime': Frankie Howerd, June Whitfield and Alan Simpson, 'The Girls I Like': Max Miller, 'Boiled Beef and Carrots': Lenny Henry, 'The Best of Milligan's Wake' (excerpt 1): Spike Milligan, 'You are Awful but I Like You': Dick Emery. Tape 2, side 2 – 'The Egg Marketing Board Tango': Benny Hill, 'Olympic Team': Spike Milligan, 'Willy': Dick Emery, 'The Andalucian Gypsies': Benny Hill, 'The Best of Milligan's Wake' (excerpt 2): Spike Milligan, 'We'll Meet Again': Tommy Cooper. Sleeve design: Brian Burrows. Castle Communications, cassette MAT MC 269, CD MAT CD 269. Playing time: 101 minutes.

Benny Hill Time

In the wake of hugely successful remarketing of the big four classics *Hancock's Half Hour*, *Round The Horne*, *The Navy Lark* and *The Goon Show*, the vaults of the BBC were further raided in 1995 to present a quartet of the best episodes from Hill's major radio series. Reinforcing his Thames Television-era persona with a peak-capped Scuttle-salute cover photograph, sales were not in the same league as the other chart-busting vintage laugh collections, and this remained the only release from the series.

Benny Hill Time. BBC Radio Collection ZBBC 1722/ISBN (0563) 390794.

On Top With Benny Hill

A 1995 American compact disc pressed in Germany featuring a compilation of old Pye recordings. 'Gather in the Mushrooms', 'Harvest of love', 'My Garden of Love', 'Pepys' Diary', 'In the Papers', 'Jose's Cantina', 'Flying South', 'What a World', 'The Andalucian Gypsies', 'Transistor Radio', 'The Egg Marketing Board Tango', 'Lonely Boy', 'Gypsy Rock', 'Wild Women', 'I'll Never Know', 'The Old Fiddler' BAM-6a 3688, 'The Piccolo Song'. (Spectrum Music 550-767-2).

A Pye in the Face

This excellent and very lengthy collection of prime comic moments from the combined vaults of Pye and Piccadilly records was put together by Barry Lazell, Peter Compton and Roger Dopson in 1996. There's the entire 'Steptoe and Son at the Palace' recording, Max Miller sparring with Lonnie Donnegan on 'The Market Song', John Cleese and the *At Last, The 1948 Show* gang, Frankie Howerd, Tommy Cooper, Arthur Mullard and (gulp) even Oliver Reed having a bash. A unique deal with the BBC even allowed a choice clip of Tony Hancock and Kenneth Williams in 'The Test Pilot' to join the two Benny Hill offerings – 'Transistor Radio' and 'Harvest of Love'.

A Pye in the Face. Diamond Records GEMCD 007.

The Best of Benny Hill

This 1996 cassette re-release of Hill's best album material was packaged with a charming black and white image from his 1950s days alongside duplicate images of a cheeky schoolboy Ben and milkman Ben. An interesting, if hardly representative cover decision in light of the era the material comes from, it is somewhat justified for the unheralded but vital inclusion of the very first Benny Hill single. Both sides of 'Who Done It?'/'Memories are Made of This' appear for the first time since the original 1956 release and make this an essential purchase. Besides, there's also a lengthy and interesting thumbnail biography of the great man by Mark Cousins.

The Best of Benny Hill. Side 1 – 'Ernie (The Fastest Milkman in the West)', 'Anna Marie', 'Ted', 'Broken-hearted Lover's Stew', 'Colleen', 'Tour Guide', 'Memories are Made of This', 'The Dustbins of Your Mind', 'The Beach at San Tropez'. Side 2 – 'Ting-a-Ling-a-Loo', 'Suzy', 'Interview', 'Rachel', 'Who Done It?', 'Making a Commercial', 'Fad-Eyed Fal', 'The Birds and the Bees'. EMI Comedy Classics Listen For Pleasure (LFPS 1551) 7243 8 52481 4 6.

Benny Hill: The Ultimate Collection

As with the *Best of Benny Hill* release, this well-compiled CD collection released in 1998 opts for a youthful image of the star for its arresting, cheerful front cover. With a brilliant selection of 23 tracks and over an hour of music, this is by far the most complete and well-packaged Hill compilation currently on the market.

Concentrating solely on the recorded musical items, it fails to deliver anything from the 1970s back catalogue save the obligatory inclusion of 'Ernie'. Its array of 1960s classics is breathtaking indeed, comprising a complete re-release of the decade's output, albeit, at the end of the day, simply a resurrection of the hard-to-find vinyl classic *A Golden Hour of Benny Hill* with the added bonus of 'Ernie'. However, despite Barry Lazell's brief, slightly condescending programme notes, this is a peerless slice of Hill's musical talent, reflecting not only his endearing performances, but also skilled talent at songwriting. Digitally remastered from the original archive tapes, this is pristine, quality stuff, quite clearly living up to the 'ultimate collection' title.

Benny Hill: The Ultimate Collection. 'Gather in the Mushrooms', 'Transistor Radio', 'Harvest of Love', 'Pepys' Diary', 'Gypsy Rock', 'The Piccolo Song', 'Lonely Boy', 'Moving on Again', 'The Andalucian Gypsies', 'The Egg Marketing Board Tango', 'BAM-ba 3688', 'What a World', 'I'll Never Know', 'My Garden of Love', 'In the Papers', 'Golden Days', 'Flying South', 'Wild Women', 'Jose's Cantina', 'Rose', 'Those Days' (duet with Maggie Stredder), 'The Old Fiddler', 'Ernie (The Fastest Milkman in the West)'. Pulse/Castle Communications (PLS CD 273) 5 016073 727329.

FILMS

Who Done It?

Benny Hill's first feature film appearance is a very old-fashioned romp bearing the distinctive comic stamp of pre-war Ealing Studios output. The title 'Who Done It?' had already been used for the 1942 Abbott and Costello picture, but more to the point, Ealing, now fighting for its own life, recruited the big new star of television – Benny Hill – and tossed him into a scenario of a 1930s music hall vehicle. Indeed, this plays as if *Passport to Pimlico*, *The Lavender Hill Mob* and *The Ladykillers* had never appeared.

Scripted by T.E.B. Clarke, he surprisingly reinvents the Ealing genre by turning the clock back twenty years to re-embrace the crime caper/star comic bumbling of Will Hay and George Formby. The plot – Hill, as a hapless crime-obsessed ice-rink sweeper, uncovers an attempt to place a scientific secret formula in enemy hands, culminating in a madcap stock car race – sounds like a slightly rearranged remake of 1937's George Formby classic *I See Ice*. The presence of familiar ATP face Garry Marsh merely heightens the sense of *déjà vu*, and this clearly stands fully in the tradition that runs through Will Hay's *Where's That Fire?* to the 1983 Cannon and Ball comedy *The Boys in Blue* – the climax to all three pictures is practically identical.

However, by 1956, Ealing comedy had really moved on. Hill had broken through via the new, threatening medium of television, as opposed to the provincial, cosy world of music hall. The script is nothing new, but Clarke happily structures a convincingly confusing espionage plot with husky, bulky victim Denis Shaw, gorgeous, eyelash-fluttering blonde attraction Belinda Lee, and delightful, aged eccentric work from Ealing veteran Ernest Thesiger. It's part of the cluster of Cold War comedies from the post-war era which saw George Cole caught up in *Top Secret* and Dirk Bogarde effortlessly grin his way through *Cold Enough for June*.

Hill turns in a natural, likeable performance, basking in his television stardom and running through the hackneyed, cliché-ridden spy tale with consummate ease. The set-up is obvious but endearing, with Harold Goodwin's sheepish man from the detective magazine arriving at the ice-rink with £100 prize money and a charming bloodhound named Fabian. This is the first of many tongue-in-cheek references to the small-screen rival, Raymond Francis's *Fabian of the Yard* – although this one is laboured several times until finally, defeated, Hill mutters that he has to leave 'Fabian in the yard'. There's the usual disastrous, accident-prone display of ineptitude as Hill, engrossed in his dime thriller, *A Date with Death* (with his wonderfully Raymond Chandleresque voice-over dragging the viewer into his crime-filled mentality), misses his cue, bumbles about the place, staggers into Belinda and ends up as part of the ice-show act 'Tropic Nights on Ice'. The slapstick is well orchestrated, and Hill's anguished cries of panic are effective, while the clever, pseudo-*Singin' in the Rain* touch of having elderly, stuffy oldies (Lucy Griffith among them) singing guff like 'Golden Afternoon' for the miming, skating hunks and lovelies adds an edge of satire to the collapsing madness.

The supporting cast is literally awash with familiar British film favourites, including a quick cough, spit and shattered classical record vignette from Charles Hawtrey, typically wolfish charm from Thorley Walters, a stunning piece of cross-banter, pedantic British scientific pundit chat from Peter Bull and Nicholas Phipps, and that glorious old Ealing stand-by Philip Stainton as the tortured, rotund and effortlessly jolly theatrical agent. Garry Marsh storms, fumes, rants, stares and explodes with perfect comic grace, flapping throughout all the fun and games like a headless chicken on amphetamines and encountering more bashes over the head than at a Three Stooges convention, while David Kossoff brilliantly opts for the other extreme, peerlessly underplaying his sinister, trustworthy, gentle and knowing Uralian bigwig. Kossoff's at the epicentre of the whole thing, hiring our hapless hero to impersonate the flamboyant foreignness of Denis Shaw for his London weather-making machine demonstration. Of course, the whole plot is lifted from the dark flip side of *The Prisoner of Zenda* – Hill is destined to be blown to bits and the secrets shipped off to European outer limits along with the inventor. However, Hill outfoxes the evil ones by sheer stupidity rather than knowledge or cunning, while the influx of freak weather pads out the initial part of the film with distinguished gents struggling through freezing conditions and flying fruit flans.

And that's the problem. No one really seems to know in which direction to take the movie. Is it an old-fashioned star vehicle from 1937 with a hip 1956 television comedian? Is it a wry, tongue-in-cheek parody of that ancient genre? Is it trying to give Norman Wisdom a run for his money in the bumbling slapstick comic stakes? Or is it a rather half-hearted spy thriller with a familiar face tossed into the mixture for added box office clout? I suppose it's a bit of all these things, although as a vehicle for Hill's brilliant skills at the time, it works well enough to be gratefully embraced. It resembles a less intense run-through of Dick Emery's shamefully undervalued film *Ooh! You are Awful*, in that this picture allows Hill a few opportunities to don various character make-ups. There's the well-padded, jargon-spouting Otto Stumpf for one, a timid, eye-rolling female television contestant, a silky Jewish mechanical chair salesman, a slick-haired display model dummy, and best of all, a frightfully pompous, Jimmy Edwards-styled toff. The pseudo-Bogart henchman pep talk into the mirror is a charming piece of work, but it's his own willing-to-please, hard-done-by, dogged personality which makes this performance such a joy.

The film embraces the cheeky comedy Hill was known and loved for – there's a classic bit of confusion with Marsh and Kossoff as unfamiliar drink is blamed for Hill's flights of wild fancy, and his misunderstanding attempts to rescue his beloved Belinda result in a pained expression as a spiked fence catches him unawares. Hill's skill for visual clowning is well used (most notably a perfectly timed street collision, with both men annoyed at the other's impertinence in reading while walking), while television importance is built into the narrative with the Earl's Court Radio Show and the crucial images-by-radio-signal invention that could cause the downfall of the British nation. Of course, the secret is just one big McGuffin, and the stock Iron Curtain characterizations are gloriously hissworthy villains dedicated to the downfall of the British Empire – their early plot is backed with a burst of 'Rule Britannia' as Hill strolls into the lion's den.

For his hapless heroine fantasy figure, Hill couldn't have asked for more than Belinda Lee. Her character is an interesting if sometimes painfully unsuccessful stab at reinventing the screaming heroine in favour of a tough cookie who could easily outhero the hero. Her strong woman act, highlighted as she effortlessly rips telephone directories, is an intriguing touch, allowing plenty of wide-eyed Hill amazement at how powerful she is. But all she really wants is a feminine lifestyle and a man to dom-inate her – it's very much of its time, but her wistful remarks about 'no real man' finding her attractive are potent indeed. Besides, there weren't many more gorgeous young actresses populating British cinema in the 1950s than Belinda Lee, so her bizarre moments can be forgiven in favour of decorative wailing, a well-judged sight gag as her drummer girl disguise knocks out the aisle-side audience members, and a whiff of poignancy as she chirpily escapes near death in a manic car chase only to succumb in real life five years later. She certainly backed Hill to the hilt while he threw himself into the off-kilter physical humour and gadget-heavy exhibition sequence, reaching the same heights of manic disaster achieved by the team in *Carry On Regardless*.

The climactic radio show event also allows a heap of quickfire gag appearances and supporting legends to have a brief say, while Hill clearly relishes all the madcap action as Basil Dearden structures a sort of comic answer to Orson Welles's *The Lady from Shanghai* mirror climax within a multiple array of television screens – effectively latching onto the tannoy announcement about BBC and commercial television celebrities – and T.E.B. Clarke fully

A stunning publicity pose for the detective dream becomes nightmare comedy of *Who Done It?*

embracing the old, more polished spectre of *The Lavender Hill Mob*. Indeed, the police radio call sign, M2GW, is the same as that used in the Guinness/Holloway heist masterpiece.

Who Done It? is at times outrageous, absurd, badly paced, hilariously pointed, unashamedly hammed, peerlessly performed, a haven for great character actor spotting and just plain bizarre. But it's always got something, and that something is Benny Hill, hardly believing his luck at headlining a movie, and having a whale of time as he does it. Personally, I love the film – a classic family comic romp.

Hill's first taste of film fame remains one of the few regular television repeats on British television – just right for a cosy afternoon on Channel 4, with roaring fire, steaming mug of tea and a plate of chocolate biscuits.

Who Done It?. A Michael Balcon Production. Ealing, RFD. Opened March 1956 (reissued in 1961 by General Era Film Distributors). Black and white. 85 mins. Hugo Dill BENNY HILL, Frankie Mayne BELINDA LEE, Zacco DAVID KOSSOFF, Inspector Hancock GARRY MARSH, Barakov GEORGE MARGO, Gruber FREDERICK SCHILLER, Sir Walter ERNEST THESIGER, Raymond Courtney THORLEY WALTERS, Frankie's Agent PHILIP STAINTON, Scientists NICHOLAS PHIPPS, PETER BULL, GIBB McLAUGHLIN, ERNEST JAY, HAROLD SCOTT, The Actress NORAH BLANEY, Disc Jockey CHARLES HAWTREY, Police Constable Roberts WARWICK ASHTON, Police Constable Coleman STRATFORD JOHNS, Otto Stumpf DENIS SHAW, Vu-Eezie Chair Customer IRENE HANDL. Uncredited: Mr Goodwin TERENCE ALEXANDER, Remote Control Tank Demonstrator ARTHUR LOWE, Man from *Detective Weekly* Magazine HAROLD GOODWIN. Guest starring JEREMY HAWK, ROBERT McDERMOTT with THE DAGENHAM GIRL PIPERS and CHAMPION APPELINE HECTOR OF WEST SUMMERLAND, with FABIAN the bloodhound as himself. Members of the *Holiday on Ice* Corps de Ballet produced by Gerald Palmer. Story and screenplay: T.E.B. Clarke. Photography: Otto Heller. Art Director: Jim Morahan. Editor: Peter Tanner. Music: Philip Green. Music played

Intrigue, mystery and a wide-eyed debutante - A wonderfully atmospheric still of Benny Hill and David Kossoff from Basil Dearden's *Who Done It?*

1.

1. Don't blame me for the script! - Benny Hill and Belinda Lee pass the buck for *Who Done It?* publicity.

2. Dare you read on... Benny's caught by the thrillers in *Who Done It?*

3. A quick snack break in between takes on the set of *Who Done It?* with David Kossoff.

4. Looks familiar!! Denis Shaw and Benny Hill are up for the part of Professor Stumpf in *Who Done It?*

5. Consultation time with Benny's first case in *Who Done It?*... who designed Norah Blaney's hat!

6. Eat your heart out Bob Mitchum! - Every inch the cool movie dude in a *Who Done It?* pose.

7. A touch of the Jimmy Edwards for *Who Done It?*

8. Roger Moore with a touch of Dudley Moore - publicity for *Who Done It?*

9. A cracking character study of Benny in Stumpf disguise - *Who Done It?*

2.

3.

4.

5.

6.

7.

8.

9.

by the Sinfonia of London, conducted by Dock Mathison. 'Who Done It?' lyrics by Norman Newell and Marcel Stellman. Production Supervisor: Hal Mason. Unit Production Manager: David Peers. Sound Supervisor: Stephen Dalby. Camera Operator: Chic Waterson. Assistant Director: Tom Pevsner. Recordist: Leo Wilkins. Continuity: Jean Graham. Sound Editor: Alastair McIntyre. Costume Designer: Anthony Mendleson. Hair styles: Daphne Martin. Make-up: Harry Frampton. Special effects: E.R. Taylor. Scenic Artist: W. Simpson Robinson. Producer: Michael Relph. Director: Basil Dearden. Made at Ealing Studios, London, England.

Did You Know?

Despite the high prestige of landing a film role at Ealing, the studio was hardly in the best position to capitalize on *Who Done It?*'s success and build on Hill's big-screen stardom. The film had the dubious pleasure of coming in at the tail end of Ealing's output (with just the more conventional but rather lacklustre T.E.B. Clark reheating of Alec Guinness glories in *Barnacle Bill* and the Harry Secombe/Kenneth Connor/Susan Shaw bitter-sweet tale *Davy* to come). The studio was running out of steam, and with the BBC buy-out just round the corner, Ealing's films were being distributed by the Rank Organisation. With their own hugely successful star film comic Norman Wisdom to promote, Rank were less than enthusiastic in pushing forward a rival's similarly styled career – even though, or more likely because, *Who Done It?* was very successful at the box office. This, coupled with Hill's own self-doubt in his ability to become a star comedian on film, meant that his big-screen career was quickly curtailed.

Following the lead of his hero, Jack Benny's, reaction to *The Horn Blows at Midnight*, and akin to Frankie Howerd's outraged reaction to *The Runaway Bus*, Hill delighted in mock disgust when discussing *Who Done It?* Informed by one reporter that his film debut was due to play on television, Hill quickly answered: 'In that case I'm taking the next plane to Marseilles!' But even escaping the country wasn't always enough – in 1975, on a flight to Paris, one of the air stewards turned out to have appeared in the film during the ice-rink sequence.

The minor character played by Denis Shaw, Herr Otto Stumpf, was later adopted for Hill's outrageous German character in *The Benny Hill Show*.

Benny Hill proposed to glamorous co-star Belinda Lee two weeks into making the movie, but she refused.

Scriptwriter T.E.B. Clark accompanied Hill on his 1954 stage tour of *The Benny Hill Show* to soak in his style of comic performance.

As a publicity stunt in reflection of the stock car climax for the film, Ealing Studios sent Hill and a couple of Windmill girls down to the West Ham track. Hill started the race by driving a jeep round the track, and awarded the *Who Done It?* trophy to the winner.

Major Hill fan Burt Reynolds first saw his idol in this film – he hated the picture, but loved the star.

Although the film didn't make Benny Hill the great movie star he had the potential to become, it did prove popular enough to warrant the comedian writing a regular column for *Picturegoer*. These feasts of comic observation would often be enhanced by jokes from his brother Leonard, who would also often ghost-write newspaper articles on his behalf.

Light Up the Sky!

Easily lumped in with the glorious cascade of low-brow, innuendo-driven, knockabout British film comedies reflecting the military (*Carry On Sergeant*, *Idle on Parade*, *I Only Arsked!*, *The Square Peg*), this vastly underrated comedy drama is a far more complex, heartwrenching affair. Taking its inspiration from the 1942 David Niven classic *The Way Ahead*, and later seeing its bitter-sweet, war-as-reality humour reflected in Spike Milligan's *Adolf Hitler – My Part in His Downfall*, this classic Lewis Gilbert ensemble piece showcases what is arguably Benny Hill's most thought-provoking work.

Clearly not at ease following in the star vehicle footsteps of Will Hay or George Formby, this major supporting role was Hill's second stab at big-screen success, happy to contribute a quite stunning piece of work while Ian Carmichael and Tommy Steele carried the film in leading roles. Indeed, in terms of screen time and narrative importance, Hill is every bit as vital, if not more so, than Carmichael and Steele, but with the freedom of lack of responsibility, Hill relaxes to give, without doubt, his finest film performance.

The genius at work in the casting lies in the use of a galaxy of familiar comic character players (Victor Maddern, Harry Locke and Dick Emery notable among them), allowing them their usual comic characteristics and brilliantly twisting the situation by throwing brutal truths at them. This is not the work-shy, corruptible, fag-smoking Harry Locke of *On the Fiddle*, but the work-shy, corruptible, fag-smoking, real face of a serving British soldier, ultimately terrified at facing death when his posting has been delayed.

Victor Maddern, in one of his most impressive roles, turns on the usual gruff, authoritative disdain, bemoaning his fate of working with the cheeky attitude of British servicemen. Throwing himself into a mock battle with Locke (which turns bitingly bitter when the real enemy danger rains down), chomping away at Locke's lovingly created cheese straws, whining about the lack of chips, hilariously embracing the fruity references of the barrack room with his fear of boiling water in the bath (peerlessly set up by Locke's disgruntled 'feet' comment) and creating havoc as he perilously bridges the working-class squaddies with the friendly, understanding but law-enforcing officer figure of Ian Carmichael (including a beautifully played scene of knowing cover-up between the two in front of an obvious countryside back projection), this is classy stuff.

Cyril Smith is a delight as the jobsworth administrative figure, dishing out free haircuts and free advice to

Next stop Broadway - Tommy Steele and Benny Hill embrace memories of ENSA and CSE for *Light Up The Sky!*

all and sundry, while Dick Emery, popping in with classic put-downs and grouchy tirades, contrasts his usual abrasive wit with quiet, understanding eye contact at moments of cold reality. His thoughts on rumoured overseas postings are brilliantly performed. Sydney Tafler, retaining the warmth of countless cockney spivs, delivers a more world-weary, experienced face of British strength, protecting the fresh-faced naiviety of Johnny Briggs, happily going along with the gentle authority-twisting of his fellow gunners and injecting heart-wrenching agony as news filters through concerning his son being killed in action.

A hard, bitter, quiet moment of emotion is heightened by the tyrannical Victor Maddern receiving the information over the radio, his reaction so believable it almost hurts to watch, and comforting the grief-stricken father with the simplest, but sincerest, of comments. Briggs, coaxed back from desertion by kindly Carmichael, becomes the surrogate figure of parental concern, easing the wounds of casual throwaway comment and haunting disbelief of loss by merely being a young, family-less figure clutched under the wing of Tafler.

Tommy Steele, typically, is all cheeky, toothy grin, girl-chasing and upbeat joyfulness, but even he accepts humiliation, rejection and foolhardiness into his light characterization. Trapped in a hasty marriage, besotted by the local farm beauty and ultimately fathering an illegitimate son, the military mates discuss the mountain of social, financial and moral outrage, and absent-minded thoughts that 'rape isn't as bad as desertion' (a hint that Maddern's past is less than pure).

Tafler's amazed reaction to a continual diet of poached duck for dinner ('Is my arse waddling?'), Locke's smoker's cough continually disguising expletives and a real sense of impending violence as Locke finally takes the hate–hate Maddern relationship to breaking point all breathe truth into the knockabout barrack room cameraderie. More than any other post-war comic reinspection of Britain's finest hour, *Light Up the Sky!* strips away the comic depiction of shared experience to weave the uniquely British reaction to threatened death into long passages of serious diatribe. However, the real revelation in the film is Benny Hill.

Allowing the sense of dramatic skill behind all his comic BBC characterizations, Hill portrays the most potent, emotive, believable and effective role of his career, brilliantly masking the deeply rooted sense of angst with the persona of familiar Benny Hill – a non-stop gush of corny gags, silly voices and cheeky grins. In an amazing exposure of the troubled man behind the comedy, Hill

relishes his upbeat, Max Miller-styled banter with his eagerly entertained comrades of the Lionheart Lighting Battery. The joker at every turn, Hill puts on the posh voice while discussing cheese straws, flamboyantly boasts about the number of female conquests he's made, ribs Carmichael with Churchill references, delivers a hilariously touching after-dinner speech (complete with some wonderfully cornball gags) and gloriously throws himself into female characterization. However, all this typical jokery works so well simply because of the strong contrast with the natural persona of Hill's character. For every hilarious assault on the farm, stealing brussel sprouts in a bath tub, there's a venomous, adamant rant concerning changed roster duties.

From his first appearance, Hill's role embraces comic contradictions, set up as a figure probably away winning the war, only to be revealed skilfully pinching a load of eggs from the local farm. But behind the ever-cheery covering up for the absence of his brother (Steele), there's the secret distress of looking after him since their mother died, and the shared understanding from his fellow gunners. Even the iron-hearted Victor Maddern, continually letting his authority slip, threatens to expose

Give Me The Moonlight! - Benny Hill and Tommy Steele strut their corny, military-geared stuff for *Light Up The Sky!*

Tommy Steele, Benny Hill, Harry Locke and Cyril Smith check the roster in *Light Up the Sky!*

Give Us A Puff!
Benny eyes Ian Carmichael's Churchill status symbol in *Light Up the Sky!*

Steele's desertion, only to sheepishly and quietly report all present and correct, much to the silent appreciation of Hill. But even this sense of friendliness in war is corrupted, and Steele ruins the sense of unity by having a military excuse for his lateness, also destroying Hill's loyalty by having secretly married. The barrage of well-rehearsed corny gags on Steele's first appearance is brilliantly counterbalanced by Hill's stunned amazement at the news, bitterly breaking up their proposed comic act and washing his hands of all responsibility. It is acted with heartfelt pain and sincerity, ripping out the emotions to reveal the true hurt of a loved one's disappointment.

The contrast between cheery tomfoolery concerning buttons on flies and the raw anger from Hill about handing bits of bloody cake about is made even more stark due to the fact that this is Benny Hill in totally new terrain. Never before or since did he land a role of such depth. Struggling through his shows of the late 1980s, one wistfully longs for the performer who could, when given the opportunity, produce a performance of this quality. The ultimate battle between Hill and Steele as the illegitimate child situation is slowly revealed is played with such intensity that the anger bursts off the screen. Hill's flaming attack on Steele, storming off with defeated outrage, is unforgettable, and it's only the helpless tears of Steele which rekindle the parental instinct in Hill's character.

The scenes outside the barracks are extremely brief, restricted to the Steele/Burnett liaisons, angst-ridden attempts to see the baby, and most celebrated of all, the unofficial excursion into town to perform at the theatre's amateur night. With Cardew Robinson's silkily smooth compere, Sheila Hancock's gloriously off-key wannabe singer, the first attraction of Burnett to Steele's boyish charms and the ultimate arrival of Hill to drag his brother back to barracks, the scene is set for enforced theatrical experience.

Caught on stage as the curtain goes up, Hill immediately throws himself into the act, with Steele fitting into the routine with cheesy ease. Condemned by off-stage critics but uproariously accepted by the low-brow, loving audience, the catchy song 'Touch It Light', corny gags aplenty and pseudo-vaudevillian style (straw boaters and canes) give the act a feel of bottom-of-the-bill, working-class comedy. As a team, Hill and Steele are dynamite, effortlessly making the most groanworthy one-liner enjoyable, and injecting a real sense of excitement into the performance. Even the sudden shock of seeing Carmichael cheerfully acknowledging them in the box doesn't stop the team in their soft-shoe shuffle tracks. It's the magical presence of an audience that dispels any animosity, forgetting the long-standing feud (several months have passed since Steele's marriage bombshell), while Hill's hard-bitten second guessing of the situation as Carmichael escorts them back to base gradually eases away as the truth concerning a regimental performance dawns, only to be brilliantly dashed as Maddern's stunned disbelief is curtailed by Carmichael's charming sentencing of punishment.

Steele's endearing habit of forgetting important words and hastily inserting 'whatsisname' at every juncture means that Hill can never fully go against him, but Maddern is the character who finally strips the comic disguise from Hill's serious-edged persona with an infuriated comment: 'We stopped laughing at your jokes months ago – you're just not funny any more!' The poignant reaction from Hill is potent indeed.

The one criticism that could be levelled at the film is the top-and-tail technique of an ageing Carmichael recounting his heady 1942 days of command. Relaxing in front of a gentle game of civilized cricket with a refined cigarette holder and a pint of beer, this dashing remnant of British military might relates the film's major action in 17-year-old flashback. The format, immediately drawing parallels with the Peter Sellers satire *I'm Alright Jack* (cannily painting a glorious military picture while visually depicting the truth – Tafler and Locke playing cards), fails to gel here because it is done with cloying affection.

The device of the educated, financially comfortable ruling class looking back at working-class chaps belongs to another less cynical age. A decade later, Michael Crawford's unintentionally sinister delivery of his experiences in *How I Won the War* works thanks to a generation familiar with Vietnam, the assassination of Kennedy and Beatles counter-culture, whereas in 1959, Carmichael's sophisticated image of upper-class victory plays like parody without the intention of making it acceptable – indeed, the credits shout that 'Lt Ian Carmichael introduces the Troop he had the honour to command: Gunner Tommy Steele, Gunner Benny Hill', etc. In the late 1950s, military officialdom was still seen as tough but likeable, and Carmichael (as with William Hartnell's Sergeant Grimshawe) clearly governed with understanding, but the perspective of upper-class privilege serves to underline the issue of class, which distorts the characterization of Carmichael in wartime.

The belated introduction of a dual role for Tommy Steele is also a far too radical gear-shift from the highly emotional final conflict of the close-knit comrades (Hill and Steele making up as the enemy aircraft fall around them, death among their number, cold real-

You can't beat Army grub... A light-hearted, somewhat misrepresentative, publicity pose for *Light Up The Sky!*

ization of fear/battle fatigue), and the hasty round-up of what the principals are now doing makes the same mistake *American Graffiti* did fifteen years later: the characterizations are so rounded and believable that a full update of progress rips apart the magical ensemble that makes most of the film work so perfectly. However, having said that, nothing can really mar the beautifully constructed performances of the cast, and Hill in particular was never so impressive. If anybody ever again quickly condemns Benny Hill as nothing but a low-brow comedian, simply introduce them to this film, it's a true revelation.

Ecky Thump! Benny Hill's Northern Fire Chief casts a knowing eye over the aerial madness of *Those Magnificent Men In Their Flying Machines.*

Light Up the Sky!: British Lion Films Ltd in association with Bryanston. Opened June 1960. Black and white. 90 mins. 'A' Certificate. Lt Ogleby IAN CARMICHAEL, Gunner Eric McCaffey and Winston McCaffey TOMMY STEELE, Gunner Sidney McCaffey BENNY HILL, Gunner Ted Green SIDNEY TAFLER, Lance Bombardier Tomlinson VICTOR MADDERN, Gunner Roland Kenyon HARRY LOCKE, Gunner Leslie Smith JOHN- NY BRIGGS, Gunner 'Spinner' Rice CYRIL SMITH, Gunner Harry the Driver DICK EMERY. Civilians: Compere CARDEW ROBINSON, Jean Jennings SUSAN BURNET, Theatre Act SHEILA HANCOCK, Mr Jenning FRED GRIFFITHS. Screenplay: Vernon Harris. Based on the play *Touch It Light* by Robert Storey. Photography: John Wilcox. Music composed by Douglas Gamley, conducted by Muir Mathieson. Song 'Touch It Light' by Lionel Bart and Michael Pratt. Art Director: John Stoll. Editor: Peter Tanner. Production Manager:

Morris Aza. Camera Operator: Dudley Lovell. Assistant Director: Jack Causey. Sound Supervisor: Stephen Dalby. Sound Mixer: Cecil Mason. Sound Editor: Alban Streeter. Continuity: Shirley Barnes. Make-up: Jim Hydes. Associate Producer: John Dark. Produced and directed by Lewis Gilbert. RCA sound recording. Twickenham Film Studios, London, England.

Did You Know?

Hill wrote the corny Army show patter act for Light Up the Sky!, resurrecting reassuringly dreadful jokes from his own wartime experiences and giving the Steele/Hill dou- ble act that warm, affectionate touch of spontaneous truth that makes it so effective. Gags like 'Two Bishops in bed together – which one wore the night dress? ... Mrs Bishop!' are pure low-brow magic, ripped off from Max Miller and blessed with Hill's confident delivery.

Those Magnificent Men in Their Flying Machines, or How I Flew from London to Paris in 25 Hours 11 Minutes

By the third film in Benny Hill's erratic big-screen career, any plans for major film stardom had gone by the wayside in favour of his BBC television specials. However, British cinema, with one eye firmly on the potent force of televi- sion and the other on the American market, was eager to inject elements of both for international and home approval. Thus by 1965, with smash-bang-wallop come- dies all the rage, 20th Century Fox poured millions into this classic, action-packed, plane-destroying, slapstick orgy. Since Stanley Kramer's 1963 film *It's a Mad, Mad, Mad, Mad World*, silent visual humour had been reworked and reinvented for the modern audience, and although *Those Magnificent Men in Their Flying Machines* never rivals the priceless bickering of Kramer's film, there are plenty of joyous moments along the way.

Playing for the American side are dashing teeth- flasher Stuart Whitman and Sam Wanamaker, but the real power of the film is delivered by a breathtaking selection of class British comedians and character players. Although limited to a very minor supporting turn as the bumbling, cheery Northern Fire Chief, Benny Hill received major star credit in the opening titles, and almost single-hand- edly humanizes the all-out madness of the film, control- ling his men with an assured sense of the Keystone Kops tradition while thankfully injecting subtle touches of con- trasting character comedy. In a film of international importance, there's something very reassuring in Hill's brief vignettes, keeping an eye on the training competitors with a telescope, relaxing with a cup of tea with his feet up, having a manic panic attack when his fire engine is messed about with, relishing the busy day of accidents ahead and reacting with bemused amazement at the behaviour of the flyers. Norman Rossington plays a second in command know-it-all jobsworth, with Hill's ringing his bell with superiority and insisting on sticking strictly to the rules, even when Terry-Thomas is steering his plane into perilous situations. However, this annoying efficiency is tempered by endearing lapses into Northern cosiness, ('ooh! eck!') and above all, allowing himself a cherubic grin at others' misfortunes. The sewage farm incident taps fully into the expected lavatorial delights of Hill's BBC telvision series.

Restricted to the English set portion of the film, Hill pops up fairly regularly through the elongated planned pre-Channel crossing race, and although his characterization has little narrative importance, the wild antics on his speeding fire engine coupled with the odd treasured moment of dumbfounded facial reaction make him a very welcome passenger aboard this comic epic. A major box office success, the film was the first American breakthrough for Hill, although his performance hardly set the country alight, and never really captures the core of his comic persona. It perfectly encapsulates the 1960s' love of excess, jam-packed with star names, seemingly having a blood-lust for wanton destruction and stretching its colourful, wide-screen canvas to breaking point – indeed, one waggish critic suggested that the film seemed to last longer than the allotted time of the winning entrant in the London to Paris race!

From the mocking, honky-tonk piano version of the familiar 20th Century Fox fanfare, the film successfully contrasts the superior modernity of the 1960s with the uproariously primitive antics of days gone by, both in terms of aviation and cinema, and Red Skelton, presenting in flashes from history the style of monochrome silent comedy, mugs brilliantly as the valiant flyer who tops and tails the film, helped along his way by a suitably assured narration from James Robertson Justice on leave from St. Swithins. A priceless four-minute introduction breaks into the staggering, Gilliamesque opening credits from cartoonist Ronald Searle and the fab Ron Goodwin theme song, again tackling the vintage with contemporary affectionate mockery. Stirring, tongue-in-cheek and irresistibly unforgettable, it lends the entire project a jaunty, easy-going feel.

The British romantic leads, James Fox and Sarah Miles, are suitably bland as a perfect backdrop for the over-played glories of the comedians, brilliantly latching onto the stiff-upper-lipped, refined images of the landed gentry with an obsessive, God-given right to fly. More importantly, the casting of Fox and Miles rekindles memories of the 1963 Joseph Losey masterpiece *The Servant*, where the two battled either side of Dirk Bogarde's camp furies and created one of the most potent of swinging sixties cinema journeys. The very notion that these icons of the decade should be thrown into uniform and lace is another major uniting force between the ancient and the now. The 'no kissing, duty comes first' persona of Fox, deliberately set in stark contrast with Whitman's wild west attitude, works against the tomboy performance of Sarah Miles – a mechanic kid under the demure finery, coupled with plenty of skirt-dropping for the lads. The love triangle that erupts forms the main rival substance of the plot, with an American need for money and a British need for pride eventually forging an unlikely bond between the two young suitors.

All this English fair play is brilliantly encapsulated by Robert Morley's grand, booming presence, establishing the whole race to increase newspaper circulation, and injecting great swathes of xenophobia, complaining about the need to involve 'blasted foreigners' in these international affairs. Mind you, the various foreign eccentrics do dominate rather too much of the film, with Italian Alberto Sordi fathering a huge family and a thirst for patriotic recognition, a less prominent but effective wry turn from Japan's Yujiro Ishihara befuddling the British judges with his elongated and pretty unimpressive route to the starting line, Jean-Pierre Cassel with sexual pursuits grabbing his attention far more than flying, and the chest-puffing Gert Frobe, in his finest film appearance bar *Goldfinger*, embracing the iron nerve of Germanic victory.

The vast gallery of comic cameos bolsters the seemingly endless shots of rickety flying machines struggling to stay aloft, with a cracking Willy Rushton flustering around the place, Sister Flora Robson giving a joyfully biased change of heart towards the Catholic Sordi, Franco-geared nonsense from John LeMesurier and Eric Barker, Scottish bravura from Gordon Jackson, and best of all, a beautifully etched picture of English amazement from Cicely Courtneidge and Fred Emney. The most potent of the starry bit parts is, of course, Tony Hancock – like Benny Hill, resigned to never finding film stardom, but giving his all as the inept aviator Harry Popplewell, bragging and boasting to anyone who cares to listen, ushering in a burst of Sousa's 'Liberty Bell' four years before Monty Python, decrying the unfairness of his genius being matched against the other competitors ('It's pathetic!') and ultimately vanishing from sight, flying backwards to Scotland. A very minor turn indeed, but bearing the mark of real comic power.

However, nobody in the cast comes within a hundred miles of the towering, black-hearted, sinister, grinning bag of corruption that is Terry-Thomas. The definitive endearing villain, flashing charm and Union Jack-flying arrogance ('Are you there, Yankee fellow?') with disarming ease, he cuts down everybody else like wheat before the sickle, and even though filmic convention dictates that the man can never win, he will still always get the biggest cheer from this quarter. With general dogsbody and put-upon aide Eric Sykes, the animation historian need look no further than this partnership for Hanna-Barbara's influence for Dick Dastardly and Mutley. Sharpening his smoothie from *It's a Mad, Mad, Mad, Mad World* and happy to resurrect Sir Percyisms for *Monte Carlo or Bust!*, Terry-Thomas steamrolls through the pomp of the occasion, bantering with Maurice Denham's hard-nosed sea captain, receiving corrective dismissal from Willy Rushton, and most treasurable of all, effortlessly allowing the painful mock seagull interlude to shine with the merest 'Buzz off!' A work of pure genius. Thus, for all the film's minor flaws, the promise of a Terry-Thomas grin and sophisticatedly puffed cigarette is more than enough to keep the interest going.

The attitude of national importance of the winner taps into the zeitgeist of the impending Common Market and European unity. The chaps who stand by their flags are either old-fashioned and ridiculed (James Fox, Jeremy Lloyd) or complete bounders and losers (Terry-Thomas, Tony Hancock). The American way, sacrificing his very independence to aid a potential enemy, is celebrated, and although the happy-ever-after, share-and-share-alike mentality of the film is endearing, there's still a sense that Annakin's underlining message is even more endearingly cynical. For a film with one foot in 1910 and the other in 1965, the ending is a masterpiece, with Miles and Whitman reacting with shock at the speeding jet plane uniting the two ages.

This is an over-long comedy, certainly, with several character and plot sags, but Annakin does wonders to keep the slapstick fresh, brings out a Terry-Thomas performance of colossal importance and delivers the last – and arguably, only – British-based comedy blockbuster. It caught the style of visual, universal comedy that Hancock yearned to discover within himself and that Hill instinctively had. More than fitting then that after just two more 1960s supporting roles, Hill would devote himself to major comic television expressions of slapstick slap and tickle for the world forum.

Those Magnificent Men in Their Flying Machines, or How I Flew from London to Paris in 25 Hours 11 Minutes. 20th Century Fox. Opened April 1965. Pinewood De Luxe Technicolor/Todd-AO. 133 mins. 'U' Certificate. TV debut: ITV Thursday Adventure Film, 26 August 1976, 7–9.25 p.m. Orvil Newton STUART WHITMAN, Hon. Patricia Rawnsley SARAH MILES, Richard Mays JAMES FOX, Count Emilio Ponticelli ALBERTO SORDI, Lord Rawnsley ROBERT MORLEY, Count Manfred von Holstein GERT FROBE, Pierre Dubois JEAN-PIERRE CASSEL, Brigitte, Ingrid, Marlene, Francoise, Yvette and Betty IRINA DEMICK, Courtney ERIC SYKES, Sir Percy Ware-Armitage TERRY-THOMAS. Special guest star: Neanderthal man/pioneer flyers RED SKELTON. Co-starring Yama Moto YUJIRO ISHIHARA, Fire Chief Perkins BENNY HILL, Mother Superior FLORA ROBSON, Karl MICHAEL VOGLER, George SAM WANAMAKER, Harry Popperwell TONY HANCOCK, McDougal GORDON JACKSON, Airline Hostess MILLICENT MARTIN, Gascoyne Tremayne WILLIAM RUSHTON, Colonel Willy FRED EMNEY, French Painter JOHN LE MESURIER, French Postman ERIC BARKER, Officials MICHAEL TRUBSHAWE and RONNIE STEVENS, Jean Pascac DAVY KAYE, Lt. Parsons JEREMY LLOYD, Chop 'n' Chips Waitress MARJORIE RHODES, Reporter STEVE PLYTAS, Fireman NORMAN ROSSINGTON, Photographer JIMMY THOMPSON, Muriel the Memsahib CECILY COURTNEDGE, Ship's Captain MAURICE DENHAM, Narrator JAMES ROBERTSON JUSTICE. With ZENA MARSHALL, ERIC POHLMAN, GRAHAM STARK. Screenplay: Jack Davies and Ken Annakin. Photography: Christopher Challis. Titles: Ronald Searle. Production Designer: Tom Morahan. Costumes: Osbert Lancaster (British Film Award for Best Costumes, 1965). Technical Adviser: Air Commodore Allen H. Wheeler. Casting Director: Stuart Lyons. Unit Managers: Colin Brewer and Pat Clayton. Sound: John W. Mitchell and Gordon McCallum. Dubbing Editor: Jonathan Bates. Second Unit Cameraman: Skeets Kelly. Second Unit Assistant Director: Jake Wright. Associate Art Director: Jim Morahan. Associate Costumes Designer: Dinah Greet. Special Effects: Richard Parker. Set Dresser: Arthur Taksen. Continuity: Joy Mercer. Hairdressers: Barbara Ritchie and Biddy Chrystal. Make-up: William Parleton and Stuart Freeborn. Animation: Ralph Ayres. Titles executed by National Screen Service Ltd, London. Music: Ron Goodwin. Production Supervisor: Denis

Holt. Editors: Gordon Stone and Anne V. Coates. Second Unit Director: Don Sharp. Assistant Director: Clive Reed. Camera Operator: Dudley Lovell. Associate Producer: Jack Davies. Producer: Stan Margulies. Director: Ken Annakin.

Did You Know?

Benny Hill was the first star signed up for *Those Magnificent Men in Their Flying Machines*. Working well with director Ken Annakin, despite severe fear of heights while filming his tower-based sequences, Hill tried to inject even more wacky silent comedy humour into his part. He suggested that as he poured his flask of tea, a gust of wind (provided by an off-screen machine) could blow it into his cup – the idea was attempted, but proved impossible to realize.

Chitty Chitty Bang Bang

For this delightful children's fantasy which continues to capture each new generation's imagination via countless holiday television screenings, blockbusting producer Cubby Broccoli turned to his most profitable source material provider, Ian Fleming, for this post- initial Bond boom classic (indeed, the film's official title is *Ian Fleming's Chitty Chitty Bang Bang*), and created a magical, hummable-

tune-filled, colourful adventure. In terms of Benny Hill's film career, it was the ideal, multi-million pound, international epic, following the overtly comedically geared bonanza of *Those Magnificent Men in Their Flying Machines*. Both this film and Hill's following big-screen venture, *The Italian Job*, came at the time of his crucial shift from BBC to Thames Television. Indeed, Hill used these small but potent film performances to bridge his two different television eras. Although prominently credited, Hill's contribution is very brief indeed, and he doesn't make his first appearance until over 90 minutes into the film. However, it was critically cited as a beautifully played piece of work, and in retrospect, remains a fine, frequently revived film appearance.

It's almost impossible to detach Hill's performance from the rest of the film, for by the time Chitty takes to the air and the Germanic nightmarish sequence starts, the senses have already been bombarded with more treats than Willy Wonka's chocolate factory. Hill's work stands out, however, thanks to director Ken Hughes' establishment of a fairy tale village populated by world-weary villagers and ruled with pantomime-sized excesses by Anna Quayle and Gert Frobe (another bit of Bond baggage, bringing touches of *Goldfinger*'s megalomaniac action). The gloriously over-the-top playing of these chief booworthy characterizations counterbalances the friendly

earnestness of the hero, Dick Van Dyke, and his delightful female companion, Sally Ann Howes.

As the town's harassed toymaker, Hill could have lapsed into eye-rolling, flamboyant mugging, but his contribution is one of subtle restraint, sincere kindness and underlined terror. Made even more potent against a backdrop of outlandish, larger-than-life acting, garish decor and mountains of toys, Hill skilfully avoids any sort of comic by-play or manic business, simply to present this quick-witted and resourceful figure as the stolid embodiment of hope in a hopeless situation. His castigation of Van Dyke's song in the face of disaster is both a brilliantly acted piece of confrontation and pillories the musical convention of 'song in the heart equals problem almost over'. Hill's guided tour of the *Oliver!*-like children hiding away in a *Phantom of the Opera*-inspired cavern is touching, momentarily stopping his diatribe to bestow affection and hair-ruffling on a particularly forlorn-looking lad. His disgruntled acceptance of responsibility for helping hide Van Dyke's children (grudgingly giving the kids toy nutcrackers) is perfectly understated, allowing this cynical, anti-social bringer of children's playthings to reveal the deep-rooted kindness of a friendly uncle. Hill's *pièce de résistance*, the Trojan horse-styled attack on the palace via intricate toys for the Baron's birthday (Sally Ann Howes and Dick Van Dyke in heavy disguise), is the one opportunity for knowing comic glances, but even here, the shared moment of triumph is tempered with dangerous exploits and successful military campaigning.

From his first appearance, bravely ushering in the newcomers while all about him run for comfort, to the climactic cannon run attack on the imprisoned children's cell and a fond wave to the departing flying car, this is Hill being allowed to craft a strong, three-dimensional supporting persona. Previously, his forte was for Keystone Kop-inspired physical comedy, and *The Italian Job* would call for a more adult, over-played comic contribution, so *Chitty Chitty Bang Bang* was very much foreign terrain for the comedian, and as a result, his performance is both thoughtful and penetratingly effective. Stripped of the need for barrel-scraping comic business and with little character traits and subtle touches such as uncontrolled twitches as Robert Helpmann's child-catcher sniffs

around, a quick grin of confidence and his heartfelt outburst about the lifestyle of the village's forbidden children, this is arguably Hill's most satisfying film performance. A complete departure from his well-known, well-defined screen image, when you first encounter this film as a child, you scarcely – if at all – register that this is Benny Hill the comedian. One can imagine Hill's smile of satisfaction at that fact.

A magical, joyfully rip-roaring children's adventure, from the catchy musical score during the elongated credit sequence (illustrating Chitty's successful motor racing career and the car's ultimate demise while avoiding a dog on the track), director Ken Hughes orchestrates a feel-good romp. With a powerful bang in the musical score as the photographer snaps a winning shot of the car, the audience are whisked off to a musical wonderland, inhabited by post-*Mary Poppins* tunes, adding a dollop of fantastic excess to the blockbuster, studio-bound musicals of the 1960s. Van Dyke, stripped of his cringe-making *Mary Poppins* cockney accent, delivers a brilliant performance of subtle emotion, spirited dancing (the 'Old Bamboo' routine almost puts 'Chim Chim Cheree' to shame, his money-making surprise and initially slightly out-of-time rendition creating a show-stopping routine) and playful comic mugging (a deliciously Stan Laurel-like Trojan doll turn for Baron Gert Frobe, counterbalanced with the faceless *Masque of Red Death*-inspired courtiers and a rousing *Bride of Frankenstein* meets *Don't Lose Your Head* via *Hue and Cry* climax). Broccoli clutches Bondian signifiers close to his chest with a telling cameo from Desmond Llewelyn (away from his duties as 'Q') as the pleasant but business-governed junk man Mr Coggins. There's room for some lip-smacking villainy from Victor Maddern (anyone who dares to kick Chitty when she's down and out has to be booed), Van Dyke mixes musical convention with heartwarming parental love with ease (if you don't get a lump in your throat when he croons 'Hush-a-Bye Mountain' to his adorable children, then feel for a pulse), and Sally Ann Howes effortlessly thaws from British ice maiden to eyelash-flashing funster. However, without doubt, it's the inspiring cast of priceless supporting character players that breathes true endearing magic into this irresistible film treat.

Lionel Jeffries, just before embarking on his own children-orientated swathe of directorial assignments, breezes through the eccentric comedy with perfection, white-suited, India-obsessed, patriotic, knowingly off the wall, and most telling of all, skilled in counterpointing Van Dyke's madness with a kindly shake of the head. He has a fine line in comic observation (on the meanness of Coggins: 'He wouldn't light your pipe if your house was on fire!') and a sense of peerless bewilderment as mistaken identity forces him into feigned scientific genius. But best of all is a marvellously rousing rendition of his solo song 'P.O.S.H.', interjecting delightful Colonial references, mugging his way through close encounters with a watery fate as his hot air balloon-abducted hut drifts across the ocean, and casually embracing the treat of tea as the answer to every problem.

In a smaller, though no less relishable role, is the ageing James Robertson Justice, just about to bow out of film appearances altogether, but happy to incorporate a familiar burst of business tycoon barking here – memorably disgruntled touring round his Victorian factory, and bluntly raining on Van Dyke's parade with 'Too late, had your chance ... muffed it!' – brilliantly cruel and final. Surrounded by all sorts of sweets like a confectionery Wizard of Oz, Robertson Justice leaves an indelible mark on the film, dismissing Van Dyke's Toot Sweets (despite a very catchy song and *Oliver!*-styled dance routine), allowing a crack of kindness to emerge with sweet-sucking, child hand-holding and old buffer laughter, struggling to control his temper as dogs invade his factory (led by the Potts family's Edison the sheepdog), and finally (after the Baron fantasy interlude), embracing Van Dyke's invention, throwing himself into toy soldier battles with his old

The fairy tale within the film comes to a happy ending - Benny Hill, Dick Van Dyke, Heather Ripley, Lionel Jeffries, Adrian Hall and Sally Ann Howes climb aboard the star of the show, *Chitty Chitty Bang Bang*

batman (Jeffries), sealing the wealth of the family, and – crucial for the happy ending – allowing the proud but penniless Van Dyke to finally marry the landed-gentry, totally rich, truly scrumptious Sally Ann Howes.

The frantic fairground sequence (effectively built up by Hughes from the touching children's serenade, via breathtaking windmill imagery, distant music and a sudden plan-hatching expression on Van Dyke's face) allows a spirited step into colourful play, with Arthur Mullard portraying ... well ... Arthur Mullard with cockney bluster, and Barbara Windsor following suit with a giggling blonde characterization of fun-filled party girl tinged with over-the-top shock reaction. The population of Gert Frobe's Vulgaria boasts brief turns from Davy Kaye, Gerald Campion and a wonderfully apt slice of gobbledegook, bizarre billiard playing from Stanley Unwin, while a music hall legend, Young Mr Grace's brother from television's *Are You Being Served?* and that charming old bloke from *Rent-a-Ghost*, joyfully drags Lionel Jeffries through the painfully optimistic 'Up from the Ashes'.

While the Baron and his wife play evil for overblown laughs, Robert Helpmann, employing his balletic grace coupled with the sinister grotesqueness of his Oberon, playfully prances through the fairy tale as the dreaded child-catcher. This is the stuff of childhood nightmare. With a charming line in niceties, sweets aplenty, a threatening cane and a huge horse-driven cage, his black-clad, sickly pleasant figure scurries round the village like a particularly dangerous spider. Travelling down the same yellow brick road as Margaret Hamilton's Wicked Witch of the West, Helpmann's villain is perfectly flamboyant and unforgettable.

The film may be over-long, with the Mack Sennett-styled bathing scene, Howes's cloying ballad at Pinewood's pond and the Laurel and Hardyesque knock-about foreign henchmen (X and Bacon) all stretching the attention span, but even waiting over 45 minutes to see Chitty back to her former glory is forgivable when so much of the film is enjoyable.

There's an undefinable magic at work in *Chitty Chitty Bang Bang*, with the eager, child-view anticipation at Chitty's resurrection, a gloriously innocent sense of xenophobic Brit in Jeffries ('I'm being abducted by for-

eigners!'), a clear understanding of both humanity and fantasy, Chitty's breathtaking first flight over the white cliffs of Dover, and most powerfully of all, the climactic, happy-ever-after closure, dispelling any doubt that Chitty's a very special car with a reprise of the unshakeable theme. If you feel yourself getting too old to enjoy this one, just fight it.

Chitty Chitty Bang Bang. Released through United Artists/Warfield Productions Ltd/DFI. Opened October 1968. Technicolor/Super Panavision 70/Todd-AO. 145 mins. 'U' Certificate. Professor Caractacus Potts DICK VAN DYKE, Truly Scrumptious SALLY ANN HOWES, Grandpa Potts LIONEL JEFFRIES, Jemima Potts HEATHER RIPLEY, Jeremy Potts ADRIAN HALL, Baron Bomburst GERT FROBE, Baroness Bomburst ANNA QUAYLE, Toymaker BENNY HILL, Lord Scrumptious JAMES ROBERTSON JUSTICE, Child Catcher ROBERT HELPMANN, Blonde at Fair BARBARA WINDSOR, Cyril 'Hair-cut' ARTHUR MULLARD, Admiral DAVY KAYE, Spies ALEXANDER DORE and BERNARD SPEAR, Chancellor STANLEY UNWIN, Captain of Guard PETER ARNE,

Mr Coggins the Junk Man DESMOND LLEWELYN, 'That Nasty Junk Man Who Wanted to Buy Chitty' VICTOR MADDERN, Chef ROSS PARKER, Ministers GERALD CAMPION, FELIX FELTON and MONTI de LYLE, Duchess TOTTI TRUMAN TAYLOR, Lieutenant LARRY TAYLOR, Orchestra Leader MAX BACON, Phillips RICHARD WATTIS, Uninventors MAX WALL, JOHN HEAWOOD, MICHAEL DARBYSHIRE, KENNETH WALLER, GERALD TAYLOR and EDDIE DAVIS. Screenplay: Roald Dahl and Ken Hughes. Additional dialogue: Richard Maibaum. Director of Photography: Christopher Challis BSC. Music supervised and conducted by Irwin Kostal. Music and lyrics: Richard M. Sherman and Robert B. Sherman. Musical numbers staged by Marc Breaux and Dee Dee Wood. Art Director: Harry Pottle. Second Unit Director: Richard Taylor. Aerial Cameraman: John Jordan. Second Unit Cameraman: Skeets Kelly. Camera Operator: John Harris. Continuity: Angela Martella. Assistant Director: Gus Agosti. Location Manager: Frank Ernst. Associate Art Director: Jack Stephens. Sound Recordists: John Mitchell and Fred Hynes. Dubbing Editors: Harry

Taking time out to smell the flowers - Benny Hill's sweetly naive Professor Plum begins to plan *The Italian Job*.

Miller and Les Wiggins. Music Editor: Robin Clarke. Assistant Art Directors: Bob Laing, Peter Lamont and Michael White. Wardrobe Supervisor: Jackie Cummins. Potts inventions created by Rowland Emett. Editor: John Shirley. Special effects: John Stears. Production Supervisor: David Middlemas. Matte effects: Cliff Culley. Production Associate: Peter Hunt. Production designed by Ken Adam. Colour costume design: Elizabeth Haffenden and Joan Bridge. Associate Producer: Stanley Sopel. Producer: Albert R. Broccoli. Director: Ken Hughes. Filmed on location in Rothenburg, Germany, and France, and at Pinewood Studios, London, England

Did You Know?

Despite his billing, Roald Dahl contributed very little to the finished screenplay of *Chitty Chitty Bang Bang*, and Benny Hill himself worked with Ken Hughes for five weeks injecting comic moments into the initial Caractacus Potts scenes.

The sound track recording for *Chitty Chitty Bang Bang* was an essential home treat for any self-respecting

kid, but apart from a namecheck on the poster-design cover, Hill was notable by his absence. However, the 1997 CD reissue of the album on the MGM deluxe edition label (RCD 10702) successfully addressed that – a wonderful package, it includes choice soundbites from the movie as well as the expected song favourites. But that's not all: in this joyful high-tech age, we now have the added bonus of the original film trailer on CD-ROM.

The Italian Job

The epitome of 'Cool Britannia', and spearheading the 1990s' hip reappraisal of the 1960s via Oasis, Blur and Loaded magazine, this classic, patriotic, laddish, Beatles Britain heist movie has been raised to cult status and headlined by Sky Sports as the perfect pre-match movie before any England–Italy footie fest because of the diverting international match within the film's narrative – indeed, Michael Caine signed up for a campaign promoting 'The Italian Job 2', cheering our lads along and into the World Cup Finals.

There's no doubt that the film stands very much as

symbolic of its era, even though its reputation does mask the fact that much of it is fairly workmanlike. Playing like a glorified episode of ATV's *The Saint*, signs of strain in the script are apparent throughout, although Caine's self-confident cockney charmer more than makes up for it. Displaying sublime comic touches in his reactions to the hang-ups, freedom and atmosphere of the period, Caine is the epitome of style, bucking the system, toeing the line with one eye on corruption, embracing sexual freedom (albeit facing the consequences when he oversteps the mark celebrating his release from jail) and tackling ever-changing trends with crestfallen acceptance. Who cares if he does little but shout instructions to his gang, this is Caine at the zenith of his career, coasting through a tailor-made character with aplomb.

The closing scene is one of the ultimate feelgood/feel sorry endings in British film. With crime almost paying, our British heroes can be seen to get away with the job, but not quite – ripping off the Italians to boost the failing British coffers, but still falling at the final hurdle. Caine's upbeat determination to solve the situation (the getaway truck balanced over a precipice), facing a life-or-wealth dilemma (die, or let the loot go), the masterly direction and the irresistably catchy burst of 'Self Preservation Society' builds up to a truly classic close. In an age of multiple sequels, the unresolved climax could have led to at least one follow-up, but there's something reassuringly British and cosy about an ending, literally left in the air, and this fondly remembered, fun picture of sharp suits, sharp tongues and sharp operators speeds along with tangible energy. A conclusive ending would have ruined it.

The chief joy, of course, is the tightly knit ensemble cast, boasting fabulous supports from the likes of Tony Beckley's cutting Camp Freddie, a super-cool, short-lived bit of advice from Rossana Brazzi (the victim of serious vendetta treatment, complete with cinematic iconology of callously crushed shades, black-suited gangsters and casually tossed wreaths), a toe-curlingly arch cameo from TV chat show host of the time Simon Dee, and interestingly, a minor turn from Benny Hill's familiar television sidekick, Henry McGee. His throwaway knowing, prison-aware comment to the recently uncaged Caine hits home perfectly.

Despite receiving prominent billing, Benny Hill has very little to do except grin with sheepish sexual angst and deploy his persona of absent-minded genius. Blessed with a gloriously dotty performance from Irene Handl as his sister, Hill's surreal creation of Professor Peach mirrors his television persona, with his unhealthy obsession with large women (before his entrance there are rumours of obscene behaviour with Annette), manic, misunderstood antics such as chomping on proffered cigars, and brilliantly contrasting his cheeky, smut-ridden expressions with the naivety of childhood. The most endearing moment comes when he merrily picks wild flowers when the gang are at the height of nervous energy.

Hill's central role in the crime itself is purely brainwork, cracking into the super-powerful Turin computer to demolibilize traffic/security systems, while somewhat letting the side down by giving into his urges with a large Italian woman, thoroughly enjoying his helping hand in squeezing her into a bus or through the doors of the police station, and injecting subversive, sheepish elements as he shiftily waddles into the hands of justice. But all the real legwork of the film's crime is left to Michael Caine, and Hill happily goes along for the ride.

A very minor performance enhanced by added comic asides and visual business, Hill's almost, but not quite, lost innocent Brit is nevertheless one of the gang in the patriotic plan to knock the Italians for six. In this, his last performance in a feature film before enjoying the new freedom ITV held in store, there's a pleasing full-circle element to the credits – support player Irene Handl and camera operator Chic Waterson had also been involved in *Who Done It?*

Often dismissed as nothing more humorous than saying 'bloody' in a petulant cockney accent, Caine's pivotal performance works perfectly with the rest of the cast. Effortlessly importing off-kilter anti-hero baggage from *Alfie* and the Harry Palmer movies, embracing the swinging *chic* culture, and barking his proud-to-be-British ideals while harbouring a lust for personal security, he is the ultimate lad's hero.

However, for me, it's the outstanding work from Noel Coward that really gives *The Italian Job* its heart. Gracefully languishing at Her Majesty's Pleasure, Coward continues to celebrate the pleasure of Her Majesty with a cell covered with magazine photographs of the Queen, while his distinguished, dignified, and more importantly, powerful position in the prison clearly foreshadow's Peter Vaughan's harder-edged top dog, Grouty, in the Ronnie Barker television series *Porridge*. Joyfully sending up his own sophisticated mannerisms, Coward injects the odd sly cockney slant into his pompous connoisseur, wandering round the cells with an air of indignant disdain, appraising Caine's charmer with a superior sniff: 'Everyone in the world is bent!'

In a smaller, though by no means less potent part, Fred Emney staggers in for some wonderfully gruff touch-

She's BIG! -
The Italian Job allows sex-mad size-mad Benny to go well over the top.

es of patriotic eccentricity, doing the dirty on the 'bloody foreigners', shamelessly sporting his Union Jack carrier bag and blustering with perfect spontaneity.

With subtle changes in pace, this delightful character work stands alongside frantic action for the stunt driving team, with the closing 20 minutes an exercise in breakneck driving through tight avenues. Amid overblown crashes, the lads drive rings round the competition in a breathtaking display, performed, suitably enough, in three Minis – one red, one white and one blue. It's this sense of a daring robbery conducted in the name of British pride that carries the action along, where not standing for the National Anthem is frowned upon, where blowing the British trumpet is still encouraged, capturing the 1960s' brash attitude of national pride, counter-culture awareness, groovy tunes and the promise of instant fortune, whatever your social background.

This recipe made *The Italian Job* one of the biggest box office successes of the decade of classless British opportunity, where Michael Caine's coolest of cool dudes can wander through life with glamorous girls, barked orders, patriotic pride and a sense of self-righteousness, where our anti-hero can happily put down foreign stereotypes and eagerly chuck in a coda about Italians driving on the wrong side of the road, a time when pleasure and iconography in the Union Jack symbolized a sense of freedom, energy and productiveness, where a sigh of regret can be heard as the trio of British-made Minis bite the dust after an encounter with an equally patriotically painted coach, and above all, when a tight-knit community spirit of wartime memories, a fast-vanishing but heartwarming respect for regal authority and laid-back, progressive film production were all at play. It's a triumph of style over content, the times were certainly a'changin', and the characterizations may be lightly sketched, but there's something comforting about checking in for 90 minutes in the company of Michael Caine and his gang.

The climactic reassurance from the main man is one of the most powerful, satisfying moments in cinema history. It's from a long gone era, but it's as fresh and emotive as it ever was, and personally, I never tire of this sparkling bit of heist roller-coasting.

The Italian Job: Paramount/Oakhurst. Opened June 1969. Television debut: ITV, 25 January 1976, 7.55–9.45 p.m. Eastmancolor/Panavision. 100 mins. 'U' Certificate. Charlie Croker MICHAEL CAINE, Mr Bridger NOEL COWARD, Professor Simon Peach BENNY HILL, Altabani RAF VALLONE, Camp Freddie TONY BECKLEY, Roger Beckerman ROSSANO BRAZZI, Lorna MAGGIE BLYE, Miss Peach IRENE HANDL, Governor JOHN LE MESURIER, Birkenshaw FRED EMNEY, Arthur MICHAEL STANDING, Frank JOHN FORGEHAM, Bill Bailey GEORGE INNES, Big William HARRY BAIRD, Yellow ROBERT POWELL, Rozzer DEREK WARE, Roger FRANK JARVIS, Coco STANLEY CAINE, Garage Manager JOHN CLIVE, Keats GRAHAM PAYN, Shirt Maker SIMON DEE, Tailor HENRY McGEE, Chris BARRY COX, Dominic DAVID SALAMONE, Tony RICHARD ESSAME, Manzo MARIO VOLGOI, Cosca RENATO ROMANO, Altabani's Driver FRANCO NOVELLI, Dentist TIMOTHY BATESON, Vicar DAVID KELLY, Computer Room Officials ARNOLD DIAMOND and LOUIS MANSI, Cinema Warder ALISTAIR HUNTER, Mrs Cosca LANA GATTO, Stand-in JOHN MORRIS, Receptionist VALERIE LEON. Screenplay: Troy Kennedy Martin. Photography:

this film. Location work: Italy, Ireland and England, and Isleworth Studios/Twickenham Studios, London.

Did You Know?

As was becoming the norm, Hill injected minor alterations to the script of *The Italian Job*, restructuring his own role, adding the obsession with overweight women, and initially playing the part as a deaf Yorkshireman who occasionally broke into shouts to combat his disability. The makers didn't like this subtle touch, and ordered him to re-dub his part.

With any thoughts of a star career in the movies behind him, Hill decided to abandon plans for pet projects. He had written the screenplay *I Love You, I Love You, I Love You*, and attracted John Borman to direct, plans had been made for a starring vehicle for Hammer Films, producers Bud Yorkin and Ben Arbeid were in discussion about major film work, while Blake Edwards courted him for an interesting supporting role in his 1969 film *Darling Lili*, starring Julie Andrews and Rock Hudson. Auditioned by Edwards, he was asked whether he could do a French accent. Naturally, Hill could, and he asked: 'Would you like a Paris accent? East side or west ...?' Edwards, not amused by this pedantic attention to detail, found somebody else.

Hill's film career was all but over anyway, with the lure of controlled television stardom far more interesting and appealing. However, he had one further crack at big-screen success in the 1960s with *The Waiters*, a special homage to all those classic slapstick comedies that had shaped his own work.

The Waiters

This delightful, short silent comedy was made during Hill's crucial transition between the BBC and Thames Television. He starred opposite familiar comedy actor David Battley (from the television series *Sykes* and *Bless This House*, the original 'George Harrison' figure in *The Rutles*) as a couple of clumsy, accident-prone waiters at an elegant dinner party.

Hill mugs with energetic slapstick splendour as the superior, refined bumbler to Battley's clumsy, unsophisticated bumbler in a feast of perverted social graces, sexual temptations, Freddie Frinton-styled food juggling and wide-eyed leering, performed with an expert touch. However, the film failed to relaunch his big-screen career, and resembles a self-contained television situation comedy. Indeed, his second and last self-penned, self-conceived half-hour film, *Eddie in August*, was planned specifically

Douglas Slocombe. Editor: John Trumper. Camera Operator: Chic Waterson. Assistant Director: Scott Wodehouse. Second Unit Director: Phillip Wrestler. Art Sound Editor: Stephen Warwick. Continuity: Helen Whitson. Sound Mixer: John Aldred. Dubbing Mixer: Gerry Humphreys. Chief Make-up Artist: Freddie Williamson. Wardrobe Supervisor: Dulcie Midwinter. Chief Hairdresser: Gordon Bond. Wardrobe Master: Roy Ponting. Production Secretary: Barbara Allen. Lighting: Lee Electric. Special effects: Pat Moore. Casting: Paul Lee Landen. Costumes: Bermans. Mr Caine's suits: Douglas Hayward. Director: Michael Knight. Construction Manager: Terry Closey. Location Manager: Cil Burgess. Production Manager: Derek Kavanagh. Second Unit Director: Phillip Wrestler. Second Unit Director of Photography: Norman Warwick. Camera Operator: Ronnie Maasz. Assistant Director: David Munro. Music: Quincy Jones. 'On Days Like These', sung by Matt Monro, and 'Getta Bloomin' Move On!' lyrics by Don Black. Italian Production Supervisor: Georgia Migliarini. Italian Assistant Director: Mauro Sacripanti. Stunt driving: L'Equipe Rémy Julienne. Processed by Humphries Laboratories. Production Designer: Disley Jones. Associate Producer: Bob Porter. Producer: Michael Deeley. Director: Peter Collinson. Our grateful thanks to Turin and Fiat for their help with

The Waiters shows a classic Hill sight gag in two easy lessons; First serve the fruit to Jan Butlin in a low cut dress ... then drop it down the obvious place.

for television.

 The Waiters itself now seems more at home on the small screen, although it has rarely been trundled out since its ITV screening on 2 October 1983 during Hill's ultimate Thames glory days. On Sunday 3 March 1996, *The Waiters* was screened as part of the Southampton Festival of Comedy at Harbour Lights Cinema, the town finally reclaiming its own.

The Waiters. Fanfare (Paramount). Opened December 1969. 30 mins. Colour. 'U' Certificate. The Waiters BENNY HILL, DAVID BATTLEY, Host ARTHUR HEWLETT, Hostess PAMELA CUNDELL, Guest JAMES OTTAWAY, Daughter JAN BUTLIN. Also featuring NANCY MACKEITH, GEORGE FENTON. Script: Benny Hill. Producer: George H. Brown. Director: Jan Darnley-Smith.

The Best of Benny Hill

While the Monty Python boys were happily refilming and rearranging vintage BBC television vignettes for their film debut, *And Now For Something Completely Different*, Benny Hill was having none of that. Delving into his 1969–1971 Thames Television back catalogue, *The Best of Benny Hill* was simply a quick edit of old television sketches packaged together for the big screen. What his loyal punters paid good money to see at the cinema, they had already seen in the comfort of their own homes. But no one seemed to mind – certainly, no one was conned into thinking this was new material – and the box office tills did ring loud and long.

 This Thames compilation has long proved an essential source of reference for documentary makers and Hill scholars ever since. Indeed, while Hill's early Thames

Benny Hill and Dave Freeman see the sights following a lunch at the House of Commons with Bessie Braddock M.P.

material is hardly, if ever, screened, *The Best of Benny Hill* is aired regularly, usually filling some graveyard shift slot on ITV. From the cheap and cheerful title credit animation, featuring Benny Hill's quick character changes via hastily created cut-outs and continually rolling eyes, this is a real whiz-bang affair. No real style, continuity or effort is used, it's just left to trusty old Thames archive highlights and Hill's energetic, remorselessly passionate delivery to create a classic comedy film experience.

Straight away, it's into slapstick speed-up territory with 'Tribute to the Lower Tidmarsh Volunteer Hospital Service', Hill's embodiment of shoddy medical staff boozing in a pub and running the gamut of head-slapping, arse-kicking comedy with Jackie Wright's aged patient. Lighting a match on his head and typical Hill chasing of sexy, willing nurses round a bed obscures the fact that this is a brilliantly cruel, surreal piece. While there's a touch of half-hearted social comment, with the patients serving the nurses tea in bed, and an over-ripe dose of *Carry On*-style mugging with the enforced stripping of a sexy patient, this piece wanders into bizarre, Pythonesque regions, displaying a glorious disregard for taste balanced by the com-

mon touch of family smut. The darts match with hypodermic needles is cleverly handled, there's an entertaining piece about smoking during operations, and a manic game of noughts and crosses on the patient's stomach before real, rich sickness is embraced when he feeds the hospital cat bits of spare flesh from the operating table. It's a pity that such ground-breaking invention ends with a pinched *Carry On Doctor* gag (Hill's watch is left inside Wright), although the situation is given a further comic twist, the startled patient handing the surgeon his own watch as a replacement before making a speedy exit. This is an inventive introduction to Hill's best slapstick comedy style, albeit overlong at eight minutes.

A throwaway old-time American serenader having a window smashed in his face hardly has time to capture the audience's attention before this compilation's masterpiece, and possibly my all-time favourite Benny Hill gem, comes into view. Starring Hill's beloved role-reversal male, Mervyn Cruddy, the ageing chorus boy finds himself interviewed *à la* Joan Bakewell on television's *The Grass is Greener*. Gloriously drenched with knowing innuendo and moments of brilliantly relaxed corpsing, Hill throws himself into the semi-autobiographical tale of this starstruck Bournemouth performer. Packed with seaside picture-postcard double meanings, his tale of standing by the water's edge and having a paddle becomes loaded simply because of Hill's knowing grin to the audience. The reversal of female, stereotyped beauty contests is brilliantly achieved here with Hill's naked embarrassment during the knobbly knees competition, and the hilarity reaches fever pitch with his suppressed laughter-edged delivery of 'tapping 'em and testing 'em'. Embracing feminists' view of beauty contests as cattle markets is clearly aimed to mock the movement, but Hill's role-reversal scenario brings the absurdity and innocence of the situation sharply into focus. Hill's bumbling, charming but naive interviewee struggles on through the less than rigorous questioning ('Played leads?' – 'And Manchester ...') with priceless name-dropping for the old school of Kathleen Harrison and clever wordplay with the drinking session deconstruction ('lived life with a big L' – 'suffered pain with a big P'). This is undiluted and totally classic Benny Hill, material to rank him alongside any of the greats of British comedy. The fact that these inspired flights of dialogue-twisting are often ignored in favour of his mugged mime remains all the more amazing when savouring a *tour de force* like this. A new peak is reached with shocked tales of a party in Chelsea with female and male witches ('Warlocks!' – 'It's true I tell you ... there were male witches there!'), before the final masterpiece is unleashed: 'What steps did you take?' – 'Bloody long ones, I can tell you!'

Beautifully obvious, performed with the perfect air of delicious spontaneity and greeted with the all-conquering, corpsing feel of a great sketch well delivered, everything else has to pale in comparison, although the following item is fairly weak in anybody's book, with Hill's penniless French actor, Claude, trapped in a silent sepia-tone movie, longing for his lost lady love and skilfully trying to continue to woo her behind the back of Pepe the wealthy banker (Jack Wright). Rushing through a string of positions disguised as a servant to get a crack at his Fifi, Hill bounds through butler, chauffeur and gardener duties before putting on the drag as the cute French maid. Sharing a bed with a fellow nubile young maid puts paid to his passionate energies, and the whole thing plays like a more pessimistic Mack Sennett two-reeler.

A delightful quickie, with Sue Bond's Juliet forgetting her lines, much to the chagrin of Hill's Romeo, fades into the classic groovy, wild-haired raver, mesmerized by the gyrating legs of mini-skirted pop groupies. A hairdressing sketch with Jenny Lee-Wright and Bob Todd is simply included so that Hill can undermine the acting performance and memorably complain to his director, 'Honestly John, he's so bloody rubbish', while the ITV audiences of old (and here, the cinema viewers) can enjoy a stunning frontal attack on television commercial conventions, notably a twist on the butter/Stork margarine tasting campaign of the time.

Next, Henry McGee grabs his chance to shine, asking questions of Hill's distinguished Edith Evans-like lady via a delayed satellite link. In an inspired extended joke at the medium's expense, after a problem with the link during the first question, Hill responds to the previous enquiry throughout, heightened innuendo resulting from each misunderstood reply.

Hill's following wordless masterpiece as the unattractive suitor embracing a handsome face mask to impress his lady love is pure Chaplin poetry, brilliantly twisted with the surreal sexual role-reversal of the mistaken female mask and the caddish sidelines reaction of Nicholas Parsons.

However, this brief, beautifully constructed piece fails to attract anywhere near as many laughs as Hill's drunken political chat show guest. Pre-empting the outrageousness of Oliver Reed, Hill's uncontrolled, disgraceful, sexist running commentary over Patricia Hayes's fashion guru diatribe is hilarious. Hayes, waxing lyrical on the new styles with 'See your wife in something long and flowing', invites the obvious but painfully funny Hill comment, 'Yes, the river!'

'The Messenger', tends to stretch the attention span to breaking point. During a mammoth journey from Sussex to Edinburgh, there's some wonderful detail, and Hill's cherubic expressions are endearing enough, but most of the sight gags are laboured or repetitive – clothes-swapping with pretty maid results in unwanted advances from soldier, the distinguished Charles I (Parsons) lights his pipe with the valued message – but it's worth sitting through if only for the inspiring piggyback ride with an aged crone. Rehashed from his old BBC shows but worthy of Monty Python, the sight is so incongruously comic that you can't help laughing.

'The Garden of Love' number, delivered with the Arthur Askey technique of fully accepting the corniness of the material, sees Hill enjoying himself, although most of the best lyrics were lifted for the vinyl release 'Brokenhearted Lover's Stew'. Fittingly, the song is followed by the married couple tolerance quickie, questioning Hill's paternal contributions before heading into television mockery territory again with McGee as a gloriously pretentious film critic chatting to laid-back French filmmaker Pierre Peteir.

Hill's performance employs a subtlety often overlooked by dissenters, responding to McGee's eulogistic praise for stark, meaningful black and white images with the downbeat explanation that he ran out of colour film. This is the perfect prelude to the classic 1930s film parody, 'Passengers of Love'. Although it would have worked even better in grainy black and white, the obvious parodying of Ray Milland and Loretta Young as Ray Hilland and Loretta Bung ushers in affectionate ribbing of Hollywood convention. Basking in the self-parody of *Singin' in the Rain*, Hill's mini-masterpiece jumps out of synchronization so that characters mouth the lines of other characters and break off dialogue to present a host of unsubtle innuendo. Again, as with many of Hill's clever techniques, the idea is overused and the speeded-up/slowed down vocal athletics set the toes curling, but there's some wonderful over-the-top pompous nastiness from Nicholas Parsons and a joyful rendition of 'Tiptoe Through the Tulips' as the dodgy plot lines are woven together and Hill's handsome hero wins in the end. Some unsubtle credit puns (Wardrobe: Fran Tick/Director: John Poppins) smoothes this shaky cinematic sea voyage into the calmer, comically safer waters of 'The Birds and the Bees'.

Perhaps Hill's most familiar piece of material from these early Thames days (extensively reproduced in documentaries and on Hill records), 'The Birds and the Bees' is the definitive slice of his rustic, knowing comedy. No 'best of' compilation of Benny Hill could be complete without a burst of Fred Scuttle, and here we are treated to a 1972 keep fit routine with the bespectacled one surrounded by an attractive array of glamorous girl recruits. It relies on low-key sexual advances to the girls, clod-hopping sight gags and knowing leers, but although Hill does chase the girls here, the final capture and stolen kiss results in disinterest from Hill and besotted pursuit from the woman. The final Chaplinesque belittling of Hill's skills, with a child lifting the defeatingly heavy weight, rounds off a rather lame slice of Scuttle, but those twinkling eyes can get away with murder.

A couple of classic quickies follow – firstly, Hill's kindly vicar interviewed by Patricia Hayes, revealing professional backbiting and sexual attraction once the 'off-air' signal is given, and best of all, a 1969 gem involving Hill's old buffer character saddled with a nagging, long-standing wife. The doddery pair walk up to a wishing well, where Hill's disgruntled husband character tosses in a coin with a fervent wish that his wife would disappear. It works. Inspired, he tosses in another coin and gets a bikini-clad babe. The girl makes a wish and conjures up a hunk in the shape of Dave Prowse, who in turn throws in a coin and makes the girl vanish. The hunk approaches the aged Hill, who makes another wish and replaces the muscle man with his well-worn wife again. The sketch ends as it begins, with the couple strolling by – that twenty or so seconds is what made Benny Hill a celebrated comic genius.

One of Hill's greatest, relentlessly hilarious pieces follows, second only to 'The Grass is Greener' as this compilation's high point. Steeped in television conventions and the coolness of Simon Dee's BBC television chat show, Hill is the super-cool Tommy Tupper, host of *Tupper-Time*. Nervously presenting his prime-time load of guff, Hill desperately latches onto hip language ('Alrighty') and bravely tries to put over a casual air while live television technology collapses around him amid disinterested audience reaction ('There's one!'). As his fund of corny quips fail to ignite, he falls off his chair ('Falling for you tonight!') and welcomes the first guest, Wright's 107-year-old Eric Molten, who dies during his entrance. Hill carries on regardless, fumbles his unwitty link, and introduces the football-loving Reverend Peter Whilby (Michael Sharvell-Martin), whose diatribe cheerfully explaining he's an ordinary sort of bloke is completely eclipsed by the fact that his fly is undone. Hill's gallant attempts to obscure the camera's view and unceremoniously drag a potted plant in front of the gaping trousers is sublime comedy of embarrassment, quickly usurped by Henry McGee's non-communicative West End star, Rodney Fairchild. Introduced with a flamboyant flick of the wrist which sends his notes flying (sort of Woody Allen's date nervousness in *Play It Again Sam* meets Thames TV convention), Hill details the press discussions of McGee's hell-raising lifestyle, only to be greeted with momentous pauses and monosyllabic answers. Hill's expression of amazed frustration is treasurable indeed – his pained 'I could go on talking with you all night!' is brilliantly developed. The introduction of a legless theatrical blonde bimbo rounds things off as Hill thankfully turns to winding up the programme, only to realize there's another 42 minutes of airtime to go. The sketch is a comedy gem, dialogue-driven and displaying Hill's great, undervalued skill as a true character comedian.

A decidedly Pythonesque burst of Alan Whicker being sucked to his death in marshland and a neat piece of performance corruption with Hill's camp chap condemning the mistimed delivery of 'What's that in the road ... a head?' plugs the gap before the self-indulgent mini-epic 'The Life of Maurice Dribble from Womb to Tomb in 5 min 46 secs'.

Its cleverness rather outbalances the humour, with plenty of speeded-up antics in his parent's wedding bedroom, childish school mugging, labour exchange visits and alcohol devotion. Army recruitment gives Hill the excuse to adopt a Scuttle salute, but time is running out, and the aged Maurice Dribble gallops through the ranks, ends up falling downstairs (look out for a hilarious moment as his eyes roll with bewilderment), an emergency operation brings on a short-lived jig of renewed energy, and he finally ends up in a nursing home. Death comes as his strip poker-winning hand prompts his sexy nurse to remove her last item of clothing.

Next, more low-grade stuff and further toying with television convention, with Hill the newly-wed struggling over the threshold with a line-fluffing Rita Webb, and Benny's director voice-over condemning the camera's lingering on cleavage ('two trophies') and stocking tops, not to mention Bob Todd's nose-picking. McGee and LeBeau snogging allows another continuity error for Hill to exploit, there's a baffling bit of madness with Hill struggling behind a naked torso portrait, and the belated appearance of beloved Chinaman Chow Mein, battling with McGee's customs jobsworth. Typically, Mein gets the upper hand, sending up the British misunderstanding with 'Bruddy trit!', and countering snooty remarks about the Isle of

Wight hardly being overseas with 'You trying walking there!' Todd's Indian immigration official mixes racial stereotypes with Hill's continual reference to 'Cookie', and there's even a pinched *Carry On Camping* gag ('No, Sir, it has to be the bull!') to enliven the proceedings.

The finale, a goodnight song with Hill in various incarnations, stands as perhaps the only dated element in this vintage compilation. Rich with the cream of variety theatre of the early 1970s, this runs like a mini-*International Cabaret*, with impressions of Shirley Bassey (complete with exposed bum cleavage), Gilbert O'Sullivan (complete with schoolboy cap and winning grin), Dorothy Squires (belting it out like a good 'un), Nana Mouskouri (rambling on and on about the story behind her few lines of performance), Moira Anderson (all teeth and no trousers) and the Beverly Sisters (a rather clumsy split-screen affair allowing Hill to be all three of the blonde ones). Hill says his farewells and the credits roll as our comic hero, as an escaped convict, runs at high speed past coppers, gay advances and drag situations.

This collection of Benny Hill's past glories may be patchy, but if you still think he's just smut and no substance, give this potted history of his best era a try.

The Best of Benny Hill: Nat Cohen presentation for EMI Film Distributors. Euston Films/Thames Television Production. Compiled from *The Benny Hill Show*. Opened April 1974. 87 mins. Technicolour. 'A' Certificate. Starring BENNY HILL. Featuring BOB TODD, ANNE IRVING, BETTINE LE BEAU, DAVID PROWSE, HENRY McGEE, NICHOLAS PARSONS, PATRICIA HAYES, CONNIE GEORGES, JENNY LEE-WRIGHT, EIRA HEATH, ANDREE MELLY, RITA WEBB, LESLIE GOLDIE, JACK WRIGHT, NICOLE SHELBY, PENNY MEREDITH, MICHAEL SHARVELL-MARTIN, JAN BUTLIN, SUE BOND, CHARMAINE SEAL, ANNE IRVING, PAMELA CUNDELL, MICHAEL MOORE, VALERIE ST JOHN, JIM TYSON, VERNE MOR-GAN, ARTHUR HEWLETT, CAROL MILLS, GERALDINE BURNETT, ROY SCAMMELL, RHONA NEWTON, JOHN TED SENTON, JOHN-NY GREELAND, TOM SYE, TESSA SCOPES, BAR-BARA LINDLEY, DAVID HAMILTON, MIA MAR-TIN, MALCOLM WEAVER, JOSIE STUART, FRED-DIE WILES, WALLY GOODMAN, PAM BECK-MAN. Script and songs: Benny Hill. Feature and Music Editor: Archie Ludski GBFE. Musical Director: Ronnie Aldrich. Music: Ronnie Aldrich and Benny Hill. Producers: John Robins and Roy Skeggs. Director: John Robins. Thames Television Studios, Teddington, Middlesex, England.

Did You Know?

The Best of Benny Hill cost just £30,000 to put together, but made millions. Hill had suggested the clips package idea, having seen reports about Sid Caesar compiling ten old *Your Show of Shows* 35 millimetre television sketches into a popular feature film, predictably entitled, *Ten from Your Show of Shows*, for a 1973 cinema release. Hill thought 'That's clever and cheap!', and followed in his footsteps. Richard Stone suggested they approach impresario Bernie Delfont, and coincidentally, their initial meeting concluded with Delfont screening the Caesar movie as a reference point.

The success of *The Best of Benny Hill* merely confirmed Hill's deep-rooted belief that television was the only medium for him. Indeed, this compilation was his last major appearance in cinemas. However, after more than a decade, and with his international reputation now firmly assured, he accepted a brief appearance in the 1986 French film *Le Miracule*, directed by its star, Jean-Pierre Mocky. But America was the entertainment capital of the world, and although several Hollywood offers were made, it took a very British rock group to capitalize on Hill's enormous US popularity.

Anything She Does

Phil Collins, a dedicated British comedy fan and major Benny Hill admirer, roped in his hero for this 1987 Genesis video. In discussion with Tony Banks and Mike Rutherford, the group decided it was strong enough to be released as a single, and since its lyrics concerned a lonely man obsessed with a woman, Collins thought Hill would be perfect.

Although its most frequent exposure was on MTV, this video was conceived as an opening film for Genesis's live shows, with Hill's initial Fred Scuttle salute to the audience greeted by huge cheers at the American concerts. There's a lengthy, hilarious Hill preamble before the song, with boot-licking devotion to the group, unconvincing promises that he will provide efficient security cover, and frantic efforts to please. Rutherford and Banks may be rather wooden as actors, but Collins brilliantly throws himself into the spirit of the occasion, effortlessly turning on the cockney charm and embracing his own bit of visual humour by incorporating a swinging light fixture into his drum kit and mugging on the opening trumpet blast.

Once the song rocks in, Hill simply relaxes in his security box as Genesis's inner sanctum is invaded and the

What sight from yonder window...
muddled Shakespeare for a Thames quickie - *The Best of Benny Hill* with Sue Bond.

Visible Touch: Genesis: Vision Video Ltd. 48 mins. 'Anything She Does', 'Throwing It All Away', 'Tonight, Tonight, Tonight', 'Land of Confusion', 'In Too Deep', 'Invisible Touch', plus a mini-documentary looking into Genesis on tour. All tracks composed by A. Banks, P. Collins, M. Rutherford. All tracks published by Anthony Banks Ltd/Philip Collins Ltd/Michael Rutherford Ltd/Hit and Run Music (Publishing) Ltd. Designed by Baker Dave at Assorted Images. Virgin Records VVD 204.

Throughout his classic years at Thames Television, Hill seriously considered writing an original feature film script to star in, but doubts about the potential, fear of losing control over the project, concern about wasting valued time on a major idea that could be aborted, and most importantly, contentment in simply continuing with his ultra-successful television work put paid to the idea.

During the 1980s, with his American popularity at its peak, Hill was continually feted by major Hollywood producers, desperate for a supporting contribution or cameo. Ironically, he was once courted by Hollywood producers on *The Queen Mary* – a ship he had lived cheek by jowl with while the luxury liner was moored in Southampton Docks. Despite several high-powered lunches and discussions, these ideas never came to fruition, mainly due to the ambivalent attitude of Hill himself. Besides, his first love was his British television show, and no amount of money could drag him away from that. Of course, after May 1989, things were very different.

In 1990, shortly after his sacking by Thames, he was approached to star in a major comedy film concerning the exploits in a burlesque house. He was offered $5 million to star. However, after much consideration, Hill turned down the huge fee because he didn't feel the part was quite right for him. Even in these bleak days when he was desperate to get back to work, it had to be the right work to get the Hill seal of approval.

after-show refreshments are devoured. Engrossed in studying the beautiful form of Maria Whittaker on page 3 of the *Sun*, he is stunned when she appears before him, flirting with him while a troupe of interlopers sneak in unnoticed, Hill's ears steaming at Whittaker's attention. Familiar face Sue Upton turns up at the last minute, resulting in a classic speeded-up chase and, yes, another example of Benny Hill chasing the girl – although here it's hardly through sexual longing, rather a fear of failing in his duties. During a panicky clear-out of unauthorized revellers, a reverse-film technique corrects all the damage and replaces food that has been consumed.

With the return of the band, Hill gives a final, cheeky salute, complete with the nice touch of having cream from the reinstated cake still on his hand. Collins, satisfied with the security, promises to see him after the show, and the three head towards the stage. During concerts, the group would emerge at this point and the gig proper would start. What a way to start a show!

TELEVISION

I f Benny Hill's entire career had consisted of only television work, he would still be the world's most famous comedian. Hill loved the medium, and in turn, the medium loved him, rewarding him with global recognition unparalleled since Charlie Chaplin. The story of his long, long journey from the days as a penniless, struggling performer eagerly watching the television sets in Curry's shop window to the world-beating Benny Hill Show being voted least favourite programme by a leading women's magazine lies ahead of us.

Despite important footholds in radio and variety theatre, Hill saw the huge potential in television well before any of his contemporaries. Indeed, as early as 1949, disenchanted with his theatrical stooge work with Reg Varney, Hill was bombarding the Head of BBC Light Entertainment, Ronnie Waldman, with scripts and sketches. Although he was more eager to write comedy for other performers on television than perform himself outside the medium, these early ideas were systematically rejected. However, ironically, it was in harness with Varney that Hill landed his first television appearance, earning the fee of 13 guineas.

Here's Mud in Your Eyes

Hill's first television chance came with Reg Varney in tow for this 1949 comedy revue, broadcast live from Alexandra Palace. (The mud, by the way, was made of thick cocoa!) The sketches featured the comic duo in the guises of soldiers and hillbilly hicks. It hardly set the world of light entertainment alight, but Hill relished the opportunity to merge the fear and quick changes of theatre with the modernity of cameras and lenses. Importantly, it embraced the unseen audience, crossed the camera barrier and invaded the sitting room by finishing the fun with bucketloads of fake mud being slung at the camera (a pane of glass prevented any damage to the equipment). Even in these very early days, Hill was aware of his destiny, telling the critic Fred Cooke: 'The future of entertainment lies with television. That's the star to which I've hitched my wagon.'

Throughout his early success, Hill continued to send comedy material to Ronnie Waldman. During a nine-week drought of theatre work, he spent all his time writing television sketches. Finally called in to discuss the work with the man himself (although some sources claim Hill arrived unannounced and barged in to see Waldman), Hill arrived for his half-hour meeting with a shoe box stuffed with 40 original sketches. To prove that every one was something he had confidence in, Hill pulled a piece of paper at random from it as an example of his work. The selected sketch involved a bowler-hatted city gent caught in the confusing and bemusing conveyor belt system in a Lyon's tea shop. With gusto, Hill mimed the frustrated umbrella by-play, impaling stray doughnuts and general slapstick nightmarishness. Waldman asked him who he thought could perform the material, and while Hill was modestly brainstorming for a name like Arthur Askey or Terry-Thomas, Waldman advised him that the only person he thought could do it properly was Hill himself. Casually, he muttered: 'What are you doing next Thursday? Would you like your own show?'

Hi There

Waldman's deputy was Bill Lyon-Shaw, who produced *Hi There*. This BBC revue show broadcast on 20 August 1951 (8.15-9.15 p.m.) featured Hill in solo spots and sketches. David Jacobs was his refined straightman, and cleverly playing safe, the first sketch Hill performed was the self-service item that had made Ronnie Waldman laugh in the first place. The comedian tried everything from bumbling waiters in a Parisian bistro to rip-roaring cockney barrow boys flogging dodgy goods down the market – the public loved it. Almost immediately, in August 1951, the *News Chronicle* prophetically commented: 'Mark down Benny Hill among the future television favourites.'

Starlight Symphony

Broadcast live from the 1951 Radio Show with Hill as compere/comic, Leonard Mosley commented that Hill 'has charm and manner and can get his tongue round some amusing dialect stories and songs, the only trouble being that people like Jon Pertwee do the same thing rather better.' On 29 February 1952, Benny starred in *After The Show*, an episode of *Kaleidoscope*.

The Centre Show

As with his variety radio performances, Hill was still very much associated with military entertainment. Landing a spot on this monthly series tailored for the services and broadcast from the Nuffield Centre in London's Soho, he graduated to regular host of this lightweight, undemanding revue. Guests included future regular stooge Nicholas Parsons and Shirley Abicair, while the resident band was Johnny Dankworth's, featuring singer Cleo Laine. With Hill telling dubious jokes and singing dubious songs in dubious costumes, notably a Yeoman of the Guard number, this was vitally important for the later development of *The Benny Hill Show*. It was the first joint venture for star Benny Hill, producer Kenneth Carter and writer Dave Freeman.

Having sold his first three jokes to Jimmy Edwards, Freeman sold his first short sketch to Hill for *The Centre Show* after meeting the comic at the American Officers' Club. He soon found himself contributing regularly to the programme. One of their earliest sketch ideas was called 'The Boy on the Bridge', but four years later, during the heyday of Hill's own BBC show, it had yet to be finished. The meagre £20 budget for the show was put together by Hill and Carter themselves. Importantly, this series also presented Benny to the general public for the first time in drag – camping it up rotten as Primrose Hill.

Continually peppering his delivery with innuendoes and retaining his stand-up persona as opposed to character comedy, Hill's saucy diatribes were even condemned by the War Office, which made an official complaint to the upper echelons of the BBC. Ironically, the offending gag quoted by the men in grey suits was one of Hill's most innocent observations, involving a lost football pool coupon in Chelsea. To claim it, the owner should phone 'Whitehall home-away, home-away'. This feeble gag (Whitehall's phone number being 1212, and the value of home wins being 1 and away wins 2 on football pools coupons) excited heated complaint from Whitehall Department AG3, which condemned it as filth, having misheard the gag as 'homo-way, homo-way', believing it implied effeminate behaviour in high office. The War Office Colonel himself wrote the official letter of outrage, insisting that all future Hill scripts should be checked before the show. In the end, the wonderful press coverage of this outrageous reaction couldn't have been bought. Happy with the viewing figures and aware that

Hill was on the up as a performer, the BBC wisely reacted by embracing the comedian and merely changing the name of the show.

Showcase

Benny Hill graduated from a one-off guest starring turn on *Showcase* to becoming its leading comic light. Quick sketches and television parodies were to the fore. The opener – Jeremy Hawk as a shopkeeper selling Hill a wonderful, compact electrical gadget before revealing the enormous battery needed to run it – was typically powerful, simple and endearing.

Already experimenting with twisting the conventions of television, Hill began performing wickedly accurate impressions of small-screen favourites. Bearded, eccentric television chef Philip Harben (younger readers should check out the climactic chase through Television Centre in Norman Wisdom's film *Man of the Moment* to catch his style) was an early target. Hill loved playing the part, tossing in old chestnuts about making gorgonzola cheese from gorgons and zolas, and even feeling confident enough to throw in an ad-lib when a potato rolled off a chicken-laden cooking tray – 'Oh! It's laid an egg!' This proved such a showstopper that in 1971, when Hill gave television cook Fanny Craddock the comic treatment, he repeated the line for maximum effect.

For *Showtime*, the follically challenged Harben made a guest gag appearance opposite Hill's phrenologist. This proved so successful that Harben was recalled for a cookery skit, but upon reading the script and watching Hill's performance, the star personality walked out of the studios fuming: 'They submitted a sketch to me which I considered degrading. It seemed to be devised to make me appear professionally incompetent. I was supposed to be half-tight and the whole thing indicated that I couldn't cook. That's no joke to me!' But who needed the real thing with Benny Hill about? Besides, Harben was back for *The Benny Hill Show* a few years down the line.

Celebrated, flamboyant hair stylist Mr Teasie Weasie became Mr Twirly Whirly, complete with curly wig, thinly disguised working-class vocal slips and luxurious smoking jacket. DIY expert Barry Bucknell was accurately parodied as a bumbling, beloved eccentric who couldn't make anything (a television age before Kenny Everett or Jasper Carrott developed similar routines). Sports commentator Raymond Glendenning was mocked. But the real eye-opener came with Hill's masterly parody of *What's My Line?* This was live television, don't forget, so Hill's quick changes from Barbara Kelly to Lady Isabel Barnett to

Gilbert Harding to David Nixon allowed Hill the danger-ous adrenaline of having to rely on skilful facial reactions rather than elaborate costume and make-up. Even by the time of his ground-breaking split-screen *Juke Box Jury* par-ody, this immediacy had vanished and studio trickery was king. Of the *What's My Line?* routine, Clifford Davis com-mented that it was 'so entertaining that all the other acts faded into nothingness'.

Did You Know?

Keen to have his name in full prominence, the star origi-nally wanted to call the *Showcase* show *Benny Hill's Merry-Go-Round* – however, Waldman didn't consider his fame big enough to warrant such an honour.

It was originally planned to begin the show with a burst of fairground organ music, but after unsatisfactory trial runs with organs in an aircraft hangar near Chichester, orchestra director Cyril Bevy created the sound illusion with his musicians, and introduced the show with a collection of glamorous girls on a carousel.

In 1998, alternative comedian Alexei Sayle launched his new series – *Alexei Sayle's Merry-Go-Round*!

The Services Show

For all intents and purposes, this is really *The Centre Show* under a different guise, with Hill still wringing out every last double meaning during his monologue presentations. However, to appease the military bigwigs, the broadcast was decamped to the cosy confines of Television Centre, Shepherd's Bush, London. A clear step up from the loca-tion-based *Centre Show*, Benny Hill was reigning supreme at BBC HQ, Eric Robinson's orchestra was backing him, and the watching millions adored the grinning clown cocking a snook at authority. Besides the increasing audi-ence figures, one grateful Benny Hill admirer, Moore Raymond, penned a glowing report in the *Evening Dispatch*, praising the BBC's decision to keep Hill on the screens and celebrating the comedian's talent: 'He is posi-tively the most original and refreshing comedian that British TV has discovered.'

The great British public were clearly in total agree-ment, voting Benny Hill TV Personality of 1953/54. The fact that televison had a surfeit of personalities at the time is beside the point. The first major television event, Queen Elizabeth II's Coronation in 1953, meant that the small flickering box in the corner was about to rivet almost the entire population's consciousness. Hill was a star from the very dawning of television's Golden Age and the advent of commercial television in Britain with the founding of ITV, mainly entertainment-based while the BBC valiantly struggled to fulfil its charter by educating and infoming as welll, spurred the BBC to spearhead tele-vision comedy by launching Hill's ultimate contribution to popular culture.

The Benny Hill Show, The BBC Years

After lengthy discussions about billing the show with Benny Hill's name as the central point (Waldman thought he wasn't quite ready for such an honour), the first edition of *The Benny Hill Show* was broadcast live from BBC Television Centre, Shepherd's Bush, London, in January 1955. Eight million viewers tuned in.

The initial format was very much a variety revue, with Hill's monologues and sketches linking musical numbers from the sublime Alma Cogan, comic business

Top of the world Ma!

Opposite Benny flogging Schweppes tomato juice through laughter.

from *Archie's the Boy* cohort Beryl Reid, and a troupe of dancing girls performing everything from a stylized voodoo war dance to a Folies Bergères number. Jeremy Hawk was Hill's Jerry Desmonde-styled straightman, and he would provide the sophisticated, petulant foil for much of the comedian's best BBC work. Hawk also hosted the ground-breaking television game show *Criss Cross Quiz* (as well as its children's variation, *Junior Criss Cross Quiz*), worked comic magic with the likes of Arthur Askey, Norman Wisdom and Arthur Haynes, directed some of Sid Caesar's shows, played the doctor opposite an alcohol-full Sid Field in *Harvey* at the Prince of Wales Theatre, and later became a commercial television immortal with his 'nuts, whole hazelnuts' chocolate ads. His daughter is actress Belinda Lang.

Although the style would change radically, Hill was warping the conventions of television from the outset. The first show's major piece was a bitingly accurate parody of the panel game *Find the Link*. Hill realized that the best thing to mock on television was television itself. Your audience knew exactly the strait-laced, pretentious and often ludicrous broadcasting techniques being parodied, and on the morning after the broadcast, this sketch was

the one everybody was talking about. In it, Jeremy Hawk plays the chairman and Hill, in a multi-character performance which would become the hallmark of his vintage television work, played all four panelists – subtle variations on the real thing (Josephine Douglas, Moira Lister, Peter Noble and Kenneth Horne).

An astounding mix of Goonish surrealism (the link is that both contestants have treacle in their shoes), primitive, ground-breaking film techniques (cutting from one Benny guise to another, with staggering results) and cheeky references to television itself (before Michael Bentine, Spike Milligan, Marty Feldman and Monty Python), this sketch caused a sensation. As a result, the variety style of the show was considered passé by many viewers, and when *The Benny Hill Show* returned for its second season, the emphasis was shifted towards Hill's comic characterizations. Even so, by only his second BBC special in February 1955, he was the *Radio Times* cover star (6–12 February).

Hill was firmly at the top. His role as variety king never really changed – even during his all-conquering Thames Television years there was a need for special guest performers and supporting players – but the first BBC

shows resurrect Hill mostly in his service show role as cheeky host. With the added emphasis on wacky sketches, the format became a winner.

The Benny Hill Show: BBC, broadcast Saturday 15 January 1955, 8.45–9.45 p.m. Saturday 12 February 1955, 8.45–9.45 p.m. Saturday 12 March 1955, 9.15–10.15 p.m. Starring BENNY HILL. Featuring BERYL REID, ALMA COGAN, JEREMY HAWK, JERRY ALLEN AND HIS TRIO, THE EDORICS, FOUR IN A CROWD, THE JACK BILLINGS DANCERS. Dance Director: Jack Billings. Orchestra directed by Eric Robinson. Script: Benny Hill and Dave Freeman. Designer: Frederick Knapman. Producer: Kenneth Carter.

Saturday Night Spectacular

Knocking himself out with a punishing workload in 1955, Hill was so grateful to Bernie Delfont for freeing him from his stage commitments that the star readily agreed to write and star in a couple of Delfont's television variety showcas-

es for ITV. Hill also cropped up as celebrity guest on the April 1955 programme *Something to Shout About.*

Off the Record

Benny Hill appeared in one edition of this occasional series of interviews and insights from the world of the hit parade hosted by Jack Payne to discuss his Prince of Wales Theatre revue, *Paris by Night,* and the film-inspired single, 'Who Done It?'

Off the Record: BBC, 13 February 1956, 9.15–9.45 p.m. JACK PAYNE with BENNY HILL, JILL DAY, LITA ROZA, BERT WEEDON, RONNIE CARROLL, SID PHILLIPS AND HIS BAND, THE CONCERT ORCHESTRA, THE GEORGE MITCHELL SINGERS. Conductor: Stanley Black. Producer: Francis Essex.

Hill enjoyed several other interview spots during 1956, on *Talk of Many Things* and *Saturday Night Out,* although these would be firmly based on his stage exploits rather than his favoured television. Indeed, thanks to theatrical commitments, he hadn't made a major television appearance for eighteen months. During this time, his special, pioneering hour spot had inspired Norman Wisdom, Ted Ray, Charlie Chester and Jimmy Wheeler to host their own eponymous BBC shows.

Saturday Comedy Hour

In early 1957, Hill was back, loud and proud, in the new *Saturday Comedy Hour* slot. Still keeping up the mock feud, Hill flamboyantly described this show as better than 'three nights on TV without Bob Monkhouse'! Guests for the opening edition reflected his love of Continental speciality acts, with Katherine Kath, a respected dancer featured in the film *Moulin Rouge,* and 'The Flying Duchess' songstress Pia Beck. Besides his usual stooges, however, this show featured *Goon Show* announcer Wallace

the need for funnies like *Bootsie and Snudge*, the Desdemona/Des O'Connor confusion) builds hilariously.

'The Intelligence Test' with Johnny Vyvyan took innuendo to breaking point and beyond with the question concerning the connection between something on a billiard table and inside a man's trousers – innocence is retained with the answer, 'pockets', and Hill wrings out the last-gasp laugh with his enraged command when he sees what Vyvyan has written: 'Rub that out!' Playing with corny innuendo within a framework of fresh, experimental television was clearly the peak of Hill's achievements.

Saturday Comedy Hour, 'The Benny Hill Show': BBC, Saturday 5 January 1957, 8.30–9.30 p.m. Starring BENNY HILL aided and abetted by JEREMY HAWK, WALLACE GREENSLADE, JOHN VYVYAN. Featuring KATHERINE KATH, PIA BECK, THE THREE DEUCES, THE TOMMY LINDEN DANCERS, THE GEORGE MITCHELL SINGERS. Dance Director: Tom Linden. Orchestra conducted by Bob Sharples. Script: Dave Freeman and Benny Hill. Designer: George Djurkovic. Producer: Duncan Wood.

Saturday Comedy Hour, 'The Benny Hill Show': Saturday 2 February 1957, 9–10 p.m. Starring BENNY HILL aided and abetted by JEREMY HAWK. Featuring KENNETH HORNE, THE STARGAZERS, CLEO LAINE, KENNY BAKER, SUSAN DENNY, ANNE REIDCERS, THE GEORGE MITCHELL SINGERS. Dance Director: Tommy Linden. Script: Dave Freeman and Benny Hill. Musical arrangement and orchestra conducted by Bob Sharples. Music Associate: Ivor Raymonde. Designer: George Djurkovic. Producer: Duncan Wood.

Greenslade, and his tinge of sophisticated surrealism was the perfect foil for much of Hill's comedy for the BBC.

Although he is seldom if ever classed with the likes of Spike Milligan, Peter Cook, Marty Feldman and John Cleese, Benny Hill's intricate television parodies and twists on everyday life delighted in quirks of fancy and often bizarre imagery. Even before Michael Bentine, *The Benny Hill Show* exposed Television Centre to an outside recording of a Pythonesque granny steeplechase culminating at BBC headquarters. Indeed, the primitive influences on Monty Python may be seen in the classic, half-forgotten taxidermist sketch, where a duck which has been left for stuffing has been eaten by the shopkeeper and unconvincingly replaced by a – wait for it – dead parrot! The ensuing argument includes Hill defending himself with: 'That's the shrinkage, Sir!' There was also a brilliantly worked out one-way telephone conversation between television commissioning producer Hill and hack writer William Shakespeare. The basic seed may have been reworked from Bob Newhart's routine about Raleigh's discovery of tobacco, but Hill's contemporary slant on the Bard (convinced he used to write *The Saint*,

The Windmill Theatre - Twenty-Five Years Non-Stop

Oh, how Benny Hill must have loved this little television assignment, as he joined Richard Murdoch and a clutch of stage veterans at the Trocadero Restaurant for a silver anniversary salute to the legendary Windmill Theatre. It was only about five years since the place had shown him the door, but who was laughing now?

The Windmill Theatre – Twenty-Five Years Non-Stop: BBC, Monday 4 February 1957, 10.15–10.45 p.m. Starring RICHARD MURDOCH with guests JIMMY EDWARDS, BENNY HILL, GEORGE MARTIN, JEAN KENT, BOB MONKHOUSE, KEELLERS

AND THE WINDMILL GIRLS. Choreography: Maisie Cryer. Orchestra Director: George Clouston. Producers: Alan Chivers and Ernest Maxim.

The Benny Hill Show

Co-writing with Dave Freeman, Hill created reams of new characters, remorselessly peppered with throwaway innuendoes and music hall smut. With the initial offer of six hour-long specials in 1954, Freeman and Hill split the 50 guinea per show fee right down the middle. Written at Hill's flat if the weather was bleak or in Freeman's back garden if it was fine, on occasion the two would work by chatting during a walk through Regent's Park. By 1958, Freeman partitioned off a large room in his flat for an office. Usually getting together a month before broadcast, Hill (with a notebook full of comic observations) and Freeman (with a brain set to 'filter') enjoyed each other's company, usually doing their best to avoid work. Hill told Peter Black in an interview for the *Daily Mail* (28 December 1958, 'The Night of the Long Laughs'): 'We talk about anything under the sun except TV. Then it's 11 o'clock and we haven't got a line on paper.'

Beginning with an early milk bottle sketch, Freeman frequently popped up as Hill's stooge, and by the late 1950s, Freeman had settled into the surreal layabout cameo of Albert the Spiv, while concentrating on successful comedy writing. There was the delightful parody of children's television series *Bill and Ben* featuring Hill and Freeman, the medieval king with a collection of advisers, all played by Hill – including a nutter with a ball and chain – and the detailed musical numbers which always closed the show, beginning with a flamboyant version of *The Student Prince* and eventually running through horror (both *Dracula* and *Frankenstein* got the treatment) and television imports (a memorable retelling of Broderick Crawford's *Highway Patrol*). A classic parody of the hip pop music show *Six-Five Special* again featured multiple Hills, notably scoring a major hit as Freddie Mills.

Whether it was a send-up of Hughie Green's talent show *Opportunity Knocks* or the lilting delivery of Alan Whicker, the scripts were original, vibrant, and above all, pointedly hilarious. For me, Freeman is the key here. Later, when Hill was both performer and writer, with no one to rein him in and suggest a different comedic approach, his work became predictable. In these golden days of BBC originality, he was ploughing fresh ground, comically addressing the very medium he loved, and unknowingly laying down the foundations for a host of television absurdists. Importantly, when in the 1980s yet another western skit or speeded-up chase was featured in his show, Hill still continually tried to include new ideas. Shows like *Juke Box Jury* and *Dixon of Dock Green* were ripe for many differently slanted skits, but Hill tried hard to avoid any hint of duplication. 'It's no good trying to widen the field,' he said in 1958, 'It's got to be in TV, that's the only thing people know about. And you can't do a thing twice.'

He had an amazing ability to take on a new character with the merest wig or false moustache, a skill needed in these glorious days of live television, when a quick change could be as quick as 30 seconds. However, despite this series containing arguably his finest work, critics were less than impressed with the new programmes, dismissing the contents as patchy and lacking cohesion. But this was a sketch show, and all sketch shows tend to lack a common, bonding structure – something even Python's bizarre links and more stream-of-consciousness approach couldn't completely overcome. Some critics took the view that this fine comedian was throwing away his career ('Benny wasted most of his talents on worthless stuff'), or worse still, that the comedian had little talent in the first place ('Benny had little to offer!').

The public, on the other hand, loved it. Although many in the corporation's boardroom considered the show's humour rather dubious, the BBC were no fools, and with the advent of commercial television, they were fully aware that Benny Hill was their single biggest property. In 1956 Hill was earning £350 per show, by 1957 that had increased to 650 guineas, and in 1958 a memo from the new Head of Light Entertainment, Tom Sloan, revealed that the BBC would happily boost Hill's income to £1,000 for each programme. BBC audience research estimated that *The Benny Hill Show* was pulling in 12 million viewers in 1957.

Although it is his 1970s material from the less constrained Thames Television era that typifies Hill's comedy for many people, I maintain that these fledgling BBC years of experiment, growth and comedy character acting represent his best work. While he always retained impersonation and television parody in his later programmes, there was a struggling affection at the BBC, breaking down barriers of comedy and taking the humour just to the boundaries of acceptability. His tongue-in-cheek, fly-on-the-wall investigative looks at the corporation brilliantly masked and revealed the identity of stars – a *Panorama* documentary report avoiding the laws of libel by referring to presenter Fred Dimbleby (for David Dimbleby) – is that any less penetrating than Python's 'Mouse Problem'? The BBC presenters became a vital part of our collective consciousness,

Show me the money - Bog dweller Benny Hill and Squire Dave Freeman sell out to sell Schweppes bitter lemon - stop them and buy one.

and Hill's painfully accurate parodies of Fanny Craddock, Lady Isobel Barnet, Cliff Michelmore, Gilbert Harding and Barbara Kelly were classics. He mocked zither plucker Shirley Abicaire (as Shirley Have-a-Car), Ingrid Bergman (Havasneezia Bergman in *Anastasia*), telly hits *Tonight* and *Guess My Secret*, but these parodies were not malicious. There was a sense of 'we're all learning this thing called television together', and the television jester's job was to comment comically on television itself.

Hill was already injecting his own personal experiences into the mixture, notably drawing on embarrassed memories as an innocent lodger in accommodation shared with rowing couples. The lovelorn failure, destined to become the core of his comedy, was not long in coming, and indeed, characters destined to be international favourites were also debuted during the BBC shows, with Fred Scuttle's first appearance in Freeman's 'The Wheelbarrow Tester', taking off in a makeshift rocket and uttering those immortal words, 'Hello Moon!'

In later years, Scuttle would come to epitomize Hill (like Chaplin's Tramp), but this opening Scuttle skit played outrageously with television conventions – breaking out of the comedy performance to expose the cameras and waiting firemen anxious about explosions in the studio. Embracing the BBC's concerns about the rickety rocket prop, Hill brilliantly stepped out of character to address the situation, as if to say: 'This is not really the moon, and I am not really Fred Scuttle. This is BBC Television Centre, and I'm Benny Hill!'

Another equally hilarious, albeit far less subtle and thus more typical sketch featured the ever-lovable Scuttle as television director Jean-Paul, coaxing Patricia Hayes's Dame Edith through her stumbling paces.

The Benny Hill Show. BBC, Saturday 2 March 1957, 8.45–9.45 p.m. Starring BENNY HILL aided and abetted by JEREMY HAWK. Featuring ALBERTO DEL PARANA AND HIS TRIO LOS PARAGUAYOS, CARL BARRITEAU, SUSAN DENNY, TONIA BERN, PATRICIA HAYES, THE TOMMY LINDEN DANCERS. Dance Director: Tommy Linden. Musical arrangements and orchestra conducted by Bob Sharples. Music Associate: Ivor Raymonde. Script: Dave Freeman and Benny Hill. Designer: George Djurkovic. Producer: Duncan Wood.

The Benny Hill Show. BBC, Saturday 30 March 1957, 8.15–9.15 p.m. Starring BENNY HILL aided and abetted by JEREMY HAWK. Featuring JUNE RICHMOND, EDMUND HOCKRIDGE, PETER HAIGH, SUSAN DENNY, PATRICIA HAYES, THE TOMMY LINDEN DANCERS. Dance Director: Tommy Linden. Music arrangements and orchestra directed by Bob Sharples. Music Associate: Ivor Raymonde. Script: Dave Freeman and Benny Hill. Designer: George Djurkovic. Producer: John Street.

The Benny Hill Show. BBC, Saturday 27 April 1957, 8–9 p.m. Starring BENNY HILL aided and abetted by JEREMY HAWK. Featuring PIA BECK, THE TANNER SISTERS, PHILIP HARBEN, SUSAN DENNY, PATRICIA HAYES, THE TOMMY LINDEN DANCERS, THE GEORGE MITCHELL SINGERS. Dance Director: Tommy Linden. Music arrangement and orchestra directed by Bob Sharples. Music Associate: Ivor Raymonde. Script: Dave Freeman and Benny Hill. Designer: George Djurkovic. Producers: Duncan Wood and John Street.

The Benny Hill Show. BBC, Saturday 1 June 1957, 8–9 p.m. Starring BENNY HILL aided and abetted by JEREMY HAWK. Featuring LUIS ALBERTO DEL PARANA AND HIS TRIO LOS PARAGUAYOS, PETULA CLARK, CARL BARRITEAU, THE PETER CRAWFORD TRIO, THE TOMMY LINDEN DANCERS. Dance Director: Tommy Linden. Music arrangements and orchestra directed by Bob Sharples. Musical Associate: Ivor Raymonde. Script: Dave Freeman and Benny Hill. Designer: George Djurkovic. Producer: Duncan Wood.

A couple of special ATV editions were broadcast on 9 November and 14 December 1957. Both were screened on Saturday evening from 8.30-9.30 p.m. and were penned by Dave Freeman and Benny Hill. Support came from the Cuddlesome Cuties, The Handsome Herberts and The Layabouts with producer/director Brian Tesler in charge of the first programme, and Albert Locke the second.

Pantomania – Babes in the Wood

At around the time of these ATV specials, Hill was interviewed on the ITV programme *Now*, and made a rare return to stand-up patter for *Late Extra* before being clutched to the BBC's bosom for its all-singing, all-dancing Christmas party.

In the days before the blessed *Christmas Night with the Stars*, the BBC's top light entertainment performers cavorted about for 'TV's Annual Frolic' – the likes of Frankie Howerd and Eric Sykes had previously filled the bill, but for 1957 an even dreamier dream team was assembled. Despite the title, this was a concoction of several traditional pantomimes. Headlining Tony Hancock and Sid James, Benny Hill mugged with comic energy as The Minstrel, accompanied by the Peter Crawford Trio, and the cast included Kenneth Connor, Charlie Drake, Ted Ray, and ventriloquist act Terry Hall and Lenny the

Lion – all in the same programme. Oh! Those were the days of real seasonal television treats.

Pantomania – Babes in the Wood. BBC, telerecorded on 35mm film 17 December 1957, broadcast 25 December 1957, 7.30–8.30 p.m. A Robber DEREK BOND, Baron Eville SAM COSTA, School Inspector/Lawyer KENNETH CONNOR, Sheriff CHARLIE DRAKE, A Robber PETER HAIGH, Minstrel BENNY HILL, Minstrel's Minstrels PETER CRAWFORD TRIO, Aladdin/Robin Hood TONY HANCOCK, Forrester and Lion TERRY HALL AND LENNY THE LION, The Genie/Friar Tuck SIDNEY JAMES, Merry Men EAMONN ANDREWS, DEREK HART, CLIFF MICHELMORE, HUW WHELDON, Merry Man/Sherwood Commentator PETER DIMMOCK, The Babes BILL MAYNARD, TED RAY, Widow Higgins JACK PAYNE, Platinum Back-scratcher PAULINE TOOTH, 1st Villager/Woodcutter ALEX MACINTOSH, Maid Marian SYLVIA PETERS, Floor Manager LEN MITCHELL, Fairy Queen JEAN METCALFE. Script: Brad Ashton, S.C. Green, R.M. Hills and Dick Vosburgh. The Eric Robinson Orchestra and The George Mitchell Singers conducted by George Clouston. Producer: Graeme Muir.

With stardom, of course, came speculation, and as early as 1958, questions arose about Hill's sexuality. A great many of his clever impressions were of female television personalities and movie stars, but this was simply part of the great British drag tradition that encompassed Arthur Askey, Dick Emery and countless others. Hill enjoyed playing in drag, in contrast to Sid James with his grin-and-bear-it attitude, but that's all there was to it. Interviewed about his 1958 BBC season, Hill proudly revealed that some £1,200 had been spent on hiring and buying female wigs for his series, but quickly added that he was no sissy. It was not enough – the lad appeared to have protested too much, for rumours abounded about his private life, and eventually, bowing to this pressure, he began to phase out a lot of his female characters, dropping completely his endearingly affectionate catchphrase 'Bless your hearts!' Instead, Hill moved towards the leering lecher persona that cleared him of accusations of effeminacy but, ironically, eventually ruined his name.

By the time of this batch of shows, he had already begun to take a saucier direction anyway. The old-fashioned line of variety chorus girls was now replaced by choreographed production numbers, opening with the Leslie Roberts girls whizzing through their critically acclaimed portrayal of animals at a jungle watering hole. The show was given a slicker look, while Hill still feverishly parodied all the latest and greatest television shows, including Cliff Michelmore in the news magazine *Tonight* and shaky broadcasts which highlighted excerpts from successful London shows. Other gems included a manic German choir and the debut of the short-lived Benny Hill signature tune, written especially for the show by Stanley Black. The typically naughty but nice lyrics were by Sid Colin. The second programme was greeted by an attacking poem by *Tonight*'s Alistair Sampson published in the *Radio Times* in retaliation for the first show's *Tonight* parody. It was all in a self-promoting, cosy, 'all friends together at the BBC and having a laugh at ourselves' spirit, but it was certainly not the last time *The Benny Hill Show* would be condemned as 'that terrible monstrosity'.

The Benny Hill Show. BBC, Saturday 1 February 1958, 8–9 p.m. Starring BENNY HILL. Featuring ANNE SHELTON, TONY BRENT, LES MARTHYS and from Paris with their music, LOS GUARANIA aided and abetted by PETER VERNON, DAVE FREEMAN, RONNIE BRODY, ROGER AVON, THE GEORGE MITCHELL SINGERS, THE LESLIE ROBERTS SILHOUETTES. Script: Benny Hill and Dave Freeman. Orchestra led by Eric Robinson. Guest Choreographer: Leslie Roberts. Designer: Tony Abbott. Producer: John Street.

The Benny Hill Show. BBC, Saturday 1 March 1958, 8.30–9.30 p.m. Starring BENNY HILL aided and abetted by PETER VERNON, DAVE FREEMAN featuring THE KAYE SISTERS and music staged by guest choreographer Buddy Bradley presenting CARL BARRITEAU, LESLIE 'JIVER' HUTCHINSON and his all-star coloured band, THE GEORGE MITCHELL SINGERS. Script: Benny Hill and Dave Freeman. Orchestra conducted by Eric Robinson. Designer: Tony Abbott. Producer: John Street.

The Benny Hill Show. BBC, Saturday 29 March 1958, 8.15–9.15 p.m. Starring BENNY HILL with a helping hand from DAVE FREEMAN, PETER VERNON featuring EDNA SAVAGE, also presenting for the first time in England THE TWO ROVITAS with THE GEORGE MITCHELL SINGERS. Script: Benny Hill and Dave Freeman. Guest Choreographer: Lisa Thawnton. Orchestra conducted by Eric Robinson. Designer: Tony Abbott. Producer: John Street

The Benny Hill Show. BBC, Saturday 26 April 1958,

8–9 p.m. Starring BENNY HILL with a helping hand from DAVE FREEMAN, PETER VERNON, RONNIE BRODY featuring ALMA COGAN and presenting ALAN KERNBLE AND CHRISTINE, THE GEORGE MITCHELL SINGERS. Script: Benny Hill and Dave Freeman. Guest Choreographer and Orchestra Leader: Eric Robinson. Designer: Tony Abbott. Producer: John Street.

The Benny Hill Show (repeat): BBC, Wednesday 24 September 1958, 7.30–8.30 p.m. (repeat of 26/4/58).

Did You Know?

Hill enjoyed the best of British in backroom crew during his BBC years, from producer Ken Carter and PA Eve Lucas in the pioneering days to junior assistant Harold Snoad (later to produce the likes of Dick Emery and the 1990s sitcom *Keeping Up Appearances*).

Tragically, although these live *Benny Hill Shows* were recorded on 16mm film at the time, the majority of these have been wiped from the BBC archives.

Once, while away with Dave Freeman writing a sketch about a friendly, misunderstood burglar, Hill returned to his own flat to find he had been burgled. The sketch was completed through gritted teeth.

One of the most hotly sought after character supports Hill wanted on his show was the cream of female co-stars, Hattie Jacques. So desperate was Hill to attract her that he threw a luscious meal of lobster at his flat with Dave Freeman in attendance, continually trying to tempt her aboard. Sadly, she didn't give in and stuck with Eric Sykes – and a new deal with Peter Rogers for something called *Carry On Sergeant*!

A further excursion into the world of commercial television on Saturday 29 November 1958 (7.55-8.55 p.m.) saw Benny Hill don his white wig and come forth with a rush of saucy madrigals and dumplings-boiling-over gags. Critics called it the slickest and funniest light entertainment programme of the year.

Meanwhile, as well as his own show, Hill enjoyed turning on his variety charms for the BBC Saturday night specials and an ITV special in December 1958. Dave Freeman said: 'I reckon he could last on TV for ever if he didn't do too much of it.' Some thirty years later, Benny Hill was still Britain's biggest comedy star.

During his formative years in London, Hill lived in a furnished room in a large house owned by the revue double act Billy Rhodes and Chica Lane in Mapesbury Road, Kilburn. He was still content here during the early years of *The Benny Hill Show*, but finally, he bought a flat overlooking the canal in Maida Vale. Furnished with freebies picked up from countless furniture shop openings, Hill escaped from it at the slightest chance. Living a simple life akin to reclusive comedian Kenneth Williams, Hill rarely entertained at home, and when he did, often fed his guests tasty but experimental meals made from tins of food bought cheap as salvage goods because the labels had come off – they might contain Irish stew or tinned peaches!

Back on television, Hill was peaking with an estimated 17 million viewers at the BBC, although these figures are fairly unreliable, being based on guesswork more than anything else. Nevertheless, he was the BBC's biggest gun against the mass-market appeal of ITV's ratings-topping low-brow military antics in *The Army Game* – so much so that BBC producers begged Hill to make guest appearances on other programmes, spread himself a bit thinner and thus increase the audiences for BBC television as a whole. Hill continually refused, mostly sticking to his commitment that his self-penned, self-performed *Benny Hill Shows* were all he wanted to do. Overexposure might damage the sense that each new Hill special was an event worth watching. However, he did agree to a small number of such appearances, although very rarely during the tail end of the 1950s, thanks to his full involvement in the theatre revue *Fine Fettle*. In response to the falling bookings for the show, Bernie Delfont replaced his usual ITV highlight *Sunday Night at the London Palladium* with an abridged promotional television presentation, *Fine Fettle*, in 1959. Along the same lines was Richard Stone's programme, *Let's Make a Night of It*, presenting highlights from Hill's summer season hit at the Pavilion Theatre, Weymouth. The television version was screened on Bank Holiday Monday (1 August 1960, 6.50–7.20 p.m.), and was presented by Albert Stevenson.

Hill's love life was still stormy. Following rejections in Margate and during the filming of *Who Done It?*, a girl involved in Hill's radio shows by the name of Elaine had come and gone from the scene, and by the start of his BBC series in 1955, he was heavily involved with Elizabeth Seal. Two relationships spanned his early television stardom, both with BBC dancers, and both coming to an end after lengthy courtships once Hill mentioned marriage (after three years and five years respectively). The real love of his life was probably actress Anette Andre, whom he had met during service shows in Australia. Close friends, Hill invited the young, struggling actress to look him up if she ever came to England. She did, and although Hill's marriage proposal came as a shock, her refusal didn't prevent him helping her out. He clearly had a sense of humour, however – her first book-

ing with him saw her dressed in a gorilla skin, a far cry from the cult TV stardom she found with 1969's ATV classic, *Randall and Hopkirk – Deceased*. Hill frequently changed television channels when she appeared, due to the heartbreak he still felt over her rejection, and a lengthy advertising campaign with Andre endorsing Matchsticks chocolates continually caught him ill prepared to see her face on screen again.

Perhaps his eagerness to settle down with a family was constantly at odds with his love of freedom, travel and self-containment. At the end of the day, he seemed more in love with the idea of marriage than marriage itself. Indeed, during his hungry years of struggle, when he was earning 27s 6d per week, Hill once gave up smoking to be able to afford to take a girl out – but he soon went back to cigarettes, explaining they gave him more pleasure and fewer problems! Later in life, his many female companions would all be codenamed 'Annie', but these were usually geared for publicity to uphold the image of Hill the saucy comedian. Happy to bask in the limelight of girl-obsessed comic greatness, Hill projected an image of a grinning King Leer surrounded by bathing beauties. Coded messages to male friends ('Don't come round, I'm a busy boy!') would mean he was entertaining a young lady, but his closest associations would be paternal love for co-stars Sue Upton and Louise English.

Commercials

Although he had endorsed Mars bars and curtain rings in print, Hill finally gave in to financial temptation in 1960 and began filming a long-running series of commercials for soft drinks manufacturer Schweppes. The pioneering idea of John Holmes, accounts executive for advertising agency Clifford Bloxham and Partners, the use of comedy to sell was immediately successful, and probably reached the peak of influence with Tony Hancock's endorsement of eggs from 1965.

Performing the adverts with regular BBC cohort Dave Freeman, Hill crafted a load of 'rustic idiot' characters to battle opposite the military bearing of Freeman's sophisticated, authoritative figure. Freeman wrote all these campaigns, practically inventing the speeded-up filming technique which Hill instantly fell in love with. Here, it was necessary to get the advertising message and laughter lines across quickly, and Hill would soon tend to rely on the technique. Fifteen of these short comic masterpieces were produced over a six-year period, employing director David Poltenghi, and later, Hill's BBC collaborator, Kenneth Carter.

In the adverts, bog-dweller Benny mumbled about the delights of bitter lemon to Freeman's Lord of the Manor. Hill as an old lady drinking fizzy water or doing canoe antics as Hiawatha successfully promoted the product. Another classic Schweppes pitch concentrated on tomato juice, with Hill's vegetable gardener crushing a plant with a cricket bat and explaining that there's an easier way to get juice – hilarious, punchy, eye-catching and convincing, all in thirty seconds. No wonder that particular episode won first prize at the 1961 Cannes International Festival of Commercials.

Held up as peerless examples of advertising, all 36 Schweppes films are preserved in the TV Library in America – a joint venture founded by Schweppes and Coca-Cola. Perversely, since the campaigns earned him more money than his own show on BBC, Hill later mercilessly parodied the 1970s Schweppes slogan opposite Henry McGee during the Thames Television years, when his distraught lady kept on hearing 'Sh ... you know who – and I don't!'

Even earlier, Hill had tackled the absurdity of television advertising with gems like 1964's washing-up liquid commercial with Patricia Hayes. Hill's whining, bubble-obsessed cherub is as relevant to today's advertising style as when it was first screened. Hill was instrumental in subverting the banality of selling, by producing comic, self-parodying adverts. Unsurprisingly, following the successful Schweppes campaign, Hill was later enlisted for commercial campaigns promoting Stork margarine and Farmer's Wife bread. His milkman iconography was further enforced during the 'There's a Humphrey About!' milk campaign, when he appeared in familiar white coat searching for his missing milk float.

In later years, when *The Benny Hill Show* for Thames was the only work he took on in Britain, Hill agreed to make commercials for foreign television. In 1983, he picked up £25,000 for a day's filming promoting German Kaiser beer for Greek television, while he promoted SABA televisions in Spain, portraying a collection of German, English, Italian and Japanese satisfied viewers. A long-running promotion for Jacques Brunch biscuits on French television from 1981 earned him £80,000 for ten 30-second spots featuring him as a leather-clad guy, a distinguished woman, a glam girl, a First World War pilot, a rugby player, a Scuttle-like scoutmaster and many more, all enjoying the tasty snack. An Australian campaign saw Hill extolling the virtues of Walton's department store. In 1984, at the height of his American popularity, Ron Rice, boss of the Hawaiian Tropic Sun Tan Lotion Company, hired Hill for a multi-million-pound promotion, and in 1991, his star comedian was enlisted as the judge for a promotional beauty competition in the Bahamas and Daytona, Florida.

Hill's only prerequisite for these international advertising jobs was two free trips and hotel accommodation, in case he wanted to enjoy the free holiday with a female companion. This seldom worked out, as Hill, a frequent traveller and thus familiar with the tourist sights, usually spent his time watching French, American or Spanish television. But these rare pieces of Benny Hill were never for use in Britain. Once, Hill appeared as a panting dog – complete with floppy ears – happy in the knowledge that his home audience would never see it. One of his last advertising jobs was for S.T.A.M.P. Inc. in 1991, for a French confectionery. Once again, Hill's Scuttle persona was surrounded by gorgeous girls and helped shift a load of sweetmeats.

The Benny Hill Show
Returned to ATV on Saturday 24 January 1959 7.55-8.55 p.m. Again utilising the Beeb dream team of Carter and Freeman, further specials were screened on 2 April, 20 April and 28 May 1960, Saturdays, 8-8.55 p.m.

Curtain Call

Four 1960 television specials for Australia's Channel 7 saw Hill decamp down under with BBC director Ken Carter and straightman Peter Vernon in tow. The surrounding cast members were all local talent, although one of the guest artistes provided some stunning small-screen entertainment when Basil Rathbone recited 'The Green Eye of the Little Yellow God'. Extremely popular, the fourth and final show was beset by a musicians' strike – a back-handed compliment, in that bandleader Tommy Tico told Hill that they had chosen his time slot to make the maximum impact on viewers. The show went on, however.

Following his return from Australia in November 1960, Hill turned his attention to more BBC work. With the first of his new series blessed with a *Radio Times* cover (4–10 February) and a wry interview by Rowan Ayers headed 'Back on the Old Telly', there's already a relaxed, 'work on my own terms' tone to Hill's answers. While his contemporaries like Frankie Howerd and Norman Wisdom were knocking themselves out taking every radio spot or TV guest role offered, Hill seemed totally at ease with his own destiny. The last-page preview would keep the best news for its opening line – 'It is a Benny Hill week' – and the star knew that no amount of publicity would noticeably boost his popularity.

Hill's comedy was as sharp and perceptive as ever, digging into television's finest and having first crack of the parody whip at that long-lived favourite, the new ITV soap opera *Coronation Street*. The programme was only months old when Hill crossed the divide between the old corporation and the new ITV. He wrote a sketch with himself as Violet Carson's much loved battleaxe Ena Sharples, and actually borrowed the prop coat from the actress for added authenticity.

The show was highly influential, breaking out of studio filming to undertake a tricky outside shoot for several sketches. Even if the gags themselves were hardly hilarious (Hill looking out of a basement window and being sprayed by a passing road cleaner), Hill was trying to be innovative with this new toy called television, filming a quickie sketch filler on Chelsea Bridge for total veracity. He also parodied new BBC offerings, notably sending up his old pal, comedian Jimmy Edwards, and the school-based delights of *Whack-O!*, but he reached his pinnacle with perhaps the best-remembered of his BBC sketches, the *Juke Box Jury* parody, 'Soap Box Jury', from 1961.

With John Street travelling down to Pinewood to discover if it was possible to fulfil Hill's ambitious idea for this sketch – playing presenter David Jacobs and the entire panel of pop pundits – the scene was set for a major television landmark. Street was told it was technically easy (simply masking off parts of the Mitchell camera lenses during four individual shots), but these ground-breaking ideas often are. It still remains one of television's most effective comedy moments. Hill does a superb job, injecting Fred Curry (read Pete Murray) with a cocky, know-all attitude, exuding cool hipness and knowledge of other recordings, pointing out the similarity to the classic album *Elsie and Doris Waters in Las Vegas*, refined posturing from an aged female dignitary, Lady Edgware, pompous, snoring boredom from crusty old Ted Grumble, and gum-chewing, air-headed enthusiasm from the blonde teenager, Liza Gasometer, reading a magazine throughout and hiding her low-cut dress to give the impression of being completely naked. With complaints from the audience, a coy rising and clever image cropping, this illusion is hilariously maintained. However, not only does Hill play all the major parts, he's also spotted playing members of the studio audience, and capturing the awkwardness when members of the public realize that the television camera has momentarily settled on them. It is by turns bold, fresh, amazing and very funny.

Eventually, this technique would be extended to self-contained playlets within the show, featuring Hill in over fifty different guises. One such example resurrected

wartime memories, with Hill playing a multitude of parachutists and marine divers.

The Benny Hill Show. BBC, Saturday 4 February 1961, 7.45–8.30 p.m. Starring BENNY HILL who is assisted by PETER VERNON and DORITA Y PEPE, RONNIE BRODY, ROBERT NICHOLS, ANTHEA WYNDHAM, CARMEN BLANCK-SICHEL, THE IRVING DAVIES DANCERS. Original music and script: Benny Hill. Musical Director: Harry Rabinowitz. Orchestra Leader: Alec Firman Choreography: Irving Davies. Settings: Robert MacGowan. Producer: John Street.

The Benny Hill Show. BBC, Saturday 4 March 1961, 7.45–8.30 p.m. Starring BENNY HILL who is assisted by PETER VERNON and VIVIENNE MARTIN with JO SHELTON, RONNIE BRODY, TOM CLEGG, THE LESLIE ROBERTS SILHOUETTES. Script: Benny Hill and Dave Freeman. Musical Director: Harry Rabinowitz. Orchestra Leader: Alec Firman. Choreography: Leslie Roberts. Settings: Robert MacGowan. Producer: John Street.

Ask Anne

In a very rare guest appearance on someone else's show, a popular television variety request programme presented by beloved songstress Anne Shelton, Benny Hill threw himself into the public's chosen songs and music. Most of the backroom staff were or would soon be working on *The Benny Hill Show*. The grinning home viewers whose favourite tunes were selected were interviewed by Patrick Feeny.

Ask Anne. BBC, Sunday 11 June 1961, 9.30–10.15 p.m. Starring ANNE SHELTON. Guests BENNY HILL, KENNY BAKER, ANDY STEWART, MATT MONRO, THE BERYL STOTT SINGERS. Musical Director: Harry Rabinowitz. Orchestra Leader: Alec Firman. Film Editor: Ken Cooper. Designer: Cephas Howard.

The Jo Stafford Show

In 1961, years before Hill's American stardom, he guest-starred on the popular comedy variety slot *The Jo Stafford Show*. His contribution, a hilarious theatrical moment inspired by his 1940s pantomime *Robinson Crusoe*, was perfect visual fare, with Hill failing to locate the prop poisoned chalice and ad-libbing his death scene at length to keep the script on the right track. This proved a successful interlude, but certainly not ground-breaking.

Blue Peter

Yes, believe it or not, in September 1961 Benny Hill made an appearance on this BBC children's show haven for sticky-backed plastic, empty washing-up liquid bottles and un-housetrained baby elephants. Valerie Willis, who had been personal assistant to *Benny Hill Show* producer Ken Carter, landed a chance to prove herself in the producer's chair with a trial run on *Blue Peter*. In order to give her new position some much-needed clout, she called Benny Hill and asked if he would agree to an appearance. Enjoying presenting prizes to the children on the show, Hill insisted that Willis wouldn't be able to afford what his agent would require, so he did the spot as a favour for no fee at all.

Hill presented his second batch of specials for 1961 refreshed and full of ideas gleaned from real-life events around him. Regular cohorts were joined by some starry guests, notably singers Matt Monro and Dusty Springfield (with The Springfields, before she went solo), while the production was in the more than capable hands of future British sitcom supremo David Croft.

The gags were reassuringly corny, and television personalities were still happy to send themselves up, gardener Percy Thrower effortlessly wandering through the water cress/gin cress routine later adapted for radio's *Benny Hill Time*.

The Benny Hill Show. BBC, Saturday 4 November 1961, 7.15–8 p.m. Starring BENNY HILL. Featuring JANIE MARDEN, THE SPRINGFIELDS, PETER VERNON, JEAN MUIR, DAVE FREEMAN, RONNIE BRODY, SCOTT PETERS, YVONNE BUCKINGHAM, PATRICIA HAYES, CYRIL ORNADEL AND HIS ORCHESTRA. Script: Dave Freeman. Dance Director: Patricia Kirschner. Designer: George Djurkovic. Film Editor: Roy Clarke. Producer: David Croft.

The Benny Hill Show. BBC, Saturday, 25 November 1961, 7.15–8 p.m. Starring BENNY HILL. Featuring IVOR EMMANUEL, JANIE MARDEN, LIONEL AND JOYCE BLAIR, STANLEY MEADOWS, PETER VERNON, TONY SYMPSON, JENNIFER BROWNE, SALLY SMITH, CYRIL ORNADEL AND HIS ORCHESTRA. Script: Dave Freeman and Benny Hill. Designer: George Djurkovic. Producer: David Croft

The Benny Hill Show. BBC, Saturday 16 December 1961, 7.15–8 p.m. Starring BENNY HILL. Featuring MATT MONRO, JANIE MARDEN, DORITA Y

PEPE, PETER VERNON, JENNIFER BROWNE, PAT HAYES, JOHN JUNKIN, THE BARNEY GILBRAITH SINGERS, THE LIONEL BLAIR DANCERS, PERCY THROWER, CYRIL ORNADEL AND HIS ORCHESTRA. Script: Dave Freeman and Benny Hill. Dance Director: Lionel Blair. Designer: George Djurkovic. Producer: David Croft.

Come Dancing

Benny Hill made one appearance on this long-running ballroom dancing contest, serving on the panel of judges in an edition broadcast in March 1962.

Benny Hill

This early 1960s experiment of live, self-contained, 25-minute situation comedy chunks starring Hill in various and multiple parts is all but forgotten today. The BBC had grown tired of the 50-minute revue format that Hill excelled at, and hankered to move all their comedy stars into the more focused, sitcom mode of Tony Hancock. Indeed, Dave Freeman had helped Charlie Drake develop as a comedy actor in a series of half-hour adventures not a million miles from these later *Benny Hill* episodes. With a justified reputation for multiple characterizations, the notion seemed perfect for Hill, and by the end of the three-series run he had created some fifty different characterizations for the show, never repeating one. This very lack of familiarity was perhaps the show's downfall, although its dismissal into the forgotten files of television history hides the fact that Hill's genius was never more pronounced or refreshing.

The brilliance at work in the scripts is quite breathtaking at times, with several plot developments and structured layers working together to form an intriguing comic whole. Hill's quickfire characterizations are played at breakneck speed and with precise detail, while Freeman's solo writing efforts further stretch the comedian with pathos-driven escapades and a galaxy of bizarre characters. The supporting cast is also top-notch throughout, whether it be regular Hill cohorts Patricia Hayes and Jeremy Hawk, or notable comedy acting guest spots from fledgling superstar Ronnie Barker and Hancock refugee Bill Kerr.

Similar in structure to Michael Palin and Terry Jones's later post-Python series *Ripping Yarns* and presenting Hill the comedian in the same multi-talented, multi-charactered light as Steve Coogan's 1995 series

Coogan's Run, perhaps *Benny Hill* was simply too far ahead of its time. In 1962, this collection of 'comedy adventures' as Hill dubbed them, was tampering with the sitcom format far too radically to succeed, and was certainly moving completely away from what both Benny Hill wanted and his audience expected – he was allowed only half his usual allotted time, and by series two, was performing material completely written by someone else. Even his *Radio Times* cover shot was crowded out with other top-lining comic talents (8–14 December 1962, 'Comedy on Parade with Ken Dodd, Harry Worth, George Chisholm, Jimmy Edwards and Brian Rix'). It was a relief when the BBC offered him his old format back, but these unsung, seldom bettered comic gems are well worth re-evaluating.

Series One

Benny Hill, 'Portrait of a Bridegroom': BBC, Friday 23 December 1962, 8.45-9.10 p.m. Starring BENNY HILL. Featuring JUNE WHITFIELD, PATRICIA HAYES, PRISCILLA MORGAN and DIANA KING, with ANNABELLE LEE, SHEENA MARSHE, RONNIE BRODY, MICHAEL STAINTON, PHILIP CARR, ALEC BREGONZI, JOHNNY VYVYAN. Script: Dave Freeman and Benny Hill. Incidental music: Ron Grainer. Designer: Tony Abbott. Producer: Duncan Wood. In the first show of series one, members of a wedding party give different insights into the blushing bridegroom, depending on their own bias – the bride's mother pictures him as an oily, worthless conman, an ex-girlfriend remembers him as the sophisticated antique dealer, and his mother presents a fond image of a playful schoolboy.

Benny Hill, 'A Pair of Socks': BBC, Friday 29 February 1962, 8.45-9.10 p.m. Starring BENNY HILL. Featuring TERENCE ALEXANDER, DAVID LODGE, RONNIE BARKER, PENNY MORRELL, PAULINE STROUD, ANNABELLE LEE, PAMELA STRONG, ARTHUR MULLARD, GWENDA EWAN, ROGER AVON. Script: Dave Freeman and Benny Hill. Incidental music: Ron Grainer. Designer: Tony Abbott. Producer: Duncan Wood. Taking up from where O. Henry's short stories and the 1943 Charles Laughton/Edward G. Robinson compendium movie *Tales of Manhattan* left off, Hill's collection of comic grotesques are linked by self-contained vignettes built round a pair of socks – from the shop assistant who sells them, through the adventures of an electrician, a waiter and a musical comedy tenor by the name of Mornington Cressant (file it under 'Harry Hill – Reinvention').

Benny Hill, 'The Constant Viewer': BBC, Friday 6 March 1962, 8.45-9.10 p.m. Starring BENNY HILL. Featuring JEREMY HAWK, HUGH LLOYD, PATRICIA HAYES, PETER CAVANAGH, ANNABELLE LEE, ANN LANCASTER, JENNIFER BROWNE, VALERIE BELL, DENNIS CHINNERY. Script: Dave Freeman and Benny Hill. Incidental music: Ron Grainer. Designer: Tony Abbott. Producer: Duncan Wood. In this near-autobiographical glimpse at Hill, the compulsive television-watcher, he plays the central figure, Bert Noggsmith, crawling through life in flights of television-based fantasy – be it a medical drama, winning a game show, investigative journalism or as a feted violinist at a major concert. Naturally, like Danny Kaye in *The Secret Life of Walter Mitty*, Hill's heroic alter ego finds a different beautiful girl in each televisual time zone – bliss! There's also room for Tony Hancock/Terry Scott cohort Hugh Lloyd, Hill's ever familiar girl Friday Pat Hayes, and old BBC stooge Jeremy Hawk.

Benny Hill, 'The Changeling': BBC, Friday 12 March 1962, 8.45-9.10 p.m. Starring BENNY HILL. Featuring MARY HINTON, PATRICIA HAYES, JOAN NEWELL, PRISCILLA MORGAN, ANNABELLE LEE, DOROTHY GORDON, SHEENA MARSHE, PENNY MORRELL, SIDNEY VIVIAN, ROGER AVON, MICHAEL STAINTON, CAROLE ALLEN. Script: Dave Freeman and Benny Hill. Incidental music: Ron Grainer. Designer: Tony Abbott. Producer: Duncan Wood. The classic 'babies switched at the age of six months' story casts Hill as an aged tramp storyteller relating his tale of misfortune to a young nanny (Penny Morrell) on a park bench. The unsettled lives of Nigel, the son of a duke, and Mervyn, the son of a shrimp-seller, allow for plenty of social comedy and myriad classic Hill characterizations.

Benny Hill, 'The Before Man': BBC, Friday 18 March 1962, 8.45-9.10 p.m. Starring BENNY HILL. Featuring CAMPBELL SINGER, PRISCILLA MORGAN, ROGER AVON, PENNY MORRELL, ANNABELLE LEE, MICHAEL BIRD, EDWIN APPS, MARGARET FLINT, VALERIE BELL, STUART HILLIER, SUSAN DENNY, SIDNEY VIVIAN, KEN ROBERTS, REG THOMPSON, STAN SIMMONS, VALERIE BROOKS, MARIA LENNARD, PAMELA STRONG. Script: Dave Freeman and Benny Hill. Incidental music: Ron Grainer. Designer: Tony Abbott. Producer: Duncan Wood. One of the prizes from this first series is this brilliantly constructed portrayal of advertising techniques, featuring an early appearance of Hill's favourite character

Daleks, dragons or dolly birds...Graham Stark and the star of the show don't know what this science fiction comedy will throw at them - *Benny Hill: The Secret of Planet Seven.*

– naive, bumbling, nice but dim Mervyn Cruddy – as a sad, lonely wimp of an actor who is continually cast as the 'before' man in before/after commercials. Mistakenly cast as the 'after' man, he goes through further Walter Mitty-like re-evaluation, strolling through life as a racing driver, airline pilot and London-based Canadian mountie.

Benny Hill, 'Aunt Mirabelle': Friday 30 March 1962, 8.45-9.10 p.m.Starring BENNY HILL. Featuring JUNE WHITFIELD, GRAHAM STARK, PRISCILLA MORGAN, PATRICIA HAYES, RONNIE BRODY, PENNY MORRELL, ROGER AVON, MICHAEL STAINTON, JOHNNY VYVYAN, LAUREL MATHER, LESLIE RAWLINGS, CARL EWER. Script: Benny Hill and Dave Freeman. Incidental music: Ron Grainer. Designer: Tony Abbott. Producer: Duncan Wood.

Benny Hill (repeat season): Wednesday, 7.30–8 p.m. – 'Portrait of a Bridegroom' (8 August 1962), 'A Pair of Socks' (15 August 1962), 'The Constant Viewer' (22 August 1962), 'The Changeling' (29 August 1962), 'The Before Man' (5 September 1962), 'Aunt Mirabelle' (12 September 1962).

Series Two

Benny Hill, 'The Mystery of Black Bog Manor': BBC, Friday 30 November 1962, 8.50–9.15 p.m. Starring BENNY HILL. Featuring GRAHAM STARK, PRISCILLA MORGAN, NIGEL GREEN, EILEEN WAY, CAMERON HALL, PATSY SMART, PETER VERNON, RONNIE BRODY. Script: Dave Freeman. Incidental music: Ron Grainer. Designer: Robert MacGowan. Producer: Duncan Wood. In the first show

of series two, billed as 'a new series of unlikely situations', Hill stars as a nervous, foolhardy newspaper reporter who cheerfully wanders into spooky, haunted house comedy territory with death threats, curses and Graham Stark's deliciously creepy old family retainer.

Benny Hill, 'Cry of Innocence': BBC, Friday 7 December 1962, 8.50–9.15 p.m. Starring BENNY HILL. Featuring JOHN GABRIEL, AMBROSINE PHILLPOTTS, JOAN NEWELL, ROGER AVON, YOOTHA JOYCE, ARTHUR MULLARD, GORDON PHILLOTT, HOWARD DOUGLAS, ANN LANCASTER, JOAN INGRAM, RONNIE BRODY, PATSY SMART, JENNIFER BROWNE, ROBERT RAGLEN, WILLIAM SHERWOOD, MICHAEL STAINTON, REG THOMPSON, MICHAEL EARL. Script: Dave Freeman. Incidental music: Ron Grainer. Designer: Tony Abbott. Producer: Duncan Wood. In a wonderfully detailed spoof on Alfred Hitchcock's vastly underrated documentary-style Henry Fonda flick *The Wrong Man*, Hill plays the much put upon and mentally troubled Godfrey Bellbine, continually arrested, for no apparent reason, by hard-nosed Detective Inspectors Jones (John Gabriel) and Williams (Roger Avon). A tight-knit, claustrophobic and bleakly played comedy of oppressive situation.

Benny Hill, 'The Time Bicycle': BBC, Friday 14 December 1962, 8.50–9.15 p.m. Starring BENNY HILL. Featuring GRAHAM STARK, ANTHONY SHARP, LAUREL MATHER, GWENDA EWEN, CAMERON HALL, KEN ROBERTS, JULIAN ORCHARD, MOLLY SUGDEN, EDWIN APPS, SIDNEY VIVIAN, REG THOMPSON, ROGER AVON, JEAN MARLOW, ALEC BREGONZI. Script: Dave

Starring BENNY HILL. Featuring GRAHAM STARK, PENNY MORRELL, COLIN DOUGLAS, ARTHUR MULLARD, JOE GIBBONS, CORAL MORPHEW, VALERIE COONEY, TRICIA MONEY, GILLIAN WATT, CARON GARDNER, VALERIE STANTON and the voice of LEON THAU. Script: Dave Freeman. Incidental music: Ron Grainer. Designer: Tony Abbott. Producer: John Street. Hill is super-spaceman Humphry Grumby, posted to an experimental observation post on the mysterious Planet Seven. Graham Stark comes along to give back-handed moral support, but the real danger lies in the planet's oath-cracking temptations. Can Astronaut Hill keep his British dignity intact? What do you think?

Benny Hill, 'The Shooting of Willie the Kid': BBC, Friday 4 January 1963, 8.50–9.15 p.m. Starring BENNY HILL. Featuring GRAHAM STARK, BILL KERR, JOHN BLUTHAL, MAGGIE FITZGIBBON, MICHAEL BRENNAN, MICHAEL PEAKE, RON-NIE BRODY, ANN LANCASTER, MARJIE LAWRENCE, KEN ROBERTS, JOE GIBBONS. Script: Dave Freeman. Incidental music: Ron Grainer. Designer: Robert MacGowan. Producer: Duncan Wood. Benny Hill's big-headed, tall tale storyteller, Mr Whittaker T. Wildfoot, is the much-respected proprietor of a wild west entertainment emporium resembling *Westworld* without the relentless Yul Brynner. Mind you, Michael Crichton may have been tuning in, for the flamboyant Wildfoot does come face with face with the heartless western outlaw at the centre of his fantasy empire – Willie the Kid, as played by John Bluthal. And come to think of it, Talbot Rothwell probably had his set switched on as another Benny Hill eccentric, Wildfoot's naive English nephew, Clarence, wandered about the place like Jim Dale's Marshall P. Knutt in *Carry On Cowboy*. A wonderful deconstruction of western terminology and the best fun down at the BBC saloon until William Hartnell had a brush with those gunfighters in 1966.

Freeman. Incidental music: Ron Grainer. Designer: Robert MacGowan. Producer: Duncan Wood. A joyous H.G. Wells parody starring Benny as Mr Bottiwell, a cheerful Edwardian chap who, one fateful September afternoon in 1902, takes a trip to Hampstead to visit his inventor friend, Hadrian, played by Graham Stark. Notorious for his wacky ideas, he plies Hill with bucket-loads of sherry, straps him into a magical time-travelling bike and sends him into the future.

Benny Hill, 'Mervyn's Christmas Pudding': BBC, Friday 21 December 1962, 8.50–9.15 p.m. Starring BENNY HILL. Featuring GRAHAM STARK, MOYRA FRAS-ER, PRISCILLA MORGAN, PATRICIA HAYES, PETER VERNON, LALA LLOYD, DAVID KEIR. Script: Dave Freeman. Incidental music: Ron Grainer. Designer: Tony Abbott. Producer: John Street. A much welcome return for Cruddy, albeit only in name, as this slight variation on the simple one celebrates the festive season with a bumbling time at a pint-and-pudding party in Pimlico.

Benny Hill, 'The Secret of Planet Seven': BBC, Boxing Day, Wednesday 26 December 1962, 8.45–9.10 p.m.

Benny Hill, 'The Vanishing Man': BBC, Friday 11 January 1963, 8.50–9.15 p.m. Starring BENNY HILL.

There's easier ways to get your call through - fending off Joan Newell and a dodgy looking mandolin in *Benny Hill: The Vanishing Man*.

Left: He laughed so much his false teeth fell out - a wonderfully seedy character study from *Benny Hill: Mr Jolly*.

Benny Hill: The Trouble Maker with a hapless trainee doing just what startled David Lodge doesn't want done.

Featuring NADJA REGIN, FRANK THORNTON, JOAN NEWELL, JENNIFER BROWNE, VALERIE BROOKS, JOE GIBBONS, EDWIN BROWN, LEON THAU, TRICIA MONEY, VALERIE STANTON, CARON GARDNER, COLIN SPAULL, GEORGE MYDDLETON. Script: Dave Freeman. Incidental music: Ron Grainer. Designer: Robert MacGowan. Producer: John Street. Another comic mystery with Hill as Harry Cruddy, a variation on the Mervyn theme. This chap is a gas-fitter's mate and slate club treasurer who suddenly disappears at precisely the time that the annual share-out money also goes astray. Valerie Brooks is his self-conscious girlfriend, Vera, while Harry's brother, Ron (Hill again), bumbles about with wild flights of espionage fancy, heading off behind the Iron Curtain to search for his lost flesh and blood. Deliciously naive, surreal and hilarious – all at the same time.

Series Three

Benny Hill, 'Mr Apollo': BBC, Tuesday 3 September 1963, 8–8.25 p.m. Starring BENNY HILL. Featuring GRAHAM STARK, JOAN NEWELL, YOOTHA JOYCE, ANTHEA WYNDHAM, ANNA GILCRIST. Script: Dave Freeman. Incidental music: Ron Grainer. Designer: Susan Spence. Producer: John Street. In the first show of series three, Hill's coughing, wheezing, chain-smoking wreck cons the nation by promoting his healthy regime with a poster campaign featuring his face superimposed on an ultra-fit, muscle-packed body-builder. A delicious touch of black humour informs this classic, with the trickster ending up in the next hospital

bed to his first suffering follower, touchingly played by Graham Stark.

Benny Hill, 'The Visitor': BBC, Tuesday 10 September 1963, 8–8.25 p.m. Starring BENNY HILL. Featuring MELISSA STRIBLING, ALLAN CUTHBERTSON with FRANK THORNTON, LEN LOWE, DIANA HOPE. Script: Dave Freeman. Incidental music: Ron Grainer. Designer: Malcolm Goulding. Producer: John Street. Hill stars as the ultimate embodiment of dullness and irritation imposed upon the hapless and helpless Johnsons, played by Stribling and Cuthbertson. The nuisance guest from hell, Hill's unaware intrusion leads to a classic comic nightmare of domestic distress.

Benny Hill, 'Mr Jolly': BBC, Tuesday 17 September 1963, 8–8.25 p.m. Starring BENNY HILL. Featuring DERMOT KELLY, PATRICIA HAYES, ANNABELLE LEE, JOE GIBBONS with RONNIE BRODY, EDWIN BROWN, MICHAEL BEINT, MAEVE LESLIE, DEREK JOHNS. Script: Dave Freeman. Incidental music: Ron Grainer. Designer: Malcolm Goulding. Producer: John Street. Twenty-five years after this classic half-hour, the legendary Peter Cook would rip through an edition of *Comic Strip Presents* ... as the murderous, humourless Mr Jolly. Here, the joke is less grotesque but equally disturbing. Benny Hill's Mr Jolly is an unsmiling, eccentric joke and comic novelty seller. With his motto, 'Laugh and the world laughs with you!', this spreader of cheap thrills and japery ambles through life until a young lad, played by Dermot Kelly, gets himself trapped in a gothic mask. The race is on to remove the object, while the comic tension is heightened by Hill's laid-back delivery and the high-octane panic of the boy's distressed mother, Mrs Wilson – a peerless performance from Patricia Hayes. The two stars adorned the cover of the *Radio Times* (14–20 September 1963).

Benny Hill, 'The Trouble Maker': BBC, Tuesday 24 September 1963, 8–8.25 p.m. Starring BENNY HILL. Featuring DAVID LODGE with DIANA KING, GWENDOLYN WATTS, JOE GIBBONS, FRANK LITTLEWOOD, DIANA HOPE, RONNIE BRODY, EDWIN BROWN, MICHAEL BEINT. Screenplay: Dave Freeman. Incidental music: Ron Grainer. Designer: Susan Spence. Producer: John Street. This is the disastrous tale of skilled electrician Jim (brilliantly brought to life by that fine character player David Lodge) and his hapless, ever-cheerful but incompetent mate, played by Benny Hill. A block of luxury flats descends into chaos thanks to Hill's manic meddling, but it's his boss who endures all the hassle as the smiling cherub looks on, the picture of innocence

Benny Hill, 'The Dresser': BBC, Tuesday 24 September 1963, 8–8.25 p.m. Starring BENNY HILL. Featuring HUGH PADDICK and ANTHONY SHARP with GEORGE WOODBRIDGE, JOAN NEWELL, LEN LOWE, JOE GIBBONS, ANNA GILCRIST. Script: Dave Freeman. Incidental music: Ron Grainer. Designer: Susan Spence. Producer: John Street. Hill as Ernie – not of the milk but of the egg, a former egg-stamper in fact – gets involved in the luvvie world of theatrics.

Benny Hill, 'The Taxidermist': BBC, Tuesday 1 October 1963, 7.45–8.10 p.m. Starring BENNY HILL. Featuring DERMOT KELLY with PATRICIA HAYES, LEN LOWE. Special guest: GRAHAM STARK. Script: Dave Freeman. Designer: Susan Spence. Incidental music: Ron Grainer. Producer: John Street. A distinguished, comfortably well off Benny meets a ragged, streetwise Irish chap (Dermot Kelly) in the park. Before long, the silver-tongued devil has sold Hill a 50/50 partnership in a taxidermist's shop. Following an intensive theory course from an old textbook, Hill ventures into business – with the expected comic results.

Benny Hill (repeat season): Tuesday, 10–10.25 p.m. – 'The Vanishing Man' (19 November 1963), 'Cry Of Innocence' (26 November 1963), 'The Time Bicycle' (3 December 1963), 'The Taxidermist' (17 December 1963) and 'The Time Bicycle' (Monday 23 December 1963).

A Midsummer Night's Dream

Filmed as ITV production company Rediffusion's contribution to the 400th anniversary of William Shakespeare's birth, the role of Bottom was traditionally one which saw a favourite comic talent of the day go legitimate, so it was perfect for Benny Hill. Very much an ITV attempt to bring culture to the masses, popular television singer Eira Heath was enlisted alongside more theatrically trained performers such as Patrick Allen and Anna Massey, while the comedy duties were left in the capable hands of priceless film character actor Miles Malleson, Alfie Bass, digging in with Bootsie-type comic delivery, and in a reunion with Bass's old co-star from *The Army Game*, Bernard Bresslaw hamming it up with wide-eyed disbelief.

A faithful retelling of the play, the production was one of the most expensive of its day, with beautifully naturalistic sets from Michael Yates constructed as semi-transparent drapes to enhance the sense of magic in the woodland scenes. The majestic score of Mendelssohn was retained, and the production was greeted with satisfaction by critics convinced this was the way to present Shakespeare to the masses – top-name popular stars with a background of traditional staging, brilliantly contrasting edited, high-brow prose with low-brow comedians, much as Shakespeare envisaged it. However, one critic rather snootily celebrated the show before commenting that none of the mainstream television audience would bother to watch it. He was wrong, and several elated reviewers went for the obvious, but sincere, comment that 'Benny Hill's Bottom was the tops!'

A Midsummer Night's Dream: Associated Rediffusion. Broadcast ITV, Wednesday 25 June 1964, 9.10–11 p.m., 110 mins, black and white 16 mm, 3,959 feet. Theseus PATRICK ALLEN, Flute ALFIE BASS, Philostrate TONY BATEMAN, Hermia MAUREEN BECK, Helena JILL BENNETT, Snout BERNARD BRESSLAW, Demetrius CLIFFORD ELKIN, Lysander JOHN FRASER, Fairy KAY FRAZER, Hippolyta EIRA HEATH, Egeus CYRIL LUCKHAM, Quince MILES MALLESON, Titania ANNA MASSEY, Starveling BILL SHINE, Puck TONY TANNER, Oberon PETER WYNGARDE, Bottom BENNY HILL. Music: Mendelssohn, performed by The London Philharmonica Orchestra. Set Designer: Michael Yates. Choreography: Juan Corelli. Produced and directed by Joan Kemp-Welch.

Did You Know?

A Midsummer Night's Dream made the cover of *TV Times* (21–27 June 1964), with Hill surrounded by his fellow am dram colleagues.

Benny Hill and Richard Stone travelled to Brighton's Theatre Royal in early 1964 to watch Ralph Richardson's acclaimed performance as Nick Bottom in *A Midsummer Night's Dream*.

Condemned by some purists for casting Hill, director Joan Kemp-Welch defended her choice with the obvious argument that the part was created for a beloved low-brow comic with the fruity gusto of a sexually charged rogue. Frankie Howerd also gave a wonderful performance of the part on stage. Hill delighted in the mixed company of Shakespearian pros and comedy actors, indeed Miles Malleson was enchanted by his energetic performance – reading the line 'Methought I was, and methought I had!' with perfect sexual emphasis. Television debutante Anna Massey claims to have been equally riveted by Hill's natural treatment of the Bard for television. Professor George Rylands from Cambridge University was enlisted as technical adviser.

A Midsummer Night's Dream was Hill's brother Leonard's favourite play.

The Benny Hill Show

Discontented with the successful, albeit disorganized, *Benny Hill* situation comedies, Dave Freeman parted company with his star collaborator. Hill in the mean time had written himself radio's revue series *Benny Hill Time*, cleared his head for another batch of television specials and fired his comic imagination with a European holiday covering Hamburg, Paris, Madrid, Nice and Marseilles. He returned refreshed and raring to go, presenting the BBC with a sparkling one-off effort.

Back in harness with producer Kenneth Carter, Hill crafted a breathtaking comic variety revue with this special prelude to his 1965 sketch season. There's an exhausting piece of television trickery with a glorious town band made up of 16 Benny Hills, all in different costumes and playing different instruments (prefiguring Charlie Drake's celebrated orchestra sketch), Hill as a greedy, rip-roaring captain of a pirate radio station, and best of all, a painstakingly constructed James Bond B-movie parody, 'The Secret of Love', casting Patricia Hayes as the sullen *femme fatale*. As usual, there are also international cabaret turns, notably American jazz singer Mark Murphy. Quite clearly, Hill was back at his peak and in his element. Goodbye, clever situation comedy constructions; hello,

happy quickies, songs, innuendo and guest artistes.

Above all, this classic edition ushered in a sharper, more cynical, streetwise, social comment-geared style. In the wake of *That Was The Week That Was* and *Steptoe and Son*, Hill tightened up his targets for a more bitter-sweet attack with some of the most biting work of his career.

The Benny Hill Show: BBC1, Friday 6 November 1964, 8.25–9.10 p.m. Starring BENNY HILL. Featuring JULIE ROGERS, PATRICIA HAYES, ALEX MACINTOSH, MARK MURPHY. Script: Benny Hill. Musical Director: Burt Rhodes. Film Cameramen: James Balfour and John A.S. Turner. Film Editor: Jim Latham. Designer: Douglas Smith. Producer: Kenneth Carter.

Christmas Night with the Stars

The annual festive get-together was joyfully mocked by *Steptoe and Son*, when the freezing cold nation gathered round their turkey carcasses, ravaged trees and flickering television sets to be entertained by the cream of BBC talent. This priceless 1964 show is a prime example, with the reassuring tones of Sergeant Dixon of Dock Green himself, Jack Warner, presenting the wealth of familiar and fresh favourites with relaxed ease. There's a sense of other-worldly innocence about the addresses to the viewing audience, referred to as 'friends and family' by our neatly bow-tied and suited host. With shaky camerawork and even shakier linking dialogue, Warner guides the half-sozzled television audience through mini-playlets from the best-loved television faces of the day.

First, if that after-dinner port had been too much for Uncle Frank, there was a bristling 'Wakey, Wakey!' from bandleader Billy Cotton, cutting a gloriously Dickensian figure with a stirring rendition of 'Food, Glorious Food' from the contemporary West End hit *Oliver!* A joyous collection of grub, short-skirted dancers and glamorous backing singers was enough to please any dad in the household, and this rousing beginning gave way to some classic comedy from Dick Emery. We can forgive Warner's truly groan-worthy linking gag ('Thanks for the Emerys!') in light of Dick's contribution, resembling a cut-price Peter Sellers with vox pop comments from distinguished thespian Seymour Bloom, a refined lady, a Pythonesque upper-class twit, a camp hairdresser, a pop groupie, a cheerful robber, and of course, a buxom blonde sexpot.

Warner's older-generation condescension towards pop groups led into a totally cringe-making round-up of parodies from The Barron Knights, with The Rolling Stones, The Animals, The Honeycombs, and naturally,

The Beatles getting the treatment, before Scottish singer and comedian Andy Stewart, looking bemused, delivered a Christmas tree to remote Unst in the Shetland Isles.

Much better stuff was offered up by Terry Scott and Hugh Lloyd for the *Hugh and I* contribution, brilliantly recreating a family Christmas, watching Andy Stewart on the box, tackling the huge mound of washing up and tripping through a myriad of angst-ridden, post-feast party games with hilarious results. Even better was the fresh-faced *Likely Lads*, having started on BBC television just two weeks earlier, with Rodney Bewes and James Bolam reliving nightmares of spending the evening watching *Christmas Night with the Stars*, planning to booze the seasonal period away, and finally letting the moment slip by, surrounding themselves in a joyfully regressive *Rupert the Bear Annual* contest.

Benny Hill's contribution, 'The Lonely One', is a masterpiece of spoof fly-on-the-wall television documentary, with Hill mumbling his way through the role of teenage delinquent Willie Treader, unemployable for eight years and happy to spend his time hanging about water. Typical of Hill's work of the period, there's an underlying sense of earthy realism and suggestiveness throughout (highlighted by the dubious dog sight gag), but Hill's cheeky expressions, peerlessly played angst and firm grasp of the acceptable level of innuendo create an achingly funny dissection of Britain's youth culture.

The uneasy commentary and firsthand reports from blasé interviewees mean that there's a hint of Monty Python's more cutting 'Ethel the Frog' of five years later, with Hill outstanding as the shrieking geography teacher detailing a deprived childhood and cagily remembering the 'vulgar songs' which the young boy 'whistled' (this proved too good a gag to leave in Christmas obscurity, and Hill reused it in a 1975 Thames Television special). With Edith Evans-like dignity and leaving perfect pauses for effect, this is Hill the unsubtle comedian scaling the heights of subtle performance. He scores another triumph as the retentive, bespectacled youth leader, turning on the sexually repressed, anti-permissive air of a pent-up pervert with laxative misunderstandings and a feeling that it's society to blame. Even in 1964, that cliché was ripe for mocking, and Hill tellingly reveals his sad-man character with a rant about the prevalence of scantily clad women on escalator posters and his dedicated effort to count all 17 adverts – over and over again! The young tearaway's mother (voiced by an uncredited Patricia Hayes – although she's in the *Hugh and I* sketch) describes him as a 'cycle-path', while Hill as the boy's hated father, a pompous, pinstripe-suited council officer, is more concerned with discussing his own popularity and position. In that unlaboured and inventive moment, Hill's comedy directly addresses the reality of juvenile crime. Comedy patches up the message before the audience can think, with the Lady Mayoress considering young Hill 'a handful', and a classic Hill authority-mocking figure in the hard-nosed works foreman, moaning about the young of today in a diatribe continually bleeped to mask expletives. With poster gags, dog biscuits, telly obsession and even a drugs reference, this is a masterly Benny Hill segment.

The show was then almost over, with a brief spot by newcomers Prunella Scales and Richard Briers plugging *Marriage Lines*, Kathy Kirby (giving no cause for worry to Judy Garland) singing 'Have Yourself a Merry Little Christmas', and finally, our genteel host raising his glass and wishing the assembled masses all the best. They just don't make Christmas Day television entertainment like this any more ...

Christmas Night with the Stars. BBC, 25 December 1964, 7.15–8.45 p.m. Host: JACK WARNER. Continuity written by Robert Gray and Jack Warner. Orchestra directed by Harry Rabinowitz. Orchestrations by Dennis Wilson, Alan Bristow, Ray Terry, Peter Moore, Jackie Brown and Arthur Wilkinson. Film Editor: Richard Barclay. Producer: Graeme Muir. *The Black and White Minstrels* – JOHN FRANCIS, TONY MERCER, BENNY GARCIA, MARGARET SAVAGE and THE TELEVISION TOPPERS. Dance direction: Larry Gordon. Vocal arrangements: George Mitchell. Orchestrations: Alan Bristion and Ray Terry. Director: George Inns. *The Billy Cotton Band Show* – BILLY COTTON AND HIS BAND, KATHIE KAY, ALAN BREEZE, THE COTTON SINGERS AND DANCERS. Staged by Malcolm Goddard. Arranged by Michael Hurll. Director: Terence Hughes. KATHY KIRBY – Orchestra conducted by Eric Robinson. Directed by Ernest Maxin. DICK EMERY with GLEN MASON – Script: David Cumming. Film Cameraman: Tom Friswell. Film Editor: Pat Holland. Director: David Croft. *Top of the Pops*: 'Greet the Groups' with THE BARRON KNIGHTS – Director: Johnnie Stewart. ANDY STEWART with IAN POWRIE AND HIS BAND – Director: Iain MacFadyen. ROY CASTLE – Orchestra conducted by Harry Rabinowitz. Director: Dennis Main-Wilson. *Hugh and I* – TERRY SCOTT and HUGH LLOYD with PATRICIA HAYES, CHARLES DYER, JACK HAIG, VI STEVENS, MOLLY SUGDEN, JILL CURZON, MAURICE PODBREY. Script: John Chapman. Director: David

Croft. *The Likely Lads* – JAMES BOLAM and ROD-NEY BEWES with SHEILA FEARN. Script: Dick Clement and Ian La Frenais. Director: Dick Clement. *Meet the Wife* – THORA HIRD and FREDDIE FRIN-TON with DARRYL READ. Script: Ronald Wolfe and Ronald Chesney. Director: Graeme Muir. *Marriage Lines* – RICHARD BRIERS and PRUNELLA SCALES with DENZIL ELLIS. Script: Richard Waring. Director: Robin Nash. *The Billy Cotton Band Show* – Ralph Reader and the London Boy Scout Gang Show. Arranged by Michael Hurll. Director Terence Hughes. BENNY HILL with ALEX MACINTOSH and PATRI-CIA HAYES. Script: Benny Hill. Film Cameraman: John Turner. Film Editor: Jim Latham. Director: Kenneth Carter.

The Benny Hill Show

This shorter but sweeter edition was the BBC's entry for 1965's Golden Rose of Montreux Award, and represented the way forward for Hill's comedy – in his later career, he would rarely vary from the format presented in this show. Wiping the dust of *Benny Hill* sitcomland off his feet, this was back to the old, familiar territory. Interviewed by David Griffith for *Radio Times*, Hill wallowed in his beloved form of 'lots of clowning in funny hats'. However, more importantly, this was deliberately constructed to appeal to a cross-section of European audiences. Thus, Hill explained, the sketches were all 'simple, universally understood comedy'. His future as the most widely known international comedy star was assured.

Still delighting in his collection of eccentrics and grotesques, this breathtaking half-hour squeezed in some 35 Benny Hill characterizations. He plays all members of a twelve-piece orchestra (male and female), gets stoned, cool and far out, man, as all members of a Rolling Stones-styled beat combo, touches Keaton-like film magic as a schoolboy influenced by his big-screen heroes, and bumbles through as a German professor (ably assisted by Gwendolyn Watts) trying to teach English via a Eurovision satellite link.

Hill's talent for visual comedy is clear in the celebrated fashion show sketch, the star injecting subtle facial disgust as a self-conscious, short-trousered male model on the catwalk opposite Jeremy Hawk and Catherine Boyle. Originally included in Hill's gloriously surreal stage show *Fine Fettle*, this skit was originally suggested to him by Michael Bentine – an inspiration which received a nod of thanks on air.

There's the spirit of traditional music hall in the

Sid Field (via Freddie Frinton) antics of an aged family retainer coping with a stately home where the mantelpiece figurines come alive, while, back by popular demand, the show includes a repeat screening of the B-movie 'The Secret Agent of Love'. A personal favourite of both Hill and producer Kenneth Carter, they were delighted to discover that this prime piece of bad movie-making was being used as a 'how-not-to' example for fledgling BBC staff.

However, best of all, here was the truly masterly 'Cha-Cha' radio breakfast sketch, which played out the morning routine of Hill, his wife (Sylvia Tysick) and mother-in-law (Doris Hare) to the strains of the wireless. A sublime piece of visual comedy, it showed Hill and his wife reacting to the morning radio show – tapping the *Radio Times* in beat to the music, slicing bread and the like – years before Eric and Ernie's more celebrated 'Stripper' routine relied on exactly the same idea. Hill would later use the technique for the even more elaborate Thames Television sketch 'Piped Music', only to be accused of pinching classic Eric and Ernie material! Such is the fate of the long-lasting pioneer.

The Benny Hill Show. BBC1, Saturday 3 April 1965, 7.25–7.55 p.m. Starring BENNY HILL. With PATRI-CIA HAYES, GWENDOLYN WATTS, JEREMY HAWK, CATHERINE BOYLE, DORIS HARE, SYLVIA TYSICK, MICHAEL MALNICK, PETER THORNTON. Script: Benny Hill. Costumes: Ena Nickalls. Make-up: Christina Morris. Lighting: Ken McGregor. Sound: Len Shorey. Film Cameraman: James Balfour. Film Editor: Keith Raven. Musical arrangements by Burt Rhodes, Basil Tait and Peter Knight. Orchestra conducted by Harry Rabinowitz. Additional material: Robert Gould. Design: Robert MacGowan. Producer: Kenneth Carter.

As was his wont, Hill holidayed during the summer of 1965, travelling through Marseilles and the Camargue, constructing new comedy sketches all the way. By now, he was very much a solo writing force. Dave Freeman had departed under quite amicable terms to write situation comedies for television, stage plays and feature films. Although no one noticed at the time and his popularity remained buoyant, Hill lost a crucial collaborator in Freeman.

It is undeniable that Benny Hill was the comedian who created, fashioned and developed the vast majority of filming techniques used in television comedy ever since, but equally undeniably, without the perceptive, critical Freeman as a sounding board, his BBC work would have been diminished. With a knowing look into the lens and a beckoning action bringing the camera closer, Hill crossed the boundary between cast and audience. This was no longer a set piece, playing like a filmed theatre play, this was live television, recreating the intimacy of music hall and variety. Hill effortlessly developed an ability to play to every home in the country.

However, having achieved almost all he could possibly want to in the sphere of television parody, with Freeman's departure Hill restyled himself as an archetype of male sexual frustration. This had always been a crucial element to his comedy, but from this point on, his male figures had never really grown up and never fully recovered from the dangerous shock attached to sexual discovery. The definitive, pioneering example was a 1965 sketch called 'Baby Boy'. Influenced by the 1956 Carrol Baker hot American drama *Baby Doll*, Hill was the fully grown male, treated like a baby by sexually charged women, and continually giving bemused looks to his unseen audience at home. Amid elongated cries of 'A new teddy bear' (with a deliciously ridiculous Southern American accent), Hill plays along as the babe in arms, fears the sexual attentions of his lusting company staying 'all day and all ... the time' and secretly revels in the attention. Although comic giants like Terry Scott (in a 1965 sketch, 'Eat Up Your Prunes') and Marty Feldman (in a 1967 *It's Marty*) trod the territory again, it became the core of Hill's comedy. He saw his regressive, infantile male amid the nervousness of the outside world as crucial to an understanding of his comic message. Indeed, this eternal sense of Benny Hill as the naughty schoolboy making rude suggestions and laughing behind his hand was the very reason that, however risqué his gags became, the basic reaction was simply laughter rather than offence.

Importantly, during this 1965 season of reinvention, Hill refilmed and reworked his celebrated spoof on the film *The Collector*, this time reversing the sexual equation to cast Patricia Hayes as the dominant vamp and himself as the weak victim. Nor had he lost his skill of embracing the new, happening trends. His take on the 1965 Richard Lester swinger, *The Knack*, was christened 'The Knock', in which contemporary cool met provincial awfulness as the predicted first prizewinner at the Chipping Sodbury Film Festival. This November edition of the 1965 season also targeted both the BBC and ITV, the ethos of ITV's Hughie Green mocked by Hill's compering of the BBC's first talent show, headlining such unsung talents as the amazing singing acrobat.

His love of the vintage golden days of Hollywood was never far from his comedy, but above all, Hill was very, very funny. As often as not, he went for the lowest possible denominator, frantically overplaying obvious jokes for maximum laughter and delightfully knocking the quality of his own painstakingly worked out script. Hill was a comedian of the people, inviting them to join him in unashamedly laughing at human nature's absurdities. One classic example came in the January 1966 show, with Hill's kilted Scottish dancer getting one hint from a fellow dancer, another hint, and finally, in a perfect three-tier joke, suddenly realizing that he's left his underpants in the dressing room. This is hardly high art, but it's certainly high comedy.

The Benny Hill Show: BBC1, Saturday 24 April 1965, 7.25–8.10 p.m. Starring BENNY HILL. With PATRICIA HAYES, JEREMY HAWK, GLORIA PAUL, PETER THOMAS, DAN MEADEN, ROGER AVON, JOHNNY CLAYTON, DAVE GRIFFITHS, VALERIE BRIEN. Guests ANITA HARRIS, TRYPHINA PARTRIDGE, THE RAINDROPS. Script: Benny Hill. Costumes: Ena Nickalls. Make-up: Christina Morris. Lighting: Ken MacGregor. Sound: Len Shorey. Film Cameraman: James Balfour. Film Editor: Angus Newton. Musical arrangements: Burt Rhodes. Orchestra conducted by Harry Rabinowitz. Producer: Kenneth Carter.

The Benny Hill Show: BBC1, Saturday 8 May 1965, 7.45–8.30 p.m. Starring BENNY HIL. With PATRICIA HAYES, JEREMY HAWK, GLORIA PAUL, PETER VERNON, ROGER AVON, PETER BAYLISS, LINDSAY SCOTT-PATTON, SUSAN CLARK. Guests JULIE ROGERS, THE COUNTRYMEN, IVOR MAIRANTS. Script: Benny Hill. Lighting: Geoff Shaw. Sound: Len Shorey. Film Cameraman: James Balfour. Film Editor: Angus Newton. Musical arrangements: Burt Rhodes. Orchestra conducted by Harry Rabinowitz. Design: Robert MacGowan. Producer: Kenneth Carter.

The Benny Hill Show: BBC1, Saturday 22 May 1965, 7.25–8.10 p.m. Starring BENNY HILL. With PATRICIA HAYES, JEREMY HAWK, RONNIE BRODY, PAT ASHTON, JOHN HOWARD, JOHNNY CLAYTON. Guests JAN WATERS, LOS ZAFIROS. Script: Benny Hill. Lighting: Geoff Shaw. Sound: Len Shorey. Film Cameraman: James Balfour. Film Editor: Angus Newton. Musical arrangements: Burt Rhodes. Orchestra conducted by Harry Rabinowitz. Design: Robert MacGowan. Producer: Kenneth Carter.

The Benny Hill Show. BBC1, Saturday 6 November 1965, 8.50–9.35 p.m. Starring BENNY HILL. With PATRICIA HAYES, JEREMY HAWK, THE HONEYS, WENDY BARRY, PATRICIA MASON, MANDY AND VERA, THELMA TAYLOR, MABEL MARKS. Guest JULIE ROGERS. Script: Benny Hill. Incidental music and arrangements: Burt Rhodes. Orchestra conducted by Harry Rabinowitz. Design: Melvyn Cornish. Producer: Kenneth Carter.

The Benny Hill Show. BBC1, Saturday 27 November 1965, 8.50–9.35 p.m. Starring BENNY HILL. With PATRICIA HAYES, JEREMY HAWK, BRIDGET ARMSTRONG, ROSEMARIE DUNHAM, FELIX BOWNESS, JOHN DERRICK, SUE DONOVAN. Guest SALENA JONES. Script: Benny Hill. Musical arrangements and direction: Burt Rhodes. Design: Melvyn Cornish. Producer: Kenneth Carter.

The Benny Hill Show. BBC1, Saturday 18 December 1965, 9–9. 45 p.m. Starring BENNY HILL. With PATRICIA HAYES, JEREMY HAWK, ELAINE TAYLOR, FELIX BOWNESS, THE KINSMEN. Script: Benny Hill. Musical arrangements and direction: Burt Rhodes. Design: Melvyn Cornish. Producer: Kenneth Carter.

The Benny Hill Show. BBC1, Saturday 8 January 1966, 8.50–9.35 p.m. Starring BENNY HILL. With PATRICIA HAYES, JEREMY HAWK, JOE GIBBONS, PAMELA CHARLES, MIRANDA HAMPTON, FELIX BOWNESS, RENE SARTORIS, SHEILA DELANEY, BELLA EMBERG, JUDY RUSSELL. Guest PATSY ANN NOBLE. Script: Benny Hill. Musical arrangements and direction: Burt Rhodes. Design: Melvyn Cornish. Producer: Kenneth Carter.

Variety Club of Great Britain Awards

This was an edited BBC presentation of the gala luncheon at the Savoy Hotel, held earlier in the day, at which Bernie Delfont dished out the prizes. Benny Hill won the much-coveted BBC Personality of the Year award, reflecting the fact that 1965 had proved one of the most popular and ground-breaking of his career.

Other winners were: ITV Personality, Patrick McGoohan; Film Actor, Sean Connery; Film Actress, Julie Christie; Show Business Personality, Ken Dodd; Stage Actor, Robert Stephens; Stage Actress, Dorothy Tutin; Radio Personality, Peter Haigh; Most Promising Artist, Michael Crawford, and there were special

awards for ITV quizmasters Hughie Green and Michael Miles.

Variety Club of Great Britain Awards. BBC, broadcast Tuesday 8 March 1966, 10.55–11.20 p.m. Introduced by PETER HAIGH. Chief Barker: SIR WILLIAM BUTLIN. Producer: Ray Colley.

Benny Hill joined BBC favourites Stanley Baxter, Jimmy Edwards, Eammon Andrews, Hattie Jacques, Miriam Karlin, Katie Boyle, Charlie Chester and Carole Carr on the Happy New Year *Radio Times* cover for 30 December 1967–5 January 1968. However, no new shows were on the cards, and his face remained on television merely through sparse repeat screenings.

The Benny Hill Show (repeat): BBC1, Saturday 6 May 1967, 8.30–9.15 p.m. (repeat of 6/11/65).

The Best of Benny Hill (repeat): BBC1, Saturday 20 May 1967 (repeat of 8/1/66).

The Best of Benny Hill (compilation): Saturday 3 June 1967, 8.25–9.10 p.m. (edited repeat of 22/5/65, with additional vintage footage featuring ROGER AVON, SUSAN CLARK, DORIS HARE, GLORIA PAUL).

Although he was at the peak of his powers, Benny Hill was becoming noticeably restless. Like Tony Hancock, he longed for international recognition, particularly a chance to crack the American market, and Richard Stone finally provided him with the opportunity.

Spotlight

Produced by Lord Grade's ATV in association with an American television company, *Spotlight* consisted of ten variety-style television specials designed for the American market. Benny Hill appeared in two of the ten editions, and although he apparently hated the experience, he relished the international cabaret feel of the show. More to the point, this was his first television appearance in colour, and proved a tempting distraction from both further BBC *Benny Hill Shows* and the productive film cameo work that now dominated his time.

Recorded in black and white for the British market, Grade employed colour cameras in tandem to record the shows for American viewing, and although legends of the calibre of Robert Goulet and Shelley Berman were assured of adoration, Benny Hill was hardly well known to

American audiences at this point in time. Nevertheless, although Tom Jones, Tommy Cooper, Shani Wallis and Frankie Vaughan were all recruited for this occasional spectacular variety series, it was Benny Hill who was chosen to headline the very first episode.

Sharing the bill with singers Abbe Lane and Noel Harrison (son of Sir Rex, and in vogue at the time for his haunting song 'Windmills of Your Mind' from *The Thomas Crown Affair* – later ruthlessly mocked by Hill's single 'Dustbins of Your Mind'), Hill performed his comedy routines to perfection, but – hard to credit considering there was such high-class competition on the show – he also sang a straight rendition of *New York, New York*. Suffice to say, he was no Frank Sinatra. His second appearance, in 1968, was alongside Lana Cantrella and Paul Anka. At the end of the show, he and Anka sang a brief duet of 'The Party's Over' – Hill cringed about it for years afterwards.

The sketches still stand up very well, many were reworked for later *Benny Hill Shows*, and the star's support team was top-notch, with old cohort Jeremy Hawk turning on the usual charm, Pat Hayes excelling in a working-class kitchen sink drama parody, and a new face, the sublime Julian Orchard, lending the star a professional hand.

Spotlight: ITV, Sunday 8 October 1967, 10.05–11 p.m. Starring BENNY HILL, NOEL HARRISON, ABBE LANE. With PATRICIA HAYES, JULIAN ORCHARD, BILL NAGY, JACK HAIG, THE DOUGLAS SQUIRES DANCERS, THE MIKE SAMMES SINGERS, JACK PARNELL AND HIS ORCHESTRA. Musical numbers staged by Douglas Squires. Designer: Richard Lake. Script: Howard Leeds and Bernard Rothman. Special material: Benny Hill. Producer: Jon Scoffield.

Spotlight: ITV, Easter Monday 14 April 1968, 8.25–9.25 p.m. Starring BENNY HILL, PAUL ANKA, LANA CANTRELLA. With PATRICIA HAYES, JEREMY HAWK, ANNETTE ANDRE, TOM CHATTO, RONNIE BRODY, MARK COLLEANO, THE LIONEL BLAIR DANCERS, THE MIKE SAMMES SINGERS, JACK PARNELL AND HIS ORCHESTRA. Musical numbers staged by Lionel Blair. Designer: Richard Lake. Script: Howard Leeds and Bernard Rothman. Benny Hill sketches written by Benny Hill. Producer: Jon Scoffield.

Neither *Spotlight* show was a hit in America, and Benny Hill hardly emerged victorious, but worse was to come. Not only had this attempt at American superstardom failed, there were worried rumblings from the BBC. To be fair, the corporation had always taken the loyalty of Richard Stone and Benny Hill for granted, and plans for future shows were never an issue. Hill wrote and performed three or four specials a year, and that was that. However, by the mid-1960s, Hill had been dallying with cinema work, and the BBC graciously backed his plans to widen his public persona. It was all part of his bid to find global fame, but the BBC never thought that his television assignments for them would cease completely. Indeed, the BBC plugged any gap in their Benny Hill output with popular compilation programmes, *The Best of Benny Hill*. In between the two guest starring turns for Lew Grade's *Spotlight* came a further shift towards ITV stardom – the commercial network's big Christmas comedy hit for 1967 was none other than *The Benny Hill Show*!

The Benny Hill Show

To all intents and purposes, this was the sort of fare that the BBC would have expected to broadcast, but even before the rise of Thames Television, Hill created this special hour-long edition for Grade's ATV network.

With more variety performers than was usual on his BBC shows, Hill dished out the familiar menu of television parody and innuendo-filled sketches, embracing straightman Nicholas Parsons for the first time, featuring the exotic sound of Dorita y Pepe, running through a bit of pre-Cilla Black *Blind Date* angst with Rita Webb, wallowing in familiar historical sketches, and more importantly, resurrecting his glorious partnership with Dave Freeman for a last time.

The Benny Hill Show: ITV, Boxing Day 1967, 7–8 p.m. Starring BENNY HILL. With THE SEEKERS, VINCE HILL, NICHOLAS PARSONS, DORITA Y PEPE, ARTHUR MULLARD, RITA WEBB, DAVE FREEMAN, YVONNE ANTROBUS, BETTINE LE BEAU, PETER DIAMOND, GERRY WAIN, JACK PARNELL AND HIS ORCHESTRA, THE PAMELA DEVIS DANCERS, THE MIKE SAMMES SINGERS. Musical Associate: Philip Casson. Producer: Jon Scoffield.

However, this brief flirtation with ITV did not lead to a long-term affair at this stage, and in 1968, Hill wrote and performed a final batch of BBC specials. Classy support from Hugh Paddick and June Whitfield graced these excellent, polished, stylish pieces of work. Hill's delivery was peerless, the writing was sparkling, and the television trickery simply heightened the professionalism.

At the tail end of the 1960s, the shows still reflected Hill's European travels and perceptive eye for British institutions (the November edition exposed the madness of the prison system and security guards), while the finger on the contemporary pulse ushered in the Benny Hill/Patricia Hayes deconstruction of the glorious, earthy weirdness of the Ken Russell musical 'Gavin Blod'. Hill was still penning original, hilarious songs at the time, and the musical numbers remain some of the most enjoyable of his career, notably an oft-resurrected vampire piece with June Whitfield (screened at the National Film Theatre's tribute in 1994, and as part of Whitfield's *Funny Women* BBC compilation).

However, the series' masterpieces have to be the hugely inventive 'double' sketches, resurrecting famous movie partnerships – be they vintage (an absolutely sublime performance as both Peter Lorre and Sydney Greenstreet from *Casablanca*, a delightful W.C. Fields and Mae West from *My Little Chickadee*, even embracing Fields's love of ancient insults with 'mooncalf') or contemporary (Richard Burton and Elizabeth Taylor from *Who's Afraid of Virginia Woolf?* – adding an extra, beloved wordplay gag and dubbing the skit 'Rich Burt and Eliza Tayl in *Who's Afraid of Virgin Wool?*). The gags may have been old – the Fields/West 'My father was a mayor.' – 'Your mother was a jockey.' exchange springs to mind – but the performance had a freshness that remains irresistible.

Another popular 'double' was Hill's take on the singing duo Esther and Abi Ofarim, who had just had a hit with 'Cinderella, Rockefella', while naturalist filmmakers Armand and Michaela Denis were parodied via *Wizard of Oz* iconography with their trek through Bert Lahr country. There was a particularly stunning celebration of the 1954 masterpiece *On the Waterfront*, with Hill affectionately sending up the 'I could have been a contender' sequence between Marlon Brando and Rod Steiger, but it was his old comedy heroes that brought the finest moments, excelling at Groucho, Harpo and Chico Marx, as well as a wonderfully detailed impersonation of Oliver Hardy. He tackled dream sequences, silent comedy, camera trickery to elongate his features, graffiti-like one-liners and much else, taking innuendo and the comedy of British embarrassment in fresh directions.

The Benny Hill Show. BBC, Wednesday 20 April 1968, 7.50–8.35 p.m. Starring BENNY HILL. With JUNE WHITFIELD, HUGH PADDICK, JANIE MARDEN, DORIS ROGERS, DONNA READING, HARRY SELTER, PAMELA BECKMAN, SANDY DUKE, EILEEN NICHOLAS. Script: Benny Hill. Original music: Art Day and Burt Rhodes. Musical Director and Arranger: Burt Rhodes. Settings designed by Malcolm Middleton. Producer: Kenneth Carter.

Showtime – The Benny Hill Show. BBC, Wednesday 20 November 1968, 7.30–8.15 p.m. Starring BENNY HILL. With JUNE WHITFIELD, HENRY McGEE, THE RITA WILLIAMS SINGERS, DONNA READING, JIM TYSON, JENNE MORGAN, RIK RICH, BEVERLY AND JOHN WRIGHT. Special guests THE KAYE SISTERS. Script: Benny Hill. Musical Director and Arranger: Burt Rhodes. Costumes: Mary Woods. Settings designed by Brian Tregidden. Producer: Kenneth Carter.

The Benny Hill Show. BBC, Wednesday 11 December 1968, 7.30–8.15 p.m. Starring BENNY HILL. With PATRICIA HAYES, HENRY McGEE, PRISCILLA MORGAN, RITA WEBB, GILLY MELVER, BOB TODD, JENNY LEE-WRIGHT, DICK GRAHAM, PAMELA CUNDELL, JOHN WRIGHT, MAEVE LESLIE. Guests THE TRIO ATHENEE. Script: Benny Hill. Musical Director and Arranger: Burt Rhodes. Costumes: Mary Woods. Settings designed by Brian Tregidden. Producer: Kenneth Carter.

The Benny Hill Show. BBC, Boxing Day, Thursday 26 December 1968, 7.15–8 p.m. Starring BENNY HILL. With JUNE WHITFIELD, HENRY McGEE, TAMMY JONES, JENNY LEE-WRIGHT, JOHN WRIGHT, DORIS ROGERS, JIM TYSON, KEDD SENTON, CAROLYN MOODY, DAVID G. MARSH, RICHARD MOTTAN. Script: Benny Hill. Musical Director and Arranger: Burt Rhodes. Costumes: Mary Woods. Lighting: Peter Wesson. Settings designed by Brian Tregidden. Producer: Kenneth Carter.

THE THAMES YEARS

Although 1964 had seen Hill become a legitimate actor for Rediffusion's *A Midsummer Night's Dream* and 1967 had seen him work for ATV, at this stage the star was still very much part of the BBC team – you don't get a special Christmas show and your face on the seasonal *Radio Times* if you're batting for the other side! However, manager Richard Stone cites Hill's three major ATV programmes as the turning point in his career. Surprisingly, Stone thought Hill and the BBC were through, so he offered Benny Hill's television contract to Philip Jones, Head of Light Entertainment at Thames Television. Understandably, Jones jumped at the chance.

Thames, a young company which had been founded in 1968, was very much dedicated to the mass appeal of ensemble, popular comedy. The sitcoms *Doctor in the House*, *Please Sir!* and *On the Buses* were all huge ratings winners, but Benny Hill was destined to become the jewel in the Thames comedy crown. Jones had initially headlined Benny Hill miming to his classic number 'Pepys' Diary' in an early Thames variety show, *Thank Your Lucky Stars*. He would go on to win 11 major television awards for the company.

The BBC was understandably displeased to hear that their biggest comedy star was about to start turning out *The Benny Hill Show* for its rival. Evidence of the alliance with the 'other side' was presented in the 1–7 March 1969 edition of the *TV Times*, where, as part of a celebrity-studded 'Let's Make You a Star Cook' course with a £100 reader's prize, cookery editor Kathie Webber enlisted Benny Hill's help for the first instalment – the starter ('Eat as much as you like but don't swallow'). Others dragged into the kitchen were Bob Monkhouse, Jimmy Tarbuck, popster Barry Ryan and wrestler Jacki Pallo, but Hill's thoughts were firmly on his new season of comedy hour specials for Thames Television.

The odd ITV guest spot and prawn cocktail recipe was one thing, but a much closer relationship between Benny Hill and commercial television was about to be forged. When news leaked out that Hill had signed for Thames, the BBC's plans for a further summer repeat series of Hill compilations to be broadcast from 5 June 1969 were immediately cancelled, and Tom Sloan took the opportunity to write a furious letter to Richard Stone. Dismissing one projected repeat (a skit on the BBC's late-night news magazine *24 Hours*) as 'hopelessly out-dated', the letter asked, not unreasonably, why the BBC should broadcast a collection of old successes just in time to launch Benny Hill as ITV's new star. Sloan paid the monies owed for any repeat season planned, and shelved the broadcasts for good.

The BBC had been waiting for Hill to deliver plans for his next season, allowing him time to work on films, but they weren't even given the chance to counter-bid against the offer from Thames, since Hill was ready for a change anyway. It was a crucial departure in Hill's career, but in retrospect, one which offered him the chance to

fully develop his saucy style and fully embrace the world market he longed for.

As it did when the BBC lost Morecambe and Wise almost a decade later, ITV tempted Benny Hill with the possibility of broadening his horizons. First and foremost, there was the bonus of broadcasting in colour, there was serious talk of allowing Hill to direct the shows, and Hill could develop films especially for television. With these carrots dangled and a sense that he should get out of the BBC while the going was good, Benny Hill happily decamped his collection of comic characters, and carried on pretty much as before.

Certainly, as far as Hill's work ideals were concerned, nothing had changed. It's interesting to note that the support Hill enjoyed for the last three BBC specials – Henry McGee, Bob Todd, Jenny Lee-Wright, Pamela Cundell and Jack Wright – all followed the comic pied piper to ITV. Hailed as a conquering hero. Hill's face adorned the 15–21 November *TV Times* cover with the legend, 'The Return of the Flyaway Comedian' (I'm sure a few BBC eyebrows were raised at that!), and he made his first official appearance under the Thames banner on 19 November 1969. Gems included the bird act with David Battley, the wishing well sketch and 'Tommy Tupper-Time'.

If you asked most people what their image of Benny Hill was, chances are that the vast majority would suggest something from these golden years of Thames Television. In an amazing run between 1969 and 1989, Hill channelled almost all his creative energies into his long-awaited hour specials for Thames. It is a huge body of work which has been seen by the biggest audience of any comedian, anywhere and at any time – not bad for a lad from Southampton. Even as far back as the mid-1950s Hill, had been labouring material that many critics considered unworthy of him, and again, his first official *Benny Hill Show* for Thames in 1969 was greeted with snooty derision. However, the audience figures were more than enough to calm any fears, and Philip Jones, with a commercial eye and broader comic landscape than the old BBC, happily allowed and encouraged Hill's troupe of innuendo-encrusted routines and scantily clad ladies. He considered them no worse than Mack Sennett's bathing beauties, and with this confident backing from the man at the top, Hill was given the comic freedom he so desired.

Whether as the delightful mime artist (early examples being 1969's Marcel Marceau-like 'trapped in a balloon' routine, performed badly for brilliant comic effect, 1970's rejected lover finding favour behind a mask) or the country yokel, knowingly revealing countryside secrets to the sophisticated (in a 1969 gem, continually turning down the job of stable boy until he discovers the intentions of the owner – Lady Godiva), Hill was the most popular television comedian around. The high quality of his early Thames work is probably best judged from the compilation film *The Best of Benny Hill* and the widely available *Ernie* album material.

The Benny Hill Show

Benny Hill's first Thames show was an excellent continuation of the old BBC formula of innuendo with an added sense of awareness. The classic 'Tommy Tupper' interview sketch, a vicar appearing on television with his flies undone, appears alongside a lengthy commentary on the supposed meanness of the French in a hotel skit and a seemingly never-ending line of stereotypical sexy nurses in suspenders and frilly underwear. The critics condemned the whole exercise as banal, but the ratings went through the roof – so much so that Benny Hill was named ITV Personality of the Year for 1969 and saw a compilation of his work entered for the Montreux Festival within months of joining Thames.

Hill was really busy that Christmas, when he was portrayed as a Thames mainstay for a *TV Times* montage (20 December 1969–2 January 1970) featuring everybody from Tommy Cooper and Spike Milligan to Barbara Windsor and Ringo Starr. More importantly, instead of joining all the comic favourites for the two-and-a-half-hour *All Star Comedy Carnival*, Hill's show followed later – top billing, an hour long and in pole position, ITV comedy show of the year. Hill also threw himself into the New Year fun in *TV Times*, donning a kilt in the 'Kilt Joys!' photo feature, and insisting: 'I was a teenage Scottish teapot.' Others similarly embarrassed were Cliff Richard, Roy Hudd, Rodney Bewes, Bruce Forsyth and Freddie Davies.

The Benny Hill Show. Thames Television, Wednesday 19 November 1969, 8–9 p.m. Starring BENNY HILL. With EIRA HEATH, HENRY McGEE, KEN PARRY, DAVID BATTLEY, THE LADYBIRDS, JOHN WRIGHT, MIGUEL LOPEZ CORTEZO, MICHAEL SHARVELL-MARTIN, JAN BUTLIN, CONNIE GEORGES, VERNE MORGAN, BARBARA LINDLEY. Script and original songs: Benny Hill. Musical Director: Ronnie Aldrich. Designer: Harry Clark. Produced and directed by John Robins. Includes: 'European Song Contest' – Hill playing all the parts, including hostess Katie Boiler (for Katie Boyle), a French singer, an Austrian composer, a Flamenco singer, plus Ernie's first appearance.

Eddie In August - Nicole Shelby and Benny Hill radiate much more fun than the programme delivered

The Benny Hill Show. Thames Television, Thursday 25 December 1969, 8.30–9.30 p.m. Starring BENNY HILL. With EIRA HEATH, NICHOLAS PARSONS, MICHAEL SHARVELL-MARTIN, THE LADY-BIRDS, TOMMY MANN. Script and original songs: Benny Hill. Musical Director: Ronnie Aldrich. Designer: Harry Clark. Produced and directed by John Robins. Includes: 'Round-up of Holiday Sport'.

The Benny Hill Show. Thames Television, Wednesday 4 February 1970, 8–9 p.m. Starring BENNY HILL. Featuring EIRA HEATH, HENRY McGEE, RITA WEBB, NICOLE SHELBY, LOS PARAGUAYOS, THE LADYBIRDS, MICHAEL SHARVELL-MAR-TIN, JOHN WRIGHT, CHRISTINE RODGERS, HAROLD GEE, VALERIE ST JOHN, CHARMAINE SEAL, DAVID HAMILTON. Script and original songs: Benny Hill. Musical Director: Ronnie Aldrich. Designer: Harry Clark. Produced and directed by John Robins. Includes: 'A Look at Paris Holiday Life'.

The Benny Hill Show. Thames Television, Wednesday 11 March 1970, 8–9 p.m. Starring BENNY HILL. With EIRA HEATH, NICHOLAS PARSONS, PATRICIA HAYES, JIMMY THOMPSON, NICOLE SHELBY, THE LADYBIRDS, MICHAEL SHARVELL-MARTIN, MAVIS ASCOTT, BILL DRYSDALE, WALTER CARTI-ER, PIPPA REYNAUD, TERRY DAY, SUE BISHOP, DAVID HAMILTON. Script and original songs: Benny Hill. Musical Director: Ronnie Aldrich. Musical Associate: Ted Taylor. Designer: Harry Clark. Produced and directed by John Robins. Includes: a Hammer horror parody with Hill as Frankenstein's monster.

The Benny Hill Show – Montreux Festival Compilation

A compilation from Benny Hill's first four Thames specials was chosen as ITV's entry for Montreux, and *TV Times* (18–24 April 1970) made him its cover star with two photos in western guise and the legend 'Benny Plots His Big Kill'. Because the competition rules stipulated that the exact programme must have been screened in the country it represented, the compilation was quickly broadcast just before the entries were announced. Hill knew that Thames stood to gain prestige, enlarged foreign sales and the prize money of £1,000 – a perfect way to impress his new bosses – so a hasty schedule was arranged for this 'best of' selection, featuring Hill as pop fan Raver, The Milky Bar Kid, and Hans Stuck, the Austrian

Eurovison Song Contest competitor, complete with host Katie Boiler and French singer Mireille Matante.

When the festival opened on Thursday 23 April, Hill was confident and planning to fly over to accept the award if there was news that it was going his way. In the end, the winner was the Czech film *Six Fugitives*, which had no dialogue at all. Hill's comedy was very visual, and already sold to Germany, Sweden, Switzerland, Holland and Belgium, as well as Australia, but this blow probably pushed him further towards the reliance on mime which would lead to global recognition. Indeed, although it had already been completed before the judgement was announced, Hill's next Thames venture, *Eddie in August*, was an attempt to reinvent the genre.

The Benny Hill Show (Montreux Compilation): Thames Television, Monday 20 April 1970, 6.45–7.30 p.m. Starring BENNY HILL. With EIRA HEATH, NICHOLAS PARSONS, RITA WEBB, THE LADY-BIRDS, MICHAEL SHARVELL-MARTIN. Script and original songs: Benny Hill. Musical Director: Ronnie Aldrich. Musical Associate: Ted Taylor. Designer: Harry Clark. Produced and directed by John Robins.

Eddie in August

'No words. No spoken gags. Just Benny Hill at his visual best.' That's how *TV Times* tried to flog this silent slapstick ego trip. In a piece by Shaun Usher entitled 'Benny Hill Heading in a New Direction – Behind the Camera', it was clear that directing was very much part of his new ambition, and he was trying to become a card-holding member of the Association of Cinematography, Television and Allied Technicians' Union. However, despite Hill's obvious involvement at every level of *The Benny Hill Show*, his directorial contributions would always be happily hidden behind the bushel of Dennis Kirkland. Despite the fact that, as with Morecambe and Wise, working for ITV allowed very little variety, Hill did manage to celebrate the beginning of the Thames era with a very personal comedy film.

A short, self-contained adventure devised by Hill to try to emulate the mime skills of Chaplin and Tati, *Eddie in August* suffered from a lack of cohesion that was seized upon by critics. The narrative was fairly typical of Hill's most poignant scenes, with the man himself as a lonely failure longing for female company. Obsessed with a pretty girl who flirts with all the muscle men, Hill is the 28-year-old, crestfallen wannabe lover at every turn, contrasting cheap laughs (a dog urinates over his foot at a low ebb) with sentimentality (even his Walter Mitty flights of fantasy are a failure, because he remains a loser here as well). He is the eternal loser, with a continually breaking-down car and unfulfilled sexual desires so strong he is finally reduced to pathetically crawling around on all fours to look up glamorous girls' skirts.

In a *TV Times* preview (2–8 May 1970), Nicole Shelby discussed the new film, and the mess was succinctly summed up with: 'She rushes through the film in car chases and races through the woods, and Benny rushes after her.' As a reviewer claimed, 'This is more sad than funny', and the programme contains all those self-deprecating, slapstick elements which would mar his least satisfactory work. Ironically, it was this very mime element that allowed him to break through in America, but in Britain, critics – and indeed, audiences – were less than impressed with this effort, and Hill returned to the safe haven of *The Benny Hill Show* very quickly. Undertaking script, music, producing and directing duties, this is Benny Hill doing Charlie Chaplin, and doing it rather lacklustrely.

Eddie in August: Thames Television, Thursday 4 June 1970, 7–7.30 p.m. Starring BENNY HILL. With NICOLE SHELBY, DOUGLAS HILL, JILL EASTER, TOMMY GODFREY, GEORGE RODERICK. Written and devised by Benny Hill. Music: Benny Hill. Musical Director: Ronnie Aldrich. Editor: Stuart Hall. Produced and directed by John Robins and Benny Hill.

The audience ratings for *Eddie in August*, just over 4.5 million viewers, put it at number 13 in the charts, which was less than impressive, certainly compared to the figures for *The Benny Hill Show*. So in a conscious effort to embrace innuendo-drenched sketches and songs (for the home market) and elongated slapstick silent romping (for the overseas market and his own satisfaction), Hill did the only sensible thing he could. After a break of several months, collecting his thoughts, writing new material and performing it, Thames Television unleashed a new series – *The Benny Hill Show*!

The Benny Hill Show

Yes, it had to be more of the same, and for me, these first few years of re-evaluated, refreshed Thames specials make up a highly impressive body of work. Hill continued to inject impersonations into comic situations, with plenty of drag (a 1971 'Fanny Craddock' sketch with Bob Todd as Johnny Craddock, and Hill as Mary Quant in a hip sixties bit of business) and subverting of television conven-

tions (he delighted in digging into 1970s favourites like *Starsky and Hutch*, playing both parts, with old Jackie Wright outstanding as Huggie Bear). The rest of the sketches were Donald McGill postcards come to life, with nagging, overweight wives, gorgeous, cleavage-exposing young girls and sexually inadequate men.

Hill was a fireman among female firefighters flashing stocking tops, Hill was a vicar getting an eyeful from some glamorous churchgoer, Hill was a headmaster teaching a load of St Trinian's-style pupils, Hill was a bank robber, excited by the sight of pursuing policewomen losing their clothes on barbed wire, Hill was a hospital patient tended to by nurses in black basques ...

With total control over the writing and performing of his comedy, Hill became a powerful man at Thames, although, naturally, he still needed the approval of Phillip Jones, but with the ratings reaching the dream figure of 20 million, Jones had much to approve of. Hill's use of glamorous girls in his shows simply reflected the British nation's consciousness at the time. Feminist objections were treated more as a joke than any serious threat – Hill himself addressed the issue in tongue-in-cheek fashion as Mervyn Cruddy, while advertising at the time was gleefully using the scantily clad female form to sell almost anything.

The feting of Hill as one of the country's most important entertainers continued in *TV Times*, with frequent cover stardom and promotional interviews. For the 23–29 January 1971 issue (with a cover photo by Gordon Moore), the magazine maintained: 'It's the twinkle that makes him a star!' The fact that the magazine also celebrated the gorgeous girls who excited that twinkle, Sue Bond and Lesley Goldie, shows that they were a vital – indeed, often the major – part of Hill's appeal. This would backfire in later years.

During those permissive days of the early 1970s, what Benny Hill was doing was innocent compared to the world at large, but ten years later, this constant reliance on 'the girls', restricted to decorative, speechless bit parts in Hill's sped-up fantasies, would blight his entire career. As a February 1972 article reported, the girls 'flit in and out of sketches', while earlier, for a *TV Times* interview (18–24 September 1971), 27-year-old Hill's Angel Marilyn Rickard likened her experience of working with him to: 'doing nothing but play hockey. You know how it is in Benny's shows. You're on and off the screen in seconds and you feel you have done nothing.' This first public expression of dissent among his female cohort was heightened by the magazine itself when Dilys Watling's rendition of 'No Way to Treat a Lady' was billed as reflecting a possible rebellion of the fairer sex against Hill's style of comedy. But more usually it was 'good old, lucky old, Benny', with a later piece in *TV Times* (18–24 March 1972) detailing Penny Meredith's constant need for massages on set – many of the crew volunteered, but the privilege usually went to Benny himself. Subsequently, this might have served to fuel accusations that he was a 'dirty old man', but here Hill was held up as the British male's champion, having a whale of a time surrounded by sexy women, getting paid for it, making everybody laugh, and becoming a familiar friend to a nation of television worshippers.

Since he had a keen interest in reinforcing links with the ITV network, Hill agreed to take on the role of guest cartoon editor in the *TV Times* funnies section, 'It Makes Me Laugh'. Everybody from Jimmy Handley to Diana Coupland was roped in at some stage, and although the editorship was in name only, Hill's tenure remains interesting. His four weeks in the editor's seat, starting in the 5–11 December 1970 issue, were peppered with purely visual gags. Indeed, the first batch to receive his seal of approval do not have a written tag line among them. His self-concious blurb, 'I don't really understand humour so I try to play it by ear', is typical of him, but in action, the situation was quite different. His all-embracing, confiding style with his audience was perfectly suited to television, typically leading the viewers down a comic, bizarre path before backtracking skilfully. He perfected Max Miller's brilliance in wide-eyed amazement at any filthy connotations his audience might attach to his totally innocent observations. This was Benny Hill, a master of his craft.

However, he was at his best as the sexual ignorant, parading a long line of wheezing, aged, impotent and nervous figures like Scuttle, Maurice Dribble and the rest which the glamorous girls could run rings round. A classic example from 1972 saw Paula Wilcox (having starred in the sitcom *The Lover* with Richard Beckinsale) flashing her legs and making advances to Hill's bespectacled, speech-impaired (continually spraying 'Exactly!'), blow-up doll-owning boss figure. Add the noises of breaking wind (from the doll), Hill's uncertain keenness, Wilcox's contrasting flights of sexual freedom and male outrage ('Bloody selfish lot of gits!') and you have a burst of definitive Hill sketch comedy. He was the naughty schoolboy who had never grown up, setting women on a pedestal, and defusing sexual tension by injecting confidence tinged with terror into his comedy. In a 1973 musical number, Hill's maracas fall off at the sight of the stunning, scantily clad dancer. This is a man's reverent reaction to real beauty, and Hill's stunned comic expression makes it pure gold.

The country bumpkin figure was a familiar Hill character, bumbling through life, and notably, in the telephone exchange scene, chatting with the vicar and getting milk sent down to him over the wires. This wasn't all smut and no content – Hill, as displayed during his BBC days, could bring surreal humour to the masses. More potently than Python, Hill, Tommy Cooper and Eric Morecambe brought attitude-questioning comedy into the mainstream arena and got their messages across.

Of course, sex was also very important to Hill's comedy, whether it be a quickie sketch, with Hill in his undies outside the window, Bob Todd the returning husband and Sue Upton the faithless wife in stockings and scanties, but the surrealism was still in place – in this case, Hill discovers a skeleton when he hides on the window ledge. However, these touches of bizarre sight humour were never as popular as Hill's legendary Fred Scuttle, an obvious but thoroughly endearing comic creation, at his best when interviewed by Nicholas Parsons or Henry McGee.

A classic 1972 sketch featured Hill as a security guard, reacting with stunned amazement to McGee's opening question, 'How long is it?', and attaining genius with his answer to the question whether a female shoplifter had been picked up by the fuzz – after a mighty, laughter-drenched pause, Hill comments: 'No, Sir! Just tapped on the shoulders!', defusing the innuendo by adding 'We never involved the police!'

One of my personal favourites is the sketch from 1972 with Hill's genteel vicar, full of good feeling for his fellow man, explaining his selfless mission to help those around him, only to reveal, with a slowly opened door, that selected capital letters from the church's noticeboard bearing his message spell out 'KNICKERS'. Hardly the height of subtlety, but you believe the sincerity in Hill's distinguished man of the cloth, and his cheeky awareness of the punchline can't help but reach your comic soul. His 1971 season with producer John Robins won a BAFTA award.

The Benny Hill Show. Thames Television, Wednesday 14 November 1970, 8–9 p.m. Starring BENNY HILL. With NICHOLAS PARSONS, PATRICIA HAYES, LIZ FRASER, BOB TODD, DAN JACKSON, JACK WRIGHT. Script and original songs: Benny Hill. Musical Director: Ronnie Aldrich. Designer: Tony Borer. Directed and produced by John Robins. Includes: 'The Return of Fred Scuttle' and 'The Underworld Water of Jacques Custard'.

The Benny Hill Show. Thames Television, Wednesday 23 December 1970, 8–9 p.m. Starring BENNY HILL. With NICHOLAS PARSONS, TRISHA NOBLE.

Guests: LIZ FRASER, THE LADYBIRDS, JACK WRIGHT, TOMMY MANN, SUE BOND, JAN BUTLIN, KAY FRAZER, CHARMAINE SEAL. Script and original songs: Benny Hill. Musical Director: Ronnie Aldrich. Musical Associate: Syd Lucas. Designer: Tony Borer. Directed and produced by John Robins. Includes: Fred Scuttle as a cut-price holiday tycoon.

The Benny Hill Show. Thames Television, Wednesday 27 January 1971, 8–9 p.m. Starring BENNY HILL. With NICHOLAS PARSONS, PATRICIA HAYES, RITA WEBB, JENNY LEE-WRIGHT, KIKI DEE, PETTICOAT AND VINE, GEORGE RODERICK, JACK WRIGHT, SUE BOND, LESLEY GOLDIE, MIA MARTIN, PETE O'DELL. Script and original songs: Benny Hill. Musical Director: Ronnie Aldrich. Designer: Tony Borer. Directed and produced by John Robins. Includes: 'Top of the Tops', with Hill's happy hippy interviewed by Nicholas Parsons, and Scuttle as a police spokesman.

The Benny Hill Show. Thames Television, Wednesday 24 February 1971, 8–9 p.m. Starring BENNY HILL. With NICHOLAS PARSONS, NANETTE, BOB TODD, LUIS ALBERTO, DEL PARANA, LOS PARAGUAYOS, JENNY LEE-WRIGHT, LESLEY GOLDIE. Script and original songs: Benny Hill. Musical Director: Ronnie Aldrich. Musical Associate: Syd Lucas. Designer: Tony Borer. Directed and pro-

duced by John Robins. Includes: James Bond spy parody, Scuttle as the curator of an art gallery, Nanette performs her latest recording 'Everybody's Singing, Like Now', and 'Pepys' Diary' reappears for the second time.

The Benny Hill Show. Thames Television, Wednesday 24 March 1971, 8–9 p.m. Starring BENNY HILL. With NICHOLAS PARSONS, ANDRE MELLY, BOB TODD, JACK WRIGHT, THE LADYBIRDS, BETTINE LE BEAU, JENNY LEE-WRIGHT, LESLIE GOLDIE, SUE BOND. Script and original songs: Benny Hill. Musical Director: Ronnie Aldrich. Designer: Tony Borer. Directed and produced by John Robins. Supermarket ballet sketch choreographed by Johnny Greenland. Includes: a resurrection of Hill's classic 1960s hit, 'The Egg Marketing Board Tango'.

The Benny Hill Show (repeat season): Thames Television, Saturday, 9.30–10.30 p.m. 23 October 1971 (repeat of 23/12/70), 30 October 1971 (repeat of 27/1/71), 6 November 1971 (repeat of 24/2/71), 13 November 1971 (repeat of 24/3/71), 20 November 1971 (repeat of 25/12/69).

The Benny Hill Show. Thames Television, Wednesday 24 November 1971, 8–9 p.m. Starring BENNY HILL. With HENRY McGEE, ANDREE MELLY, BOB TODD, JENNY LEE-WRIGHT, THE LADYBIRDS, JERROLD WELLS, CAROL MILLS, JOSE STEW-

Self deluding authority - A Scuttle variation with ever patient Nicholas Parsons .

Opposite: **The Thames dream comedy line-up: Robin Nedwell, Benny Hill and Richard O'Sullivan promise to deliver the laughter you are after! Look-In magazine cover**

ART, MARILYN RICKARD, BETTINE LE BEAU, JACK WRIGHT, BELLA EMBERG, CONNIE GEORGES, LILLIAN PADMORE, BRIAN NOLAN, YVONNE PAUL, MIA MARTIN, DAVID WATERMAN, VIC TAYLOR, DENNIS PLENTY. Script and original songs: Benny Hill. Musical Director: Ronnie Aldrich. Musical Associate: Syd Lucas. Designers: Norman Garwood and Tony Borer. Directed and produced by David Bell. Includes: Hill as Chow Mein and a Frenchman, a look at cinema, and antics with a camera-festooned American tourist.

The Benny Hill Show. Thames Television, Wednesday 22 December 1971, 8–9 p.m. Starring BENNY HILL. With NICHOLAS PARSONS, BOB TODD, RITA WEBB, CLOVISSA NEWCOMBE, THE LADYBIRDS, KAY FRAZER, BETTINA LE BEAU, RONNIE BRODY, CAROL MILLS, JOHNNY GREENLAND, MIA MARTIN, JOHN TRAYHORN. Script

and original songs: Benny Hill. Musical Director: Ronnie Aldrich. Designer: Tony Borer. Produced and directed by David Bell. Includes: The Ladybirds singing 'Say a Little Prayer'.

By 1971, Benny Hill was quite clearly the country's biggest comedy star, with his Thames Christmas Special watched in an estimated 8,550,000 homes and ranking as the season's most watched programme. Even Morecambe and Wise, at the height of their powers for Bill Cotton over on BBC1, couldn't outdo Hill, and indeed, Benny's 1971 award for Funniest Person on Television beat them and fellow nominees The Two Ronnies and Dick Emery. Wendy Craig's embodiment of sitcom niceties gained her the position of Funniest Woman, but it was always clear that Hill was the kingpin of British light entertainment. His show won three of the British Screen and Television Awards, held at the Albert Hall, including Best Light Entertainment Programme, and most importantly to Hill, Best Scriptwriter. Vindicated, he naturally continued to dish out more of the same. His face again adorned *TV Times* (18–24 March 1972, photograph by Ron McFarlane), he allowed a brief investigation of his years of struggle in the article 'Turning Point – The Day Benny Quit ... and Bought a Ticket to Stardom', and cheerfully welcomed back his first Thames producer, John Robins.

The Benny Hill Show. Thames Television, Wednesday 23 February 1972, 8–9 p.m. Starring BENNY HILL. With HENRY McGEE, PAULA WILCOX, BOB TODD, PERCY THROWER, SYLVIA McNEIL, THE LADYBIRDS, JENNY LEE-WRIGHT, BETTINE LE BEAU, CAROL MILLS, PENNY MEREDITH, JACK WRIGHT, JIM TYSON, ROY SCAMMELL, MALCOLM WEAVER, GERALDINE BURNETT, MIA MARTIN, KEVIN O'LEARY. Script and original songs: Benny Hill. Musical Director: Ronnie Aldrich. Musical Associate: Syd Lucas. Designer: Tony Borer. Produced and directed by John Robins. Includes: Sylvia McNeil's singing interlude and 'Fred Scuttle's Health and Keep Fit Group'.

The Benny Hill Show. Thames Television, Wednesday 22 March 1972, 8–9 p.m. Starring BENNY HILL. With NICHOLAS PARSONS, BOB TODD, ZIENIA MERTON, THE LADYBIRDS, JENNY LEE-WRIGHT, LESLEY GOLDIE, CAROL MILLS, PENNY MEREDITH, JACK WRIGHT, JIM TYSON, PAMELA CUNDELL, YVONNE PAUL, GERALDINE BURNETT, VERNE MORGAN, JOSIE

STEWART, BRIAN NOLAN, ROBERT HOWE. Script and original songs: Benny Hill. Musical Director: Ronnie Aldrich. Musical Associate: Syd Lucas. Designer: Tony Borer. Hospital ballet choreographed by Johnny Greenland. Produced and directed by John Robins. Includes: 'A Revelation ... Chow Mein Has a Wife', played by Zienia Merton, and a look at Hill's comical world of children.

The Benny Hill Show – repeat season: Thames Television, Friday 25 August 1972, 8–9 p.m. (repeat of 24/11/71), Friday 1 September 1972, 8–9 p.m. (repeat of 22/12/71), Saturday 8 September 1972, 8–9 p.m. (repeat of 23/2/72), Saturday 15 September 1972, 8–9 p.m. (repeat of 22/3/72).

The Benny Hill Show. Thames Television, Wednesday 25 October 1972, 8–9 p.m. Starring BENNY HILL. With HUGH PADDICK, BOB TODD, THE LADYBIRDS, THE MIKE SAMMES SINGERS, JACK WRIGHT, BETTINA LE BEAU. Script and original songs: Benny Hill. Musical Director: Ronnie Aldrich. Designer: Roger Allan. Directed and produced by Keith Beckett. Includes: a 'Woodstock'-style pop festival freakout for old age pensioners, and Hill performing both sides of his new record release, 'The Dustbins of My Mind'/'Fad-Eyed Fal'.

The Benny Hill Show. Thames Television, Wednesday 27 December 1972, 8–9 p.m. Starring BENNY HILL. With NICHOLAS PARSONS, BOB TODD, JIMMY THOMPSON, DIANA KING, PAT ASHTON, JENNY LEE-WRIGHT, JACK WRIGHT, THE LADYBIRDS, WALTER GOODMAN. Script and original songs: Benny Hill. Musical Director: Ronnie Aldrich. Musical Associate: Syd Lucas. Designers: Neville Green and Darnell Lass. Produced and directed by Keith Beckett. Includes: a visit to the Funboy Club with Fred Scuttle's commissionaire interviewed by Nicholas Parsons, and the musical number 'Common Market Square Dance'.

The Benny Hill Show. Thames Television, Thursday 22 February 1973, 9–10 p.m. Starring BENNY HILL. With HENRY McGEE, BOB TODD, PAT ASHTON, THE LADYBIRDS, THE ORANGE BLOSSOM SOUND, JACK WRIGHT. Script and original songs: Benny Hill. Musical Director: Ronnie Aldrich. Musical Associate: Syd Lucas. Designers: Neville Green and Darrell Lass. Programme Associate: Dennis Kirkland.

Directed and produced by Keith Beckett. Includes: Scuttle as a security guard, Chow Mein as an interpreter and a guide to package tours.

The Benny Hill Show. Thames Television, Thursday 29 March 1973, 9–10 p.m. Starring BENNY HILL. With HENRY McGEE, BOB TODD, LEE GIBSON, JON JON KEEFE, TRUDI VAN DOORN, JACK WRIGHT, THE LADYBIRDS. Script and original songs: Benny Hill. Musical Director: Ronnie Aldrich. Musical Associate: Ted Taylor. Designers: Bill Palmer and Darrell Lass. Directed and produced by Peter Frazer-Jones. Includes: solicitor Fred Scuttle is called to the bar, the musical delights of a railway porter choir, western antics with Deputy Hill, McGee's Fiery Fred and Todd's Desperate Dave, plus poets' corner.

Churning out an irregular but extremely popular stream of hour-long specials, totally in tune with the gloriously smutty philosophy of his comic world and surrounded by a hand-picked collection of acting colleagues, Hill may have been at his zenith, but still 'the girls' seemed to be the focus for any critique of his success. In a March 1973 piece for *TV Times*, photographer Dave Lanning skilfully filled his three-page spread of Hill girls 'Cheryl [Gilham], Laraine [Humphries], Jenny [Lee-Wright], Helli [Louise] & Sue [Bond] ... All Benny's birds ... and Trudi [Van Doorn] makes six ...' with some of the raunchiest poses imaginable.

Displaying double standards that would later become all too familiar, the piece hinted at sexism in Hill's comedy. A black and white picture of Hill peers and leers in the girls' direction, and although the 'Programme Planner' image is from an earlier Thames sketch, there's no avoiding the fact that the comedian is depicted as a Svengali-like figure, controlling his comic harem with a self-satisfied grin on his face. The image was a clever and comically geared interpretation of what made *The Benny Hill Show* great, and Hill wasn't denying anything. Why should he? Maybe his shows were becoming predictable, it was almost a guarantee that Chow Mein would crop up somewhere, and Scuttle's beloved 'Yeth Thir!' would accompany a juddering salute, but the audience loved it. Indeed, although his hour-long specials were being screened much more frequently than would be the case later, the nation's feelings were summed up in a letter written by Mrs B.L. Foster of Southend (*TV Times*, 26 January–1 February 1974), stating: 'He is so entertaining that I cannot imagine how anyone could tire of a diet of non-stop Benny Hill every night of the week.'

With Hill as cover star for *TV Times* yet again (he was 'ITV Minstrel 1974 in the Style of Benny Hill' for 2–8 February 1974, and once more in familiar Scuttle mode – 'Good Evening Viewers' for the 24–30 May 1975 issue), his image was guaranteed to excite anticipation in the audience. Indeed, as one of the linchpins in the Thames canon, Hill was embraced as a comic strip favourite for *Look-In* magazine. Billed as 'The Junior TV Times', it was Hill's second taste of cartoon stardom, having scored a hit during the late 1950s in *Radio Fun*.

The *Look-In* strips usually concentrated on the manic antics of Fred Scuttle or highlighted the misadventures of Hill's historic ancestors from stone age man via roundheads and onwards – like Blackadder without the bite. In a magazine which was essential playground reading, Hill's section also cast him as the lisping anti-hero Captain Scuttle, in response to David Jason's vintage character, Captain Fantastic. His life story in words and pictures, 'The Fastest Milkman: The Benny Hill Story' (mainly an interview discussing his extensive foreign travel), was featured in the 1975 *Look-In TV Comedy Annual* (published by Independent Television Books), and by the following year, his regular strip, 'The Benny Hill Page' by Andy Christine, was the magazine's prize attraction.

Back in mainstream television land and the pages of *TV Times* itself, Hill was still a major player on ITV, highlighted as part of 'The Big Season' in the edition of 30 August – 5 September 1975, caricatured by Stephen Nemethy alongside those other comic powerhouses Michael Bentine and Tommy Cooper, feted as cover star ('Benny Rides Again', 13–19 December 1975) for his new show of the season, and again ('Making You Laugh Can be Murder' – employing a gun-to-the-head image from his Casanova sketch) during World Cup 1978 fever. Although he was interviewed about football, giving a nod to his home team of Southampton, admitting to childhood allegiance alternating between Chelsea and Fulham, and even relating the time he visited the Penang Cup Final in Singapore, the fact remains that *The Benny Hill Show* dominated the football-obsessed month.

Hill's well-known love of travel and independence was shamelessly employed in the February 1974 *TV Times* 'Roger Elliot Predicts' piece, which risked its reputation by daringly proclaiming that Hill was someone who liked travel and independence. Early 1970s travel also brought Hill peace of mind. On 23 June 1971, he had taken his father on holiday in Spain. The two had enjoyed each

other's company, seen all the sights that the star son had seen before, and settled their differences without having to discuss them. Hill's father died shortly afterwards.

The Benny Hill Show. Thames Television, Thursday 5 July 1973, 9–10 p.m. Starring BENNY HILL. With HUGH PADDICK, BOB TODD, THE LADY-BIRDS, THE MIKE SAMMES SINGERS, JACK WRIGHT, BETTINE LE BEAU. Script and original songs: Benny Hill. Musical Director: Ronnie Aldrich. Designer: Roger Allen. Directed and produced by Keith Beckett. Includes: the pop festival to end all pop festivals (not again, Ben!).

The Benny Hill Show. Thames Television, Wednesday 5 December 1973, 8–9 p.m. Starring BENNY HILL. With HENRY McGEE, BOB TODD, LESLEY GOLDIE, LOS ZAFIROS, BERRY CORNISH, KAY FRAZER, JACK WRIGHT, NICOLE SHELBY, BELLA EMBERG, BARBARA WISE, JIM TYSON, JOHNNY GREENLAND, JON JON KEEFE. Script and original songs: Benny Hill. Musical Director: Albert

Pure Scuttle.

Elms. Musical Associate: Ted Taylor. Designer: Tony Borer. Directed and produced by John Robins. Includes: songs from Los Zafiros and Berry Cornish.

The Benny Hill Show. Thames Television, Thursday 27 December 1973, 9–10 p.m. Starring BENNY HILL. With HENRY McGEE, ANDREE MELLY, BOB TODD, ANNE SHELTON, THE LADYBIRDS, LESLEY GOLDIE, BELLA EMBERG, JACK WRIGHT, MALOU CARTWRIGHT, JON JON KEEFE, CAROLE JOHN BALL. Script and original songs: Benny Hill. Musical Director: Albert Elms. Musical Associate: Ted Taylor. Designer: Tony Borer. Directed and produced by John Robins. Includes: a vintage disappearance case performed in handed-down rhyme and in the style of popular television, Anne Shelton sings 'Galilee Song', and Scuttle lectures on the Channel tunnel.

The Benny Hill Show. Thames Television, Thursday 7 February 1974, 8.30–9.30 p.m. Starring BENNY HILL. With HENRY McGEE, BOB TODD, LESLEY GOLDIE, DESIGN, DIANA DARVEY, DAVID HAMILTON. Script and original songs: Benny Hill. Musical Director: Albert Elms. Designer: Tony Borer. Directed and produced by John Robins. Includes: musical numbers from Design and Diana Darvey, Darvey and Hill recreate the classic *Baby Doll* scenario.

The Benny Hill Show. Thames Television, Wednesday 13 March 1974, 8-9 p.m. Starring BENNY HILL. With NICHOLAS PARSONS, BOB TODD, DIANA DARVEY. Guests: JUDITH DURHAM AND THE HOTTEST BAND IN TOWN, THE LADYBIRDS, JACK WRIGHT, BELLA EMBERG, JERROLD WELLS. Script and original songs: Benny Hill. Musical Director: Ronnie Aldrich. Musical Associate: Ted Taylor. Designer: Tony Borer. Director Mark Stuart.

The Benny Hill Show (repeat season): Thames Television, Friday 19 July, 1974 8–9 p.m. (repeat of 27/12/72), 26 July 1974, 8–9 p.m. (repeat of 29/3/73), 2 August 1974, 8–9 p.m. (repeat of 29/3/73, the same as previous week's repeat billed in *Radio Times*; if this was a transcription error, it's likely that 05/7/73 was screened in the time slot), 9 August 1974, 8–9 p.m. (repeat of 5/12/73), 16 August 1974, 8–9 p.m. (repeat of 7/2/74), 23 August 1974, 8–9 p.m. (repeat of 13/3/74), 30 August 1974, 9–10 p.m. (repeat of 27/12/73)

The Benny Hill Show. Thames Television, Wednesday 8

January 1975, 8–9 p.m. Starring BENNY HILL. With HENRY McGEE, BOB TODD, STELLA MORAY, LEE GIBSON, DIANA DARVEY, JACK WRIGHT, SAMANTHA STEVENS, BILL WESTON, YVONNE DEARMAN, ANNE BRUZAC. Script and original songs: Benny Hill. Musical Director: Ronnie Aldrich. Musical Associate: Ted Taylor. Designer: Bill Palmer. Producer: Mark Stuart. Includes: Kung Fu sketch – Kwai Chang.

The Benny Hill Show. Thames Television, Wednesday 12 March 1975, 8–9 p.m. Starring BENNY HILL. With HENRY McGEE, BOB TODD, PATRICK NEWELL, ANNA DAWSON, DIANA DARVEY, LEE GIBSON, JACK WRIGHT, SAMANTHA STEVENS, EARL ADAIR, BILL WESTON, YVONNE DEARMAN. Script and original songs: Benny Hill. Musical Director: Ronnie Aldrich. Musical Associate: Ted Taylor. Designers: Bill Palmer and Darrell Lass. Producer: Mark Stuart. Includes: Chow Mein, more martial arts with 'Kung Phooie', Scuttle as a TV director, 'Orson Buggy presents "The Catch" in The Orson Buggy Mysteries'.

The Benny Hill Show. Thames Television, Monday 26 May 1975, 8.30–9.30 p.m. Starring BENNY HILL. With HENRY McGEE, STELLA MORAY, DON ESTELLE, EDDIE BUCHANAN, CHERYL GILHAM, MOIRA FOOT, LIBBY ROBERTS, DEBBIE GREENHILL, JEANNIE COLLINGS. Script: Benny Hill. Musical Director: Ronnie Aldrich. Musical Associate: Ted Taylor. Designer: Mike Hall. Directed and produced by Ronald Fouracre. Includes: 'Lana's Performing Males', talent show *New Faces* discovery Eddie Buchanan sings 'Going Nowhere' – and did!

The Benny Hill Show, Thames Television, Bank Holiday Monday 25 August 1975, 8–9 p.m. Starring BENNY HILL. With HENRY McGEE, BOB TODD, STELLA MORAY, LEE GIBSON, DIANA DARVEY. Script: Benny Hill. Musical Director: Ronnie Aldrich. Musical Associate: Ted Taylor. Designer: Mike Hall. Directed and produced by Ronald Fouracre. Includes: the return of Fred Forsythe Scuttle, Hill as composer Gavin Blod, and the talent show parody, 'Newer Faces'.

The Benny Hill Show. Thames Television, Wednesday 24 September 1975, 8–9 p.m. Starring BENNY HILL. With HENRY McGEE, STELLA MORAY, DON ESTELLE, EDDIE BUCHANAN, CHERYL GILHAM, MOIRA FOOT, LIBBY ROBERTS, DEB-

BIE GREENHILL, JEANNIE COLLINGS. Script: Benny Hill. Musical Director: Ronnie Aldrich. Musical Associate: Ted Taylor. Designer: Mike Hall. Directed and produced by Ronald Fouracre. Includes: Hill as pop idol Tex Cymbal, Golden Boy doing the television rounds with appearances on the 'Parking Space' show and 'The Old Grey Whistle Tester', Hill as mum in a spoof on the fly-on-the wall documentary *The Family*, and of course, Fred Scuttle.

The Benny Hill Show (repeat before the big James Bond film *Dr No*): Thames Television, Tuesday 28 October 1975, 7–8 p.m. (repeat of 12/3/75).

The Benny Hill Show: Thames Television, Wednesday 17 December 1975, 8–9 p.m. Starring BENNY HILL. With HENRY McGEE, JACK WRIGHT, DILYS WATLING, EDDIE BUCHANAN, CLARE RUANE, LORNA NATHAN, LEANNE ROBINSON, JENNY WESTBROOK. Script: Benny Hill. Musical Director: Ronnie Aldrich. Musical Associate: Ted Taylor. Designer: David Marshall. Directed and produced by Mark Stuart. Includes: Dilys Watling sings 'That Ain't No Way to Treat a Lady', Hill as Meg Richardson from the soap *Crossroads*, and Scuttle the mindreader.

Promoting his 1976 season, Benny Hill promised his familiar format would be enhanced by new, dangerous satire, including a vicious parody of Edward Heath. In the end, that sort of thing was best left to Mike Yarwood, and audience figures were so impressive that during the late 1970s, nothing about the show was altered. With his collection of comedy experts in tow, Hill successfully rehashed every old visual gag in the book, reshaping and rearranging material picked up from across the world, and making the familiar but still funny struggle between the sexes the heart of his work. Hill's businessman getting an eyeful of young thigh was always funny, and the shows fell into an unshakeable pattern.

Beginning with Hill's musical number, populated with eccentric, sex-obsessed figures and overloaded with glamorous girls, *The Benny Hill Show* became as much part of the ITV holiday season as James Bond and *Digby – The Biggest Dog in the World*. Influenced by American television's *Rowan & Martin's Laugh-In*, which revisited all the corny gags from vaudeville, Hill continued his obsession with wordplay and quickfire, corny one-liners on a common theme, emulating the *Laugh-In* joke wall with unsubtle graffiti quips, as well as increasingly groanworthy exchanges such as 'How did you come to break your leg?' – 'I didn't come to break my leg, I came to mend the roof!' or 'I gave my secretary the sack. She said, "I'll do anything if you'll forgive me." So I forgave her four times!' and desperate visual gags, such as the one-armed bandit that aims a revolver at Benny's gambler. However, even this mostly barrel-scraping material was given an endearing edge via Hill's cheery delivery, and when the creative juices were really flowing, few could be funnier or more clever.

Fresh characters for his Thames years included the immediately popular Chinese character, Chow Mein, whose crude grasp on the English language led to myriad hilarious, unintentionally outrageous-sounding conversations (at their best opposite the shocked bumbling of Bob Todd's Indian waiter). Famously, Hill wrote the original Chow Mein script on the back of some launderette shirt-back stiffener cardboard, and posted the almost illegible jottings to the production office. It was ages before Kirkland, Robins and personal assistant Rennie Bloomsteen finally realized that this rubbish about 'Sirry iriot!' and the like was to be delivered by an Oriental character.

Hill delighted in wordplay, and later accusations of racism in this portrayal were countered with the observation that it's the British people who are mocked because

they misunderstand this Chinaman's delivery of the language – after all, how many of us can speak Mandarin as well as Mein speaks English? Besides, if it was funny, it was in the show. Obsessed with the use of language and delighting in spoonerisms, malapropisms and every other ism, Hill continually peppered his Scuttle and other bumbling sketches with lines like 'How can you define the intangerine?' to great effect.

His comedy was straight out of Joe Miller's bottom-drawer book and Max Miller's blue book, but Hill was an assured ratings winner for the family audience of ITV, and whether it be one of countless gangsters, cowboys or corny songs, his humour delivered the goods. From Fred Scuttle struggling through an interview with Henry McGee to the wild-haired, bewigged madrigal singer Herbert Fudge, Benny Hill was very much part of the fabric of the British way of life. Although mime had become central to his work, the Max Miller influence was still very potent – not least in his Miller impersonation from 1977, complete with saucy song and eager 'Here's another!' interjections. Clearly, Hill was in nostalgic mood during 1977, since his show also included a spot of Punch and Judy – typically baiting those who labelled him sexist when a gorgeous girl changed in his booth. In 1979, in a saucy take on Ronnie Barker's tongue-twisting sermons, Hill recited the poem 'Faith, Hope and Charity', as it was originally written twenty years before, as if produced on a typewriter with no letter H. Contrived, predictable but always hilarious, Hill's chirpy delivery is a master class in comedy performance, with the likes of 'Tuesday, Marc the Tird' building up to the almighty laugh on 'O, sit! ...' addressed to his dog. That innocence lurking behind the dubious is pure Hill genius.

By 1979, he was very much part of the Thames furniture, posing with his girls with *Minder* star Dennis Waterman and adding to his packed trophy cupboard – BAFTAs for Best Light Entertainment Programme/Light Entertainment Production and Design (1972), a CRAFT Award for Best Script, a Variety Club of Great Britain, the Radio Industries Club Award, and ITV Personality of the Year for 1976. That same year, he was voted The Funniest Man on TV in The *TV Times* Awards (Yootha Joyce picked up Funniest Woman for the sitcom *George and Mildred*), he repeated the feat in 1977, and was inducted into Television's Hall of Fame in 1978.

The Benny Hill Show. Thames Television, Wednesday 18 February 1976, 8–9 p.m. Starring BENNY HILL. With HENRY McGEE, JACK WRIGHT, EDDIE BUCHANAN, LOVE MACHINE, MOIRA FOOT. Script and original songs: Benny Hill. Musical Director:

Ronnie Aldrich. Musical Associate: Ted Taylor. Designers: David Marshall and Norman Garwood. Directed and produced by Mark Stuart. Includes: a spoof of *World of Sport* – Hill appears as host Dickie Davies, a weight-lifter, a cyclist and myriad other sportsmen – and Moira Foot as historic sexpots Delilah, Salome et al.

The Benny Hill Show. Thames Television, Wednesday 24 March 1976, 8.30–9.30 p.m. Starring BENNY HILL. With HENRY McGEE, BOB TODD, JACK WRIGHT, BRENDA ARNAU, EDDIE BUCHANAN, JENNY LEE-WRIGHT, LEANNE ROBINSON, MONICA RINGWALD. Script and original songs: Benny Hill. Musical Director: Ronnie Aldrich. Musical Associate: Ted Taylor. Designers: Mike Hall and David Marshall. Directed and produced by Mark Stuart. Includes: 'Murder on the Oregon Express' with Hill brilliant as multiple TV detectives (McCloud, Ironside, Cannon, Poirot and Kojak), Hill and Todd as Fanee and Jonee Claddock, a rousing Robin Hood adventure, Brenda Arnau sings 'Tell it Like it is').

The Benny Hill Show. Thames Television, Wednesday 21 April 1976, 8–9 p.m. Starring BENNY HILL. With PAUL EDDINGTON, JACK WRIGHT, EDDIE

Bob Todd and Benny Hill
Chinese banter for *The Benny Hill Show*, February 1973.

counteract hunger with appetite-curbing amphetamines. It is believed this behaviour worsened his kidney problem. Also, following his father's death in 1972, Hill's beloved mother passed away peacefully at her Southampton home on 10 February 1976. True to her wishes, Hill never sold the family home.

The Benny Hill Show. Thames Television, Wednesday 26 January 1977, 8–9 p.m. Starring BENNY HILL. With RITA WEBB, HENRY McGEE, JACK WRIGHT, JENNY LEE-WRIGHT, REFLECTIONS, EDDIE BUCHANAN, DIANA DARVEY, SUE UPTON. Script and original songs: Benny Hill. Musical Director: Ronnie Aldrich. Musical Associate: Ted Taylor. Designer: Peter Le Page. Directed and produced by Mark Stuart. Includes: a number from Reflections, a female singing group which featured familiar Hill girl Linda Robinson (in this edition playing Joanna Lumley's Purdy in a classic *New Avengers* parody, Hill, of course, playing Patrick Macnee's Steed, while, rather more surprisingly, little Jackie Wright portrayed the macho power of Gareth Hunt's Gambit), parodies of *Mastermind* and *I, Claudius* plus 'Bionic Baby' – addressing the influx of US import fantasies such as *The Six Million Dollar Man* and *The Bionic Woman*.

The Benny Hill Show. Thames Television, Wednesday 23 February 1977, 8–9 p.m. Starring BENNY HILL. With HENRY McGEE, JACK WRIGHT, RITA WEBB, EDDIE BUCHANAN, LOVE MACHINE, JENNY LEE-WRIGHT. Script and original songs: Benny Hill. Musical Director: Ronnie Aldrich. Musical Associate: Ted Taylor. Designer: Tony Borer. Directed and produced by Mark Stuart. Includes: a *Starsky and Hutch* parody.

The Benny Hill Show. Thames Television, Wednesday 23 March 1977, 8–9 p.m. Starring BENNY HILL. With HENRY McGEE, RITA WEBB, DILYS WATLING, JACK WRIGHT, EDDIE BUCHANAN, FROGGY, SUZY MANDEL, KEN SEDD, ELLIE REECE-KNIGHT, PENNY RIGDEN. Script and original songs: Benny Hill. Musical Director: Ronnie Aldrich. Musical Associate: Ted Taylor. Designer: Tony Borer. Directed and produced by Mark Stuart. Includes: Chinese package holidays with Chow Mein, Casanova –

BUCHANAN, SUSIE BAKER, LOVE MACHINE, BELLA EMBERG, KEN SEDD. Script and original songs: Benny Hill. Musical Director: Ronnie Aldrich. Musical Associate: Ted Taylor. Designer: Rod Stratford. Directed and produced by Mark Stuart. Includes: 'Sale of the Half Century', 'Moving' On', 'Top of the Pops', 'Who's Afraid of Virgin Wool?', Eddie Buchanan and Love Machine perform the musical number 'Dancing in the Nude'...Quite!

The Benny Hill Show (repeat season): Thames Television, Wednesday 4 August 1976, 8–9 p.m. (repeat of 24/9/75), Wednesday 25 August 1976, 8–9 p.m. (repeat of 17/12/75), Thursday 9 September 1976, 8–9 p.m. (repeat of 18/2/76), Wednesday 6 October 1976, 8–9 p.m. (repeat of 24/3/76), Wednesday 13 October 1976, 8–9 p.m. (repeat of 21/4/76).

Although it was never apparent in his work, during 1976 Benny Hill was plagued with health problems and emotional strain. Continually putting off all matters medical if it would disrupt the smooth running of the show, Hill finally had a kidney removed in 1976. With a passion for losing weight and depicting himself on screen as the lean, mean comedy machine he had always been in his dreams, Hill would deny himself food for days, eat to excess and with Jack Wright's naked chest bearing the legend 'Betty May', while Hill's cheekily reads 'Freda Does'.

The Benny Hill Show (repeat season): Thames Television, Wednesday, 8–9 p.m., 7 September 1977 (repeat of 26/1/77), 14 September 1977 (repeat of 23/2/77), 2 November 1977 (repeat of 23/3/77)

The Best of Benny Hill

This vintage compilation of Hill's greatest bits, including Hurricane Hill (read snooker champ Hurricane Higgins) in 'Spot Black', wrestling and the bizarre tale of Fam and Fufan, is a celebration of his Thames material, mostly from his earliest years with them.

The Best of Benny Hill: Thames Television, Boxing Day, 26 December 1977, 8.30–9.30 p.m. Starring BENNY HILL. With BOB TODD, NICHOLAS PARSONS, HENRY McGEE, JACK WRIGHT, LESLEY GOLDIE, TOMMY MANN, THE LADYBIRDS.

Folk circuit comedians like Billy Connolly and Jasper Carrott were now getting their own ITV specials, newcomers and world-beaters like Rowan Atkinson and Lenny Henry were making their mark, Jim Davidson, Michael Barrymore and Pauline Quirke were breaking through, and veteran comic heroes like Les Dawson, Tommy Cooper, Morecambe and Wise, Eric Sykes and Frankie Howerd were more frequently gracing British television screens.

Hill's policy of restricting himself to only a handful of shows a year was coming perilously close to backfiring – for the next few years, his shows were even less frequent, and Thames failed to help keep his face on screen by abandoning their usual repeat screenings. His usual quiet Christmas at home, alone, would involve continual television-watching, but when by 1978 his prime Thames position had been usurped by the Magnificent Two – Morecambe and Wise – Hill contributed, without bitterness, to the seasonal *TV Times*, quoted on the Boxing Day pages as eager to settle down for the festivities, 'watching Eric and Ernie on Christmas Day and my own show today'.

Benny Hill Down Under

Hill's Thames shows had proved huge ratings winners in Australia, so, like Frankie Howerd, Peter Cook and Dudley Moore and many other British comic greats, he decided to give his audience down under an hour-long show tailor-made for them, using an Australian cast and crew, and filmed in and around Sydney. This explains the lack of much new Hill material on ITV during this time – indeed, apart from the Christmas 1977 compilation, this was his first new television special in just over a year. Hill's Australian connections stretched back to the days when he first met actress Anette Andre, and his sister Diana and brother-in-law Noel now lived in Swan Hill, Victoria, but he didn't visit them.

Hill resurrected beloved old favourites like Scuttle, Chow Mein and, yes, even dear old Ernie the milkman for this special, but he also served up Benny Kelly, son of infamous Australian outlaw Ned Kelly. The scenario involving nubile, naked girls in the shower distracting Hill so much that he beats the flowers off his grandmother's carpet is definitive late 1970s Hill material. A *TV Times* interview ('Boomerang Benny' by Alan Ken) was, as usual, girl-obsessed, hinting that the Australian actresses were running around naked most of the time, and that he had a different squadron of girls in every port across the globe.

Benny Hill Down Under: First broadcast in Australia, 11 October 1977. Wednesday 12 April 1978, 8–9 p.m. Written and performed by BENNY HILL.
The Benny Hill Show: Thames Television, Tuesday 30 May 1978, 8–9 p.m. Starring BENNY HILL. With HENRY McGEE, JACK WRIGHT, CHARLES STAPLEY, DEE DEE DARLINGTON, EUNICE BLACK, JILLIANE FOOT, DENISE BROWNLOW, DONNA SCARFF, THE COTTON MILL BOYS, JENNY WESTBROOK, FRANK CODYA, PENNY CHISHOLM, KENNETH SEDD. Script and original songs: Benny Hill. Musical Director: Ronnie Aldrich. Musical Associate: Ted Taylor. Designer: Robin Parker. Produced and directed by Keith Beckett. Includes: more Scuttle, 'South Blank Show', The Cotton Mill Boys perform 'Orange Blossom Special', Australian detective Digger Blue (obviously a left-over from the Australian special), Hill plays Irish harp for his parody of Mary O'Hara, learned for a 1960 show with long time friends Dorita y Pepe of the nightclub The Blue Angel.

The Benny Hill Show (repeat): Thames Television, Wednesday 13 September 1978, 8–9 p.m. (repeat of 30/5/78)

The Benny Hill Show: Thames Television, Boxing Day 1978, 7.15–8.15 p.m. Starring BENNY HILL. With HENRY McGEE, JENNY LEE-WRIGHT, FELICITY

BUIRSKI, JOHN QUAYLE, CYRIL CROSS, JOHN-NY VYVYAN, EDDIE CONNOR, LEN KEYES, STEPHANIE LAWRENCE, ERICA LUDLOW, LOUISE ENGLISH, SUE UPTON, SUE BOND, TINA BOND, MANDY PENNYMENT, VICTORIA SHELLARD. Script and original songs: Benny Hill. Musical Director: Ronnie Aldrich. Musical Associate: Ted Taylor. Choreography: Samantha Stevens. Designer: Michael Minas. Directed and produced by Ronald Fouracre. Includes: Professor Marvo and his naked models, Felicity Buirski making her television debut, Hill as Wild Jack McCraw and Fred Scuttle.

The Benny Hill Show. Thames Television, Wednesday 14 March 1979, 8–9 p.m. Starring BENNY HILL. With HENRY McGEE, JACK WRIGHT, JENNY LEE-WRIGHT, GERALDINE, JOHNNY VYVYAN, SUE UPTON. Special guest: PATRICIA HAYES. Script and original songs: Benny Hill. Musical Director: Ronnie Aldrich. Choreography: Dee Dee Wilde. Designer: Robin Tarsnane. Produced and directed by Dennis Kirkland. Includes: 'Leprechaun TV' with Wondergran and Hot Gossamer, National Health antics told through speeded-up film (yet again), Irish singer Geraldine does a turn.

The Benny Hill Show. Thames Television, Wednesday 25 April 1979, 8–9 p.m. Starring BENNY HILL. With HENRY McGEE, JACKIE WRIGHT, HELEN HORTON, ROGER FINCH, ANIKA PAVEL, PAN'S PEOPLE. Script and original songs: Benny Hill. Musical Director: Ronnie Aldrich. Produced and directed by Dennis Kirkland. Includes: Hill as jazz singer Cleo Laine, Kojak, Esther Rantzen, a parody of the big ITV imported American 'Best Sellers' dramas, the comic side of TV festivals and Pan's People gyrate to 'Love for Sale'.

The Benny Hill Show (repeat season): Thames Television, Wednesday 20 June 1979 (repeat of 26/12/78), Wednesday 1 August 1979, 8–9 p.m. (repeat of 14/3/79).

BENNY'S SUPPORT

With the Australian show behind him, Hill gratefully returned to the Teddington Studios and the familiar cast of supporting actors he had gathered around him. He instinctively knew the vital importance of his crowd of regular stooges, who became almost as famous as he was.

In many ways, Hill relied on the familiarity of both his fellow performers and the well-known jokes, convinced that if he changed anything, his audience would be disappointed. Like Peter Rogers, he wisely understood the home audience's sense of humour, warming to familiar situations and laughing loudest when the expected, tried and tested sight gag or risqué one-liner was forthcoming.

Jackie Wright, with the most slapped bald head in Britain, was, like Bilko's Doberman, cast for his appearance rather than any great acting ability. One of 12 children, Wright had been a music hall trombonist in the 1930s, playing in 1941 during the only German bombing of Dublin (he frequently joked it was the only time he nearly brought the house down) and frequently figured as a television extra on shows like the police series *Z-Cars*. But it was later that Wright found fame as the non-speaking stooge for everybody from Dick Emery to Frankie Howerd in *Whoops Baghdad!* Hill had first employed him during his latter BBC days, and loved the old trouper's comic expressions, bizarre ad-libs and almost non-acting performances, admitting that he featured in one of the few totally original gags he wrote (the 'secret interview', with Wright's victim inadvertently in the light and Hill's interviewer in the dark). Hill cast Wright as the Moore-Marriott/Harbottle-like figure to his Will Hay in a fireman sketch, and the results were priceless.

Hill saw a refreshing, unpretentiousness about Wright's comedy, and he became a major American cult in his own right. An especially dedicated fan club, run by Christopher S. Hood and Bob Buche of Lowell, Indiana, sprang up, Wright was provisionally offered his own American television series, and Hill was often bombarded with requests for 'the bald guy'. Sadly, he had to retire through ill health in 1984, but Hill insisted on editing in old footage of Wright head slaps just to keep him as part of the team – and more importantly, keep those vital pay cheques coming in for Wright's old age. He died in 1989 at the age of 83 in his home town of Belfast, his 'crumbling old man' characters by then being played by the variety performer Johnny Hutch.

Rita Webb, usually in tow with Jackie Wright, was the perfect comic crone in everything from *Up Pompeii* and *Sykes* to *Confessions of a Pop Performer*, and an inspired skit had Wright and Webb as a newly married couple. While Hill was reluctant to appear on anybody else's shows, the supporting cast were hard at work, and Webb joined Bob Todd in a suitably Hill-like swimming pool sketch on *3-2-1*, while Jenny Lee-Wright and Henry McGee teamed for Norman Wisdom's ITV series *A Little Bit of Wisdom*.

Patricia Hayes, a highly gifted foil to comedy actors

I Can Resist Anything Except Temptation -
Benny indulges his love of chocs.

from Dick Emery to Peter Sellers, was a fixture in Benny Hill's career. The regular sourpuss female on radio's *Benny Hill Time*, she cropped up in many BBC television assignments, and was part of Hill's team when he moved over to Thames. She would probably have remained a familiar team member if she hadn't been offered the starring role in *Edna, The Inebriate Woman*. Hill graciously released her from the Thames contract, saw her accept the BBC film, win the Best Actress BAFTA award and pursue a fulfilling career embracing both serious drama and comedy. She gratefully returned as guest star for one last *Benny Hill Show* in 1979.

Additions to the Hill team came thick and fast during the Thames days: Kathy Staff, a favourite from *Crossroads* and comedy series *Last of the Summer Wine*, nagged for England; Bella Emberg, later to find bigger success with Russ Abbot, personified the dictatorial female, while Jon Jon Keefe, discovered by Hill in the London nightclub The Talk of the Town, was the everyman simpleton from 1974 until the end, greeting life's bizarre situations with a bemused shake of the head. The Ladybirds – Marian Davies, Gloria George and ex-Vernon Girl Maggie Stredder – were the regular backing singers for Hill's greatest flights of fancy during the 1970s. Reaching their peak with choruses of 'Ernie' on Hill's number 1 single, they had previously worked with Rolf Harris, Des O'Connor and Sandie Shaw, performing on her classic Eurovision hit, 'Puppet on a String'.

Nicholas Parsons, who can rightfully claim to be the busiest and most prolific straightman in British comedy, enjoyed a wonderful era with Arthur Haynes, valiantly tried to keep control of Kenneth Williams in the BBC radio panel game *Just a Minute*, found ITV stardom 'live from Norwich' with *Sale of the Century* and effortlessly sent himself up for *The Comic Strip Presents ...* classic *Mr Jolly Lives Next Door*. As a comedy actor, he graced the Sid James heist gem *Too Many Crooks*, flirted with Joan Sims in *Carry On Regardless*, dithered opposite Margaret Rutherford in *Murder, Ahoy!* and turned on the charm for the Boulting's *Brothers-In-Law*. Parsons was called on by Hill to impersonate Eamonn Andrews in a *This Is Your Life* skit. This proved so popular that Parsons was invited back for another 'Eamonn' slot, in which guest victim Robertson Hare was stuck with Hill's Fred Scuttle, who has no memories of who Hare is or what he's done. Having met Hill during a charity show at the Prince of Wales Theatre in the 1960s, Parsons happily performed his comic routine to cover for Hill in one stage assignment when he was suffering from tonsilitis, and eventually became a regular supercilious, upper-crust stooge during the 1970s.

Helen Horton was often cast as the typically downbeat British wife, memorably playing Miriam to Hill's hen-pecked Barney. A later valued asset was Anna Dawson, best remembered for playing Jack Warner's daughter in *Dixon of Dock Green*. Having cropped up opposite Charlie Drake in *Slapstick and Old Lace*, guested on ITV's *Starburst* and appeared with Henry McGee and Hugh Futcher in *Cinderella* at Leatherhead in 1961, she was no stranger to low-brow family entertainment, working brilliantly with Hill on such classics as 'The Love Duet' and the bird sketch during shows of the 1980s. Dawson was to become a frequent supporting player opposite Leslie Crowther in *The Crowther Collection* and *The Dick Emery Show*. However, three faces stand out:

Sue Upton, Henry McGee and Bob Todd.

Sue Upton originally came into *The Benny Hill Show* as part of Love Machine (alongside troupe leader Libby Roberts and Claire Lutter), a sexy dance group which fashioned the style that Hill's Angels would later perfect. Upton was quickly picked out of the line-up and moulded as a supporting actress by Hill. Her comic timing impressed him, and her physical attractiveness exactly fitted the bill. Indeed, an early, very scantily clad *TV Times* publicity shot of Upton probably doubled the audience ratings for that week's show. Married to musician Richard Whatling of Tonix, Upton was, along with Louise English, cited as the most famous Hill's Angel, whereas they were usually credited separately from the rest of the group. Hill was delighted with the actress, developed more character roles for her, and despite her happily claiming the position of 'head girl', moved her career away from glamorous parts when he cast her as an aged superhero, Wondergran, battling Hill's cowardly Count Dracula. Hill's toothy vampire nearly gets hit by a car, finds himself on the wrong side of a belisha beacon and finally succumbs to Upton's dogged old lady. Of all the cast, Hill was closest to Upton, and she was happy to prance along with the other girls or sink her teeth into more meaty comic roles – one of their happiest collaborations being as Laurel and Hardy. As with her Benny Hill assignments, Upton's other credits alternated between the glamorous (*What's Up Superdoc?*) and the unattractive (*Confessions from a Holiday Camp*).

Henry McGee, who had become the successor to Jerry Desmode's perfect type of authoritative stooge, found national television fame as the petulant employment exchange clerk opposite Charlie Drake in *The Worker*, and served similar purposes in farce, *3-2-1*, *Carry On Emmannuelle* and as Richard Bligh in the Lance Percival/Norman Bird sitcom *Up the Workers*, written by Tom Brennard and Roy Bottomley. He found major fame as the bemused feed in the Honey Monster breakfast cereal commercials, and regularly stooged for Hill's old partner, Reg Varney, in his ITV specials, uninventively titled *Reg Varney*. McGee starred with Cilla Black in 1975's *Comedy Six*, and has showbusiness connections reaching back to Kitty Clive, who was part of David Garrick's touring company. His mother, Clarice Batchelor, was a singer, so she was keen to support her son's theatrical ambitions. His father was less impressed. His first stage performance was as a spear carrier in *Comédie Française*, but more typical stage fare would be glorious farces like *Uproar in the House*, *Run for Your Wife* and *One Good Turn*. However, having forged a successful straight acting career on stage

and television (*Z-Cars*), McGee found his mark with straight-faced comic stooging. He had already worked with Benny Hill during the BBC days (as well as appearing in *The Italian Job*, albeit not opposite Hill). Admitting that Hill's timing was quite unique, it took him a good two years to fully settle into his delivery style – eventually, his officious types became an essential part of the programmes.

Finally, Bob Todd, who became almost as comically vital to *The Benny Hill Show* as Benny himself, was an ex-RAF squadron leader and Sussex farmer who fell into acting only to become one of the most familiar comedy character actors in the country. He took to hanging around the BBC corridors looking for work, waiting for Tony Hancock and his team. Although he never got on the show, Ray Galton and Alan Simpson did cast him in their new situation comedy for Sid James and Bill Kerr, *Citizen James*. With featured roles in *Carry On Again Doctor*, *That's Your Funeral*, Hammer's *Scars of Dracula*, *Carry On Again Christmas* and *Confessions of a Pop Performer*, alongside television work in the sitcom *In for a Penny*, *Funny Man* with Jimmy Jewel, *The Marty Feldman Comedy Machine*, *Cooper*, *On the Buses*, *Cribbins* and Spike Milligan's *Q* shows, Todd was convinced he would fit in with *The Benny Hill Show*. Indeed, in an early 1970s interview, Todd linked the two totally different comic talents together: 'I think Benny Hill is a comic genius. He is like Spike Milligan – his mind works in a different way from most people. He has to find some way to make it intelligible. And he finds an outlet in comedy.' Continually writing to the Thames shows producer with no luck, Todd finally accepted defeat, only to be contacted almost immediately with an offer to appear on the show. Todd accepted with gusto, and was rarely out of the Hill family from then on. He would appear in the West End opposite Tommy Steele in *Hans Anderson*, team up with Jack Wright for Jim Davidson's shows and spar with Anna Dawson in *The Steam Video Company*, but for all of them, television with Benny Hill was always best. Delighting the star with his larger-than-life performances, he would often crack Hill up with laughter, particularly when the two hammed it up as bumbling German officers. A classic *Bonanza* skit with Ben as Hoss and Todd as the Indian, and a *Gone With The Wind* parody with Hill as Massa Gaylord/Miss Abigail and Todd as the black servant proved a winning comic partnership. Benny Hill wasn't concerned who got the big laugh – be it Todd, Upton or the Little Angels, the next day everybody would be saying, 'Wasn't Benny Hill funny last night?'

However, this safety curtain of a familiar, loyal team

also made the great comedian lazy. While McGee, and earlier, Parsons, took on the suave interviewer persona of Jeremy Hawk from the BBC era, the multi-character performance of Hill was no longer required. As a rule, he starred in each sketch as just one character, while many other characterizations tailor-made for Hill were played by Bob Todd, thus losing the edge from his comedy and diluting the laughter, turning away from the groundbreaking technique of split-screen performance and allowing Hill to rest on his laurels while the team filled the gaps.

Perhaps his most overused gimmick was Hill's Angels, who wiggled their scantily clad behinds for a generation of rapt male viewers. Although the title Hill's Angels wasn't coined until the Dennis Kirkland era from 1979, Benny Hill comedy was synonymous with glamorous girls from the outset. The BBC days delighted in Dee Dee Wilde's troupe, and Jason Donovan's mother, Sue Macintosh, was a Hill chorus girl in the 1950s under the appropriate stage name of Sue Menlove. Ex-DJ and television announcer David Hamilton, himself a guest on Hill's shows, fully made the connection with a Thames link, jealously muttering: 'Lucky Benny and all those gorgeous girls ...' Those gorgeous girls appeared even more frequently during the Thames years, peppering Hill's speeded-up sketches and comic songs.

Sue Bond, misleadingly dubbed the first Hill's Angel, was indeed the first Thames glam to support Hill's shows in the early 1970s. Making her first stocking and suspender-clad appearance in a fireman sketch, she appeared many times, and went on to feature in the popular Patrick Cargill situation comedy *Father, Dear Father*. Another early Hill beauty, Yvonne Paul, went on to open London's most successful glamour-girl agency, Blondes – according to her 1992 tribute, at the suggestion from Hill himself, who frequently helped her out during the 1980s not only by hiring girls for his show, but by suggesting the agency to other Thames projects.

Other notable attractions included Olivia's sister, Rhona Newton-John, who appeared during the early 1970s, and Kay Frazer, who danced with The Young Generation and cropped up in several comic sketches. Bettina Le Beau, who had immortally uttered those eternally seductive words 'Fifi Le Beau' to Kenneth Connor in the film *Dentist on the Job*, was another Hill charmer, as was Susie Baker, one of the Baker Sisters, co-hostessses from *The Golden Shot*. Alison Bell (memorably rescued by Hill's cheeky fire chief) appeared as hostess on Bruce Forsyth's *Play Your Cards Right*. Bristol-born Diana Darvey, whom Hill had discovered in Spain, was that rare

British commodity, a vedette who could sing and perform comedy. Indeed, her earliest Hill appearances were as guest musical performer, although she quickly threw herself into revealing comic poses, and later graduated to Dave Freeman's *Carry On Behind* and Bob Monkhouse's game show *Quick on the Draw*.

Perhaps most memorably of all, Jenny Lee-Wright stripped off with excellence on many Hill shows throughout the 1970s. Beginning her career as one of Lionel Blair's dancers, she had graduated to BBC comedy shows with Dick Emery, coming fully to the fore as Bo Bo, the striptease girl who never got to strip at the close of Morecambe and Wise's shows. She went on to work with comedians Mike and Bernie Winters, Norman Wisdom, Des O'Connor, Les Dawson and Frankie Howerd.

Dee Dee Darlington, whose real name was Diana, was another invaluable asset, and Laraine Humphreys enjoyed credits in *Up Pompeii, Carry On Girls, Ooh! You are Awful* with Dick Emery, 1973's *Carry On Christmas* and a bit of sexy decoration on ITV's *Whose Baby?* with, believe it or not, kindly old David Nixon. Lorraine Doyle graduated to sitcom acting as Penelope Keith's secretary in *Executive Stress*. Helli Louise was born in Copenhagen and sprang to fame baring all in her prominent stage part as an au pair girl in *Pyjama Tops*. She later glammed up *Carry On Behind* in 1975.

Moira Foot was another stunning blonde heralded for *The Benny Hill Show* in a major *TV Times* article from February 1976 ('The Girl Most Likely to Put Her Foot in it') by Anthony Wall. Her father, the late Alistair Foot, had co-written the classic farce *No Sex Please – We're British*, and young Moira had studied acting at the Aida Foster School. She made her professional acting debut as a 17-year-old, playing the whispering maid, Effie, in Ronnie Barker's comedy playhouse series *Hark at Barker*. Later small-screen comedy credits included *On the Buses, The Dick Emery Show, Are You Being Served?* and *Doctor at Large*. Her most recent stage appearance before Benny Hill assignments had been a Bournemouth summer season of *The Man Most Likely* with Robin Stewart and a certain Henry McGee.

Karen David, as often as not, the petite, sweet nurse tending to Benny's exaggerated ailments, was married to comedian Roger Kitter, and frequently decorated the Saturday night Ted Rogers banter as *3–2–1* hostess. Louise English was a 16-year-old dancer with Pan's People on *The Benny Hill Show* in April 1979 when Hill spotted her and signed her up for solo spots. She would later become a successful West End musical star, guest several times on *Mike Yarwood in Person* and was part of *Elkie and*

Our Gang opposite singer Elkie Brooks on television. As with Sue Upton, she was usually billed apart from the Angels, although she recognizably became their leading figure, singing cabaret numbers while flashing her legs as accompaniment.

Jenny Westbrook, the original Hill glam girl, saw her daughter, 3-year-old Jade Westbrook, become the first (unofficial) Hill's Little Angel in a 1984 Montreux-winning sketch as an annoying girl disturbing Hill's artistic pursuits. Other Little Angels were Adam Jonstone (son of Libby Roberts, and the Jackie Coogan to Hill's Charlie Chaplin), Upton's two children and Kirkland's daughter. Benny, the elder statesman of British slapstick, could surround himself with naughty children, fall foul to their mischievous antics and keep his comic dignity intact. Blessed with a Bix Beiderbecke-like soundtrack, the spirit of Keaton and Chaplin behind him, and a sense of playful energy, the episodes which featured the Little Angels saw some of Hill's most inventive moments. This was probably the most promising direction in which to develop his comedy, but attempts to promote the Little Angels (a *TV Times* feature of 9–15 January 1988 saw Benny in the kitchen with them) failed to overcome the widespread impression that his shows relied too heavily on scantily clad females.

We all adore-a a Kiaora...Bemused cinema antics for *The Benny Hill Show*.

BENNY INVADES THE STATES

New Benny Hill shows may have been thin on the ground in Britain, but he was still hitting the ratings jackpot. However, at the end of his most creative decade, Hill was about to be launched into superstardom – and maybe lose some spontaneous freshness as a result. The next stop was America. Philip Jones was eager to experiment with the American market, and from 1968, Don Teffner was trying to break into it with Thames Television programmes. Everything failed, and through the early 1970s, even Benny Hill was repeatedly turned down by American television moguls when screened at the trade fair for National Association of Television Programme Executives in Los Angeles. Like Capital Records' comment on The Beatles, they considered the programmes of poor quality and unintelligible to the American public.

Nevertheless, in 1976, Philip Jones grabbed the chance to buy a week's worth of American airtime. Acutely aware of Hill's ambitions for the American market and confident that his visual style would appeal to American audiences, Thames Television's flagship presentation for their hired week of transmission from New York's RKO studio was none other than *The Benny Hill Show*. While the broadcasts were popular, the hoped for landslide of interest in Benny Hill was not forthcoming. However, by 1978, with Benny Hill quite simply the biggest thing on British television, Teffner found interest from Ron Gold, manager of the struggling WTAF station in Philadelphia. Insisting that these hour-long specials needed to be cut to half an hour for broadcast, Thames recruited John Street, ironically Benny Hill's old director from the BBC days, who came out of retirement to work on the shows. Initially using four full-hour specials to make one half-hour American pilot, he was instructed to compile 40 of these, with the first broadcast going ahead when three completed shows were available.

The first Hill compilations went out on 8 January 1979 (boosted by a glowing review by Lee Winfrey in The Philadelphia Inquirer under the heading 'Honest Vulgarity'), and over and over again those three priceless 22½ minute bursts of Hill were screened five nights a week in the 11 p.m. slot. A cult following began to take shape, and Hill practically saved the station single-handedly. Further edited shows were already in the can, ready for the American invasion. So popular were the shows that soon, Benny Hill appeared in the 7 p.m. slot as well – an amazing ten hours' airtime a week.

Stripped of all their British references, television in-jokes and impenetrable one-liners, the shows were top-heavy with Hill's inspired mime performances for the foreign audience. However, the cornball, vaudeville-style innuendo and wealth of attractive, scantily clad females were hardly a distraction for the American market, and the shows proved the biggest success of the week's programming. It was back to the format of Jackie Gleason and Dean Martin – both had girl troupes, the June Taylor Dancers and the Golddiggers, respectively – and the audience loved it, so much so that a one-hour special was bought, cut in half for two syndicated slots, and proved hugely popular in both New York and Los Angeles.

The invasion progressed. Hill was being screened twice nightly on some stations, Channel 20 transmitted his shows every night from Tuesday to Friday, WOR Channel Nine scored a huge hit, and it is estimated that every Thames scrap has been broadcast in America over a hundred times. With no planned syndication, the individual stations simply picked up on the vibes. In America, it was suddenly cool to dig the show. Car bumper stickers emblazoned with 'I Love Benny Hill' and T-shirts bearing 'I Understand Fred Scuttle' were quickly endorsed by Thames, and even a door hanger stating 'Do Not Disturb! We Are Watching Benny Hill!' flooded the market.

Early criticism of Hill's smut level (*Village Voice* magazine condemned him as 'pornographic grubbiness') was quickly swept away by a tidal wave of adoration. In 1979, David Lewis of the *Daily Mail* wrote about Hill's American success, and even the legendary *Washington Post* couldn't ignore the massive impact of this gloriously low-brow British comedian. Under the headline 'Delightfully Bad Benny', Tom Shales wrote: 'It is marked by a bawdiness and slap-happy vulgarity unlike anything on American television ... Hill, who looks like Rod Steiger playing Jonathan Winters, will stoop to anything – we hope. His smorgasbord of the ridiculous is delightfully bereft of redeeming social value. Bad British drama is unbearable; bad British comedy can be sublime.'

Taking a similar stance to British critics and audiences, celebrating the very awfulness of Benny Hill's comedy as its endearing quality, the American public simply fell in love with his seemingly spontaneous energy, recreating that lost age of vaudeville from television pioneers Red Skelton and Sid Caesar. A near permanent fixture on the USA Cable Network, Benny Hill had become a cultural icon, and the importance of such a crucial breakthrough did not go unnoticed at home. In an April 1980 edition of *TV Times*, a debate ('Benny – British, Bawdy –

and Brilliant?') pitted Howard Rosenberg of the *LA Times* against Hilary Kingsley of the *Daily Mirror*. The American's opinion, full of comparisons with Charlie Chaplin, Milton Berle and Ernie Kovacs, stood against the British feminist's muted praise of his BBC work, subdued distaste at his early 1970s persona, finally crossing him off the 'hiss list' to celebrate his self-contained, self-penned, non-showbusiness-like style. Both sides of the Atlantic were in agreement that Benny Hill might be corny, but he was certainly funny. His genius, Kingsley concluded, 'makes the Americans envious'. And let us not forget the loyal audience of British expatriates who seized on all things from home as a constant reminder. Perhaps the most celebrated, John Lennon, would counterbalance continued devotion to Gene Vincent and Elvis Presley by tuning into Benny Hill. In his last major interview on 6 December 1980, with Andy Peebles for the BBC, Lennon jokingly answered thoughts about the feminine side of society with: 'You mean Benny Hill!', explaining that 'he's on over here all the time. Tommy Cooper. There's so many English programmes on, in New York especially, that you see everything.'

Hill had made a massive impact. New York screened a special two-hour edition to mark New Year's Eve, and enjoyed the added bonus of a specially filmed minute-long interlude of Hill, backed by Big Ben, counting down the seconds to midnight. A series of trailers featuring him were filmed, but publicity was hardly needed any more. His shows were screened in the lounges of Las Vegas venues for afternoon entertainment, while Greta Garbo spent a vast deal of her time alone smoking cigarettes and laughing uproariously at Benny Hill on television. Clint Eastwood doggedly tried to contact Hill on his rare trips to America, and his restaurant, The Hog's Breath in Carmel, California, is packed with framed Benny Hill photographs. Michael Jackson cited him as 'the funniest comedian in the world'. Mickey Rooney, Jack Lemmon, Liza Minnelli and Burt Reynolds were fans. Arriving at Heathrow Airport, Frank Sinatra once told waiting reporters: 'I only want to do two things. I want to sing with The London Philharmonic Orchestra and I want to go to a Benny Hill rehearsal.' These guys were not being ironic or cryptic or sarcastic. This was real American devotion.

Benny Hill was offered a fortune to perform live in America, but never accepted. Indeed, an advert for Benny Hill in cabaret with his full television cast in Atlantic City was published without the knowledge of the star – the show, of course, didn't go ahead. He refused all offers of television interviews, and rarely visited. Before his first official appearance to promote the Thames shows, many

American fans thought the comedian was dead. Hill couldn't quite believe that America was gripped with this Bennymania, and secretly, he didn't want to find the impact was less than people made out. However, friends kept coming back from the States and convincing him – Eric Morecambe said Florida was full of Benny Hill merchandise, Ernie Wise reputedly couldn't get a drink in Fort Laundendale when *The Benny Hill Show* was playing because everywhere was shut, and when his English accent was noticed, everyone asked him 'Are you English? Do you know Benny Hill?' Even when *The Benny Hill Show* was nominated for Emmy awards in 1980 and 1981, the star still refused to attend the ceremonies.

Finally, in 1984, Hill visited San Francisco, arriving at Bayshore airport and being greeted by a couple of luvvies, Laurie Tollefson and Colleen Neeham. Wanting to avoid any fuss, no interviews or press releases were organized. On the third day, after a few people had recognized him in the street, Hill went public, and the country exploded. Benny Hill had arrived, and the saucy image was to the fore. Turning down a trip to be Frank Sinatra's guest at his concert in Las Vegas in favour of being guest of honour at a Hugh Hefner party with heroes like Cornel Wilde and Buck Henry, Benny cheekily commented: 'No disrespect, Frank, but the Bunny Girls won!' It was good for his image, even though Dennis Kirkland was a bit upset, to say the least – but the real reason was that the Hefner invitation had come first, and since Hill had already accepted the offer, that was that. Hill discussed comedy at the University of California, Berkeley. A special party at Chasen's Restaurant was attended by Steve Allen and Jack Lemmon.

A drinking session in Los Angeles with Burt Reynolds and Dom De Luise resulted in a brief Hill appearance from the audience of Burt's interview on *Starsearch*, and their legendary night on the tiles was related by the two Hollywood stars on *The Johnny Carson Show*. During a New York awards dinner, Audrey Hepburn chatted with Hill about who had earned less from London theatre work forty-five years earlier. She insisted on a photograph together, 'so that my sons will believe me!', and Bob Hope celebrated him as part of the glorious vaudeville tradition. Invitations to visit Michael Jackson in Los Angeles went unfulfilled, no television station managed to get an interview with the elusive Hill, and the cult fandom which had been bubbling under for years suddenly went mainstream ballistic. Twiggy welcomed her fellow Britpacker backstage to her Broadway show *My One and Only* and saw her childhood favourite mobbed by chorus girls, the Home Box Office cable channel presented Benny Hill marathons, fans held flamboyant Benny Hill parties, devotees who latched onto his burlesque comedy as a security blanket basked in being called 'Benny Babies', and eventually, some 120 half-hour episodes were flowing through the national consciousness.

John Street was now less fussy about what he included – seven-minute sketches, thought too detailed for American interest, were devoured, British references were confusing but forgiven, and the bumbling Scuttle became a hero-worshipped icon. Amazingly, the BBC material was never marketed in the same way.

In his book *Double Take and Fade Away*, Leslie Halliwell pinpoints the arrival of Benny Hill on American television screens as the watershed event prompting the country's comedy writers to venture further than they had previously dared. A feigned lesbian relationship in *Kate and Allie*, the uncompromising Joan Rivers, the adult-aimed brilliance of *Dream On* and *The Simpsons* could all now follow the trail blazed by Benny Hill.

Benny Hill's Ten of the Best

This collection of early 1970s Thames highlights culled from material familiar from the feature film *The Best of Benny Hill* was billed as a repeat, although it was a new, albeit hastily put together, compilation of wheezing old fare to launch Hill into a new decade.

Benny Hill's Ten of the Best (compilation): Thames Television, Wednesday 2 January 1980. Starring BENNY HILL. With JENNY LEE-WRIGHT, BOB TODD, JACK WRIGHT, RITA WEBB, DAVID HAMILTON, DIANA DARVEY, EDDIE BUCHANAN, BETTINE LE BEAU, BRENDA ARNAUD, HENRY McGEE. Script and original songs: Benny Hill.

During his formative years at Thames, Benny Hill's chief producer/director was John Robins. Coincidentally, the floor walker from that first Thames *Benny Hill Show* was Dennis Kirkland. Having directed *The Epilogue* and the children's series *The Sooty Show* and *Rainbow*, Kirkland would go on to work with this country's finest comedians – Frankie Howerd, Tommy Cooper, Billy Dainty, Chic Murray, Eric Sykes, Dick Emery, and most frequently of all, Benny Hill. Together, Hill and Kirkland fashioned the internationally recognized look of *The Benny Hill Show* from 1979 until 1989. Therefore, it is important to examine Benny Hill's strict routine in preparing his Thames specials.

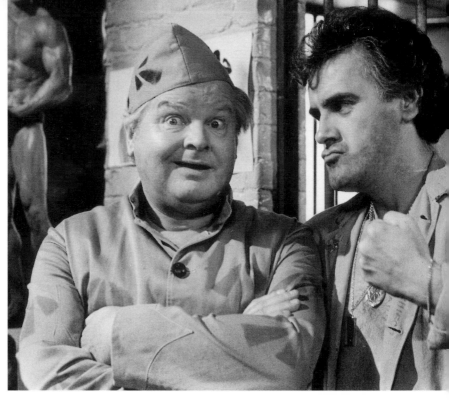

Cell Mates - Hill reverts to stock, instant laugh expression doing a prison punch up with Jon Jon Keefe.

It was a process that changed very little over twenty years. Two completed scripts would be delivered by May, with a further six or seven ready by July. Although this was far too much material for one season, Hill insisted on over-writing to keep the standards high. By August, the scripts for the following year would be set in stone and the cast contracted. The entire location work for the three shows would be completed in just three weeks during September. In order to let Hill return home every night, these shots were usually restricted to the London area, frequently filmed around Ashstead, Surrey. A week would be put aside for Hill rewrites, musical numbers with the girls would be choreographed (from 1982, by 1972–75 Hill girl Libby Roberts) under the star's watchful eye, and a further four days would be taken up with Hill's added gag spots.

Rehearsals for *The Benny Hill Show* were usually held in a deserted Hammersmith church. During filming, Hill would take the number 27 bus to Teddington Studios. The making of *The Benny Hill Show* was a riot of fun, everybody got on well, practical jokes were rife, and at the centre of it all, with the biggest satisfied grin on his face, was Uncle Ben himself. Hill's birthday would usually fall during the shooting schedules, and that day nothing but celebrating was tolerated. The quickies and filmed sketches, which were all recorded during an intensive three-day shoot at Teddington, would have music and special effects dubbed over a five-day period. Sound effects were of crucial importance to Hill, and he would

spend hours with Kirkland in experimental stages trying to ascertain the exact sound he wanted. The sound of him slapping Jackie Wright's bald head was finally discovered by wacking a balloon and slowing down the resultant noise. The sketches would finally be ready for the Friday studio recording at Teddington. Make-up and costume were also instrumental to the show's success, as an early December 1975 piece for *TV Times*, 'Everyone has a Giggle and a Licorice Allsort when Emperor Benny Holds Court' by Peter Genower, illustrated. Behind-the-scenes secrets were revealed in *Inside Benny Hill*, (with the story by Alix Coleman, pictures by Bernard Fallon and Bert Hill) detailing the intricate work of make-up girl Christine Morell.

Although the majority of items would be filmed, Hill listened for the studio laughter and cut or rearranged the pieces accordingly. Hill, with producer/director Dennis Kirkland in tow, would warm up the audience (this would set the smutty seal perfectly, with one infamous occasion, from 1977, having Hill in drag with Kirkland's hand on his breast – Hill curtly asked, 'Would you move that?', Kirkland did, and Hill muttered blissfully, 'That's better!'). That gag, recounted to Maureen Cleave for a 1977 *Evening Standard* interview, captures those free days of the 1970s. Ten years later, Hill would never have dared repeat the joke.

The warm-ups consisted of a few throwaway one-liners and a Hill monologue, but the star was quickly whisked away to allow the filmed gems to build the laughter. The major items recorded in front of the live audience were the musical numbers, picked from a fresh Hill collection or his massive back catalogue. Items like 'Graffiti' ('Don't put your cat in a washing machine, or you might get a sock in the puss.') and 'Just Wanna be in the Band' (with Hill as *The Monte Carbolic Show* host Patrick Wayne and guest star Kenny Rogers, with lyrics like 'She hollered from the kitchen,/"Kenny, would you truss the chicken?"/I said, "Of course I would, my darlin', with my life!"') revelled in the most painfully contrived lines and often scanned so clumsily as to trip up their singer-songwriter's performance, but they all had endearing charm, and the corny jokes were eternal winners. On these studio days, Hill would be at Teddington Lock from 9.30 in the morning until after 10 at night.

. Once the star was satisfied, Kirkland had the month-long job of editing the material into one-hour slots. Often, with the speeded-up film technique and fast pace of the material, there would be as much as three hours of film to work through. Even here, if Hill considered the pace of the show wrong, he would insist on re-editing or even re-filming the items, aiming for total perfection. Hill and Kirkland were a close-knit team, and the star performer often referred to his director/producer as his 'writer's labourer', developing countless sketch ideas into his own unique style.

The regular slapstick silent homage chase sequence at the close of the show graduated from its humble BBC beginnings into six-minute masterpieces at Thames. Using a technique called 'undercranking', the mini-epics were filmed at 18 frames per second, but printed at 24 frames per second to give the illusion of jerky, hand-cranked silent comedies. Hill was obsessed with the technique, and to be fair, probably milked it to death by the early 1980s. The original speeded-up reverse camerawork inventiveness of a sketch like 'The Three Musketeers' or Hill's sublime reversed routine of replacing the skin on fruit was soon lost in favour of popular, clichéd suspender and stocking-clad park chases. Utilizing the unforgettable strains of Boots Randolph's standard 'Yakety Sax' (if played on saxophone), or 'Yakety Axe' (if played on the guitar by Chet Atkins), these knockabout classics became the hallmark of Benny Hill for millions of people.

However, in the end, the show was made for the total satisfaction of just one person – Benny Hill himself. With the common touch, ability to gauge his own limitations and knowledge of innuendo/slapstick comedy, Hill judged the show by his own tastes, and found the winning formula, but the most nerve-wracking times were actually watching the finished show. He would rush from the studio once editing was complete, and study the programme on video tape before broadcast. On the day the show was due for transmission, Hill would get himself relaxed with a glass of claret half an hour before the programme, watch and record the show, and file it away – constantly trying to avoid duplicating jokes. But it became increasingly harder to avoid this by the mid-1980s.

The Benny Hill Show. Thames Television, Wednesday 6 February 1980, 8–9 p.m. Starring BENNY HILL. With HENRY McGEE, BOB TODD, JACK WRIGHT, HELEN HORTON, PAT ASHTON, SUE UPTON, ROGER FINCH, KEN SEDD, CYRIL CROSS, HILL'S ANGELS. Script and original songs: Benny Hill. Musical Director: Ronnie Aldrich. Designer: Bill Laslett. Produced and directed by Dennis Kirkland. Includes: 'The Scarlet Pimple' and a comic look at women's lib.

The Benny Hill Show. Thames Television, Wednesday 5 March 1980, 8–9 p.m. Starring BENNY HILL. With HENRY McGEE, BOB TODD, JACK WRIGHT, RITA WEBB, HELEN HORTON, JENNY LEE-WRIGHT, ROGER FINCH, HILL'S ANGELS. Script and original songs: Benny Hill. Musical Director: Ronnie Aldrich. Choreography: Linda Finch. Designer: Bill Laslett. Produced and directed by Dennis Kirkland. Includes: Benny the Court Jester, Hill and Jack Wright as Butch Caffety and the Fundance Kid, plus Chow Mein trapped in the British legal system during an industrial tribunal.

The Benny Hill Show. Thames Television, Wednesday 16 April 1980, 8–9 p.m. Starring BENNY HILL. With HENRY McGEE, BOB TODD, JACK WRIGHT, HELEN HORTON, PAT ASHTON, SUE UPTON, LOUISE ENGLISH, ROGER FINCH, HILL'S ANGELS. Script and original songs: Benny Hill. Musical Director: Ronnie Aldrich. Choreography: Linda Finch. Designer: Bill Laslett. Directed and produced by Dennis Kirkland. Includes: Fred Scuttle puts Dimpton-on-Sea on the cultural map with his new Arts Centre, Hill has a dig at the Montreux festivals that feted him, the Musketeers dash across Europe on an urgent mission for the Queen of France, and the Hill's Angels perform a dance number in celebration of the streets of New York.

Benny Hill Down Under (repeat): Thames Television, Wednesday 14 May 1980, 8–9 p.m. (repeat of 12/4/78).

Benny Hill

With Hill's invasion of American television taking everybody by storm, the British press and media were full of praise for this comic genius, newly discovered via international elevation. Always a huge star in Britain, his face had been less frequently seen around the place in the late 1970s, but suddenly Hill was everywhere.

With old BBC editor John Street in tow again, Hill helped orchestrate this major season of half-hour cobbled-together repeats akin to his American slots. Although the American transmissions initially omitted the Scuttle pieces, thought far too wordy and lengthy for the wham-bam style for that market, these British-aimed shows mixed Hill's vocal and visual comic style. However, it wasn't long before the American audiences eagerly devoured every morsel of Thames Hill comedy.

These compilations successfully repackaged Dennis Kirkland-directed Hill alongside older Thames items. With new Tommy Cooper shows on Tuesday nights, new Morecambe and Wise material on Wednesday and sliced Hill on Thursday, ITV embraced the cream of British post-war comedians in a ratings-winning line-up that would make today's programme planners' mouths water.

Benny Hill (compilation): Thames Television, Thursday 4 September 1980, 8–8.30 p.m. Starring BENNY HILL. With HENRY McGEE, RITA WEBB, JACK WRIGHT, JENNY LEE-WRIGHT, JIMMY THOMPSON, EDDIE BUCHANAN, THE LADYBIRDS, SUE UPTON. Script and original songs: Benny Hill. Musical Director: Ronnie Aldrich. Designers: Harry Clark and Tony Borer. Directed and produced by John Robins and Mark Stuart. Includes: Hill's timid nudist losing all inhibitions when faced with a girl facing suspender problems, and scoutmaster Hill.

Benny Hill (compilation): Thames Television, Thursday 11 September 1980, 8–8.30 p.m. Starring BENNY HILL. With HENRY McGEE, PAULA WILCOX, JACK WRIGHT, BOB TODD, PERCY THROWER. Script and original songs: Benny Hill. Musical Directors: Ronnie Aldrich and Albert Elms. Designer: Tony Borer. Directed and produced by John Robins. Includes: Hill's Terry Wogan hosting *Come Dancing*, Scuttle's health farm, and guest gardener Thrower happy to be humiliated in a tangled old English garden.

Benny Hill (compilation): Thames Television, Thursday 18 September 1980, 8–8.30 p.m. Starring BENNY HILL. With HENRY McGEE, BOB TODD, HUGH PADDICK, RITA WEBB, JACK WRIGHT, JENNY LEE-WRIGHT, EDDIE BUCHANAN, THE MIKE SAMMES SINGERS. Musical Director: Ronnie Aldrich. Designers: Peter Le Page and Roger Allan. Directed and produced by Mark Stuart and Keith Beckett. Includes: TV awards, spoofs on *The Avengers*, *Mastermind* and *I, Claudius*, and Hill's German Choir.

Benny Hill (compilation): Thames Television, Thursday 25 September 1980, 8–8.30 p.m. Starring BENNY HILL. With HENRY McGEE, BOB TODD, JACK WRIGHT, RITA WEBB, JENNY LEE-WRIGHT. Designers: Tony Borer, Mike Hall and David Marshall. Directed and produced by Mark Stuart. Includes: Hill's marriage for money with regret for past loves, 'Murder on the Oregon Express', 'Confessions of Eskimo Nell' and 'Candid Camera'.

Benny Hill (compilation): Thames Television, Thursday 9 October 1980, 8–8.30 p.m. Starring BENNY HILL. With HENRY McGEE, BOB TODD, JACK WRIGHT, JENNY LEE-WRIGHT, RITA WEBB. Designer: Tony Borer. Produced and directed by John Robins and Mark Stuart. Includes: Hill as a Victorian servant, and the 'Villain of the Year' awards.

W.C. Fields meets Frank Randle via Rod Steiger - Hill borrows from the best for his drunken stagger home and note the hat rammed tightly over his ears - a trait from his beloved German characterization from the 1940s.

Benny Hill (compilation): Thames Television, Thursday 16 October 1980, 8–8.30 p.m. Starring BENNY HILL. With NICHOLAS PARSONS, HENRY McGEE, BOB TODD, JENNY LEE-WRIGHT, LEE GIBSON, THE LADYBIRDS. Designers: Bill Palmer, Darrell Lass and Tony Borer. Directed and produced by Peter Frazer-Jones and John Robins. Includes: Hill on bongo drums, wild west antics and 'The Railway Choir'.

Benny Hill (compilation): Thames Television, Thursday 23 October 1980, 8–8.30 p.m. Starring BENNY HILL. With HENRY McGEE, BOB TODD, JACK WRIGHT, EDDIE BUCHANAN. Designers: David Marshall, Bill Palmer and Darrell Lass. Directed and produced by Mark Stuart. Includes: 'The Ballad of Lulu Belle', 'Pearl & Plain Film Presentations' and a profile of musician Garvin Blod.

Benny Hill (compilation): Thames Television, Thursday, 30 October 1980, 8–8.30 p.m. Starring BENNY HILL. With HENRY McGEE, PATRICIA HAYES, BOB TODD, JACK WRIGHT. Designer: Tony Borer. Produced and directed by John Robins. Includes: 'The Underworld Water of Jack Custard' and the search for forward-walking crabs, the 'Brother Ted' monologue and Chow Mein tackling customs/immigration.

Benny Hill (compilation): Thames Television, Thursday 6 November 1980, 8–8.30 p.m. Starring BENNY HILL. With HENRY McGEE, BOB TODD, JACK WRIGHT, JENNY LEE-WRIGHT, DIANA DARVEY. Designers: Bill Palmer and Darrell Lass. Produced and directed by Mark Stuart. Includes: 'Kung Phooie'.

Apart from making Hill a major figure in American culture, the show saw his regular supporting cast elevated to superstardom. Bob Todd and Henry McGee were greeted like Hollywood legends, while Jenny Lee-Wright once arrived in New York, mentioned her work on *The Benny Hill Show*, and within 45 minutes found herself talking about Hill on a live chat show.

This huge success obviously affected the creative direction of Benny Hill's work, for although it is fair to say that movie influences and cowboy American hayseed characterizations had always been part of the Hill experience, American-geared dance numbers became more and more prevalent. Throughout his career, Hill had successfully walked the line between devotion for Max Miller innuendo and devotion for Charlie Chaplin slapstick. Of these two major comic influences on his work, Hill had clearly come down on the side of Chaplin. Although the corny gags were still very much in evidence, Hill was very aware that America equated him with speeded-up mime and beautiful girls, so that was exactly what he was going to give them.

During the 1980s, the television skits became fewer – although priceless examples included a *Crossroads* parody (with Hill as the simple-minded Benny, fittingly enough, and the rest of the cast brought to life by the usual suspects – McGee, Keefe and Anna Dawson), a sparkling spoof of *Cagney and Lacey* (with Hill as both female protagonists, squashing his facial features to capture Tyne Daley's expression perfectly) and an inspired bit of Hill drag, playing Anna Ford caught in the *News at Ten* studio engrossed in a magazine, seemingly studying a pornographic male pose judging by an extended erection-like fold-out, her innocence preserved as the photo is revealed to be a soldier with his gun jutting forward. However, whiskery schoolyard howlers like '*Je t'adore* – Shut the door', '*Coup de grace* – Mow the lawn', '*Coq au vin* – Pass' and obvious remarks such as 'I'd love to see her in 3D. That's my hotel room' were taking the style to breaking point. The BBC had clearly moved on from this sort of comedy: Monty Python's 'Nudge, Nudge' routine had pricked the bubble of self-aware innuendo in 1970, and the short-lived but potent Frankie Howerd classic *Up Pompeii* constantly mocked its own corniness.

Hill, however, went on relentlessly. An overlong slapstick sequence set aboard an ocean liner (Wright afflicted with seasickness swaying and abandoning his food; a naked girl picture revealing a drawer by pulling her nipples; the crew demonstrating bouncing crockery, until Hill breaks in and smashes it; a religious meeting with Hill's vicar being devilish with a devil hand-puppet and clinking glasses to give the effect of bell-ringing; a glam girl drying herself and dropping the towel to catch a thrown gift) stretched the attention span to breaking point, but thankfully, some moments touched genius once more. One sequence had Hill and Todd as two distinguished, ultra-xenophobic British gents watching a French chap drown in the pool. Obvious sight gags like Hill grudgingly taking down one of the 'O's from the sign 'POOL' and tossing it into the water rest alongside sublime throwaway barbs like Hill's classic answer to screams of 'I can't swim!' – 'I can't play the Japanese nose flute but I don't go round shouting about it!' In that brief instant, we find the great Benny Hill of old.

Hill could still play a delightful self-opinionated old buffer, and with his own hair greying and his midriff expanding, these 1980s shows were brought to life by skilful characterizations. The gags may have been awful, but Hill spun his magic effortlessly, trying to light a cigar in a club, and using the 'no smoking' sign to get a light from the fireplace, or discussing his fine wall-mounted tiger with McGee, happily explaining that shooting it was easy, but getting it out of the zoo was more difficult. In the hands of a lesser comedy actor, these would be brief interludes of banal unimportance; in the hands of Benny Hill, they are treasurable bursts of insane, eccentric humour. Clearly, he was still at his best with quick, throwaway skits, as when discussing youth in Asia with Henry McGee, the euthanasia expert – the bemused Hill reactions to camera are still priceless.

Sadly, a repetitive reel of slapstick antics stretched out in front of him. Musical items like the Mexican 'El Bronco' repeated lyrics from the song 'Anna Marie' of ten years earlier, relying on shameless sight gags (O'Keefe removes Hill's black cloak to reveal 'naked woman' padding inside, a caged wanton harlot swaying her hips brings down the pawnbroker's balls – perhaps lifted from Bernadette Peters' seductress in the 1976 Mel Brooks film *Silent Movie*), and even older classics like 'Pepys' Diary' were resurrected. But Hill was always endearingly watchable. In that same Mexican number there are several moments, including his quick vacating of a seat resulting in a fallen lady and an injection of meanness over food, that never fail to amuse.

The 1980s saw an overwhelming reliance on the popular silent slapstick Hill humour, and many of these routines, thankfully, gave the comedian a chance to return to multi-character playing. 'A Rainy Day', for example, sees Hill as an elderly gent with a dog approached by a glam girl and ignored in favour of the hound, Hill as a rustic old gardener hanging his hat on a suggestively placed tool (in front of a statue of a naked man), Hill as a hassled bill poster directing McGee's foreign visitor by painting on his car bonnet, and Hill as a randy soldier losing out to Jackie Wright's ancient colonel. All smut, sexy walk to the beat of the music and flashing knickers this

isn't. The military situation cries out with the power of rank, Henry McGee's pompous motorist is mocked (his disgruntled companion, Bella Emberg, has 'Lisa' on her side of the car windscreen – McGee has 'Moaner', so here the man's treatment of the woman is criticized), while Hill's soldier gets the last laugh by lighting his cigarette butt with McGee's cigar, then switching the two.

Hill's passion for visual comedy and the silent traditions of Keaton and Chaplin is perfectly highlighted in 'The Vagabond'. Blessed with dewy-eyed intros and outros from Louise English, Sue Upton and the girls, Hill beautifully staggers through social (fooling a guard dog to pick up a wallet), prideful (playing oneupmanship with the hostel keeper), primitive (some dubious bodily function japery with a beery Jack Wright) and sexual (blissfully sticking paper in his clothes to keep warm, and shoving page 3 of the *Sun* down his trousers) problems, while standard extramarital bedroom scenes (Hill tries to tie his bow tie, but discovers it's the judo black belt of his lover's husband) are tired but reassuringly old-fashioned in their style. The television repair sketch (with Jon Jon Keefe fixing the upside-down image by turning the set upside down) is skilfully performed, exploiting Hill's ever-endearing gaze into camera to enlist support and understanding.

Can you hear me mother! Benny's confused yokel battles modern technology for *The Benny Hill Show*.

Increasingly, the musical numbers became more American in tone, featuring corn-sucking hayseeds, leather-jacketed streetwise hip guys and the evangelist representative of The League of Helping Hands – allowing Hill to trundle through some deliciously ancient gags with a Southern swagger.

In a show from 1983, Benny Hill addressed the use of beautiful girls with frankness and comic candour. Filling in a spare two minutes, encouraging rapturous applause with an Eric Morecambe-like movement of the hand and dressed in an untypically smart tuxedo, he explained everything in showbusiness is illusion, pleaded that he got the blame for everything, and helplessly explained: 'I don't design the dresses!' Hill's self-mocking 'I'm not against naked girls ... not as often as I'd like to be ...' precluded serious discussion on the subject.

By now, Hill's Angels had very much come of age. Although sexy dance troupes had been used before (indeed, two of his best loved co-stars, Sue Upton and Louise English, graduated from guest dancers on the show – from Love Machine and Pan's People, respectively), they had never stepped over the comedy border into the slap-and-tickle universe of Sue Bond, Jenny Lee-Wright et al. Replacing the suspender-flashing girlies of the 1970s sketches, this was Hill's answer to Kenny Everett's even more tantalizing Hot Gossip (indeed, in 1980, Thames had tried to launch Everett's ITV shows in America, with moderate success). Uncharacteristically taking on board a fellow comic's remark, Hill had read that Everett's BBC show of anarchic skits was proving very popular. Ever the modest comedian, Everett had commented: 'Thank heaven for Hot Gossip!' So it was that Hill groomed his usual collection of females, and combined the titles of ITV's American import crime-busting series *Charlie's Angels* and the Hell's Angels motorbikers to come up with Hill's Angels.

The Angels were officially launched in *The Benny Hill Show* broadcast on 6 February 1980, in response to the demands of the American market. In order to inject commercial breaks and keep the shows focused on Hill, American programme planners began cutting out the various female dance routines. Kirkland and Hill, feeling the girls were an integral part of his vaudevillian variety show for the television age, decided to incorporate them into Hill's slapstick routines, thus making it impossible to edit them out. With more laughs, more airtime and much more naked flesh, the Hill's Angels seemed the perfect support for Hill's comedy. He was satisfied, men across the nation were satisfied, and Thames were satisfied. Now, not only did the girls feature in sketches, they were allowed to display their other talents. Elaborate dance routines were staged, and Louise English became the star turn with a series of singing spots, performing in English, French (in Can-Can gear) and Spanish (with bullfighting antics), usually wearing little but paper flowers.

Gradually, the clothes became less and less apparent. A lengthy slapstick sketch set in a Continental hotel includes several intercuts of Hill's laboured routines (an image of a maintenance man weeing in the pool, whereas he is really filling it with a hose; a telephone engineer arriving merely to set up an 'out of order' sign) with shots of girls in the slightest of bikinis. Nothing could save him, even the occasional glimpse of Hill's own surrealism – the expected response to 'There's a fly in my soup' ('Don't talk too loud, everybody will want one!') following the unexpected retrieval of a trouser fly from the bowl, or the priceless Hill performance as a drunk, explaining that the hotel has 'call girl roulette' – six girls, and one of them is writing a book.

By the mid-1980s, Hill's Angels were the focal point for the show, with Hill's longing gazes, and Kirkland's lingering shots of bare backsides and even more prominent cleavages. Ironically, the girls were always in control. The frequent flashes of knicker and lingering shots through the parted legs of glams were sexy, of course, but never offensive. Even a gym sequence with the girls literally sitting on Hill's face in the showers and playfully dancing in and out of shot with towels covering their embarrassment are no more titillating than the 1930s musical numbers of Busby Berkeley. They are beautiful girls having a good time – and firmly putting sex-mad no-hopers like Benny Hill in their place.

However, as the bikinis continued to get smaller and smaller, the complaints started. In one particularly suggestive dance routine, the girls, complete with ever-reliable Sue Upton, performed a mock striptease. Since they were already wearing the bare minimum acceptable to Thames Television at the outset of the routine, nothing more could come off, but the pouting, finger-sucking actions (removing imaginary gloves) and leg-stroking (one girl removing another's imaginary tights) went well beyond slap-and-tickle, innuendo-fuelled giggles from Max Miller or Donald McGill's Brighton. Having said that, this particular routine led directly into one of Benny Hill's all-time masterpieces: the silent slapstick homage. The circus clown made up some of Hill's own personal favourite moments from the shows, injecting pathos (the poignant red rose ballet with Louise English's poster girl), music hall business (the easy drinking technique of wrapping his tie round the bottle and pulling) and vaudevillian tradition (a W.C. Fields-like touch of drunkenly letting his mouth feel its way to the top of the bottle).

His unforgettable 1982 striptease is in the ancient line which runs from Arkady Raiken, through Grock and on to Charlie Cairoli. Hill's sheepish clown, appearing as a smiling face at the end of the glam girl line-up, shows the girls a trick or two by cannily stripping down to his boxer shorts (desperately trying to cover his nipples *à la* Norman Wisdom in *The Square Peg*), enjoying some comic business with his hat and a hat stand, becoming surreal by removing his eye and bouncing it back into place, cheekily removing his wig to avoid going full-frontal, and finally, eerily, beginning to strip away his skin to reveal his skeleton. Literally stripping down to the bone, there are priceless moments involving a detached arm playing a brief tune as its bony fingers tap on the floor, a typical Hill grunt of pain as the pelvic structure goes for a burton, and a cheery vanish into nothingness as the second arm peels away. Like much of Hill's material, this wasn't an entirely new idea – the unfairly neglected 1980 Vincent Price comic horror film *The Monster Club* boasted a stripper who went the whole hog – but nevertheless, Hill's performance is beautiful and poetic. French critics cite this particular example as evidence for the fact that Hill should be considered on the same level as Buster Keaton – and you'll get no argument from this writer. Nervous of performing something so radical, Hill put it off for three years before finally committing himself to it, but this single sketch won a special award in France.

'The Loser' was another beautifully constructed piece of visual pathos, depicting Hill as a depressed figure ending it all by attaching himself to a huge rock and throwing it into a lake, only to be passed by an equally downhearted fish tied to a balloon, floating out of the water. Another *pièce de résistance* was 'Me and My Shadow' from 1983, with Hill, discovering an ability to feel the actions of his shadow. Leading to plenty of fondled females and cheating at chess, with McGee's bemused reaction hilarious every time, the scene takes a fascinating turn into darkness with the murder of his nagging wife, Kathy Staff. Nabbed by Bob Todd's policeman, Hill's collar felt by the copper's shadow, the final pathos-ridden moment, with Hill's white suit covered in shadow arrows, is Benny Hill at his best. This is a clever, well-played and brilliantly polished piece of television mime, but sadly, classics like these were far too often overshadowed by low-level smut.

Much of his other material was dreadfully thin at the time, resorting to very old jokes indeed, including this exchange between a stunning brunette and Hill: 'My boyfriend calls me Dimples.' – 'I don't see any dimples.' –

'You're not my boyfriend!' (Tommy Trinder *circa* 1942, I think). Hill's authority figures were seen as sex-mad (he begins to arrest Todd's peeping Tom, watches the female action until lights out, then completes his duty – with police superior Wright falling from a nearby tree), and while the best sketches were still highlighting male paranoia (a classic example shows the regulars running screaming out of a vasectomy clinic followed by two nurses, one banging two brick-like lunchboxes together). However, the debate about 'the girls' had already begun.

The never-ending line of skirt-dropping lovelies was beginning to affect Hill's comic credibility. Like Sid James in the tail-end *Carry On* films, Hill was now fast approaching 60 years of age, and even some of his admirers began to look upon him as nothing but a dirty old man. Although he would counter such taunts in public with 'Wrong. I'm a rich and famous dirty old man!', the days when he could acceptably surround himself with young actresses playing Miss Foam Rubber, Miss Unwed Mother of 1983 and Miss Ballcock were certainly numbered. In a 1983 piece, Hill starred as the definitive naughty schoolboy, creeping into a strip club and watching amazed as the dancer paraded on stage with just the briefest of briefs and a balloon to cover her charms. Despite Hill's usual touch of surrealism (the catapult attempt to pop the balloon results in deflating the stripper), this was merely a continuation of the sexually nervous male of 1965's 'Baby Boy'. Nearly twenty years later, Hill's comedy universe had stayed disconcertingly unaltered. Several charming slapstick pieces pointed the best way forward – including the 1985 gem with Hill's doorman dealing with a slightly worse for drink Bob Todd, brushing down his spoiled coat by simulating the brush with his hand while he is really cleaning himself up. But these touching, ingeniuous moments of a maturing, ageing comedian were still relentlessly counterbalanced by flashes of thigh and tired ideas.

Although his shows were still very popular, the quality was noticeably slipping from the peak years of the late 1970s. However, even the most obvious routine could be redeemed by Hill's tireless trickery with the medium of film. A standard medical routine with Hill's white-coated, sex-mad chap chased by scantily clad female patients and nurses, wallows for an age in the area of Dopey-like bed-hopping for more blanket baths, cleavage-staring and stocking-top ogling. But, just as the undercranking goes into overdrive and the chase is on, a hair is caught in the camera gate and plays over the image. In the next shot it is gone, and you're left thinking Hill the perfectionist has missed an error. It's back in the next shot, but this time

Hill stops in his tracks, reaches out and plucks the offending hair from the screen.

Hill's performance was still excellent, and the supporting cast did their job to perfection. It was the corny, repetitive scripts that let the side down. The banana republic criminal line-up with Todd's outstanding law enforcer and Hill's distressed masked villain plays well enough, but at the end of the day it leaves an embarrassed smile rather than a belly laugh. Needless to say, these shows were still hugely successful, and to be fair, even if Hill himself realized that his material was becoming tired, uninspired and unfunny, who would change course when the ratings were so high? The awards continued to come (The Funniest Man on TV in 1981, the TV and Radio Industries Club ITV Personality of the Year in 1982 and a coveted Golden Rose at the 1984 Montreux Comedy Festival), and his 60th birthday was marked with a pleasant party aboard a boat moored at Teddington Lock with friends and colleagues Richard Stone, Philip Jones and Dennis Kirkland. But the times were quite clearly a-changin'.

The Benny Hill Show: Thames Television, Wednesday 7 January 1981, 8–9 p.m. Starring BENNY HILL. With HENRY McGEE, BOB TODD, JACK WRIGHT, SUE UPTON, LOUISE ENGLISH, ABIGAIL HIGGINS, CLAIRE SMALLEY, ROGER FINCH, KEN SEDD, BELLA EMBERG, HILL'S ANGELS. Script and original songs: Benny Hill. Music Arrangements: Ronnie Aldrich. Choreography: Julie Hervieu. Designer: David Richens Directed and produced by Dennis Kirkland. Includes: fun in the gym, Wondergran battles Dr Jackal and Mr Hyde, and French schoolboy Young Gaston Le Clerc confuses McGee with impressions of London.

The Benny Hill Show: Thames Television, Wednesday 11 February 1981, 8–9 p.m. Starring BENNY HILL. With HENRY McGEE, JACK WRIGHT, SUE UPTON, LOUISE ENGLISH, ALISON BELL, ROGER FINCH, BELLA EMBERG, HILL'S ANGELS. Script and original songs: Benny Hill. Music Arrangements: Ronnie Aldrich. Musical Associate: Ted Taylor. Choreography: Linda Finch. Designer: David Richens. Produced and directed by Dennis Kirkland. Includes: 'The Hill Billies', Hill's love for the girl on the poster, the undercover Sanitary Inspector set to clean up the world, and 'The Lower Tidmarsh Fire Brigade' with Alison Bell in black stockings and sexy basque rescued by Hill's Chief.

The Benny Hill Show: Thames Television, Wednesday 25 March 1981, 8–9 p.m. Starring BENNY HILL.

With HENRY McGEE, BOB TODD, JACK WRIGHT, HELEN HORTON, SUE UPTON, LOUISE ENGLISH, ROGER FINCH, HILL'S ANGELS. Script and original songs: Benny Hill. Music Arrangements: Ronnie Aldrich. Musical Associate: Ted Taylor. Choreography: Julie Hervieu. Designer: David Richens. Associate Producer: Nigel Cook. Produced and directed by Dennis Kirkland. Includes: a best-selling epic of the American dream with Hill as 'Big Poppa' and most of the family, behind the scenes at a new TV studio, musical fun in a Greek taverna, and Hill as a penniless handyman wooing a squire's daughter.

The Benny Hill Show (repeat season): Thames Television, Wednesday, 8–9 p.m. 22 April 1982 (repeat of 6/2/80), 6 May 1982 (repeat of 5/3/80), 13 May 1982 (repeat of 16/4/81).

Benny Hill

This was the usual summer madness of Benny Hill, with a fresh season of compilations/revised repeats/hastily cobbled together editions – call them what you will – saturating the schedules.

Benny Hill (compilation): Thames Television, Bank Holiday Monday 31 August 1981, 8–8.45 p.m. Starring BENNY HILL. With HENRY McGEE, BOB TODD, JACK WRIGHT. Designers: Tony Borer and Michael Minas. Produced and directed by John Robins and Ronald Fouracre.

Benny Hill (compilation): Thames Television, Wednesday 16 September 1981, 8.30–9 p.m. Starring BENNY HILL. With HENRY McGEE, JACK WRIGHT, JENNY LEE-WRIGHT, EDDIE CONNOR, REFLECTIONS. Designers: Peter Le Page, Norman Garwood and David Marshall Produced and directed by Mark Stuart. Includes: 'Lovely Bianca', 'Political Correspondence', Hill and Wright as vaudeville team Luke and Tinker.

Benny Hill (compilation): Thames Television, Wednesday 23 September 1981, 8.30–9 p.m. Starring BENNY HILL. With HENRY McGEE, JACK WRIGHT, DILYS WATLING, RITA WEBB, EDDIE BUCHANAN. Designers: Tony Borer and Robin Parker. Produced and directed by Mark Stuart and Keith Beckett. Includes: 'Married Life with a Beautiful Wife', Hill joins the backing singers on Watling's rendition of

'Fever', Hill and Wright are the Carpenter brothers, and the Milk Marketing Board's Band.

Benny Hill (compilation): Thames Television, Wednesday 30 September 1981, 8.30–9 p.m. Starring BENNY HILL. With NICHOLAS PARSONS, BOB TODD, JACK WRIGHT, DIANA DARVEY, BELLA EMBERG. Designers: Tony Borer and Michael Minas. Produced and directed by Mark Stuart and Ronald Fouracre. Includes: German TV's culinary experts the Kraddocks, Scuttle's escort agency, and a Spanish finale with Darvey.

Benny Hill (compilation): Thames Television, Wednesday 7 October 1981, 8.30–9 p.m. Starring BENNY HILL. With HENRY McGEE, JACK WRIGHT, HELEN HORTON. Designers: Robin Tarsnane, Mike Hall and David Marshall. Produced and directed by Ronald Fouracre, Dennis Kirkland and Mark Stuart. Includes: 'Scuttle's Space Race', 'Cheapo Film Productions'.

Benny Hill (compilation): Thames Television, Wednesday 14 October 1981 8.30–9 p.m. Starring BENNY HILL. With HENRY McGEE, DON ESTELLE, EDDIE BUCHANAN, JO THOMAS. Designers: Tony Borer and Michael Minas. Produced and directed by Mark Stuart and Ronald Fouracre. Includes: Clyde Jarrow interview.

Benny Hill (compilation): Thames Television, Wednesday 20 October 1981, 8.30–9 p.m. Starring BENNY HILL. With HENRY McGEE, PATRICIA HAYES, JACK WRIGHT, DIANA DARVEY, ROGER FINCH, JENNY LEE-WRIGHT. Designers: Robin Tarsnane and Tony Borer. Produced and directed by John Robins and Dennis Kirkland. Includes: 'Baby Doll', 'Wondergran'.

Hill's new hour-long shows were quickly becoming restricted to just two editions a year, and as often as not, his face was frequently seen in new compilations from last season's shows, complete repeats of last series' shows and even vintage clip packages of his 1970s work.

The Benny Hill Show: Thames Television, Wednesday 6 January 1982, 8–9 p.m. Starring BENNY HILL. With HENRY McGEE, BOB TODD, JACK WRIGHT, JON JON KEEFE, ALISON BELL, BELLA EMBERG, HILL'S ANGELS. Script and original songs: Benny Hill. Choreography: Francesca Janes. Music Arrangments:

Ronnie Aldrich. Musical Associate: Ted Taylor. Designers: Bill Laslett and Robin Parker. Associate Producer: Nigel Cook. Produced and directed by Dennis Kirkland. Includes: a typically high-speed look at schooldays, holidays, traffic wardens and the pleasures of the Riviera.

The Benny Hill Show: Thames Television, Wednesday 10 February 1982, 8–9 p.m. Starring BENNY HILL. With HENRY McGEE, BOB TODD, JACK WRIGHT, JON JON KEEFE, JENNY LEE-WRIGHT, ALISON BELL, BELLA EMBERG, HILL'S ANGELS. Script and original songs: Benny Hill. Music Arrangements: Ronnie Aldrich. Musical Associate: Ted Taylor. Choreography: Linda Finch. Designer: Robin Parker. Associate Producer: Nigel Cook. Produced and directed by Dennis Kirkland. Includes: 'The Master of Mischief' at The Little Dimpton street party, Hill's autobiographical look at life as a TV fanatic, and Hill romancing as Romeo.

The Benny Hill Show (repeat season): Wednesday, 8–9 p.m. 7 April 1982 (repeat of 25/3/81), 9 June 1982 (repeat of 11/2/81), 9 June 1982 (repeat of 7/1/81).

Hill at his happiest - the laughing on the outside, laughing on the inside clown. Note the unsubtle tie gag in reaction to the revealing charms of Louise English.

LEE-WRIGHT. Designers: Norman Garwood, Tony Borer and Michael Minas. Produced and directed by David Bell and Ronald Fouracre. Includes: 'San Tropez', Bob Dylan parody and Melly's interview with Hill's film idol.

Benny Hill (compilation): Thames Television, Tuesday 14 September 1982, 8.30–9 p.m. Starring BENNY HILL. With NICHOLAS PARSONS, BOB TODD, HENRY McGEE, JACK WRIGHT. Designer: Tony Borer. Produced and directed by Mark Stuart and David Bell. Includes: Hill's fantasies about dance hall girls.

Benny Hill (compilation): Thames Television, Tuesday 21 September 1982, 8.30–9 p.m. Starring BENNY HILL. With HENRY McGEE, BOB TODD, JACK WRIGHT. Designers: Neville Green, Darrell Lass and Harry Clark. Produced and directed by Keith Beckett and John Robins. Includes: package holidays, wrestling and Scuttle.

Benny Hill (compilation): Thames Television, Tuesday 28 September 1982, 8.30–9 p.m. Starring BENNY HILL. With HENRY McGEE, BOB TODD, JACK WRIGHT, LOVE MACHINE. Designers: Norman Garwood, David Marshall and Rod Strard. Produced and directed by Mark Stuart. Includes: 'Sale of the Half Century', 'Bonnie and Clyde'.

Benny Hill (compilation): Thames Television, Tuesday 5 October 1982, 8.30–9 p.m. Starring BENNY HILL. With HENRY McGEE, EIRA HEATH, DAVID BATTLEY. Designer: Harry Clark. Produced and directed by John Robins. Includes: 'Eurovision Song Contest', 'European Honeymoon', 'Lower Tidmarsh Cottage Hospital'.

The Benny Hill Show. Thames Television, Wednesday 5 January 1983, 8–9 p.m. Starring BENNY HILL. With HENRY McGEE, JACK WRIGHT, BOB TODD, KATHY STAFF, JENNIE LEE-WRIGHT, LOUISE ENGLISH, JON JON KEEFE, HILL'S ANGELS. Script and original songs: Benny Hill. Music

Yet another season of cobbled together Benny Hill shows featured vintage gems from the John Robins era alongside more contemporary items under the guidance of Dennis Kirkland. Kicking off with a 45-minute Bank Holiday Monday special, these compilation shows kept Hill's face a familiar Thames fixture throughout the rest of the year.

Benny Hill (compilation): Thames Television, Monday 30 August 1982, 8–8.45 p.m. Starring BENNY HILL. With HENRY McGEE, BOB TODD, JACK WRIGHT, ANDRE MELLY, JENNY LEE-WRIGHT, MALOU CARTWRIGHT, LESLEY GOLDIE. Musical Directors: Albert Elms and Ronnie Aldrich. Produced and directed by John Robins and Dennis Kirkland. Includes: 'Leprechaun TV', Hill in the grips of a husband killer, and a detective's investigation of a flock of missing sheep.

Benny Hill (compilation): Thames Television, Tuesday 7 September 1982, 8.30–9 p.m. Starring BENNY HILL. With HENRY McGEE, JACK WRIGHT, BOB TODD, ANDRE MELLY, CYRIL CROSS, JENNY

Arrangements: Ronnie Aldrich. Designers: Peter Elliott and David Ferris. Produced and directed by Dennis Kirkland. Includes: adventures of an Australian lifeguard attacked by bikini babes with oars, the return of Chow Mein, and 'Superman II' – the bumbling schoolteacher!

The Benny Hill Show. Thames Television, Wednesday 16 March 1983, 8–9 p.m. Starring BENNY HILL. With HENRY McGEE, JACKIE WRIGHT, KATHY STAFF, BOB TODD, JENNY LEE-WRIGHT, LOUISE ENGLISH, JON JON KEEFE, KEN SEDD. Script and original music: Benny Hill. Music Arrangements: Ronnie Aldrich. Backing vocals: The Ladybirds. Designer: David Ferris. Produced and directed by Dennis Kirkland. Includes: holidays, 'Spain's Gay Caballero', wild west antics, Hill as a mad Scottish teacher, a bovver boy and on a winter break.

The Benny Hill Show. Thames Television, Easter Monday 4 April 1983, 8.30–9.30 p.m. Starring BENNY HILL. With HENRY McGEE, BOB TODD, JACK WRIGHT, JON JON KEEFE, JENNY LEE-WRIGHT, ALISON BELL, BELLA EMBERG, HILL'S ANGELS. Script and original songs: Benny Hill. Music Arrangements: Ronnie Aldrich. Musical Associate: Ted Taylor. Cheography: Linda Finch. Designer: Robin Parker. Associate Producer: Nigel Cook. Produced and directed by Dennis Kirkland. Includes: 'The Dimpton Street Party' and Hill's sailor surrounded by leather-clad lovelies.

More revised repeats from the overflowing Thames Benny Hill file followed. As usual, the season began with a 45-minute Bank Holiday extravaganza, but Hill's public persona was becoming somewhat tired by now. His new material was even scarcer than before, and his vintage form was being flogged to death by his employers.

Benny Hill (compilation): Thames Television, Bank Holiday Wednesday 23 August 1983, 8-9 p.m. Starring BENNY HILL. With HENRY McGEE, PAT ASHTON, JENNY LEE-WRIGHT, BOB TODD, JACK WRIGHT. Designers: Tony Borer, Bill Laslett and Ian Watson. Produced and directed by Mark Stuart and Dennis Kirkland. Includes: 'The Gay Lussar' and Hill's clown.

Benny Hill (compilation): Thames Television, Monday 5 September 1983, 8–8.30 p.m. Starring BENNY HILL. With HENRY McGEE, PAT ASHTON, BOB TODD, JACK WRIGHT. Designer: Bill Laslett. Produced and directed by Dennis Kirkland. Includes: 'Hollywood', 'Angels on the Riviera', 'Women's Lib TV'.

Benny Hill (compilation): Thames Television, 2 November 1983, 8.30–9 p.m. Starring BENNY HILL. With HENRY McGEE, BOB TODD, JACK WRIGHT, JENNY LEE-WRIGHT. Designer: Bill Laslett. Produced and directed by Dennis Kirkland. Includes: court jester, 'Butch Caffety and the Fundance Kid', 'Angels' Fashion Parade'.

Benny Hill (compilation): Thames Television, 9 November 1983, 8.30–9 p.m. Starring BENNY HILL. With HENRY McGEE, BOB TODD, JACK WRIGHT, HELEN HORTON, PAT ASHTON. Designer: Bill Laslett. Produced and directed by Dennis Kirkland. Includes: 'The Scarlet Pimple', 'Sale of the Half Century', 'Charlene's Angels'.

Benny Hill (compilation): Thames Television, 16 November 1983, 8.30–9 p.m. Starring BENNY HILL. With HENRY McGEE, BOB TODD, JACK WRIGHT, HELEN HORTON, JENNY LEE-WRIGHT. Designers: Bill Laslett and Ian Watson. Produced and directed by Dennis Kirkland. Includes: electrical appliances take over mankind, and 'Hill's Angels in New York'.

Benny Hill (compilation): Thames Television, 23 November 1983, 8.30–9 p.m. Starring BENNY HILL. With HENRY McGEE, BOB TODD, JACK WRIGHT, HELEN HORTON, JENNY LEE-WRIGHT. Designer: Bill Laslett. Produced and directed by Dennis Kirkland. Includes: edible paintings in the gallery, Chow Mein's industrial tribunal and the American family of Fudpuckers.

The Benny Hill Show. Thames Television, Monday 16 January 1984, 8–9 p.m. Starring BENNY HILL. With HENRY McGEE, JACK WRIGHT, JON JON KEEFE, LOUISE ENGLISH, ERICA LYNLEY, SUE UPTON, DEBI GAYE, HILL'S ANGELS. Script and original songs: Benny Hill. Music Arrangements: Ronnie Aldrich. Musical Associate: Ted Taylor. Choreography: Libby Roberts. Designer: Anthony Cartledge. Associate Producer: Nigel Cook. Produced and directed by Dennis Kirkland. Includes: 'Scuttlevision', Hill plays Cupid, Todd's Inspector Dibbs is on the trail of Hill's bank robbery gang, and a cabaret turn at the Club Bizarre.

Benny Hill (compilation): Thames Television, Tuesday 31 January 1984, 8.30–9 p.m. Starring BENNY HILL. With HENRY McGEE, BOB TODD, JACK WRIGHT, HELEN HORTON, PAT ASHTON.

Includes: musical quiz, electric domination and a New York number (yet again!).

The Benny Hill Show. Thames Television, Wednesday 25 April 1984, 8–9 p.m.. Starring BENNY HILL. With HENRY McGEE, BOB TODD, JACK WRIGHT, JON JON KEEFE, JENNY LEE-WRIGHT, LOUISE ENGLISH, ERICA LYNLEY, SUE UPTON, LEN KEYES, ANDREW FRANCIS, LISA JACKMAN, KAREN DAVID, HILL'S ANGELS. Script and original songs: Benny Hill. Vocal backing: The Ladybirds and Jon Jon Keefe. Music Arrangements: Ronnie Aldrich. Musical Associate: Ted Taylor. Choreography: Libby Roberts. Designer: Anthony Cartledge. Associate Producer: Nigel Cook. Produced and directed by Dennis Kirkland. Includes: an Angels gym workout, 'The Hot Shoe Show' and Hill's bungled ballet routine with Louise English.

The Benny Hill Show – Montreux Television Festival Entry (compilation of the best of 1984's shows): Thames Television, Thursday 3 May 1984, 8.45–9.30 p.m. Starring BENNY HILL. With HENRY McGEE, BOB TODD, JACK WRIGHT, JENNY LEE-WRIGHT, JON JON KEEFE, LOUISE ENGLISH, ERICA LYNLEY, SUE UPTON, DEBI GAYE, HILL'S ANGELS. Script and original songs: Benny Hill. Musical Director: Ronnie Aldrich. Music Arrangements: Ted Taylor. Choreography: Libby Roberts. Designer: Anthony Cartledge. Associate Producer: Nigel Cook. Produced and directed by Dennis Kirkland.

The Benny Hill Show (repeat): Thames Television, Bank Holiday Monday 28 May 1984 (repeat of 5/1/83).

By now, a Benny Hill compilation for the August Bank Holiday was as expected as rain on the first day of your week in Brighton or the start of the cricket season, and by the same token, a half-hour clip season followed the 45-minute holiday special as sure as night followed day. 1984 was no different.

Benny Hill (repeat): Thames Television, Bank Holiday Monday 27 August 1984, 8–9 p.m. (repeat of 16/3/83).

Benny Hill (compilation): Thames Television, Wednesday 5 September 1984, 8–8.30 p.m. Starring BENNY HILL. With HENRY McGEE, BOB TODD, JACK WRIGHT. Designer: David Richens. Produced and directed by Dennis Kirkland. Includes: 'Big Poppa' and 'News at 10'.

Benny Hill (compilation): Thames Television, Wednesday 12 September 1984, 8–8.30 p.m. Starring BENNY HILL. With HENRY McGEE, BOB TODD, JACK WRIGHT. Designer: David Richens. Produced and directed by Dennis Kirkland. Includes: 'Love Will Find a Way', McGee's interview with 'French' brother and sister.

Benny Hill (compilation): Thames Television, Wednesday 19 September 1984, 8–8.30 p.m. Starring BENNY HILL. With HENRY McGEE, BOB TODD, JACK WRIGHT. Designer: David Richens. Produced and directed by Dennis Kirkland. Includes: 'Gypsy Song', Chinese tour operator and circus antics.

Benny Hill (compilation): Thames Television, Wednesday 26 September 1984, 8–8.30 p.m. Starring BENNY HILL. With HENRY McGEE, BOB TODD, JACK WRIGHT. Designer: David Richens. Produced and directed by Dennis Kirkland. Includes: 'Poster Girl', 'Jackanory' and 'Amazonian Beauty Problems'.

Benny Hill (compilation): Thames Television, Wednesday 3 October 1984, 8–8.30 p.m. Starring BENNY HILL. With HENRY McGEE, BOB TODD, JACK WRIGHT. Designer: David Richens. Produced and directed by Dennis Kirkland and Mark Stuart. Includes: 'Boy Scout Jamboree', the return of '*enfant terrible*' Scuttle.

Benny Hill (compilation): Thames Television, Wednesday 10 October 1984, 8–8.30 p.m. Starring BENNY HILL. With HENRY McGEE, BOB TODD, JACK WRIGHT. Designers: Michael Minas and David Richens. Produced and directed by Ronald Fouracre and Dennis Kirkland. Includes: 'Wondergran'.

The Benny Hill Show (repeat): Thursday 4 December 1984, 8–9 p.m. (repeat of 16/3/83).

Bring Me Sunshine – A Tribute to Eric Morecambe, OBE

For the first time in many years, there was to be no new Morecambe and Wise special for Christmas Day. Instead, Thames showcased the Palladium tribute hosted by Ernie Wise. Guests of honour were Mrs Joan Morecambe and Prince Philip, President of The British Heart Foundation, the charity helped by this fund-raising event. A 72-page souvenir brochure was produced to further boost the cof-

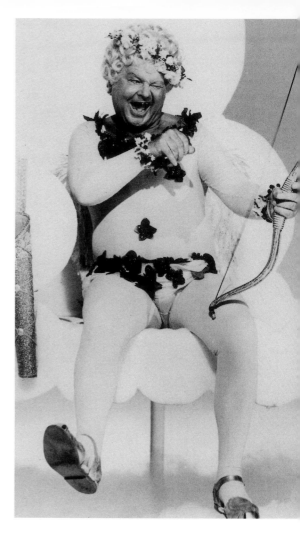

**Butter wouldn't melt -
Benny as a gloriously over aged and over ripe Cupid.**

fers. The show marked Benny Hill's first live stage performance in twenty-five years.

Bring Me Sunshine – A Tribute to Eric Morecambe,
OBE: Broadcast Thames Television, Christmas Day
1984, 6–8.30 p.m. Starring MICHAEL ASPEL,
KENNY BALL, ALISON BELL, LIONEL BLAIR,
MAX BYGRAVES, TOMMY CANNON AND
BOBBY BALL, JAMES CASEY, ROY CASTLE,
PETULA CLARK, LESLIE CROWTHER, BARRY
CRYER, SUZANNE DANIELLE, JIM DAVIDSON,
DICKIE DAVIES, FRANK FINLAY, BRUCE
FORSYTH, JILL GASCOINE, CHERRY GILLESPIE,
HANNAH GORDON, THE HALF WITS, SUSAN
HAMPSHIRE, DICKIE HENDERSON, BENNY
HILL, DIANE KEEN, BONNIE LANGFORD,
LULU, FRANCIS MATTHEWS, FULTON MACKAY,
NANETTE NEWMAN, DES O'CONNOR, MICK
OLIVER, ELAINE PAGE, MICHAEL PARKINSON,
BERTICE REDDING, ANGELA RIPPON, WAYNE
SLEEP, JIMMY TARBUCK, JOHN THAW, THE
TILLER GIRLS, ARTHUR TOLCHER, BRYN
WILLIAMS, ELI WOODS, MIKE YARWOOD, THE
IRVING DAVIES DANCERS, THE STEPHEN HILL
SINGERS. Orchestra: Harry Rabinowitz.
Choreography: Irving Davies. Script: Barry Cryer and
Sid Colin. Staged and directed by Mark Stuart and
Robin Nesbitt. Thames Consultant: Billy Marsh.
Designer: Peter Le Page. Director: Mark Stuart.
Executive Producers: Philip Jones and Louis Benjamin.

By the end of 1984, the Thames comedy scene had radically changed. When Tommy Cooper, Eric Morecambe and Leonard Rossiter died in harness at ITV, their genius was celebrated by a flurry of repeats, but Hill was considered part of a fast-vanishing tradition (having long since been given Tony Hancock's old handle, 'the lad himself'), and British comedy tastes were changing.

Hill doggedly went on with the same routine, his infrequent new shows were supplemented by countless repeats and looked dangerously old-fashioned in schedules which also boasted Ben Elton, *Girls on Top* and Rowan Atkinson. With less and less original material being produced, Hill's image was most frequently showcased via dodgy Scuttle impressions on *The Grumbleweeds Show*, while Thames continued to churn out 25-minute

Benny Hill compilations. These might have been perfect to top or tail *Coronation Street* or plug the gap before *Miss World*, but the result was that Hill was seemingly always on screen with yet more reheated, extremely familiar material, and his links with outmoded beauty contests and the traditional TV fare of their parents meant that he was considered a boring dinosaur of British comedy by the younger generation. Seen as sexist or old-fashioned, *The Benny Hill Show* wasn't attracting the audience figures it once enjoyed.

On the international scene, of course, the situation couldn't have been more different. Hill attended the 1984 Montreux Festival to be greeted as a comic genius of world-wide importance. In 1985, he attended the special 25th anniversary festivities to pick up a specially created award for a past winner whose work had been seen in the most countries. The comedian was still nursing ill health, and eighteen months earlier had been admitted to Cromwell House with a bleeding ulcer, but to the outside world, Benny Hill was still the saucebox of old, and European travel happily came to a grinding halt if a pretty girl was available for publicity pictures. Hill now insisted that he had to have a scantily clad lovely on his arm whenever he appeared in public – while eating at one of his favourite restaurants, he even grabbed a waitress from her duties so photographers would not snap him alone.

The Benny Hill Show. Thames Television, Easter Monday 8 April 1985, 8–9 p.m. Starring BENNY HILL. With HENRY McGEE, BOB TODD, JON JON KEEFE, LOUISE ENGLISH, JENNY LEE-WRIGHT, SUE UPTON, LEN KEYES, HILL'S ANGELS. Script and original songs: Benny Hill. Music Arrangements: Ronnie Aldrich. Choreography: Libby Roberts. Backing vocals: The Ladybirds. Designer: Jan Chaney. Associate Producer: Nigel Cook. Produced and directed by Dennis Kirkland. Includes: Scuttle tries to save the British film industry – with disastrous results, Hill takes a look at the hazards of life on the street, the evils of drink are explored, and the Angels perform on the beach

The Benny Hill Show. Thames Television, Bank Holiday Monday 27 May 1985, 8-9 p.m. Starring BENNY HILL. With HENRY McGEE, BOB TODD, JACK WRIGHT, KERRY GALLAGHER, ALISON BELL, ERICA LYNLEY, JON JON KEEFE, LOUISE ENGLISH, LORAINE DOYLE, LEN KEYES, SUE UPTON, JEROLD WELLS, JADE WESTBROOK, HILL'S ANGELS. Script and original songs: Benny Hill. Musical Director: Ronnie Aldrich. Musical Associate: Ted Taylor. Choreography: Libby Roberts. Backing vocals: The Ladybirds. Designer: Jan Chaney. Associate Producer: Nigel Cook. Produced and directed by Dennis Kirkland. Includes: weather house man meeting weather house girl, Hill as a lovelorn Scots chappie, and a version of *Carmen* with Bizet's music and Hill's lyrics (he had seen three productions very recently, and decided the time was right for a parody).

The Benny Hill Show (repeat): Thames Television, Wednesday 28 August 1985, 8–9 p.m. (repeat of 16/1/84).

The Benny Hill Show (compilation): Thames Television, Thursday 14 November 1985, 8–8.30 p.m. Starring BENNY HILL. With HENRY McGEE, BOB TODD, JACK WRIGHT. Designers: Bill Laslett and Mike Hall. Produced and directed by Dennis Kirkland. Includes: Hill as maternal family head and 'The Monte Carbolic Show'.

The Benny Hill Show (compilation): Thames Television, Thursday 21 November 1985, 8–8.30 p.m. Starring BENNY HILL. With HENRY McGEE, BOB TODD, JACK WRIGHT, BRENDA ARNAU, DILYS WATLING. Designers: David Marshall and Mike Hall. Produced and directed by Mark Stuart. Includes: Kojak and Fanny Craddock parodies.

The Benny Hill Show (compilation): Thames Television, Thursday 28 November 1985, 8–8.30 p.m. Starring BENNY HILL. With HUGH PADDICK, BOB TODD, JACK WRIGHT, LEE GIBSON. Designers: Bill Palmer and Roger Allen. Produced and directed by Keith Beckett and Peter Frazer-Jones. Includes: Hill as a New York family man and 'The German Navy Choir'.

The Benny Hill Show (compilation): Thames Television, Thursday 5 December 1985, 8–8.30 p.m. Starring BENNY HILL. With HENRY McGEE, BOB TODD, JACK WRIGHT, JENNY LEE-WRIGHT, LOUISE ENGLISH. Designers: Robin Parker and David Richens. Produced and directed by Dennis Kirkland. Includes: 'The Lower Tidmarsh Fire Brigade'.

The Benny Hill Show (compilation): Thames Television, Thursday 12 December 1985, 8–8.30 p.m. Starring BENNY HILL. With HENRY McGEE, BOB TODD, JACK WRIGHT, STELLA MORAY, BELLA EMBERG. Designers: Robin Parker and Bill Palmer. Produced and directed by Mark Stuart and Dennis Kirkland. Includes: the adventures of a video machine, Hill's Southern Belle, and the Angels at a street party.

The Benny Hill Show (compilation): Thames Television, Thursday 19 December 1985, 8–8.30 p.m. Starring BENNY HILL. With HENRY McGEE, JENNY LEE-WRIGHT, STELLA MORAY, EDDIE BUCHANAN. Designers: Mike Hall and Tony Borer. Produced and directed by Mark Stuart and Ronald Fouracre. Includes: 'Eskimo Nell' and 'Villain of the Year Awards'.

The Benny Hill Show (compilation): Thames Television, Thursday 30 December 1985, 8–8.30 p.m. Starring BENNY HILL. With HENRY McGEE, BOB TODD, JACK WRIGHT, JILLIANE FOOT, CHARLES STAPLEY. Designers: Robin Parker, Mike Hall and David Marshall. Produced and directed by Mark Stuart and Keith Beckett. Includes: room service at the Hotel Sordide with Hill as a waiter, and Hill's variation on *The*

South Bank Show.

Benny Hill had lived at No. 2 Queensgate, West London, for over a quarter of a century, and when the next-door flat became vacant in 1986, he took on that property as well. This uncharacteristic branching out was to be short-lived, however, for the increased building work in the block – a complete new floor was being constructed – forced Hill out in June 1986. By now, the press speculation was clearly getting to Hill, and when he heard that this was the start of a two-year building programme, he feared for his privacy, dreading that an unsuspecting worker hanging from scaffolding outside his window might catch him with a young lady and sell his story to the press.

Despite the length of time he had lived in the flat, it had never really become a home. He rented most of the furniture, the only framed photograph from his illustrious career was one of him meeting the Queen and Prince Philip at the 1955 Royal Variety Show, and most of the floorspace was littered with half-finished script ideas and photographs of Hill's Angels. Although he owned two television sets and three video recorders, he mainly frequented the tiny bedroom and dining room, leaving the huge living room untouched unless he was expecting guests. A cleaner by the name of Lynne could make little headway, although Hill frantically tidied up before she arrived! The living room had been decked out by *TV Times* for a photograph spread of Hill at home, and as usual, several of Hill's Angels were invited. When the charade was over, Hill gave the girls all the ornaments and pictures the magazine had provided.

He had never sold the Southampton property of his mother, so he returned home to No. 22 Westrow Gardens, cheered by the cosmopolitan lifestyle, hooked on the new Ocean Village with its wealth of restaurants and clubs, and at home with family (his cousin, Christopher) and friends (including Mimi Vevy, who had known him since the 1930s). The Southampton residence had all his parents' old furniture in place, so the contents of the London flat went into storage (where they remained until Hill died in 1992). He wanted to buy a house in Hampshire, and having been advised by financial experts to find a property worth at least £1 million, he began to search. The New Forest was a favourite location, but soon the Isle of Wight seemed a better option. Its thriving community spirit, good theatrical traditions and plenty of familiar faces – Billy Whittaker and Mimi Law, who had played with Hill at the Palace, Plymouth, and stood in for him at the Wellington Pier, Great Yarmouth, when he had suffered from appendicitis; Sylvia Thorley, who used to audition

You dirty old man - Down and Out with Benny Hill.

the girls for his show and had known the star since US blast-off in 1979 – meant that he visited the island frequently. However, no suitable property was available, Hill found himself getting used to life in Southampton again, and what had been planned as a brief stopgap became a much more permanent arrangement. Sue Upton's husband, Richard, helped redecorate the Southampton property, while preserving the spirit of his mother's house, and Hill seemed perfectly happy to settle there.

His problematic housing situation took up all of Hill's time, and he made no episodes for Thames for 1987 transmission. This was his first real break since 1969. However, full of fresh ideas, he spent the summer of 1988 eagerly filming at Teddington, by which time, in addition to his Southampton property, he also had a flat near the studio. Concern over his public image had made a few changes to Hill's life – indeed, he only modernized the house in Southampton because press speculation had claimed it was a *Psycho*-like shrine to his dead mother which highlighted the comedian's madness and/or meanness. His Teddington flat was chosen simply because it had no garden, which meant no gardener, which meant no one would be hanging around the place to pick up Hill stories to sell to the papers.

The Benny Hill Show. Thames Television, Wednesday 12 March 1986, 8–9 p.m. Starring BENNY HILL. With HENRY McGEE, ANNA DAWSON, BOB TODD, JON JON KEEFE, LOUISE ENGLISH, LEN KEYES, SIDNEY ARNOLD, HILL'S ANGELS. Designer: Jan Chaney. Directed and produced by Dennis Kirkland. Includes: a meeting with Hollywood producers in Cannes, a tango dance routine, the world's worst handyman, and a 1930s sea cruise on 'The Love Ship' with Hill as Captain and Dawson as the daughter of the ship's owner.

The Benny Hill Show. Thames Television, Easter Monday 31 April 1986, 8–9 p.m. Starring BENNY HILL. With HENRY McGEE, BOB TODD, ANNA DAWSON, JON JON KEEFE, LORRAINE DOYLE, SUE UPTON, JEROLD WELLS, ALISON and REBECCA MARSH, JADE WESTBROOK, HILL'S ANGELS. Musical Director: Ronnie Aldrich. Designer: Jan Chaney. Produced and directed by Dennis Kirkland. Includes: Hill haunted by luscious lovelies, Parisian escapades, a *Dynasty* parody, and the German version of *Crossroads*.

The Benny Hill Show. Thames Television, Wednesday 16 April 1986, 8–9 p.m. Starring BENNY HILL. With HENRY McGEE, ANNA DAWSON, BOB TODD, JON JON KEEFE, HELEN HORTON, KATHY STAFF, LORRAINE DOYLE, LEN KEYES, SIDNEY ARNOLD, HILL'S ANGELS. Musical Director: Ronnie Aldrich. Choreography: Libby Roberts. Designer: Jan Chaney. Produced and directed by Dennis Kirkland. Includes: Resurrection of the spirit of vaudeville, a look at our funny old world in song, and a camera trick sees Hill edited out of his own show.

Despite returning to the family home, Hill was still estranged from his brother and sister, Leonard and Diana. When Diana – whom he once described, accurately, as looking like 'me in drag' – died from leukaemia in Swan Hill, Australia, in 1984, he didn't go to her funeral. He loved her deeply, and he hadn't visited her purely because her death followed so swiftly the announcement of her illness, but still very nervous about the public's reaction to her outspoken socialist beliefs, his natural distrust of left-wing politics escalated to self-protective denial of any controversy.

After their sister's death, brothers Benny and

Leonard got on marginally better. During 1987–88's research for his book *Saucy Boy*, the hunched figure of retired headmaster-turned-comic historian Leonard would frequently be seen wandering up to Teddington Studios, with comically feigned expressions of impatience from the star of the show. Hill helped with his brother's book (published posthumously in 1990), but the picture of the two brothers on the inside cover engaged in a 'friendly stranglehold' spoke volumes.

The Benny Hill Show (repeat season): Thames Television, Wednesday 21 May 1986, 8–9 p.m. (repeat of 8/4/85), Wednesday 9 July 1986, 8–9 p.m., Bank Holiday Monday 25 August 1986, 8–9 p.m. (repeat of 27/5/85).

The Benny Hill Show (compilation): Thames Television, Monday 8 September 1986, 8.30–9 p.m. Starring BENNY HILL. With BOB TODD, JOHNNY VYVYAN, JENNY LEE-WRIGHT. Designers: Michael Minas and David Richens. Produced and directed by Ronald Fouracre and Dennis Kirkland. Including: Greek song, 'Old Age Olympics'.

The Benny Hill Show (compilation): Thames Television, Monday 15 September 1986, 8.30–9 p.m. Starring BENNY HILL. With HENRY McGEE, JACK WRIGHT, DILYS WATLING, EDDIE BUCHANAN. Designers: Tony Borer and Robin Parker. Produced and directed by Dennis Kirkland and Mark Stuart. Includes: 'Casanova', 'The Milk Marketing Board Choir', and clown stripping.

The Benny Hill Show (compilation): Thames Television, Wednesday 26 November 1986, 8.30–9 p.m. Starring BENNY HILL. With HENRY McGEE, BOB TODD, JACK WRIGHT, BELLA EMBERG. Designers: Bill Laslett and Robin Parker. Produced and directed by Keith Beckett and Dennis Kirkland. Includes: 'Digger Blue'.

The Benny Hill Show (compilation): Thames Television, Wednesday 3 December 1986, 8.30–9 p.m. Starring BENNY HILL. With HENRY McGEE, JACK WRIGHT, NICOLAS PARSONS, DIANA DARVEY. Designers: Tony Borer and Robin Tarsnane. Produced and directed by Dennis Kirkland and Mark Stuart. (Includes: 'The National Health'.)

The Benny Hill Show (compilation): Thames Television, Wednesday 11 December 1986, 8.30–9 p.m. Starring BENNY HILL. With HENRY McGEE, BOB TODD,

JACK WRIGHT, GERALDINE. Designer: Peter Elliott and Robin Tarsnane. Produced and directed by Dennis Kirkland. Includes: 'Chow Mein's Chinese Show' and Hill's Dracula versus Upton's Wondergran.

The Benny Hill Show (compilation): Thames Television, Wednesday 17 December 1986, 8.30-9 p.m. Starring BENNY HILL. With HENRY McGEE, BOB TODD, JACK WRIGHT, JENNY LEE-WRIGHT. Designers: Peter Elliott and David Ferris. Produced and directed by Dennis Kirkland. Includes: 'The Gay Caballero' and clown mime.

Wounded by feminist critiques, Hill's later Thames work reflected the niggling self-doubt that what he was doing was flying in the face of the new wave of political correctness. The BBC had abandoned *The Black and White Minstrel Show* in 1986, ITV had dropped *Miss World* in 1988, and it wasn't long before Benny Hill followed.

For his final shows, filmed for Thames during 1987–89, Hill desperately tried to refine and reshape his work. As a result, the total freedom that had allowed him to pen his most satisfying material was gone. Libby Roberts was asked to tone down the Hill's Angels choreography, and began injecting opera-styled pieces, stronger female characters and less raunchiness. With a sense of battling against current trends, *The Benny Hill Show* set sail for its last rocky seasons.

As it happens, much of the material is very good, ultra-careful Hill, successfully moving away from seductive dance routines with Hill's Angels to seductive dance routines with slightly more fully-clothed, certainly more streetwise, man-angry Hill's Angels. The role of the girls moved away from just flashing bare thighs to injecting clear – albeit laboured and half-hearted – attempts to address the feminist viewpoint. A typical example sees the girls in dresses (very tight, admittedly, but dresses nevertheless), dancing to Elton John's 'I'm Still Standing', causing feeble male heads to turn and Hill's Toulouse-Lautrec to wobble like a child's toy. The situations are reversed with a change of record ('It's Raining Men') and strip club setting. Hill is a mistreated 'Bunnyboy' figure, one of the girls knees a male in the groin to dry her hands on his forced outbreath, and all the usual lads are used as makeshift vehicles to get the girls out of the rain.

Hill's Angels, hardly qualifying for the title in their new guise, were now even more in command of their sexual destinies. Even in familiar, thigh-slapping Country & Western mode with Hill's Bronco Billy, girl power ruled, OK, with the sexually inadequate Hill of old fantasizing *à la* Peter Cook about film stars – 'Jane Fonda, Jane Seymour and me!' Hill's delightful country bumpkin still relates his innuendo-fuelled stories and songs, surrounded by glamorous, square-dancing hayseeds and Anna Dawson's superior lady of the night, but even with a final offer of a passionate night, Hill needs to be helped off stage – a charming comment on advancing years and continued sexual keenness.

The Angels were still used as decorative fillers between the struggling sketches, but now they couldn't rely on saucy costumes to get male temperatures rising, so they were featured as boxers caught on the boxing ropes, a cringe-making routine as snooker balls prancing about the studios in coloured chiffon, and a decidedly saucy appearance in cricket whites. Hill redeemed this dross somewhat with W.C. Fields-like cue-chalking antics, a wild-haired player employing golfing techniques on the snooker table

Still reversing the sexual roles -
A Benny boy Bunny boy pose for the tail -end Thames years.

and 'The End' emblazoned across his split trousers (you can't keep a good man down!), but this sort of material wasn't going to win him any awards. Before this sporting madness, Hill made a rare public address – out of character and taking on Kenneth Horne-like authority – to answer to the most frequently asked questions ('Yes!', 'The ostrich!') and his own most asked question (concerning the Angels).

Performed in his usual nervy, self-aware style, it's refreshing to see the real man behind the disguises. But this was not the nervous Benny Hill of the late 1940s, struggling to make a name for himself on the post-war comedy scene, this is the nervous Benny Hill of the late 1980s, a multi-millionaire who could rightfully claim to be the world's most famous comedian. Still, little had changed in forty years, and Hill's personality shone through his embarrassment at presenting the truly dreadful one-liners and quips that were to follow. Instead of a man who knew his shows were world-beaters, Hill now pleaded with his audience, almost ashamed at trawling out the same old barrage of reheated smut and predictable sight gags – but the audience still wanted it! Beloved old favourites like Fred Scuttle, embracing political comment and the gutter journalism of the tabloid press with 'The Daily Scuttle', were met with howls of appreciation. Sparring with Henry McGee and shooting cheeky grins to the audience, Hill was quite clearly in his element.

Other sketches exposed the private persona of Benny Hill – arriving late for a charity dinner, gorging himself, and struggling through a public address to the assembled masses. The throwaway sketches were just as sharp, with Hill's performance as effective as ever. With Anna Dawson as the definitive nagging wife, Hill took his hen-pecked husband character towards a new decade. Jokes like his reaction to Dawson's condemnation of his coy peck on the cheek, 'If you kissed me like that ten years ago you'd still be single!' – 'Now she tells me!', have a Jewish comedy quality. This new man seems to have to justify his passion for booze or spending time with the lads as part of his family duties. It doesn't wash, of course, but the attempt is made to undermine the male ego at all times.

However, Hill's Angels could still be complete bimbos within the confines of the sketches, with Hill's beautiful new bride confusing the cooker with the record player, while depression over a housekeeper with no culinary skills leads to Hill's consuming a mustard/toothpaste sandwich – the humour was all very tired and predictable, but there was an unfathomable comic magic in that strained expression. The smoke pouring out of the mouth might not make you laugh, but those frustrated eyes certainly did. Henry McGee's contribution was as potent as ever, and even a return to one of Hill's favourite comedy terrains, the western, produced a real classic in the shape of 'The Halitosis Kid'.

The techniques employed in the sketch were nothing new, but it didn't seem to matter. The speeded-up visuals, Bob Todd as the overbearing, nagging wife and the fanfare of Mexican trumpets heralded the appearance of the stunning silhouette of our hapless hero, a bespectacled clone of Fred Scuttle, his curse of bad breath described in Hill's brilliantly on-form ballad. The performance was outstanding, Hill's crestfallen gaze into camera never too sentimental it let the laughs drift away, and Henry McGee's petulant doctor figure was the perfect pillar of authority, suggesting the Kid take horse manure to tone down his problem a bit! The audience reaction was wildly enthusiastic, and one can imagine Hill's off-stage smile of satisfaction as his new material hit home. The comedian embraced the endearing naivety of his slapstick heroes, greeting the black-hearted, black-suited villain of Bob Todd, treating his horse to a Harrods nosebag and injecting a typical western clichéd portrayal of women as either sweet and innocent lucky Lulu Belle or the stocking-flashing tart with a heart. However, while the bad breath sight gags (peeling wallpaper, killing cuckoo-clock cuckoos, knocking out the baddies) are vintage Hill, the unsubtle camp cowboy in the pink suit from Keefe doesn't scan, and merely highlights the fact that Hill was out of touch. However, the Chaplinesque sunset finale is a charming close to a very effective late-period Hill romp, complemented with a few good quickies, such as Todd's doctor thinking it's the drink to blame, half-heartedly looking after McGee's cat only to put himself out, middle-aged sexual advances, and a further domestic snippet with a boiled egg overcooked for half an hour – Hill's bemused look is the stuff of comic greatness.

Perhaps the most celebrated throwaway from 1988 is the black and white commercial with Hill, Todd and the others as bowler-hatted businessmen. The pink blush to Todd's embarrassed face and the reference to the *Financial Times* advertising slogan with the 'No F ... T. No comment' tag is both brilliantly original and totally unsubtle – like all the best Benny Hill material.

It's interesting to see that Hill made a concentrated effort to balance the expected slapstick with clever wordplay sketches. One of the most effective sees Hill as a petulant waiter, discussing the celebrity-based menu for his clients. Edwina Currie with Anneka Rice, Magnus Pyke and the like gives way to much more inventive/barrel-scraping examples. There are the joyous ('Torvell and

Dean?' – 'Skate, Madame!' delivered with eyes reaching for the heavens), the cruel ('Oliver Reed' – 'Thick slice of ham!'), the tragically dated ('Charles and Diana Salad' – 'Lettuce alone!'), the cheeky ('Samantha Fox' – 'Game bird without dressing!', at which Hill cracked up, to the delight of the audience), the obvious ('Joan Bakewell Tart') and the obviously brilliant ('Vera Lynn' – 'Whale meat again!'). It may be packed with old jokes, but this single routine shows the old Benny Hill at his best. He certainly wasn't in the tired gangster musical number, with Hill hamming it up shamelessly as Brooklyn Benny, running through some crummy old gags, his coming-out-of-jail party packed with 1920s flappers and culminating in a strained, innu-endo-fuelled lament about his sad life story.

In a move away from the total domination of Hill's Angels and in an attempt to bring to the screen the lov-able 'uncle' figure that Benny Hill was off-camera, the shows introduced a new element – Hill's Little Angels. Occasionally slightly irritating, other times acting Hill off the screen, these kids, mainly made up from the families of Sue Upton and Dennis Kirkland, made Hill's aged authority figure's life a misery. Here, it's scouting antics, with chocolate-munching, fine fresh air and exercise. The young blonde still flashes her knickers, but the effect is more endearing than stimulating, while the silent slap-stick atmosphere is heightened with a 1920s jazz score like those imposed on the Robert Youngson movie com-pilations of the late 1950s and early 1960s. In a twist on Woody Allen's film weaklings, Hill can't beat the girl at an arm-wrestling contest, the kids outplay him in a less than friendly game of cricket, and a bit of golf business allows Hill's comic overacting to go into overdrive.

There's something endearingly old-fashioned and bumbling in Hill's performances from this period, and perhaps this was the right direction for his comedy to take, but he tended to rely too much on the Little Angels, as with Hill's Angels five years earlier, and he still happily gave some of his most potent work to his team of sup-porting players (Todd as a kindly vicar who gets all his ladies pregnant). The quickies don't quite gel, but there's decaying elegance in Hill's crusty old teacher bumbling through an incongruous but pleasing rhyming lecture ('Buttress – female butt!'), resembling a Ronnie Barker tongue-twister delivered with affection. The wall gag con-cerning Jackie Collins joining a nunnery is pretty good, and 'Smile Week' mixes Pythonesque bizarreness with Hill's usual sped-up chase into eternity. There are no sus-penders here, though, just the familiar farceurs bumbling through disasters (including a punk relieving himself in a policeman's helmet). There's a smile on everyone's face

until the unlikely event comes to an end and everybody chases Hill to a spectacular conclusion in a water park.

Female mockery may have been out, but xenopho-bic material certainly wasn't, with Hill and Todd playing a couple of dithering Jews debating about lending $50, while McGee's policeman tackles Hill's thick Irish shop-keeper. The male ego is questioned again with Anna Dawson finding the library book *Man: The Superior Sex* in the fiction section and there's a bit of politics as Johnny Hutch (who had replaced the aged angst of the late Jackie Wright) comments on his miserable pension, telling his butcher he's on a 'salary-controlled diet'. 'Just married' scenarios, Dawson's Edith Evans-like Norfolk turkey dia-tribe and Hill's dropped trousers are all pretty standard fare, as is the skit on the latest keep-fit fad, jogging (a milkman on his rounds making butter), Hill's Olympic flame lighting a cigarette and Upton's aged one toppling over a cliff like Wile E. Coyote. Sketches like the reverend eating from a dog bowl were neither original (Peter Sellers in *Heavens Above!* springs to mind) or amusing, Bob Todd was being increasingly asked to play the hopeless drunk, and even Fred Scuttle seems wasted in a circus routine with the Little Angels, but as Senora Benny surrounded by the familiar leggy girls and reprising snatches of his 1970s classic 'Anna Marie', Hill is at full comic power – chucking in slang smut ('meat and two veg') and delight-ing in the near-the-knuckle mention of sweetbreads.

Some of the sketches (pocket calculator, leather boy with zips on everything including his mouth, the sad-voiced anti-punk chap) were well below standard, while the Little Angels were getting more and more airtime, Hill now floundering as an underemployed stooge, as in the obvious yet charming 'Stinky Jones' telephone routine and the Ancient Rome/Edgware Road museum misun-derstanding. But when the Little Angels routines worked, they were delightful. Perhaps the most effective sketch had Hill as an aged buffer, family retainer to Todd's fruity, monocled gent. In a never-never land of maids with frilly knickers, croquet on the lawn and glorious vintage cars, Hill's put-upon butler brilliantly juggles scoops of ice-cream and deals with the troublesome kids with an air of heightened insanity. Again, the idea may go on too long, but there's a definite charm at work here.

The original Hill's Angels were still allowed to do some of their own stuff (Hutch's demand for 'a cheap

overnight bag' gets him Sue Upton for £5 with a lot of wiggling poses thrown in), while the laboured, albeit enjoyable, 'Swiss Miss' routine sees the girls bashing their behinds with tambourines to 'Toot Toot Tootsie'. However, some of the most obvious quickies were still hitting home, with Hill intriguingly cast as the 92-year-old man visiting Doctor Henry McGee and explaining that every time he goes to toilet in the middle of the night, God turns the light on. Dawson's petulant outburst that he has mistaken the toilet for the fridge again brings on a sublime look of amazement from Hill in definitive form.

The slapstick history lesson may go on too long, but there are some good moments along the way, from the Stone Age (a cool Hill, looking like an overweight Kris Kristofferson, battling Todd), Vikings (Hill blowing his own trumpet and riding Todd's mother figure), Cromwellian (wenching and sword-fighting with snooker rules) and First World War (with Todd's Germanic antics) to, best of all, the Second World War section. A lot of the previous sight gags may have been reheated, but Hill really hit form with this last portion, embracing the spirit of *Oh! What a Lovely War* with the Hitler shooting gallery, including collective television knowledge with a snatch of the *Dad's Army* theme music, and injecting a brilliant sight gag when religious salvation turns to Nazi domination – as the image of a cross through the window becomes a swastika on closer inspection. Finally, Hill even gets the female Nazi officers down to black underwear and suspenders, even though this striptease is merely a

ruse to steal their uniforms. Examples may be few and far between in these last shows, but Hill was still the top television comedian around when his foot was fully on the accelerator. With a cheerful whistle and Chaplinesque stroll off into legend, this is Hill in vintage form. However, Hill was clearly at his best and most polished when consciously twisting the conventions of his own past. It was funny when the old format was revisited, hilarious and wise when the old format was readdressed.

With Hill's Angels inhabiting the ritzy Chicago-Go Club, it's full steam ahead for one of Benny's landmark pieces – 'Tanya and Her Performing Men'. Tanya (Lorraine Doyle) is certainly stunning in her outfit, but again the female is in complete control of the situation, reversing the old regime of girls as comic props, and using the ugly, comically eccentric men as objects of fun. Indeed, this was a direct rehash of a 1975 sketch, 'Lana's Performing Men', which, although Moira Foot's female leader was in control, relied on acres of bare flesh, suspender belts and black panties. Bowler-hatted, bow-tied, wearing heavy boots and white long johns, Hill, Todd, Deadman and the rest are hilariously undermined, Doyle's sexually charged power is heightened with swathes of 'Russian' jibberish, her dominance enforced when she balances a chair in her mouth, and Hill's desperate, sheepish attempts to impress her result in him attempting to cheat at his tricks. Complete with a quick burst of the *Match of the Day* theme, this is funny, fresh and interesting. Sadly, it was all probably too little too late. No, if Hill was to fully reinvent himself, he would have to return to the satirical glories of his early BBC work. There is a hint of an attempt to do just this in the skit involving the murder victim who wasn't quite dead when the crime squad arrived (hence the painted outline on the floor has arms and legs akimbo), but the real gem of these final Benny Hill shows is the undervalued but totally brilliant parody of *The Cook Report* – 'The Crook Report'.

Hill, in the title role, is an arrogant television journalist, dragging his crew around with him, causing a hard time for all, and desperately trying to preserve his on-screen crusader image against the reality of conniving unpleasantness. Cleverly using the television medium itself for the humour (as in the early days), Hill panics when he thinks an outrage has been caught on microphone, banging the door when trying to talk to some champagne socialist who runs an exploitative carpet factory. In a single sketch, Hill is xenophobic (the Asian figures of Albert Moses and Anna Dawson are mocked – 'That's a good old English name, innit?'), sexist (he complains to Dawson that he wants to talk to the organ grinder not the monkey, and dismissively calls her 'darling') and cruel to animals (the escaping van runs over a cat), but there is a self-mocking, self-reflective edge here that had been missing for years. Forced to let his cool slip and swear on camera (a hasty 'Piss off!' blurred by a car horn), bashing through the gates when his mistake and bad conduct are discovered, brilliantly parodying the fly-on-the-wall camera angles of 'real TV' and finally hoist by his own petard when the comic chase ends in a car crash surrounded by reporters trying to hound him during his last seconds, it's the old Benny Hill retold in post-modernist fashion. This is a cynical, richly inventive, hilarious and thought-provoking piece of work. The masterpiece of his final Thames days, it was one of the last items he filmed for the network. Tragically and ironically, it was also one of the best.

The Benny Hill Show: Thames Television, Wednesday 13 January 1988, 8–9 p.m. Starring BENNY HILL. With HENRY McGEE, BOB TODD, ANNA DAWSON, JON JON KEEFE, LORRAINE DOYLE, SUE UPTON, JEROLD WELLS, DEREK DEADMAN, JOHNNY HUTCH, MIKE MULLEY, ZOE BRYANT, SHARON KIEL, HILL'S ANGELS, HILL'S LITTLE ANGELS. Script: Benny Hill. Musical Director: Ronnie Aldrich. Designer: Alison Wratten. Produced and directed by Dennis Kirkland. Includes: 'The Halitosis Kid', 'Celebrity Menu' and 'Keep Fit with the Little Angels'.

The Benny Hill Show: Thames Television, Wednesday 27 April 1988, 8–9 p.m. Starring BENNY HILL. With HENRY McGEE, BOB TODD, ANNA DAWSON, JON JON KEEFE, SUE UPTON, LORRAINE DOYLE, DEREK DEADMAN, JOHNNY HUTCH, CHRISTINE PILGRIM, GARY O'BEE, DUNCAN PETTIGREW. Script: Benny Hill. Musical Director: Ronnie Aldrich. Musical Associate: Ted Taylor. Designer: Alison Wratten. Produced and directed by Dennis Kirkland. Includes: Hill as a pigeon chatting up a budgie, a Mexican revolution in a graffiti-covered town, and 'Lana and Her Performing Men'.

The Benny Hill Show (repeat): Thames Television, Wednesday 4 May 1988, 8–9 p.m. (repeat of 16/4/86).

The Benny Hill Show (compilation): Thames Television, Thursday 8 September 1988, 8.30–9 p.m. Starring BENNY HILL. With HENRY McGEE, BOB TODD, JACK WRIGHT, LESLEY GOLDIE, JON JON KEEFE. Designers: Anthony Cartledge and Bill Laslett. Produced and directed by Dennis Kirkland and Mark Stuart. Includes: Hurricane Hill and Fred Scuttle.

The Benny Hill Show (compilation): Thames Television, Monday 19 September 1988, 8–8.30 p.m. Starring BENNY HILL. With NICHOLAS PARSONS, JACK WRIGHT, BOB TODD, BELLA EMBERG, DIANA DARVEY, JERROLD WELLS, JON JON KEEFE, LESLEY GOLDIE, JIM TYSON. Designers: Tony Borer and Bill Laslett. Produced and directed by Mark Stuart and Dennis Kirkland. Includes: 'Colditz', and the mad Scottish schoolmaster.

The Benny Hill Show (compilation): Thames Television, Monday 26 September 1988, 8–8.30 p.m. Starring BENNY HILL. With HENRY McGEE, BOB TODD, JACK WRIGHT, RITA WEBB, JENNY LEE-WRIGHT, PAT ASHTON, ROGER FINCH, KEN SEDD, EDDY CONNOR, EDDIE BUCHANAN. Designers: Tony Borer and Bill Laslett. Produced and directed by Mark Stuart and Dennis Kirkland. Includes: Scouts, a Victorian scandal, and a *Blind Date* parody.

The Benny Hill Show (compilation): Thames Television, Monday 3 October 1988, 8–8.30 p.m. Starring BENNY HILL. With HENRY McGEE, BOB TODD, JACK WRIGHT, RITA WEBB, JENNY LEE-

WRIGHT. Designers: Peter Le Page and Bill Laslett. Produced and directed by Mark Stuart and Dennis Kirkland. Includes: Dickie Davies hosts The *Sun* Awards, and 'The Scarlet Pimple'.

The Benny Hill Show (compilation): Thames Television, Monday 10 October 1988, 8–8.30 p.m. Starring BENNY HILL. With HENRY McGEE, BOB TODD, JACK WRIGHT, HELEN HORTON, PAT ASHTON, JENNY LEE-WRIGHT, RITA WEBB, EDDIE BUCHANAN, ROGER FINCH. Designers: Bill Laslett and Tony Borer. Produced and directed by Mark Stuart and Dennis Kirkland. Includes: 'Barry Norman's Hollywood Grates' and 'Holy Matrimony'.

The Benny Hill Show (compilation): Thames Television, Monday 17 October 1988, 8–8.30 p.m. Starring BENNY HILL. With HENRY McGEE, NICHOLAS PARSONS, BOB TODD, JENNY LEE-WRIGHT, JON JON KEEFE, BOGDAN KOMINOWSKI, ERICA LYNLEY, LOUISE ENGLISH, LEN KEYES. Designers: Anthony Cartledge and Tony Borer. Directed and produced by Dennis Kirkland and John Robins. Includes: Indian–Chinese clash, night club life and Hill's drunk act.

The Benny Hill Show: Thames Television, Wednesday 8 February 1989, 8–9 p.m. Starring BENNY HILL. With HENRY McGEE, BOB TODD, ANNA DAWSON, JOHNNY HUTCH, ALBERT MOSES, JON JON KEEFE, SUE UPTON, LORRAINE DOYLE, DUGGIE SMALL, HILL'S ANGELS, HILL'S LITTLE ANGELS. Script: Benny Hill. Musical Director: Ronnie Aldrich. Choreography: Libby Roberts. Designer: Ian Russell. Produced and directed by Dennis Kirkland. Includes: 'The Daily Scuttle', a West Country singer, and 'The Crook Report'.

The Benny Hill Show: Thames Television, Wednesday 22 March 1989, 9.30–10 p.m. Starring BENNY HILL. With NICHOLAS PARSONS, BOB TODD, JENNY LEE-WRIGHT, CLOVISSA NEWCOMBE, ROGER FINCH, JOHNNY VYVYAN. Designers: Tony Borer and Michael Minas. Produced and directed by David Bell and Ronald Fouracre. Includes: Bob Dylan parody, the German professor, and the abbreviation language, OK.

The Benny Hill Show: Thames Television, Wednesday 5 April 1989, 8–9 p.m. Starring BENNY HILL. With HENRY McGEE, BOB TODD, ANNA DAWSON, JOHNNY HUTCH, JON JON KEEFE, SUE UPTON,

LOUISE ENGLISH, DUGGIE SMALL, HILL'S ANGELS, HILL'S LITTLE ANGELS. Script: Benny Hill. Musical Director: Ronnie Aldrich. Musical Associate: Ted Taylor. Choreography: Libby Roberts. Designer: Ian Russell. Produced and directed by Dennis Kirkland.

The Benny Hill Show: Thames Television, May Day, Monday 1 May 1989, 8–9 p.m. Starring BENNY HILL. With HENRY McGEE, BOB TODD, ANNA DAWSON, JOHNNY HUTCH, JON JON KEEFE, DEREK DEADMAN, JERROLD WELLS, LORRAINE DOYLE, SUE UPTON, HILL'S ANGELS, HILL'S LITTLE ANGELS. Script: Benny Hill. Musical Director: Ronnie Aldrich. Musical Associate: Ted Taylor. Choreography: Libby Roberts. Designer: Ian Russell. Produced and directed by Dennis Kirkland. Includes: Angels do television titles from *The Bill* to *Tales of the Unexpected*, Hill goes fishing with the Little Angels, the final resurrection of 'Pepys' Diary' with Henry McGee.

This season also featured Hill's Little Angels – ADAM JOHNSTONE, JOANNA KIRKLAND, JADE WESTBROOK, LOUISE WHATLING, RICHARD WHATLING – and JENNY WESTBROOK, MARTIN SLATER, CARLA DE WANSEY. Vocal backing: The Ladybirds and Francesca Boulter. Casting Director: Pat Hayley. Music Executive: Joyce Sharpen. Production Managers: Bruce Englefield, Peter Ernster and Del Randall. Studio Supervisors: Brian Kerr, Del Randall and Peter Ernster. Lighting Directors: Stuart Gain, Bob Newman, Andy Andrews and Peter Bower. Sound Supervisors: Richard Churchill, Paul Gartrell and Clive Hall. Vision Control: Bob Mason, Ian Coram, Bill Marley and Allan James. Vision Mixers: Martin Perrett, Peter Boffin, Nick Ames and Peter Phillips. Videotape Editors: Terence E. Badham, Grant Goodwin, Roger Holmes, Mark Dobson, Ray Ball and Colin Bocking. Senior Cameramen: Chris Watts, Peter Howell, Adrian J. Fearnley and Albert Almond. Film Cameramen: Ted Adcock and Ray Sieman. Film Editor: John Wright. Location Manager: Eamonn Duffy. Costumes: Allard Tobin, Fran Bolwell and Keith Rosson. Make-up: Gillian Wakeford, Ann Briggs and Pearl Rashbass. Graphics: Lester Halhed and Geoff Alexander. Stage Manager: Auriol Lee. Floor Managers: Peter Beaven, Fizz Waters and Aidan Bouler. Production Assistants: Angela Carter, Angela Morgan, Maria Finnis, Ann Tivendale and Debbie Newman.

BENNY ABROAD

'I can get my face slapped in six different languages!'
Benny Hill

Despite lower ratings at home, Benny Hill was still Thames's biggest international success, and he was more than happy to travel the world to promote his series. Some of his favourite times were spent walking in the Camargue or wandering around old Roman towns like Nimes or Arles. As early as 1969 (in an interview with Dennis Reveille, published 4 October 1969), Hill had spoken candidly about his passion for travel: over the years he would entertain prospective American buyers, attend functions throughout Europe, and even when accompanied by Dennis Kirkland and two of Hill's Angels for a holiday to Athens, he was happy to talk to the waiting reporters. Since only one interview had been promised, some sixty newspaper personnel welcomed the flight, and with Kirkland borrowing the captain's hat, Hill happily posed as Fred Scuttle on the steps of the plane. A photocall at the Acropolis was interrupted by a huge crowd of onlookers, while in Athens, a quiet beer with Kirkland was interrupted by the traffic grinding to a halt amid cries of 'Beeny 'Eel!'

A *TV Times* piece, 'For Benny There's No Hiding Place From Fame' by Larry Ashe (1–7 December 1973), told of his unease at being recognized in out-of-the-way places (once, while enjoying an Amsterdam circus, the spotlight was trained on him), but he revelled in travel. In an earlier edition of *TV Times* (20–26 November 1973), he allowed his passport to be reproduced, with his face blanked out, for the feature 'Do You Know This Man?', which revealed that he had journeyed some 120,000 miles. His profession was given as 'Actor', and indeed, he would become arguably Britain's most widely known actor of all. Much of his travelling was for pleasure, of course, but work was always on his mind. Another *TV Times* article, 'How the East was Won ... By Fred Scuttle, Ernie the Milkman ... and Benny Hill', detailed a visit to the Kung Fu film factory of Run Run Shaw in Hong Kong simply to get the flavour for his forthcoming martial arts parody. As usual in interviews, Hill couldn't resist bragging about the attraction stardom held for women – he candidly talked of escort agencies and the Far East equivalent of Soho before dropping in lusty comments about a party involving eight Australian women and him.

At the start of his world fame, Hill had used the BBC Eurovision link to talk at length to Yugoslavian fans in their own language. Russian viewers, illegally picking up Hill transmissions by tuning their receivers to Finnish broadcasts, finally saw the comedian's official debut on New Year's Eve 1988. Hill recorded a specially filmed introductory link in Russian, welcoming his viewers with warm wishes for a 'Happy and festive 1989'. All non-English-speaking screenings of Hill shows would include this personal touch, relating to the viewers in their mother tongue and then letting the mime slapstick speak for itself.

Thames Television, having won a special award in America, basked in glory when Hill starred in *A Salute to Thames*. After repeated refusals, Hill finally agreed to headline with a bit of Fred Scuttle and his usual stand-up diary-reading routine, thus giving him reassurance if he forgot his lines. America worshipped him – New York cops would greet each other with the Scuttle salute if nobody else was about. Prisoners in the San Jose Penitentiary, California, rioted because their lights-out time had been brought forward by an hour to 11 p.m., half an hour before Benny Hill's show was screened. In 1988, a survey of schoolchildren in Florida revealed that few knew London was Britain's capital, but when asked the one person they associated with Britain, the most mentioned name was Benny Hill.

That same year, Hill had been chosen to represent British comedy when in February 1988 the British Academy of Film and Television Arts presented *Hollywood Salute to British Comedy* at the Bel Air Hotel, Los Angeles. The Duke and Duchess of York attended, and Dudley Moore responded to Anjelica Huston's introduction – but the main man had the last laugh, the speech included this comment: 'the British bigot Alf Garnett begat the American bigot Archie Bunker; Benny Hill, of course, begets himself.' The 'Wishing Well' clip received a great response.

Trips to New Zealand and Australia saw Hill using the flight time to write even more material. His global fan following meant that he could no longer enjoy wandering quietly around Europe. Indulging his passion for watching bullfighting in Spain, he was disrupted by adoring fans, a trip to a Sicilian hamlet miles from anywhere provided no peace since the television was screening Benny Hill, and secret trips to the centre of Hong Kong's red light district were greeted with huge cheers from the late-night workers who watched Hill on television at 3 a.m.

CRITICAL MISJUDGEMENT

'Thames are not going to turn round and say they don't want me any more just because of a bit of criticism in the papers, are they?' Benny Hill, May 1989

When John Howard Davies, the new Head of Light Entertainment at Thames Television announced at the Montreux Festival in 1989 that Thames was about to go through some radical changes, there was something in the wind. For Benny Hill it would blow no good. Philip Jones had retired in March 1988, and his successor, Davies (who had produced the first series of *Monty Python's Flying Circus* and Frankie Howerd's ill-fated *Whoops! Baghdad*), interrupted one of Hill's studio rehearsals to introduce himself and thank him for all his efforts on behalf of Thames. He even insisted on giving his biggest star a pay rise. As usual, Hill had taken less than the usual money to allow a bigger budget for the rest of his show. Despite the changes at Thames, Hill was unworried. At that time, every climactic, television-linked disaster sketch would culminate with Hill walking off-camera shouting 'Philip!', an affectionate tribute to Jones. When Jones retired, Hill told him 'Philip!' would still be the cry, because 'John Howard' didn't have the same ring to it. In the end, that really didn't matter.

Hill promoted his work at the 1989 Cannes MIP-TV Festival at the luxury Loew's Hotel, La Napoule. Marking the 21st anniversary of Thames from Friday 21 April to Monday 24 April, the Thames press information heralded Hill as 'the world's most successful comedian and Thames' longest serving artist'. Hill was the only star in attendance at the reception at Le Château – mobbed by adoring fans and hailed as a comic master. In France, his shows were being screened five nights a week to record audiences.

After their triumphant return from Cannes, Hill and Dennis Kirkland were invited to Thames. Hill naturally assumed it was to discuss and iron out any problems for the next batch of programmes. At 10 a.m., Benny Hill walked into Davies's office. At 10.02 a.m., Benny Hill was no longer a Thames employee, dismissed 'like a schoolboy', in the words of Richard Stone. Kirkland was asked into the office, only to be greeted by an ashen-faced Hill. The simple words of the man in charge were: 'I don't want to do any more Bennys.'

The expense of the show had also been causing some concern at Thames – at £500,000 for an hour slot, it took up about four times the average budget – but when Thames published pre-tax profits of £31 million on 25 May, Benny Hill was responsible for a large proportion of that, and *Variety* would soon dub Hill 'Global TV's Top Banana'. Hill had given twenty years' loyal service, during which time Thames had made millions through international sales (the American market alone was bringing in $5 million a year). In 1984, Thames Television

International (a company set up almost solely to distribute Benny Hill shows across the world) had won the Queen's Award for Industry, with 127 out of 142 countries with broadcasting facilities taking the show. In 1985, *The Benny Hill Show* had been awarded the specially commissioned prize at the Montreux Festival for a past winner seen in most countries, and in 1986, foreign tourists hardly registered images of royalty, pop stars or murderers when Hill's Madame Tussaud's effigy was unveiled. Photographed with a host of Angels, including Louise English and Sue Upton, Hill was delighted with the representation of Fred Scuttle, and tourists queued for hours to pose with the mannekin.

However, these facts and figures were not enough. John Howard Davies was a new broom with new ideas. Benny Hill was very much part of the old regime. Cable, American imports and a host of other factors meant that television executives had to come to terms with a fast-changing industry. In a decision to radically reshape the company, Benny Hill was axed. As for Kirkland, his contract, which had some five months to run, was bought off, and both star and producer/director were suddenly jobless.

Stunned, Hill and Kirkland made for their favourite local, The King's Head, known affectionately as 'Jim's pub', and Hill immediately contacted Richard Stone to give him the news. Indeed, it was very much news to him, and he was justifiably very annoyed. His client had been Thames's biggest success for over twenty years, but had been dropped without so much as a fond farewell. Craftily, Roy Addison and Melanie Louis of the Thames press office asked Hill to agree to a press release explaining that he wanted a break from television for a year or two, to collect his thoughts and write some new material, or as the press blurb had it, 'time to travel around and observe things'. This nonsense was published on 31 May 1989. Worse was published in other papers, with the *Daily Mirror* claiming that Hill didn't want to make any more shows, the *Sun* revealing that Hill felt too old to continue, and most upsetting of all, the *Daily Star* saying that Hill's decision 'had stunned Thames TV bosses'. By 4 June, the truth had leaked out, and the *Sunday Mirror* screamed: 'Benny Hill did not retire from ITV – he was sacked.'

So, was *The Benny Hill Show* just harmless fun? Was Thames justified in ditching their biggest comedy success? Was it the fault of 'alternative comedy'? Did he fall from grace, or was he pushed? The debate about sexism in Hill's comedy has raged for years, and since his death, it is this issue that is most commonly connected with his name. But was his work an extension of saucy seaside postcards, or was it far more sinister than that?

His sacking was the culmination of events that had shaped Hill's private and public persona since the mid-1970s. Looking at Hill's work from this period, it is clear that the girls were filmed in less and less clothing, but to be fair, all British comedy of this era exploited the female form in one way or another. Be it *On the Buses* and the short-skirted, sweater-filling clippies, the later, more flesh-free *Carry On* pictures or the array of chorus girls in every variety show, this was a period when cars were sold using images of models in basques, when Madeleine Smith as an ancient Briton could be portrayed eagerly awaiting a Viking's rape and pillage in an advert, when Valerie Leon slinked through Hi-Karate after-shave commercials in a black leather catsuit, and when schoolgirls such as Penny Spencer and Carol Hawkins in *Please Sir!* could get adult male viewers hot under the collar. Hill was simply one of the leading figures in a national consciousness that saw red-blooded, girl-loving lads like Sid James, Peter Wyngarde and Roger Moore as cool.

It was a time when European unity was unheard of, when the slogan 'I'm Backing Britain' was on everyone's lips, and when opinions later condemned as politically incorrect were commonplace. *TV Times* could promote Hill's guest star, *Oh! Calcutta* performer Brenda Arnau, as 'Benny's Black Beauty!' and kit her out in 'native' skins alongside the star in 'white hunter' outfit; 21-year-old French actress Anne Bruzak was nicknamed 'Froggy', and was actually billed on the show as such, and what's more, she happily posed for Hill publicity shots in a Union Jack bikini.

This is not to say all those attitudes were right, merely that Hill's humour meant no harm. His collection of girls reflected British national culture at a time when, in mainstream cinema, British comedy featured full-frontal female nudity in films like *Adventures of a Private Eye* and *Rosie Dixon – Night Nurse*. They may have been 18-rated, but the cinemas were packed, and everybody from Hill cohort Bob Todd to old-time family comic Arthur Askey appeared in such films. Benny Hill has come to symbolize the attitudes and excesses of the era mainly because of his success and the longevity of his career.

By 1980, the *Carry Ons*, *On the Buses* and the like had vanished from view, leaving only the increasingly frowned upon national institution of Miss World, but Benny Hill soldiered on with a highly successful breakthrough into video entertainment when Thames compiled a 58-minute video 'of superb slapstick humour' entitled *Benny Hill and Friends*. The overemphasis on the friends notwithstanding, this tape handily catalogues the state of

Hill's comedy in the mid-1980s. Bumbling, laboured, inept and swamped by the Angels prancing about in G-strings, it's not surprising that the feminist movement went on the warpath, although I still find it harmless – if often unfunny.

Another major watershed quickly followed in October 1985, when the *News of the World* published the story 'I was Benny Hill's Love Slave!' Written by 35-year-old fallen Angel and ex-page 3 stunner Stefanie Marianne, this shoddy piece of journalism claimed to lay bare the shocking truth of the comedian's system of vetting his young female co-stars. Having auditioned for *The Benny Hill Show* in 1966 at the age of 16, this innocent girl had served the clown for six years, patiently awaiting her chance to get a few lines on his show. Hill was pictured as a sad, lonely, wealthy figure who couldn't manage a proper relationship but relied on his 'love slaves' to act as masturbatory fantasies. Described as a sex-obsessed 'white whale', Hill's private life was suddenly public property.

It was an unbelievable piece of fiction, but dirt, however unfounded, tends to stick. Hill had been plagued by rumours about his sexuality for years, but finally, in 1982, he told the *Daily Mirror*'s Clifford Davis: 'I'm not gay and I'm no weirdo.' This was the start of his downfall. From then on, the connection between dithering sex-obsessive on television and millionaire sex-obsessive off-camera was blurred for good. Despite his apparent kindness and gregarious nature with friends and admirers, 'the filthy comic who never sexually matured' was an image that stuck with the public. Soon afterwards, ex-Angel Nikki Critcher jumped on the Benny slur bandwagon when she claimed he had grabbed her breasts so hard during a recording that she had had to slap him to release herself.

Hill's supportive Angels tried to protect him like a cuddly, beloved, eccentric child (for one birthday in the mid-1980s, the cast, mocking his press-revealed habit of using carrier bags, bought him a leather briefcase – packed with carrier bags), and the truth behind his relationship with his cast was revealed by Erica Lynley, 19 years old and fresh from ballet training college when she was interviewed for a part on the show by Hill. Invited back for a further chat, she had been tested for talents other than her looks by singing along to Hill's guitar-strumming. He made no sexual advances, and she was given a contract. Privately, it is believed that frequent trips to Hamburg, Marseilles, Bangkok and Tokyo served as a way of satisfying his sexual desires by means of prostitution. Still, a feminist journalist in Bangkok had already berated Hill's comedy, drawing parallels with stories of Hill's private life and branding him 'immoral'. However, no matter what activities he undertook abroad, there is no evidence that he ever exploited his television power on the casting couch.

Nevertheless, suddenly Hill was all over the papers, whether they were expressing amazement at his perceived miserly hermit lifestyle, carrying out further sexual probing or publishing a wildly exaggerated news flash that he was dying (Peter Charlesworth phoned the Cromwell Clinic where he was staying, to find him fit, happy and enjoying the expensive pampering of charming nurses). The papers built up the myth of his meanness and eccentric behaviour, while wild claims were made that this multi-millionaire took just one week's holiday a year, at Hornchurch – totally unjustified in the light of his packed travelling diary. In fact, Hill made a weekly pilgrimage to Hornchurch to visit friend Sue Upton and family. The cheapness of the journey wasn't a factor, it just happened to be where they lived.

He was condemned for not behaving like a star, although he did enjoy socializing with friends, and often turned out for showbusiness occasions. Again, he did himself no real favours by always insisting on a different beauty to accompany him – from Jenny Lee-Wright invited to a Cafe Royal award dinner to any one of countless wannabes who yearned to get a break on his show. Attending Thames parties throughout the 1980s, Hill would always have someone new on his arm, but with real actor friends, he could relax – whether it be Peter Butterworth and Janet Brown celebrating the Lakeside Country Club being awarded Club of the Year in 1970, publicity poses with everybody from Bernard Delfont to rap star Vanilla Ice or celebrity hob-nobbing backstage with Rula Lenska and Bernard Cribbins for pantomime pictures. A modest man, he turned down invitations for a Variety Club of Great Britain lunch or a Water Rats gala, although he always bought a table at their charitable events, and gave away the tickets to friends.

Harry Segal, the man who had fought to give Hill a chance in wartime shows all those years ago, battled again on behalf of his friend. Without work, and having suffered a heart attack, Segal had received a note from Hill in 1988 which read, 'Dear Harry – Just a wee cheer-up pressie, cos yor a luverly feller!' – attached was a cheque for £1,000. In a two-day featured interview with Hilary Boer for the *Daily Mirror*, Segal detailed what a kind man Hill was. But stories of that kind, however heartwarming for the comic admirer, don't sell newspapers; stories questioning both the private life and public work of Benny Hill most certainly did.

By the end of the 1980s, even his beloved *TV Times*

succumbed to the pressure – his last two feature articles during the show's lifetime kitted out the girls in less revealing fashion ('Angel's Delight', with Ben surrounded by Sue Upton, Miki Harvey, Zoe Bryant and Liz Jobling, 23–29 August 1988), and his financial arrangements were assessed by astrologist Martine Delamere (4–10 February 1989, with a charmingly relaxed photo by Francis Loney). The revelation about his returning from trips to Tesco's laden with carrier bags was countered with the bemused response: 'What else do I have to use in a supermarket?'

Newspaper articles usually didn't bother Hill. Indeed, in the early 1980s, when the *Evening Standard* went against the tide of popular press opinion and published a major article in praise of Hill's work, Henry McGee was amazed that he seemed embarrassed by it. The myth of 'comic genius in his ivory tower' was being formed at the time, and even a 1986 piece in *The Sunday Times Supplement*, 'Wise Enough to Play the Fool' by Russell Miller, seemed keener to rubbish his taste in decor than celebrate his talent – 'he barely notices the beige sculpted carpet on the ceiling, the similar green carpet on the floor, the dark blue walls and the buttoned velvet banquette seats in cream and maroon'. Suggesting there was a complex relationship between Hill's love of European travel and his 'winkles and chips' comedy, the verdict seemed to be in favour of Hill. However, Kenneth Williams's opinion (secretly recorded in his 16 January 1984 diary entry, but published in 1993 in *The Kenneth Williams Diaries*, edited by Russell Davies) was more forthright – 'It was as if they'd given an overfed cretin unlimited opportunities in a TV studio. There aren't words to describe the tedium, the jaded banality ... the overwhelming tat.' In 1980, he had considered it 'a show of which any network can be ashamed'.

Criticism was not just confined to the inner thoughts of a great comedy actor. As early as February 1981, the *Sun*, of all papers, had pompously published a leader comment headed 'Ban it, Benny!' In an astounding display of hypocrisy, the paper condemned the use of scantily clad girls on the show, complaining that it 'is put out at a time to catch the family audience, but Benny seems intent on appealing only to the dirty-raincoat brigade'. At this stage, such a comment from the 'family paper' which thrived on publishing pictures of topless models in every edition was more amusing than threatening to Benny Hill. While he mocked these opinions, he was safe; it was when he took them seriously that the trouble would begin.

Worse was to come. In 1987, just over a year after the *News of the World* revelations, Ben Elton launched a brief but potent attack on Benny Hill during a television interview and Channel 4's *Friday Night Live*. Alternative comedy, which had quickly grown out of the universities via London clubs The Comic Strip and The Comedy Store, had successfully fought its way onto television. Today's mainstream talents were yesterday's bright young things. Elton, a major force in the movement, had already co-written BBC2's student comedy *The Young Ones*, while Alexei Sayle, Dawn French, Jennifer Saunders, Rik Mayall and Adrian Edmondson were already spreading across the channels like wildfire. Like the post-war Goon generation, the post-Goon Fringe generation and the post-Fringe Python generation, they brought a much-needed breath of fresh air to blow away a tired collection of mainstream familiarity. Their heroes were those comic groundbreakers that had gone before them, and with an ever-increasing hold on British television comedy, the new comics grabbed the chance to work alongside them in *Blackadder*, *Friday Night Live* and *The Young Ones*. Peter Cook, Graham Chapman, John Bird, Terry Jones, Tim Brooke-Taylor, John Cleese and Jonathan Miller were very much part of this hip new wave, bringing baggage from the ground-breaking era of dangerous satire. Benny Hill was very much part of the low-brow, working-class, tried and tested earthy innuendo humour which had bonded a nation without taxing its intellect.

Was Hill really any more reliant on sexy females than the great comedians Ben Elton admired? Spike Milligan, the grandfather of anti-mainstream post-war British comedy, happily combined xenophobic comic genius with totally nude rear-view shots of young women and bra-busting, sexy figures such as Julia Breck. Monty Python continually used Carol Cleveland in a wide range of scantily clad roles. But there was one crucial difference. Milligan, Cleese and the rest were clever enough to comment on the smutty excesses in their comic narrative before anybody else could, presenting each example as a self-deprecating joke. Benny Hill, on the other hand, merely followed the lead of Max Miller and Donald McGill – a pretty girl was sexy; a pretty girl gazed at by a pathetic man was hilarious. There were no hidden messages or tricks of irony, it was pure seaside comedy for the masses. But the masses were changing. His humour most often relied on the obvious, not the bizarre, so Hill's depiction of sexy females was denounced. No longer would Hill's boss looking lustfully at his secretary's legs be acceptable, nor 'dumpling' gags about breasts, short-skirted mothers looking into their prams or throwaway marital nightmare one-liners like: 'What would people think if I walked around naked?' – 'They would think I married

you for your money!' Good-hearted smut was suddenly taboo, and those days when audiences could safely fall about at sketches concerning wife-swapping and blonde bimbos were fast disappearing. Indeed, Hill even decided to remove such innuendo as the Mexican routine starring Buenos Knockers and Senor Willie.

Tossed into the beer 'n' chips sexist pot alongside the *Sun*'s page 3 and Jim Davidson's end-of-the-pier shows, Hill suddenly found himself yesterday's news. As early as 1983, he had mocked the self-righteousness of Mary Whitehouse, reading sexual connotations into everything, and in one of his last Thames shows, the classic 1989 'Roger Crook' sketch, Hill used the characterization to speak for himself when he barked: 'I don't want those plonkers at the IBA investigating me!' It had already started. In 1988, Ben Elton's comment was followed by the more affectionate, wry observation from Hywel Bennett in Andy Hamilton's *The Return of Shelley* on 11 November. Back after a five-year absence in America, the first thing the main character says when he switches on the television is: 'Is Benny Hill still doing that?' More damning and truthful than any other criticism of the time, the line pinpoints Hill's problem perfectly.

By 1988, television was changing radically. Even the BBC had been shocked into action by outside forces, threats of disunity and political control. With Michael Grade in the chair, perennial favourites like *Dr Who* were about to bite the dust, while comic sitcoms of the traditional kind (*Terry and June*) were ousted, however much they worked at self-parody. The old-time family entertainers of the Bruce Forsyth, Jimmy Tarbuck and Bob Monkhouse school were running around like headless chickens. A lot of the blame for all this was laid on Ben Elton.

In my opinion, Elton, the finest comedian of his generation, had unwittingly sown a seed in 1986 that contributed to Hill's Thames sacking in 1989. With a comic routine reporting Elton's lack of surprise at the rise in reported rape cases when most of the British male population was tuning in to watch Benny Hill's girls, a career was set to destruction. Without going into a huge debate about the comment (it could be argued that the police and general public's more enlightened and sympathetic attitudes towards those who had been raped meant that more victims were reporting the offence), this was more than a flippant comment that really hit home. The *Sun*, in a feeble attempt to protect Hill's style and in a complete u-turn from their self-righteous condemnation from 1981, probably did more damage by repeating the quip in print to its millions of readers. Of all those who hadn't watched Channel 4, one per cent probably thought, 'Poor old Benny', while the rest probably raised an eyebrow and muttered: 'Hold on, that Ben Elton bloke has a point.'

Hill's reaction was to rely on his usual bravuro and love of smutty comedy, joking about the situation with the clever, funny but unwise quip: 'I can honestly say I have not been to bed with one of the Hill's Angels. I think her name was Sandra!' Unfortunately, Elton's 'What mugs we are' bigot character surrounded by Hill's Angel-style girls set the new public image of Hill as an old-fashioned, smutty comedian in stone. Few realized that in the same series, 1987's season of *The Man from Auntie*, Elton used the technique of upside-down talking heads – cleverly used by Hill in a Noel Cowardesque song from a trio of sharks in a sketch from 1984. Hill exposed the technique by finishing the number and revealing the artists behind the scenes with the sharks' faces painted on their chins. Elton's collection of glorious comic stereotypes was funny, but rarely unique or innovative. So the debate raged on, and Hill's comedy was channelled into one overbearing image – girls, girls, girls.

High-brow Hill scholars added further fuel to the fire by going totally overboard about the man's talents.

Anthony Burgess and John Mortimer fell over themselves to celebrate Benny Hill as 'one of the great artistes of our age'. To them, Hill's work symbolized the eternal earthiness of man's primitive sexual needs; it was real burlesque, filling the gap left by Sid Caesar and Milton Berle on American television, bringing back the sexually liberating innocence of Max Miller, and representing the pent-up angst of the entire world.

The satirical magazine *Private Eye*, mainly owned by ultra-cool Peter Cook, stoked the problem some more, memorably printing a hilarious mock ad for a Benny Hill video collection offer ('The World's Greatest Comic! Benny Hill's Immortal Legacy of Laughter Can Now Be Yours for Only 2p'), while the magazine *Viz*'s unforgettable 'Battle of the Bennys' comic strip took the joke even further, with Messrs Hill and Elton reduced to fisticuffs to prove who was the funniest comedian.

Benny Hill himself did the worst thing possible at the height of this furore – he went public. At any chance he had, Hill expressed amazement that another comedian could criticize him. Hill, an old-school professional, who either worked closely, knew well or at least played golf with some friend of another entertainer, just couldn't

Bliss! At his happiest relaxing in the park.

Benny with Sue Upton.

accept that his work was seriously being questioned. The tradition of mock in-fighting was part of the game. Des O'Connor's career was noticeably boosted by Eric Morecambe's continual jibes, and Bernard Manning was fair game for everybody – indeed, Hill himself once presented the following wall gag on *The Benny Hill Show*: 'Why does Siberia have blizzards while Britain has Bernard Manning? – Siberia had first choice' (Manning was probably the first to chuckle as he counted the box office receipts at his comedy club). But what Ben Elton had said was very different – this was not a joke, this was a serious comment. Hill was accused of provoking men to go out and rape women.

Certainly, looking back, some of those Hill's Angels routines were a bit near the knuckle, and an aged Hill schoolmaster clasping a sexy, leather-suited schoolgirl on his knee was undoubtedly ill-advised, but this underlines Hill's naivety. Granted, it is no defence to say, 'Well it's only a joke, so it's alright', but the humour of Benny Hill was just funny, pure and simple. It was not malicious.

Hill rose to the taunts, accusing the new wave of alternative comedians of producing material far more dubious than anything of his own. He counted the profanities. He told interviewers that he was shocked by the detailed bodily function routines Elton was performing, and amazed that these comics who seemed to have no taste boundaries could condemn him: 'I watched one episode of the alternative comedy shows where a naked man was bouncing up and down on another man's lap. Is that a very good idea in the middle of the AIDS crisis? And I was amazed by an episode of *Filthy, Rich and Catflap* when one chap buried an axe in another man's groin with tremendous force. I couldn't believe my eyes. For one minute I thought I was seeing my first snuff movie.'

This is fair comment, and while devotees of the comedy of Rik Mayall and Ade Edmondson, myself included, clearly see their violent antics as surreal twists on *The Three Stooges* and *Tom and Jerry*, Hill's generation of comedian was understandably appalled at finding his 'dumpling' gags and glam girls considered unacceptable when such alternatives were not. Certainly, although more informed and open in his comedy, Ben Elton's gynaecological diatribes surely offended more people than a flash of stocking top. The major difference, of course, was that Elton's comedy was not visual – his flights of sexual fancy and reams of 'knob gags' were reassuringly a stream-of-conciousness rant, allowed to form pictures in the mind of the listener and the listener alone.

Fundamentally cruder in content, Elton stripped sexuality bare to reveal the reality behind the innuendo, whereas Hill happily continued depicting the glories of a seemingly never-ending line of sexy girls, celebrating the beautiful female form through the hopeful and hopeless male gaze. In the end, Elton's detailed discussions of intricate female plumbing successfully deglamorized women with the comedy of shared knowledge, not mocked difference. Now whether that is degrading or liberating is up to you, but it's clear that often, the audience's laughter wasn't so much coming from knowing acceptance of the truth, but embarrassed unease at the truth being revealed.

In Elton's comedy, sex had become a topic for discussion rather than nudging references, hence the inference that Hill's comedy, which prepetuated the old attitudes, had contributed to the growing trend of sexual attacks in Britain. In other words, Hill's depiction of women was like a pornographic magazine; Elton's was like a medical textbook. Hill made women desirable; Elton made them human. The very attractiveness of women was suddenly a dubious area to investigate.

Unfortunately, Hill accused Elton of not even understanding his comedy. Continually complaining to interviewers that he never chased the girls, they always chased him, Hill dug himself into a hole. Although the vast majority of his finale speeded-up chases see him as the pursued victim, 'never' is a very big word, and in this case a word he couldn't use. Indeed, at the conclusion of the widely available *Benny Hill and Friends* video, Hill's robber quite clearly backtracks (along with fellow crooks and policemen) to chase the policewomen who have lost their clothes – not only that, but the usually speeded-up film slows down to capture every breast roll and lustful, tongue-lolling gaze.

As an admirer of Elton's scripts for *Blackadder* and a professional himself, Hill would have been better advised to just keep out of the debate. Instead of discussing his shows or comedy from his own perspective, every interview became a battle to prove his crowd of dissenters wrong: 'A good source of humour is the relationship between the sexes. And it is always the man who comes off worst in what I do – never the woman. Terrible things happen to me and the other men in my shows. Teeth come out, we get knocked on the head hard. But the girls retain their dignity. It is the men who are the idiots. And that is true in real life as well. Nothing nasty happens to the girls. They show their knickers but it is never dirty.' And so he went on and on.

You could see Hill's point of view. His comic characters often ran away from sexual encounters. A 1972 example has Hill chase Sue Upton, corner her against a tree, steal a kiss, pull a face of disinterest, then being chased by her, wanting more. However, for every twisting of the sexual struggle (Jon Jon Keefe, Jackie Wright and Hill seduced by a girl, only to end up as victims to her vampiric desires), there was mounting disgust at the gratuitous, clichéd flaunting of the female form, such as rows of traffic wardens in black stockings and suspenders doing a Can-Can routine. In a 1976 sketch, Hill the frustrated, work-loaded boss, counts a huge pile of papers, spies a seductive secretary bending over and flashing her stocking tops. The man loses count, and disgruntedly pulls the pile of papers back to start again. That's what Benny Hill's comedy was all about – the power of beautiful women over a collection of helpless besotted men. However, the Benny Hill debate had got out of control, and few were even bothering to consult the shows as reference any more. Simply, Benny Hill equalled unacceptable smut, and the label refused to budge.

Which ever way you look at it, Hill's disappearance from British television in 1989 was a tragedy. You may not have enjoyed his comedy, but he deserved at least some respect. After all, Benny Hill had been a *Radio Times* cover star before Ben Elton was born. Here was a man who had served his country, slept rough in London, desperate to find work, struggled on the halls from the mid-1940s, climbed the ladder through hard graft, became the first major personality made by television, stayed at the top of the popularity polls for over forty years, was fluent in French, German, Spanish, was musically inspired on cornet (learnt solely for an embryonic Scuttle sketch), guitar and Paraguayan harp, composed great swathes of incidental music for his shows and instinctively had his finger on the pulse of what made the world laugh. Now, suddenly, here was a young upstart of an alternative comedian branding everything he did as degrading rubbish. But was it as simple as that? Hardly.

Ben Elton may have been the motor-mouth calling for radical change throughout comedy, but one comment couldn't have brought down a career, however convincingly it was delivered. The fact remains that John Howard Davies simply considered Benny Hill's work was falling well below par. After forty years of sketch comedy, the man was out of original ideas. Certainly, the ratings had been very disappointing. From 1977, the new system took into account 2.2 people per viewing household as part of the total. This obviously doubled figures overnight, but Hill's audience was on the decline. In January 1981, *The Benny Hill Show* was number 1 in the ratings with figures of 20 million. By September 1988, the show had slipped to number 18 with 9.3 million viewers. Although this figure fluctuated and was still very healthy, to lose half of your audience in just over five years obviously gave cause for concern.

It is more than a little ironic that Hill's attempts to move away from his over-reliance on his Angels probably lost him many of the loyal male audience who used to tune in mainly because of it. As far back as 1979, Thames had disapproved of a clear nipple shot during a dance routine. Once edited out, the sequence of a scantily clad girl sliding down a pole had to be lengthened to fit the musical score. The resulting jerky movement looked even more suggestive, and the original sequence was reinstated. Indeed, the only time Thames successfully censored Benny Hill was concerning a joke considered cruel to animals. Based on a real-life tragedy, Hill had a visual gag of a dog being hung when its lead became caught in a remote-controlled garage door. Sick, perverse and bleak in the best Python tradition, Thames thought this went too far – although microwaving cats in the name of comedy was soon fine, if you were in the alternative tradition of Hale and Pace.

Whatever the decisive factor in Hill's unceremonious sacking, in his place John Howard Davies signed up the Montreux Golden Rose-winning *Mr Bean* pilot starring Rowan Atkinson. Ironically, it was co-scripted by Ben Elton, and its visual style led to international recognition on a par with Benny Hill.

What does a comedian do when he has no outlet for his comedy? Well, let us not be naive here – of all his many contemporaries, Benny Hill was in the best position to dig himself out of the hole. With a fortune estimated at £7 million (although it could have been much more, since he received 50 per cent of the American sales, some $2.5 million a year at their height:, commenting in 1986, 'I do get some awfully big cheques from America. I'm a bit ashamed of it really!'), Hill could have produced a series of specials independently and sold them to the highest bidder. Equally, he could have accepted one of dozens of American television offers to make a series especially for the American market. He turned down a $6 million offer to make 26 half-hour shows in America simply because he preferred his old one-hour format and the security of home territory. But why stop at America? What about any of the over one hundred countries that regularly broadcast *The Benny Hill Show*? At one stage in 1990, with 97 countries concurrently screening Benny Hill, it seemed the only place you couldn't watch him was England – the one country he wanted to live in and work in. Instead, he decided to take defeat gracefully and wait until Thames begged him back.

Jon Jon Keefe put the independent production idea to Hill, but a meeting with Dennis Kirkland in the Meridian Hotel, Piccadilly, saw no progress, and Philip Jones, eager to emerge from retirement, Richard Stone and Don Taffner discussed the possibility as early as autumn 1989. Greg Dyke and Marcus Plantin were interested, even deciding on a half-hour Saturday night slot for London Weekend Television, to be called *The New Benny Hill Show*. These promising plans finally collapsed when a meeting of ITV network bosses dismissed Hill's comedy as dated and unviable.

It seems that no approach was made to the BBC at this time, and one would suspect that the corporation, still quietly nursing a twenty-year grudge, would hardly want to pick up the pieces of a career its main competitor had just dropped. Besides, while mixing glorious smut with intelligence in the *Blackadder* series, the BBC was unlikely to latch onto a comedian whose social and cultural reputation was one of dire, old-fashioned repetition. The Broadcasting Complaints Commission was keen to wipe all smut and innuendo off British screens. Indeed, when Hill had been dropped by Thames, Colin Shaw of the Broadcasting Standards Council had issued an unconnected but ironically relevant mandate. Published on 13 November 1989, he dictated that 'the half undressed woman has been a staple element in farce and light entertainment shows, the convention is becoming increasingly offensive to a growing number of people and should be used only sparingly ... It's not as funny as it was to have half-naked girls chased across the screen by a dirty old man. Attitudes have changed. The kind of behaviour that gets a stream of men sent to magistrate's court each year isn't at all amusing.'

The time was hardly right for Benny Hill to try to make a speedy comeback, so instead, he simply got on with life. With financial security and a lot of free time, Hill enjoyed foreign travel (watching boxing in New York, bull-fighting in Spain, writing sketches at the writers' cafe, Les Deux Magots in Paris, performing three impromptu songs in a German bar in Florida), visiting his local cinemas in Kingston and Richmond, being driven by chauffeur David Goodall in his Volvo 714 to his favourite cathedral towns such as Winchester and Salisbury, spending time with close friend Dennis Kirkland, and sharing in the family life of Sue Upton.

Loved like a favourite uncle by Upton's children, Richard and Louise (who had been part of his Little Angels), Hill delighted in taking trips to Southend-on-Sea with the family, and enjoyed frequent theatre visits (he took Upton to The Talk of the Town as a birthday treat, fell asleep and was woken by her nudge just in time to make an appreciative bow in response to the celebrity mention from singing duo Peters and Lee, which he hadn't even heard!). He would pick the children up from school (much to the joy of teachers and parents) and treat them to sweets like any normal, kindly old relation. Upton saw the situation as Hill embracing a surrogate family, and this was the real Benny Hill – a man of complex feelings certainly, but also of kindness and sincerity. One of Hill's most enjoyable times was taking the kids to the pantomime. Upton accompanied Hill to the Mill Theatre, Sonning, after a lunch at The Compleat Angler, Marlowe, to see Louise English in performance, and he went to see her perform again in Bournemouth in December 1989. A Christmas celebration of Thames Television introduced by Jim Davidson was a pleasing show, including a Benny Hill clip, while his 1990 birthday was a less glamorous affair than usual – although champagne came from the still grateful Thames International. But 'Uncle Ben's Panto Party' was the ultimate treat, taking the children to see *Babes in the Wood* at Southampton's Mayfair Theatre, starring Cannon and Ball.

Fan mail still continued to pour in, and as he had always done, Hill aimed to answer each letter personally. It was a common occurrence for Hill to lock himself away for two or three days at a time to sign photographs and respond to the hundreds of gifts fans sent – from boxes of tea to chocolates. He took time to correspond with author Roger Lewis during his Peter Sellers research – a letter from Hill, dated 28 February 1991, is printed in *The Life and Death of Peter Sellers* (Century, 1994). Meanwhile, Hill indulged his other hobbies such as country walks, but two passions outstripped all others: television and food.

Indulging his love of old movies (his favourite was *The Third Man*) and sport (particularly boxing), he would watch multiple television screens in his Teddington flat.

But, as for the last forty years, he wasn't just watching for pleasure – this was work. Scanning the channels for further comic ideas from across the world, he would sit alone, waiting for inspiration. As for food, Hill would always lecture people who didn't wipe their plates clean about starving children in Africa. As a result of this genuine concern, justifying his own rule that if it was eatable, it must be eaten, Hill had always enjoyed a healthy appetite. Now, with very little to occupy his mind, food became an obsession. His biggest delight was eating a plate of fish fingers in front of the television, but latterly, his eating had turned to major restaurant binges which were putting a further strain on his already weakening heart.

The Benny Hill pub crawl begins with his favourite haunt, The King's Head pub near his Teddington flat. Hill would often sit outside with a pint and a sandwich, jotting down yet more comedy ideas and willingly signing the occasional autograph for passers-by. Then he would adjourn to The Three Pigeons on Kingston towpath, Skindles at Maidenhead, The Compleat Angler at Marlow and a bumper feed at the Roux Brothers' establishment, The Waterside at Bray.

Over-eating and over-drinking, coupled with more socializing time and no real pressure to plan comedy shows, saw Hill's weight increase drastically. His inability to stop writing comedy material even when there was no outlet for it may appear tragic – just as Stan Laurel still constructed Laurel and Hardy routines even after Hardy's death in 1957 – but for Benny Hill, this rest from television was only ever going to be temporary. His old habit of carrying a newspaper around with him in case an idea struck and needed to be captured in feverish scribbling in the margins was not about to fade away. He wanted to be ready when that phone started ringing.

In 1991, Thames were still making millions from world-wide sales of *The Benny Hill Show*, but no repeats were screened on British television. However, in August 1991, recognized internationally as a vital part of world comedy, Benny journeyed to the 11th Vevey Comedy Festival, Switzerland, to accept The Charlie Chaplin International Award For Comedy. Hill, the honorary chairman of the jury, received the 18-inch statuette of The Little Tramp from Chaplin's granddaughter, Kira, as her father, Eugene Chaplin, announced the special honour. Awarded on the last night of the festival in an open-air arena, Hill made his thankyou speech in French, and was clearly moved by the reception he received. On returning to his seat, he gave the award to Dennis Kirkland.

Even more emotive was Eugene's guided tour of his father's private study, allowing Hill to sit in the great man's chair, and revealing Chaplin's complete collection of Benny Hill videos. Having been hurt by comments during a university lecture by veteran producer Hal Roach, singling out Hill as the successor of Chaplin and Laurel and Hardy, but adding the coda 'I just wish he'd clean his act up!', Hill took solace in the fact that Chaplin had considered him the best in the business.

Sir Ewen Fergusson, British Ambassador in Paris, who, along with his wife, was a huge Hill fan, welcomed the star to a special gala lunch in October 1991 to mark his fifty years in showbusiness. He had donned various comic guises for a French confectionery commercial, and Channel 3 in France continually re-ran old Hill shows. Ironically, these were often peppered with Hill, speaking in French, defending his non-sexist comedy while backed by schoolgirl-chasing and other corny antics. Even today, Benny Hill shows are screened constantly in France, and articles about him pack French journals. However, even more importantly than this international recognition of 1991, a reassessment was in progress back in Britain. A BBC documentary was being made, capturing the feted Hill at his proudest, and destined to relaunch the television dreams of its subject.

Omnibus: 'Benny Hill – Clown Imperial'

To all intents and purposes, this vitally important insight into the mind of a comedy great, was Benny Hill's personally controlled obituary – less than six months after the show was first broadcast, he died.

There is much to enjoy and treasure about this rare television documentary, and on many different levels. For once, the BBC output of its star subject is given equal credibility to the more familiar, successful Thames back catalogue. Indeed, the clips are of the highest quality, selecting visual material (the split image of Hill's top with female legs divided by a clothes line), surrealism (the two-headed dog, police trapping a gangster in comfort behind a self-contained brick cell), graffiti groaners ('God is dead – Fred.' 'Fred is dead – God'), influences (a saucy 1981 twist on Chaplin's *A Dog's Life*, with a goose protruding from his trousers, a 1984 Frank Randle-inspired 'drunk returns home' act with Oliver Hardy hat business) and impressions (Michael Caine dishing out schoolboy howlers from 1981, W.C. Fields's mayor sparring with Jackie Wright from 1974). There are plenty of glimpses of the girls, from sophisticated glams (the 1988 *London by Night* routine) back to the glorious days of slapstick flesh-flashing (Hill's short-sighted plumber chased into infinity).

Thankfully, the programme also takes some time –

albeit brief – to mention Hill's radio and stage successes before television claimed him, and there are plenty of impressive talking heads defending his comedy against the politically correct, including Michael Caine claiming that the feminist movement has no sense of humour.

The familiar team are dragged out to remember filming Hill's shows, there's some gorgeous footage of the troupe posing for publicity photographs, while Sue Upton and Louise English demonstrate the Hill school of tap-dancing. Dear old Bob Todd says not a word as he slowly moves his hand onto Bella Emberg's knee and allows Henry McGee to celebrate the man who employed them for so long. Even people in the street are invited to voice rejection of his smutty, deprecating style or praise his head-slapping, no-nonsense, laughter-making talents. There's a very rare opportunity to cast your eye over one of Hill's working comedy scripts, separated down the middle, with visual gags on one side and dialogue on the other. But by far, the best and most valuable aspect of the show is the Benny Hill interview footage itself.

Relaxed, cheerful, focused and happy, Hill relates his life story in lengthy sound bites and *Comic Roots*-style strolling – the scenes in Southampton are particularly fun, calling out 'Milk-o!' in his old haunt of Market Street, remembering the Woolworth's job and chatting with his cousin Christopher. The Teddington scenes are no less precious, with the celebrated, jobless comic hero calling from his flat window, taking his rubbish out, running through a painfully uneasy jokey charitable appearance at The King's Head, strolling through the streets, mopping his brow with a clutch of £50 notes in his local launderette, boasting of his 'friends the stars' as he nips off to post a letter to Mickey Rooney, and brilliantly staging a comic vignette at Belfour's newsagent with his 'usual' *Times* and *Herald Tribune* joined by *Men Only* and *Mayfair* thanks to a helpful, well-briefed assistant. Moreover, Hill was in such buoyant mood because he was not only on the way out of the wilderness, he had plenty to brag about, with footage of his honoured guest status at the Chaplin Comedy Awards in Switzerland.

He is also allowed to address the sexism question again, jokingly putting an imaginary gun to his head and muttering 'I think I'll go now ...' following an onslaught of condemnation, dismissing claims that he is reclusive with mock amazement, protesting vehemently about his sacking from Thames, and revealing his inner shyness with the totally endearing mumble, 'I'm far too shy to answer that ...'. Hill comes across as a likeable, down-to-earth, charming man. It seems such a shame that the backlash against the condemnation of him never led to

complete reappraisal. In work, Michael Caine eloquently summed him up as an 'evil cherub'; at home, Benny Hill seemed a thoroughly nice bloke.

Omnibus: 'Benny Hill – Clown Imperial': Saffron Production for BBC TV in association with Thames Television International and FR3, broadcast BBC1, Friday 20 December 1991, 10.20–11.20 p.m. Starring BENNY HILL. With RONNIE ALDRICH, MICHAEL CAINE, EUGENE CHAPLIN, WALTER CRONKITE, BELLA EMBERG, LOUISE ENGLISH, SIR EWEN FERGUSSON, CHRISTOPHER HILL, PHILIP JONES, DENNIS KIRKLAND, HENRY McGEE, SABINE MIGNOT, JOHN MORTIMER, BURT REYNOLDS, MICKEY ROONEY, RICHARD STONE, JOHN STREET, BOB TODD, SUE UPTON. Omnibus Editor: Andrew Snell. Omnibus Unit Manager: Paula Leonard. Rostrum camera: Ken Morse. Sound Recordist: Les Honess. Additional sound recording (USA): John Lusitana and Etienne Sauryet. Photography: David Feig and Graham Smith.

Additional photography (USA): Philip Hurn and Peter Sternberger. Dubbing Editor: Steve Fishwick. Dubbing Mixer: Michael Narduzzo. EFC Editors: Richard Knapman and Robin Fish. Researchers: Colin Campbell and Liz Heasman. Production Manager (USA): Victor Bank. Production Assistant: Sue Innes. Associate Producer: Christopher Dixon. Film Editor: Rob Wright. Producer: Victor Pemberton. Director: David Spenser.

Did You Know?

In the *Omnibus* show, Hill fan and friend Mickey Rooney reveals in the show that he's writing a comedy film script to star Benny Hill and himself, provisionally entitled *Wait Till the Swelling Goes Down.*

Hill first met Messrs Pemberton and Spenser at the 1991 Emmy award ceremony. He had been greatly impressed by their recent documentary on the veteran actress Gwen Ffrangcon-Davies, and eagerly listened to their planned project on his life and work. Uncharacteristically, he seriously considered taking part in the project almost immediately – this would have been almost unthinkable if Hill had been enjoying television exposure via *The Benny Hill Show*. As it happened, another production company were already negotiating about a Hill documentary, although the comedian knew which proposal he preferred. In the end, Saffron Productions was in the unique position of recording the last few glorious months of a great comedy performer. However, as with new television shows and American-financed film deals, Hill was still careful of the work he accepted. During filming of *Clown Imperial,* he baulked at a sudden live spot for French television at the Embassy. Instead, the problem was solved by including a pre-recorded item.

Des O'Connor Tonight

During the last few years, Benny Hill had repeatedly turned down offers to appear on the television chat shows *Wogan* and *Aspel & Company*. Even during his major years of initial success in America, he had rejected generous offers from Johnny Carson and a chance to star on the show of one of his childhood comedy heroes, Bob Hope. However, following the Thames sacking, Hill was keen to say his piece and get on television in any way he could.

Initially, he made brief appearances on a couple of Spanish chat shows. These proved so popular and confidence-building that he accepted an offer to do a television interview with a chap called Evo in Holland. Even so, this was pre-recorded, and Hill was allowed approval at the editing stage, with the audience baying for their hero following some choice classic clips. Accompanied by Dennis Kirkland and staggering on with his back to the audience, turning and giving the Scuttle salute, Benny Hill was a tremendous success. Maybe talk was the way back onto British screens. Having seen Russ Abbot perform a major interview/performance piece on Des O'Connor's show, juxtaposing serious 'this is me' chat with character sketches, Hill telephoned Dennis Kirkland and asked him to set the wheels in motion. It was to be his first British television interview for almost thirty years.

There are the expected comedy moments with Scuttle and Chow Mein, and even the customary duet with the host, an old friend of Hill's. Hill was so relaxed and fluid that another routine as an aged lady had to be cut because it overran. However, the major treasure is the interview material itself. Hill is charming, looks fit, and makes an entertaining and enjoyable guest. The sexism question is still at the forefront of his mind, and he spends much of his time proclaiming innocence. What's more, he addresses the press reports about his 'lonely, reclusive private life', making great fun out of the misunderstanding, proving his point with a fictitious quote from his packed diary: 'Went to showbiz party ... met Jim Davidson, a fine comedian and a gentleman. Had drinks with all three of them!' He hadn't been so spontaneously funny for years.

Relaxed and obviously eager to get on with the new material that was bubbling in his brain, he talks about the amazing American reaction to his shows, frowns with indifference at the idea of live performance, and most tellingly of all, refers to his television work as 'my meat'. With a winning wink, Hill is set for a major return, and you can tell he's looking forward to it. The recording proved so relaxed and successful that O'Connor invited Hill back on the show – an hour-long, purely conversational edition was scheduled for the autumn of 1992.

Des O'Connor Tonight: ITV, Wednesday 30 October 1991, 8–9 p.m. DES O'CONNOR with guests BENNY HILL, NEIL SEDAKA, MARIAH CAREY, KIM APPLEBY. Directed and produced by Brian Penders.

Benny Hill's World Tour

Having waited for three years without a television series, 1992 was clearly the right time to re-promote the comic talents of Benny Hill. Frankie Howerd had weathered the stormy seas of the late 1980s to become the darling of the university set, Dave Freeman was about to set sail with reheated innuendo for *Carry On Columbus*, and amazingly, many of those alternative comedians who had condemned Hill's work were about to sign up for the ill-fated voyage.

For *Benny Hill's World Tour*, an independent production, the old family of supporting faces would be back with a vengeance. Dennis Kirkland was at the helm, and old friend and Thames champion Philip Jones joined Don Taffner as the show's executive producers.

Projected as a series of three one-hour specials reflecting the world-wide following of Benny Hill, episodes set in the Far East and Australia were taking shape for later in 1992. However, the natural starting point for the series was America, filmed in New York, and at Hill's spiritual home for twenty years, the Thames Studios at Teddington based at Teddington Studios (for the convenience of Hill's flat rather than any 'told you so!' back-biting at Thames). It was familiar, it was local and it was cheap. Costing £500,000 to make, Hill excitedly told British journalists: 'I reckon this is among the funniest work I've ever done.' Ranking a little higher than Laurel and Hardy's *Atoll K* and a little lower than Hancock's Australian shows, it was hardly that, but as a career coda, Benny Hill left in style.

All of the British-based stuff could have come from a five-year-old edition of *The Benny Hill Show*, and there's something comfortingly familiar about the sketches. The bank robbery with Todd ordering the staff to lie face downwards and Hill's bemused boss admonishing Sue Upton's face-up secretary 'This isn't the office party!' is reassuringly old-fashioned, despite the rather disconcerting flash of naked bottom as she turns over. Hill's bedside call of nature/praying misunderstanding with a Little Angel is a delight, and when he bellows at his off-camera child about wearing too much make-up, the punchline is a frustrated 'Do you hear me, Malcolm?'

Henry McGee interviewing Hill's sluggish drugs baron plays idly with television convention, with the unscrambled face and scrambled lower region hiding the wanted man's unzipped fly – remember that vicar from the first Thames episode in 1969? There is ironic xenophobia in Hill's crew-cutted barman chatting to Todd's Germanic customer in a fractured German accent. Talking to McGee's frightfully British bowler-hatted gent in a refined British accent, convinces Todd that Hill is mocking him, but Hill reveals he was mocking the British bloke. With an amazed 'Did I really get away with that?' expression to camera, Hill has mocked everybody – but what's the point?

McGee has more to do with the 'Our Music' slot, with aged Doctor Johnny Hutch getting to grips with a glamorous blonde in a simulated sex romp behind curtains and Hill's semi-Scuttle figure, Andrew Melonyellow, suffering from a cold and donning a bobble-hat. It's a good idea – a common cold research centre organizing a musical event with the obvious but effective bunged-up noses misunderstandings. That's all fine and dandy for the first few minutes. The dickless/dickheads link to a tenuous mention of Dickens is hilarious, but the coughing in tune routines are plain dreadful, while the bald head-slapping is done on auto-pilot. A thankfully quick cut to ever-watchable Bob Todd taps into the endearing innocence of kids with the 'drink like a fish' reference bringing on simple embarrassment from guilty parents Hill and Dawson. All this material looks like ideas in development for the 1990 season of *The Benny Hill Show* which never happened.

Finally, it's time to hit the streets of New York and the major experiment for Hill's comedy – tailoring his humour for the audience that loved his British stuff the most. A Fred Scuttle type bumbles about in the back of a yellow cab, falling foul of New York cops and trying to catch the eye of power-dressing women. As usual, Hill's pathetic male is ignored with contempt, but in Robert Benchley/goofy 'How to ...' guide style, Hill's Americanized commentary ('Hi there!') leads our hapless hero through 'How to meet beautiful women'.

The sight gags are fairly bland, with Hill showering fully clothed, reacting to the all-knowing voice-over, splashing cologne over his naked body and trying the flawless ways to attract the opposite. Again the handkerchief trick is predictable: strike one, girl picks it up and walks away; strike two, she avoids the thing, and strike three, she blows her nose. Hill is ready to give up, but pretends to faint to get the kiss of life from a passing sexy nurse, only to land a macho medic.

Car trouble provides the chance for Hill's main man to impress the glamorous girl with the 'knight in shining armour' approach, but naturally, Hill's privates are trapped and that line of enquiry fails. Leaving oily marks all over the young lady, there's a Chaplinesque walk to the park, more car antics pretending to own a luxurious model, homosexual advances when the real male owner takes a fancy to our hero, and more macho protection stuff when he hires a stunt man to insult a lady and fall victim to Hill's mock punches. Yep, you've guessed it, the stunt man is late arriving, and Hill tackles a real hard nut. It's still funny in a very low-grade Three Stooges sort of way, but Hill seems to sleepwalk through most of it – and his audience can't help but follow his example.

Glamorous hospital angels are replaced by Todd in

drag, but wait – worse is to come with a reprise of the singing cold sufferers, blowing their noses in tune to the music. Todd's petulant waitress serving McGee with a half-bitten sugar cube and Hill with a load of treacle is just pointless, while better fare is to come in Hill's major parody of *A Streetcar Named Desire*, 'A Streetcar Named Desiree'.

Dawson's frustrated wife works well, and there's good support from Todd and Deadman, but it's Hill, repeating his 1968 filmic doubles, who really shines. His coy Vivien Leigh impersonation may wear a bit thin after a while (with a multitude of 'honey' and 'sugar' interjections), but there's real gusto in his mumbling, arrogant Marlon Brando characterization, all black, greased hair, looking cool and injecting a real sledgehammer ignorance into the part. This is class stuff in a less than classic environment. The screamed 'Stella!' is perfect, but as so often during his later work, Hill the wonderful comedy actor is let down by Hill the desperate comedy writer. The jokes here are so old that Hill whizzes through them almost apologetically ('It was so hot a dog was chasing a cat – and they were both walking!', 'Slept like a baby – wet the bed!', and the three-tier chestnut, 'Look at that dog with one eye' – puts hand over eye; 'Look at that dead bird' – looks to the sky; 'Look at that!' – 'I know!' – 'So why did you tread in it?'). Apart from being cornball quips used by Hill decades earlier, there is no attempt to build them into a structured sketch. Hill delivers them in one long succession with the odd amazed shrug to the audience.

As in the original film, the card game with his pals is used to undermine the presence of Blanche, but again Hill drags out one of his oldest one-liners, returning from the toilet to the enquiry, 'Could you hear us in there?' – 'No.' – 'Well, we could hear you!' The joke is that female Hill beats male Hill here: she talks mean ('And up your's dog breath!') and dances off into the sunset with bizarre prancing. Most of the sight gags (her green knickers hanging out of the back of her skirt) are far too unsubtle, the enjoyable ones (cutting the cards with a meat cleaver) are pinched from better things (a fifty-year-old Harpo Marx trick), and the mocking of male bastions (the card game is 'Happy Families', with greased Hill thrilled with Mr Bun the Baker) just sags. It's a real shame, for as I have said, Hill the actor is clearly up to the performance. But now, it's back to those pesky coughing singers – Oh God! Where's the remote! – with a female with a moustache joining in the fun for some reason. The audience love it.

Much better is to come, with the American stance embraced by Benny on a park bench in Central Park, New York. At his most charming when chatting to the audience as himself, his little speech is interrupted by a tramp searching through Hill's pockets for a match. When challenged by Hill, the bum tells him that he never talks to strangers. The arrival of one of New York's finest asking 'Is this man annoying you?' sees Hill, the foreigner, dragged away. It's a simple, predictable piece, but there's a fine underlying message of anti-xenophobia, and Hill's performance is masterly.

Less impressive is his work as the sex-obsessed television therapist in the 'Ask Dr Ruth' section. The dreadful rolled 'R's of the speech, the clumsy attempt to project her smallness with a huge chair and frantic over-acting just plays as desperation. Hill's Rosanne Barr is no better, injecting a sarcastic, knowing, anti-men attitude which leaves the viewer completely cold. The discussion between the two is ultra-laid back and fails to ignite, and even the jokes ('manizer' being coined as the female equivalent of 'womanizer') are mocked within the structure of the sketch. The best material comes from the sketch audience (Bob Todd's Germanic chap with an obvious Yale/jail misunderstanding and his tale of making love almost every night – 'almost Monday, almost Tuesday ...'). However, fittingly, Hill's audience member is the scene's gem. Personifying every ounce of the male chauvinist pig, moaning about his wife, crew-cutted, opinionated and exciting heated reactions from the women in the audience, he runs the gamut of sexist references. Declaring he is sick of her bird impressions ('watches me like a hawk, eats like a vulture'), the most potent aspect is Hill's clever reversal of the situation. This man is a loud-mouthed bigot whose clichéd attack on his wife, 'fat, but she's the only woman I know ...', stops short of the expected punchline, leaving the relationship with a strange poignancy. A handy phone call is the perfect get-out for the sketch, with a Morecambe and Wise-like skipping exit for the host and guest (would American audiences get that reference?).

After an enjoyable quickie – Dawson chatting with Hutch's dying old man, and denying his last request for some ham because 'that's for the funeral' – it's back to Benny Hill on top form with a resurrection of his vintage favourite, Chow Mein. Sue Upton and Henry McGee conducting an audition set up the usual one-joke experience of the misunderstood Chinaman. Still, however many times you see McGee's petulant Brit desperately trying to keep a straight face at Hill's torrent of bumbling antics, this is hilarious.

The hopeless ventriloquist routine really dates back to Sandy Powell's classic comic sketch, but Hill does an excellent version of it here. The dummy, initially appearing with one leg, is a treat ('He's a singer not a dancer!'), and the Greenpeace/aerosols mispronouncements hits my sense of humour every time. More importantly, Hill is clearly enjoying the experience of performing again, and there's a sense of fun and enthusiasm about the sketch. It may be old-fashioned, it may be predictable, and it may be considered offensive, but Hill ad-libbing 'It's true!', struggling to down a pint of beer, putting his foot through a chair and finally reacting to McGee's dismissive comment about not requiring a vent, reveal a comedian of true class.

A return to the New York voice-over and Hill as himself standing in front of the Rockefeller Center (panning away to reveal a 'Made in Japan' sign), leads to the priceless 'tarts and bent cops' speakeasy scenario. Hill is the fresh face in town, facing long-legged, money-grabbing *femmes fatales*, a knowing barmaid and the black-suited gangster boss (Bob Todd). Some of the material (the belching cash registrar) doesn't work, but Hill's canny skill with money, foxing the young lady on the make (complete with action replay) and replacing a teddy bear with the ill-gotten money of the crooks all retains a sense of warm invention. Complete with atmosphere-setting movie posters (*A Tree Grows in Brooklyn*) and the same old trouser-ripping material of old, this was the last speeded-up chase Benny Hill filmed.

Finally, Hill attempts an attack on the new musical scene, with a muddled rap parody. Sporting a T-shirt bearing the legend 'I Love NY' (the back reads 'I Love LA Too'), Hill goes into bumbling Scuttle mood for this, his last musical performance. The girls, Todd and Hutch get down with the arm movements, you can hear every word of Hill's delivery, even the corniest of gags ('She said, "That's my husband at the door!"/I said, "I'll jump out the window! He sounds vicious!"/She said, "We're thirteen floors up!"/I said, "I'm not superstitious!"') is achingly funny, and there's a real sense of emotion about his closing remark: 'So let me shout it loud and clear!/I'm glad to be alive and I'm glad to be here!' Quite clearly, he was.

Benny Hill's World Tour: D.L. Taffner UK for Carlton Television. First screened on ITV as *Benny Hill Unseen* in two parts: Tuesday 12 April 1994, 9.30-10 p.m. and Monday 16 May 1994, 8–8.30 p.m. Starring BENNY HILL. With HENRY McGEE, BOB TODD, ANNA DAWSON, JON JON KEEFE, JOHNNY HUTCH, LORRAINE DOYLE, SUE UPTON, MIKE MULLOY, HILL'S ANGELS, HILL'S LITTLE ANGELS. Script and original songs: Benny Hill. Musical Director: Ronnie Aldrich. Musical Associate: Ted Taylor. Vocal backing: The Ladybirds. Hill's Angels choreography: Libby Roberts. Studio Production Manager: Peter Ernster. Lighting Director: Peter Bower. Sound: Richard Churchill and Clive Hall. Senior Cameraman: Adrian J. Fearnley. Vision Control: Allan James. Vision Mixer: Peter Boffin. Videotape Editors: Dave Lewinton and Perry Widdowson. Costumes: Fran Bolwell and Derek Hayward. Make-up: Dianne Millar. Graphics: Jeff Harrison and Graham Walker. Production Co-ordinator: Lorna Cameron. Stage Manager: Auriol Lee. Floor Manager: Fizz Waters. Production Assistant: Debbie Gregory. Designer: Ian Russell. Executive Producers: Philip Jones and Don Taffner. Produced and directed by Dennis Kirkland.

Did You Know?

During filming, Hill took time out to present Alexei Sayle, a comedian he greatly admired, with an Emmy award in New York. Audrey Hepburn was a fellow guest – a long way from when Hill had spotted her star potential as a dancer in Bob Monkhouse's revue *Sauce Tartare*.

The New York show used discarded location footage from the final batch of Thames filming.

A planned sight gag outside Trump Tower was later abandoned – Hill dropping a coin, and Donald Trump walking past, picking it up and pocketing it.

GOODNIGHT SWEET PRINCE

Although the one completed episode of *Benny Hill's World Tour* wasn't screened in Britain until after his death, the two other planned hour-long specials had already bitten the dust. Don Taffner, Thames's overseas marketer, knew the potential of more Benny Hill. Strangely, he couldn't secure a good enough deal for this latest show, and the finance for possible Paris, Berlin, Australia and Far East ventures was not forthcoming. Hill wasn't that bothered. At last he had more important fish to fry, and after three years of waiting, the pressures on British television had finally began to crack the surface. Not only were British fans bombarding Thames with requests for, if not new shows, then at least some Hill repeats, more powerfully, over a hundred countries were clamouring for more and more Benny Hill material. The fact was that all the existing material had been used up. Thames needed to make some new shows.

In the end, Hill started 1992 with the satisfying prospect of three major television companies vying for his services. Carlton presented an interesting package and was based locally, but had no plans to make programmes itself: the shows would be independently produced by Fred Nerk Productions exclusively for Carlton. This sense of vanished control and split interests put Hill off.

Working with Thames would, of course, be like going home with a justified, vindicated smile on his face, although none of the Hill 'family' could believe he was seriously considering working for them again. In the end, he decided to turn down the Thames offer, and although I'm sure he got more than a buzz of pleasure from that, the company's days were numbered anyway. Having lost its broadcasting franchise in October 1991 and with no outlet to screen its own programmes, it was simply filming material for distribution.

Benny Hill decided to make a fresh start with Nottingham-based Central Television, a deal being signed for three hour-long specials in the old style. Philip Jones had written to Andy Allan, formerly of Thames, now at Central Television, on 22 August 1991, suggesting it was time to bring Hill back to British screens and giving the idea his total approval. Central's bosses were hardly impressed by the New York show, which they thought tired and old-fashioned, but they appreciated it was designed for the American market. Once Hill had agreed to give them indispensable old favourites like Fred Scuttle within a fresher, 1990s-geared environment, the wheels were set in motion. The final deal was for two hour-long comedy specials, with a budget of £510,000 each. Hill would have the final word on editing, Dennis Kirkland would be retained to direct only, while Central's Controller of Entertainment, Richard Holloway, would produce. An option for a third show was part of the contract.

Full of ideas for the new series, Bob Todd, Henry McGee, Jon Jon Keefe, Anna Dawson, Sue Upton, Louise English and the gang had already been told to stand by for another batch of *The Benny Hill Show*. Hill and Kirkland had already discussed the material in preparation for the new season. Fred Scuttle and Chow Mein would spearhead the laughs, while the fun of filming the *Streetcar* parody for the American show had prompted Hill to write some more film/television parody 'doubles'. He was eager to parody Gérard Dépardieu's interpretation of Cyrano de Bergerac. However, the most exciting of these spoofs was a proposed running piece called 'Miss Marbles', which would see Hill playing both skits on Miss Marple and Hercule Poirot. A huge admirer of David Suchet's performance, Hill was eager to have a comic bash at the outrageous Belgian accent and shifting step. Finalized in the first week of April, the contracts were drawn up for signing, and a provisional date for broadcast was set for Christmas 1992.

Towards the end of 1991, the *Sun*'s Garry Bushell strolled through Teddington High Street with Hill, and kids were screaming out: 'Yo! Benny – you are brilliant!' Hill was pleased, and his television relaunch was still

around the corner. But the national press were still on his back, amazed and suspicious of a multimillionaire who didn't live the multi-millionaire lifestyle. Where were the country mansion, the yacht, the swimming pool and the expensive divorce settlements? Benny Hill was happy to shop for himself, stroll through the park, stay at home to watch television and quietly spend time writing new material in a local cafe or pub. He wasn't wildly eccentric, just easily satisfied. But the press wouldn't let go.

In November 1991, Hill and Kirkland were rushing to the funeral of Jack Brecken, picture publicity boss for Thames. It was pouring with rain, and the two were in a hurry. Hill needed cufflinks urgently. Asking the driver to stop at the first place he saw, and after trying a few shops that didn't stock them, Hill and Kirkland galloped into an Army and Navy Store, grabbed the first pair they found and bought them for £10.99 – which almost got Hill arrested. Immediately on setting foot outside, a trainee manager by the name of Robert Doncaster stopped them. Panicked and eager to get to the church, Hill tried to claim celebrity immunity for the first time, spluttering 'I'm Benny Hill' without much luck. The problem was soon ironed out, but the trainee sold his story to the *News of the World*, which published it under the banner headline, 'Why I Nicked Benny Hill', explaining that the two looked scruffy and suspicious. The slurs and backstabbing had clearly got out of hand, and no amount of friendly ribbing between the two (Kirkland dubbed his friend 'Benny the Bandit') could completely erase the situation.

Christmas 1991 was spent, as usual, watching television on his own, but he threw himself into the social season for New Year's Eve. Driven by David Goodall to friends in Petersfield, Hill ambled out at midnight and said he was enjoying himself so much he would stay the night and be picked up at lunchtime the following day. His birthday was spent at Browns restaurant with an old friend who ran a boarding house in Southampton and six girls from the local pantomime. On 30 January, he visited a married couple who were old school friends, and arranged to meet up again after Easter.

For Hill, it was a moving few months, with an alarming number of funerals to attend. Apart from Brecken's in November, there was family friend Mimi Levy (buried in Southampton's Hollybrook Cemetery), Brecken's memorial service at the journalists' church, St Bride's in Fleet Street, London, on 5 February 1992, and Ted Taylor, his Thames musical associate and rehearsal pianist. Hill stayed to the wake and enjoyed meeting old cohorts The Ladybirds, but recent times were tinged with a lot of sadness.

His health was also suffering. Plagued with heart problems, Hill attended a meeting to discuss the Central shows on 9 February, but later suffered chest pains. He was admitted into the Royal Brompton National Heart and Lung Hospital, Chelsea, South West London, after suffering a heart attack on 11 February 1992. A heart by-pass operation was suggested, but Hill was keen to let himself mend with time rather than take the risk. Returning home after eight days in hospital, he joked with the press and still cheekily twisted the news-dominating stories (General Election fever), commenting: 'It's a long time since I had an election, so now I'm going home to sort out my love life.' After his first stay in hospital, on 18 February 1992 Hill emerged on the arm of a nurse, the ever-ready comedian eagerly giving a Fred Scuttle salute for the cameras. However, within hours of leaving, Hill was back in hospital, at the Cromwell, with a suspected second heart attack. Keen to let his fans believe he was perfectly fit, Hill donned his beret and again adopted a Scuttle salute for the waiting journalists. In reality, this attack was diagnosed as his single kidney malfunctioning, leading to water settling on his chest, making it hard to breath. The problem, which could have caused his heart attack, slowed the rate at which blood was being pumped around the body. Rest was needed.

Prescribed a course of tablets to alleviate the condition, Hill stayed in hospital for seven days, typically visiting other patients and cheering them up. His own stay in hospital was brightened by a visit from one of his biggest fans, Michael Jackson, popping in to wish him well on 22 February. Jackson had a huge collection of Benny Hill videos, specially kept in their own designated room. Chatting happily and posing for Barry Breckon's lenses (with Jackson joining his hero in a Scuttle salute), this visit was a real tonic for the ailing Hill. Offering the superstar a Coca-Cola and quickly correcting himself, 'Oh crickey, no, it's Pepsi you support isn't?', Hill had Jackson giggling for most of their fifty minutes together. Dennis Kirkland simply looked on amazed. So relaxed was the atmosphere that there was even serious discussion about the possibility of Hill starring in a Michael Jackson pop video. The idea was to film Jackson dancing slowly and Hill dancing as fast as he could – doubling the speed of the film to make Jackson appear normal and Hill boogying frantically.

Sadly, this wasn't to be. Less than a fortnight after leaving the Brompton, he was back in the hospital on 8 March – the third visit in less than a month. This time it was just a panic attack, but doctors advised him that he needed to lose 2 stone (Hill was 5 foot 10½ inches, but weighed 16.5 stone) and go on a diet eliminating the fried

A Benny Hill publicity shot from the Golden days .

breakfasts he loved so much. Although shaken by the attack, he was clearly excited about getting back on British television, eager to screen his American special as a prelude for his newest and freshest material. Plenty of walks and healthy eating were still punctuated by the occasional eating binge (notably a huge Chinese meal allegedly with a Sun reporter), but Hill was happy with prospects for the year ahead. To further dispel any press and fan speculations about his poor health, he agreed to a photo shoot at the beginning of April with Hill's Angels choreographer Libby Roberts. Promoting her new fitness video, the stills show Hill in good spirits, tackling the dubious delights of an exercise bike. In reality, Hill never went near an exercise bike for any serious activity, and the photographs disguised the fact that he was very ill indeed.

Meanwhile, Thames, bombarded with viewers' letters demanding Hill repeats, finally gave way and asked Dennis Kirkland to quickly edit some of the old shows into half-hour compilations. An immediate ratings-winner, the first show emerged quietly on Tuesday 31 March at 8.30 p.m. No Thames fanfare sounded, but the viewing population reacted immediately. The episode broadcast in the same slot on 7 April ripped into the top 20.

During his final stay in hospital, Lynda Rona had come with a camcorder to record Benny's contribution to Richard Stone's 50th anniversary celebration in April. Since this would take place in America, Hill couldn't make the journey, but agreed to be on the special video message. Ruffling his hair, attaching himself to myriad electrodes and slumping into his hospital bed, Hill muttered a few words of congratulations in a quavering voice. After a few seconds, he pretended to think the recording was over, straightened up in bed and said: 'Are we off? Good, let's have some champagne!' A cheeky comment to Richard's wife, Sara, about not 'coming up' (referring to an early occasion when she declined the invitation to see Hill's flat) completed the hilarious vignette.

But whatever the picture he was portraying to even his closest associates, Hill was far from well. With no further treatment on offer, Hill left the Brompton on 13 April. The following day, *The Benny Hill Show* compilation screened on Tuesday 14 April reached number 15 in the ratings, attracting a very healthy 11.1 million viewers. On that same day, he spoke to old friend Sylvia Thorley (who had auditioned Hill's girls since 1979) about seeing a George Formby tribute show in Southsea, but he refused the offer. Hill confined himself to very brief walks around Teddington, but was determined to embrace the showbusiness fraternity for the sake of an ex-Hill's Angel.

Continually delighted by the success of his family of performers, he had promised Louise English that he would make the trip to see her starring in *Me and My Girl* at the Adelphi Theatre. Hill had wanted to brave the publicity spotlight of the opening night performance on 9 March, but he was too ill to attend that performance. Although clearly unwell, he dined with Sue Upton at the Savoy, saw the matinee show together on 16 April, and unusually, asked English if he could come on stage after the performance and pose for photographs. Donning a bowler hat and posing with English and Les Dennis, he chatted backstage with Alfred Marks about the old variety days and BBC radio times. A pleasant dressing room chat with Louise English followed, although the memory of that fateful Thames sacking was still as fresh as ever. Hill stayed and stayed, right up to the 7 p.m. bell for the evening performance, then went home to Teddington. Both Angels consider that this indicates Hill sensed the end was approaching. His energy was flagging, a sense of impending doom was casting a shadow over his new shows, and for the last week or so of his life he sounded distressed in conversation to friends. Explaining that he couldn't walk more than ten steps without the need for someone to help him, Benny Hill was an extremely sick man.

Returning from the performance of *Me And My Girl* on the evening of Thursday 16 April, Hill had made his very last public appearance. Frankie Howerd, the comedian whose career paralleled Hill's so closely, was also in the news with a health scare, so he sent his old friend a tongue-in-cheek telegram: 'Stop stealing my act – I do the heart attack jokes!' It was to be Hill's final gag.

Frankie Howerd died on Easter Sunday at the age of 75. Dennis Kirkland quickly delivered a Benny Hill response to the news of Howerd's death, but in reality, Hill never heard the news. Unknown to anybody at the time, Benny Hill had died alone the previous day, Saturday 18 April 1992, aged 68. Ironically, Howerd had died in the middle of filming a new series for Central Television. Four of the planned series of six *Frankie's On ... shows* were completed. Benny Hill's contract for Central television was never signed, part of the unopened mail found in his flat, delivered after his death.

Over a weekend of tremendous sadness for British comedy admirers, two of the greatest post-war talents died. On the surface it seemed Howerd was at the zenith of his popularity, beloved by all generations and busier than ever. Hill was seemingly ignored. Happily, the truth was that Hill was at his most optimistic. With a new show in the can and the prospect of a new ITV series, he was back in business. It's tragic that we never got to see those Central shows, but at least the comedian was back with his hands on the driving wheel.

The events of his last few hours are, of course, unclear. Hill's Fairwater House neighbour, Bill Greenham, distressed that no one had seen their famous resident for some four days and noticing that the light had been on throughout the day and he had not heard the usual sound of records playing in the evening, telephoned Dennis Kirkland on 20 April 1992 to see if Hill had gone away. Kirkland told him no. He hadn't spoken to Hill for two days. Having phoned the previous day and received no answer, he had assumed Hill was taking a walk. However, following the phone call from Greenham, Kirkland sensed something was wrong and once again telephoned the flat. The two had a secret ring which let Hill know it was Kirkland calling. When there was still no answer, the police were informed at 8.07 p.m., and Kirkland hastily journeyed to his friend's flat, propped a ladder against the wall and gingerly made his way up to the second-floor flat window.

Breaking into the comedian's final moment of privacy, policemen Peter Valvona and Marcus Bass smashed a 2 foot by 2 foot pane of glass in the door to gain entry just after 8.15 p.m. Kirkland already knew he was dead.

Nervously balancing outside the flat window, he could see Hill, dressed in casual blue trousers and pink shirt, barefooted, two empty plates and a half-consumed fizzy drink by his side. Lying back in his chair and looking totally at peace, his bloated features clearly showed that death had occurred some days before – aptly, while he was watching television. Ceefax was on the screen – Hill loved to read viewer's critiques on television shows – and Hill had died peacefully, alone in his flat. It was probably the ideal way to depart stage left. The police telephoned Hill's agent, Linda Ronan, to ascertain whether Dennis Kirkland could be considered his next of kin, the keys to the flat were handed to him, and Hill's home was locked up at 10.30 p.m. Dr Ravindra Fernando, of Kingston Hospital, South West London, who conducted the post mortem, concluded that Hill had died of coronary thrombosis over the Easter Weekend.

In terms of the media reaction, Hill's death immediately overshadowed that of Howerd. The popular press gave over pages of prose in celebration of this comic genius. From the *Sun* to *The Times* (which included a gloriously high-brow celebration of low comedy, 'The True Words of Jesters', by Bernard Richards, fellow of Brasenose College, Oxford), the British press paid homage to a lost master. Condemning the recent slurs of sexist content, Hill was praised as one of the land's most treasured institutions. Indeed, the *Sun*, which just over a decade earlier had been calling for Hill to be banned, pulled out all the stops for a major salute which included lengthy eulogies and a rewritten version of 'Ernie' in his memory. The ITV news, hosted by John Suchet, did the old boy proud, showing some choice clips and putting searching questions about Hill's sacking to Richard Dunn. Toeing the Thames line, he celebrated Hill's legacy, but commented that after four decades he was on the decline. The most potent moment was a live link with dear old Bob Todd in a Sussex pub. Clearly stunned at the news, he painted an endearing, likeable picture of his friend. The BBC coverage was even more heartwarming, with the news item cutting back to newscaster Michael Buerk still crying with laughter at 'The Halitosis Kid' clip featured in the tribute. The cracked-up face of a well-respected journalist on live television was the best tribute Benny Hill could have hoped for.

Perhaps most ironic of all, Thames television, whose season of Hill repeats had just begun, told journalists that they were 'urgently examining the possibility' of replacing the listed Hill compilation with a special programme. The hurriedly put together celebration of their best-loved comedian was a half-hour tribute.

Benny Hill – An Appreciation

The hasty Thames eulogy for its most popular comedian was presented by Chris Dunkley, television critic for *The Financial Times*. Obviously distressed, Dunkley began the tribute with a brief bit of 'Scuttlevision'. Suddenly, watching this at home, I felt a pang of real loss. Here was Hill hamming it up like a good 'un, with McGee and Todd in tow. Despite the sadness, Todd's naked musician greeted with Hill's outraged 'No, I said play "In the Mood"!' still brought laughter.

The impressive line-up of talking heads included John Mortimer and Michael Caine (in footage from the recent *Omnibus* show), Ernie Wise, Nicholas Parsons and Derek Nimmo, describing Benny Hill as the most famous British actor for decades. In the studio, a shell-shocked Henry McGee fondly recalled his friend's self-contained contentment. Remembering his 50th birthday, when Hill explained that he could die tomorrow and be happy with his life, this memory was linked to France's devotion to his mime (ranked above Marcel Marceau and screened all over Christmas week), illustrated with the touching, Chaplinesque scene where Hill's tramp and Louise English's girl in the poster come to life. One of the masters of mime, his unshaven, emotive character bumbles through a brief love affair, extinguishes a lamp with a catapult, is jerked out of fantasy by the shock of arrest, and poignantly concludes with the red rose still left on the park bench – a real masterpiece.

A bit of Chow Mein from the 1980s, a snippet from Hill's Des O'Connor interview and a brief tribute from Philip Jones were followed by Sue Upton and Dennis Kirkland reacting to Hill's death. Words were really not needed, but images of Upton's kids with Hill and Kirkland's recalling of stage work as 'fingernails and aspirins' were enough to lead into the final skit, with suspender-clad beauties, black stockings and bikini babes all disturbed in the search for a lost child. A suitably touching walk into the sunset faded into black with the legend, 'Benny Hill 1924–1992 – Thank you'. One can imagine Hill's quiet smile of ironic satisfaction.

Benny Hill – An Appreciation. ITV, Tuesday 21 April 1992, 8.30–9 p.m. A rather tasteless media circus saw comics of a certain age, such as Bruce Forsyth, Norman Wisdom and Derek Nimmo, worried about the sudden deaths of their illustrious contemporaries. Jack Douglas said: 'The first thing I thought this morning was to make sure I stay in bed all day in case I'm number three!' Even more tasteless were the infamous, outspoken Judge Pickles's words just a week after Hill's death. Published in the *Sun*, would you believe, he commented that there 'should be more to humour than smirk and smut but he never managed it'. Now that *is* ill-informed. Notables from Ernie Wise to politician Tony Benn celebrated Hill's legacy, and actor Peter Bowles (speaking out against the Thames dropping of Hill on *TV-AM*) started a backlash of celebrities, including Hughie Greene, Bobby Ball and Paul Daniels, who criticized the company for its treatment of a great star.

Despite all this, John Howard Davies was still maintaining he had made the right decision in sacking Hill in 1989, despite press knowledge that Thames had tried and failed to entice him back for another series of shows just weeks before his death. Thames Chief Executive Richard Dunn was slightly more tactful, celebrating Hill's comic genius and kindly manner, but dismissing Hill's comedy as outmoded. However, whatever some may have felt, Benny Hill's shows were still bringing in millions from across the world, and indeed, with Hill still on their books, Thames's attempt to retain its broadcasting franchise in 1991 could have been successful. At the time of Hill's death, Richard Holloway was in Montreux ready to break the confirmation of Benny's Central show. The announcement was planned for a special dinner on 26 April – the meeting went ahead, but of course, no announcement was made.

The long-standing money question obviously came to a head following Benny Hill's death. To the man himself, personal belongings meant very little, frequently taking a cut in salary at both BBC and Thames in order to be able to inject more money into the production. Even during his very early days at the BBC, David Croft recalls tracking down £30,000 in uncashed payment cheques, while holidays would be restricted to a budget of £1,500 in travellers' cheques. A money magazine's 1988 estimation of his worth being in excess of £10 million resulted in vehement denial. But despite the fact he had no wish to be the wealthiest British comedian in the cemetery, he did have a very hefty bank balance. His two companies, Benny Hill Entertainments Ltd and Benny Hill Productions Ltd were market successes, with conservative estimates that he had personally earned £933,073 after tax for the financial year 1986/1987.

Just before Christmas 1991, the ailing Hill had told an interviewer that with all his immediate family gone, 'two very special, lovely ladies' would be the main beneficiaries of his will. Throughout his life, Hill had secretly befriended and helped three handicapped fans. One lady had passed away some years earlier, but those two very special people were Jeanette Warner and Phoebe King. Typical of Hill's numerous pet names for everybody ('Little Heart', 'Little Sausage', Kirkland was 'Nature Boy'), these friends became 'Netta' and 'Kitten', whom Hill visited regularly, cheered up and helped. He would cook for them, clean their homes, take them out for meals and treat them to theatre trips. Netta, whom Hill had met at Great Yarmouth and considered a brilliant natural comic talent and prospective scriptwriter, had died in February 1992 at the age of 58. Her death deeply upset Hill, and left just Phoebe King. She had first written to Hill in 1950, when he was performing in Uxbridge, North London. Welcomed backstage during his summer show at the Spa Pavilion, Felixstowe, the 15-year-old fan immediately befriended the star, and kept in touch for the following forty-two years. Suffering from cerebral palsy, Phoebe lived in sheltered accommodation in Felixstowe, phoned Hill on a regular basis, and enjoyed a summer visit from her hero during June or July every year. Sometimes Hill would visit up to seven times in one year. Rather than staying in a posh hotel, Hill stayed in a special guest room attached to Phoebe's home, for which she paid the minimal fee, unbeknown to Hill. Nurses said her room was a beloved shrine to Benny Hill.

Naturally, with the death of Hill in April 1992 and the prospect of a legacy of over £7 million, the press seized on the relationship. For days, interviews were recorded, prose was presented and an image of true love was hinted at. Indeed, King herself didn't help matters by suggesting that Hill had been considering marriage. This was far from the truth, and their relationship was purely on friendly terms – to use the old cliché, Hill looked upon her as a sister. But with Hill's death, the full details of this extraordinary friendship emerged – coupled with vast amounts of money, possible sexual overtones and a juicy piece of family-versus-friend legal wrangling, the papers couldn't resist. Brenda Garrison of the Felixstowe sheltered accommodation continually repeated that Hill was like a brother to Phoebe King, but the press wouldn't let go.

As it happened, all this speculation came to naught when Hill's will was published. Always maintaining that he thought 'money is a bit overrated', Hill probably had no idea how rich he was. Indeed, most of the huge amounts pouring in from international royalties for *The Benny Hill Show* were either banked unchecked or automatically given away to charity. The only legal will uncovered dated from 1961, and it left the entire estate to his parents. Having never got round to changing the will following his parents' death in the 1970s, the money would have legally belonged to Hill's brother and sister, but since both Diana and Leonard also predeceased him, the estate went to Leonard's children Caroline, Barnaby, Jonathan and Madeleine, Madeleine's handicapped daughter Hannah, Diana's three teenage children in Australia, Michael, Peter and Tessa, and a beloved elderly Aunt Mo, in Bexleyheath. The final amount distributed was £7,548,192. Phoebe King told the press that she never wanted the money, just Benny, and the debate was curtailed.

Hill had probably planned to thank his loyal team of players and production crew with bequests. A sheet of blue Basildon Bond notepaper was found among his personal effects, listing the likes of Henry McGee, Bob Todd, Sue Upton, Louise English and Dennis Kirkland beside annotations detailing huge sums of money, but because it was unsigned and unwitnessed, it had no legal standing.

Benny Hill's funeral was held on Tuesday 28 April 1992. Organized by Dennis Kirkland, Leonard Hill's daughter Caroline and Linda Ronan of Richard Stone's office, the star's home town of Southampton came to a virtual standstill to pay respect to one of its favourite sons. Louise English noticed a little boy giving the Fred Scuttle salute as the hearse moved through the crowded streets. Although Michael Jackson, Frank Sinatra and Burt Reynolds had all sent faxes vowing to attend the memorial service, the funeral congregation was not a showbusiness affair, with close friends in the business, Henry McGee, Sue Upton, Nicholas Parsons, Jon Jon Keefe, Bella Emberg, Thames stuntman Ken Sedd and Army saviour Harry Segal mingling with the ninety or so mourners.

One moment of high farce which would have no doubt tickled Hill himself was the non-appearance of beloved stooge Bob Todd. Travelling from his Sussex home to London's Moss Bros for his suit, he was due to meet McGee and Keefe at Maidenhead for his train connection to Southampton. Delays on the road and track caused him to be late and miss the train. McGee and Keefe had no option but to leave without him, and on discovering that he couldn't make it, Todd found the nearest pub and drank to Hill's memory there. Sadly, Bob Todd himself would die less than six months later. Hill's long-standing agent, Richard Stone, was also missing from the service. Still in California marking his silver wedding anniversary, he had been very shocked by Hill's final video message.

The 3 p.m. service was held in the tiny chapel at Southampton's Holly Brook Cemetery, presided over by local vicar Peter Cooper, who remembered Benny Hill as someone who 'came to be known and loved by millions, a man with a natural instinct for entertainment'. Torrential rain came down as Benny Hill was laid to rest alongside his mother Helen and father Alfred, some 25 feet from the chapel. His name was added to the marble headstone with just the single word 'Reunited'. Over a hundred wreaths surrounded the grave, with tributes from Louise English, Yvonne Paul and Donna Scarfe joined by a flamboyant, kitten-shaped wreath in white chrysanthemums from Phoebe King. The card read: 'To Teddy Bear. I love you very much, Kitten (Phoebe)'. Some three hundred fans waited outside the churchyard and paid their own personal respects. Benny's memorial service was held on 24 September 1992. Max Bygraves, Ronnie Corbett, Les Dennis, Davy Kaye, Henry Mcgee, Alfred Marks, Nicholas Parsons and Freddie Starr were in attendance.

EPILOGUE

Cheers!

With the death of Benny Hill, British comedy lost one of its most prized assets. His talent, overshadowed to some extent by the feverish debate about the effects of his work, was more than enough to endear him to an international audience of billions. He is the most widely known comic of all time. However, after the tributes had been paid and the blame for his decline allotted, nothing had really changed. Benny Hill was still a touchstone for the crass, unacceptable face of humour. However, political correctness was quickly condemned as taking the freedom out of comedy, and although, jokesters were careful to avoid dubious subject matter, at the end of the day a joke is a joke.

Following Hill's death, the cultural shifts that had begun in the late 1980s became a clear sea change in what was and what wasn't acceptable. Comedy like *Men Behaving Badly* and *They Think It's All Over* reinvented the ideals of 'laddish' attitudes as the ultimate in cool. Pop stars, politicians and fashion icons embraced the feelgood passion for football and lager. It was cool to love old macho values. Britpop and *Loaded* magazine ushered in the age of 'New Lad', with New Labour and new everything else making it great to be different. Even the Spice Girls, symbols of the 'laddette' attitude of Girl Power, still played to every male fantasy in tight dresses and panty-revealing poses. It was all intended to be trendily ironic and postmodernist, but Girl Power's fashions revealed just as much as Hill's Angels ever did.

However, despite this, Benny Hill was still noticeably absent from British television. Across the world, he still reigned supreme, but in his home country an almost blanket denial was in force. He cropped up briefly in John Fisher's 1992 New Year's Eve salute to British humour, *Heroes of Comedy* on Channel 4, although again he was questioned rather than praised. Ironically, Fisher, who had been John Howard Davies's deputy at Thames, launched the unconvincing Hill renaissance.

In 1993, Channel 4 presented six half-hour compilations of his 1988–89 work as a new series of repeats, *Benny Hill – Hero of Comedy*. Despite Fisher's guidance, this was nothing but an unedited rehash of Thames programmes, while the Classic Pictures video release *The Golden Years of British Comedy – From the 60s* simply relied on familiar clips from *The Best of Benny Hill*. That same year, on 4 October 1993, The Dead Comics Society paid tribute to Benny Hill with a blue plaque unveiled by Phil Collins at Hill's luxury flat in Queensgate, Knightsbridge. Hill's was the star event on a day that also marked the society's tribute to, fittingly enough, Charlie Chaplin. But even with this blue-plaque respectability, further repeats were not forthcoming, and even that haven for classic old television, the satellite channel UK Gold, didn't buck the trend. The National Film Theatre celebrated Benny Hill's underrated gems from the vintage BBC archive in their praiseworthy 'Funny Men' season – at home in the five-week season with Marty Feldman, Frankie Howerd, Sid James and Peter Sellers. Nevertheless, Hill's rehabilitation was still stuck in neutral.

By 1994, an overwhelming obsession with post-war British comedians resulted in the masterly Terry

Johnson play *Dead Funny*. Although it namechecked everybody from Tony Hancock to Eric Morecambe, it focused on Benny Hill, with perverse fantasies, affairs with ex-Hill's Angels and a sad, obsessive Dead Comics Society which pandered to the sad people who worshipped at the Hill shrine. This was hardly the sort of image fans needed, but the play's brilliance was enough to fan the flame of serious interest in old comedy, with the nation hitting nostalgic overdrive as we rocketed towards the new millenium. Thames bowed to public pressure and released a massive 100-minute compilation video, *Benny Hill's Big Time Bonanza*. The following year, Thames Video repackaged and re-released *Benny Hill and Friends*. Also in 1997, in a metamorphosis from the old society, Comic Heritage unveiled a blue plaque to Benny Hill at the old Thames studios at Teddington. Although rather overburdened by the multiple unveiling – which also included Eric Morecambe, Tony Hancock and Irene Handl – Phil Collins once again did the deed for Hill.

Still cited as the epitome of uncool humour, Hill's reputation in the media world had become a joke, a byword for naff British comedy. Even now, the world-wide popularity could not break through the deaf ears of some people. By now, of course, Ben Elton had entered the mainstream, happy to praise Morecambe and Wise, the Two Ronnies and the *Carry On* movies, resurrecting the spirit of *Dad's Army* with his sitcom *The Thin Blue Line*, still as sharp as a box of knives live on stage, and a prolific writer of best-selling novels and successful West End plays. Therefore, vehement Hill devotees took Elton's guest appearance in the first ever *Harry Enfield and Chums* as a real slap in the face. Combining a brilliant parody of Benny Hill with a classic piece of self-mockery, Elton's shiny-suited ranter of old speeds through a park covering up scantily clad women, splitting up loving couples and spouting a barrage of 'little bit of politics' aggression.

Thames, on the other hand, were not having a laugh when they signed up Freddie Starr for a semi-regular series of comedy specials. The gangster/cowboy/police routines chock full with visual gags, speeded-up film and innuendo-stuffed one-liners could have been Benny Hill resurrected. Even Derek Deadman and Bella Emberg were enlisted to join in the fun. With the fan (Freddie Starr) and the old cohort (Dennis Kirkland) writing the scripts, Kirkland back in harness as producer/director and the spirit of Hill apparent in every frame, this was a weak fulfilment of the aborted Central contract the star comedian never signed.

While the recorded legacy collected dust in the archives, the image of Benny Hill in the collective consciousness grew in stature. Channel 4's 1992 series of *The Jack Dee Show* included his observation that Tony Hart, the children's television artist for a generation, was like 'Benny Hill on acid', while singer-songwriter Donovan's comparison of Benny Hill's television parody to Trevor and Simon's comic version of 'Jennifer Juniper' was received with snooty arrogance by the duo. Glamour model Jo Guest, appearing on *The Jack Doherty Show* (Channel 5, 20 November 1997), cited her sort of work as typically British and 'as innocent as Benny Hill'. VH-1's American Classics trailer ended with the sight of a young flasher revealing his underpants, holding out the promise of 'enough subtle humour to appease the land of Benny Hill'. The very first episode of detective serial *Jonathan Creek*, 'Joker in the Pack', cast John Bluthal as the ill-fated, old-fashioned comedian whose dubious sight gags and un-PC style are frowned upon. Grey-haired, rotund and dismayed at the reaction to his slapstick routine, this is the spectre of Benny Hill having his quiet say again. At the close of *The Lily Savage Show*, television critic and Hill admirer Garry Bushell chased Janet Street-Porter outside Television Centre in typical, speeded-up Benny fashion, and even the new advertising campaign for Kleenex's family-sized tissues burst into high-speed antics and the 'Yakety Sax' theme (it even included homage touches, with one of the girls stripped down to her bra and the three female friends chasing the man – here a naughty young boy). *Soccer A.M.* on Sky 1 presented scantily clad glam girls, mock beauty contest questioning, and the offer of a date with a famous milkman – naturally Ernie's name was blasted out by all audience members. Fan Jim Davidson named Benny Hill as the first choice of comic heroes on *Steve Wright's Show*, Saturday 31 January 1998, protecting the memory of a fine comedian.

As part of British heritage, Benny Hill had remained a cultural icon through reputation alone. In an age of leggy bimbos on that ultimate of bad taste, *Endurance UK* on Challenge TV, wall-to-wall soft porn on cable, imported *Italian Stripping Housewives* on Bravo and *Topless Darts in the Millennium Dome* on Live TV, old Benny Hill plays like an innocent, naive and coyly funny breath of fresh, restrained air. Finally, John Fisher stepped back into the ring to present a full documentary tribute to Benny Hill.

Heroes of Comedy – Benny Hill

Eventually reaching Benny Hill in his whistle-stop celebrations of British comedy greats, John Fisher had started the tradition with a Frankie Howerd pilot, an initial batch of four (Max Miller, Terry-Thomas, Arthur Haynes and

Joyce Grenfell) and another quartet (The Goons, Kenny Everett, Les Dawson and Alastair Sim) before headlining his third season with this tribute (the next subjects were Peter Cook, Arthur Askey and, at long last, Tony Hancock).

This Benny Hill showcase broke a major British television dearth for the comedian, but really had very little to say that had not been said already. A thumbnail gallop past early variety and BBC television allowed the vast majority of (cheaper) clips to be culled from the Thames years, while friends, colleagues and fans discussed the great man. Still the sexist debate made up about a quarter of the airtime, and Caroline Aherne stood up for the 'harmless' angle with charming pride. Hill soundbites came from the familiar *Omnibus* programme, but the show's two chief rarities were a glorious (albeit brief) interview at the unveiling of his Madame Tussaud's model and a heartwarming (if poignant) snippet of him leaving hospital in February 1992. The perfect introductory package for any non-follower, Benny Hill was back on television, where he belonged, but this oasis caused no major re-evaluation of the man's work.

Heroes of Comedy – Benny Hill: Thames – Pearson TV Company production for Channel 4, 12 January 1998, 9–10 p.m. Contributions from CAROLINE AHERNE, STEVE ALLEN, PETER CHARLESWORTH, PHYLLIS DILLER, JEREMY HAWK, DENNIS KIRKLAND, HENRY McGEE, BOB MONKHOUSE OBE, ANTHONY NEWLEY, RICHARD STONE, DON TAFFNER, BARRY TOOK, SUE UPTON, DICK VAN DYKE, REG VARNEY. Also featuring GILLIAN ADAMS, SUSI BAKER, KATIE BOYLE, JAN BUTLIN, FANNY and JOHNNY CRADDOCK, DEREK DEADMAN, CONNIE GEORGES, LEE GIBSON, JON JON KEEFE, SHARON KIEL, MAX MILLER, HUGH PADDICK, DAVE PROWSE, PAM RATTIGAN, CORINNE RUSSELL, CHARMAINE SEAL, KATHY STAFF, ELAINE TAYLOR, BOB TODD, DILYS WATLING, PAULA WILCOX, JACKIE WRIGHT. With special thanks to the Benny Hill estate, DAVE FREEMAN, MARGARET FORWOOD and PHILIP JONES. Written and produced by John Fisher. Director: Tom Atkinson.

This long-overdue tribute to Hill's career seemed to make little difference, for on Easter Monday 1998, BBC2 gave their evening over to a look at politically incorrect television. Hill clips were branded as some of the worst 'horrors' of small-screen entertainment, and a *Radio Times* cartoon pictured Ben Elton pelting Hill, Bernard Manning and John Boulter with tomatoes, but when it finally came down to it, no Hill clips joined comic masters Frankie Howerd, Kenny Everett, Dick Emery and Les Dawson. Perhaps Hill was considered just too unacceptable even in this framework, or perhaps, even in death, Benny Hill just wouldn't set foot into the minority realms of BBC2. Still, Granada Plus, home of the hits, screened Thames work every week night from 1 March 1999. Postmodernist irony, great swathes of foreign screenings and Hill's place in British public affection still seem to count for absolutely nothing.

However, let's be loud and proud and say this once and for all: the man practically invented British television comedy. His work has been seen by more people in more parts of the world than anybody else, and at his very peak, Benny Hill was a comedy actor of extraordinary talent. The most frustrating fact remains that even after such a shift in social acceptability, the moment you mention the fact you admire Benny Hill, you instantly feel the need to justify yourself. Even now, Benny Hill is seen as the benchmark for everything that is bad about British comedy. I just hope that this book goes some way towards redressing the balance.

'The sun may have gone down on the British Empire but it has yet to go down on Benny Hill.'
Henry McGee

'I want the show to be a joyous thing. I want everyone to have a giggle.'
Benny Hill

FURTHER READING

Forwood, Margaret, *The Real Benny Hill*, Robson Books, 1992

Hill, Leonard, *Saucy Boy: The Life Story of Benny Hill*, Robson Books, 1989

Housham, David and Frank-Keyes, John, *Funny Business: The Greatest Names in Comedy*, Boxtree, 1992

Joseph, Michael, *25 Years of ITV: 1955–1970*, A & C Black, 1980

Kirkland, Dennis with Bonner, Hilary, *Benny: The True Story*, Smith Gryphon, 1992

Morecambe, Gary, *The Illustrated Benny Hill*, Elm Tree Books, 1989

Parsons, Nicholas, *The Straight Man – My Life in Comedy*, Weidenfeld & Nicolson, 1994

Staveacre, Tony, *Slapstick!*, Angus & Robertson, 1987

Took, Barry, *The Life and Times of Benny Hill and Frankie Howerd*, Weidenfeld & Nicolson, 1992

Quinlan, David, *Quinlan's Illustrated Directory of Film Comedy Stars*, Batsford, 1992

VIDEOS

Benny Hill and Friends, Thames Video TV8257

Benny Hill's Big Time Bonanza, Thames Video TV8236

Benny Hill's World Tour: 'Benny Hill's World: New York!', 4Front Video 639 0743

Benny Hill – The World's Favourite Clown: The Full Story of the Comic Genius, (Omnibus: Benny Hill Clown Imperial), Thames Video TV8168

The Crazy World of Benny Hill, Comedy Club

The Golden Years of British Comedy – From the 60s (features clips from *The Best of Benny Hill*), VVL 0884783. Re-released in 1997, 4Front Video 046 540 4

The Italian Job, Paramount BRP 2925. Also available on widescreen videodisk, Paramount PLFEB 35241

Those Magnificent Men in Their Flying Machines, 20th Century Fox Home Entertainment 10336

The Very Best of Benny Hill (repackage of *Benny Hill's Greatest Hits*, Thames TV8116), Thames Video TV8199

The Very Best of Benny Hill - Clown King of Comedy, Pearson TV 8199

Visible Touch: Genesis (featuring 'Anything She Does'), Vision Video VVD 204